CLASSIC KITS

ARTHUR WARD
CLASSIC KITS
COLLECTING THE GREATEST MODEL KITS IN THE WORLD
FROM AIRFIX TO TAMIYA

DEDICATION

For Eleanor and Alice. Study this book carefully. It features part of your inheritance – you lucky girls!

First published in 2004 by
Collins, an imprint of
HarperCollinsPublishers
77-85 Fulham Palace Road
Hammersmith
London W6 8JB

Collins is a registered trademark of HarperCollinsPublishers Ltd.

everything clicks at www.collins.co.uk

10	09	08	07	06	05	04
7	6	5	4	3	2	1

A catalogue record for this book is available from the British Library

ISBN 0-00-717695-3

Designed by Christine Wood

Printed and bound by Printing Express Ltd, Hong Kong.

contents

Daddy Prog reading his book.
Saturday January 10th 2004

by Eleanor 14

**Illustration of author by
Eleanor Ward. Age 7½**

An apology

This book is not a list of every kit made by each kit manufacturer. There is simply not the space to do so and, frankly, I lack the ability and desire to do it. Many of today's companies simply re-package kits which originated elsewhere; keeping track of everything is almost impossible. The commercial marketplace features a great deal of 'mould sharing' whereby old kits are re-badged and re-boxed by value-added resellers in the manner common in the IT industry. Consequently it is very difficult to keep track of the provenance of mould tools which may have originated in England years ago – especially those made by FROG – or even with kits which originated more recently in Japan or Korea. Apart from a few exceptions most of the brands shown in this book originated some time ago.

There are many worthy checklists in print. Probably the best available is published by John Burns of America's 'Kit Collector's Clearinghouse'. I admire the ability of men such as John – although I have no idea where they find the energy required to compile such directories – but my interest is simply to try and capture some of the 'essence' of what plastic modelling means and has represented to generations of enthusiasts. I want to engender a feeling of warm nostalgia – the memory of happy days building plastic kits, encouraging recollections of relaxed and innocent times when, apart from the odd occasions when one lost a tiny but essential part deep into engulfing carpet pile, making kits was fun.

Introduction

By the late Victorian age, industrialisation and the increased shift from rural to urban dwelling compelled massive lifestyle changes amongst Britain's population.

The coming of the 20th Century hastened this revolution. Individuals — mostly men — went from their homes to a separate place of work and came back at a regular hour each day to enjoy a certain amount of free time. Time at ease could be spent in pursuit of sport, in the pub or club or, of course, at home in the fulfilment of a personal interest. The hobbyist was born.

During this period of social and economic reform, the aforementioned industrialisation also delivered mass production, enabling the manufacture of a vast range of components, previously the province of skilled artisans. So now, along with Ford Model 'T's, an assortment of much smaller machined gears, cranks and con rods rolled out of factories every-where. With the avail-ability of standardised minia-ture components, the scale model enthusiast was born.

As the title of this book suggests, the focus of the narrative is a survey of the most famous and enduring kit brands. Other than Bill Bosworth's late lamented Accurate Miniatures from the 1990s or Freddie Leung's Hong

¼₄th scale Spitfire Mk1a the first of the 'Superkits' (1970)

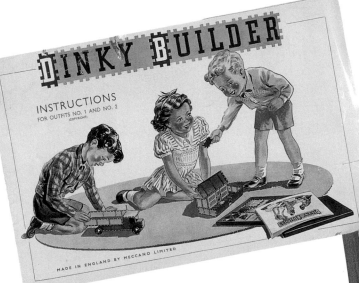

Dinky Builder, 1950's.

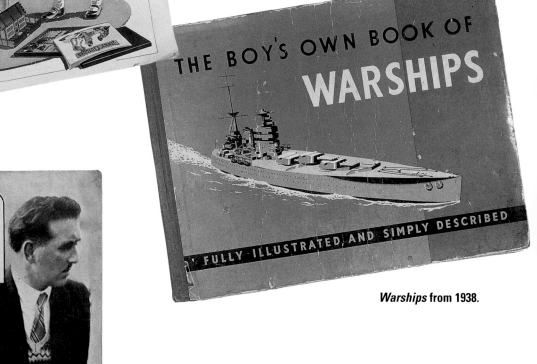

Warships from 1938.

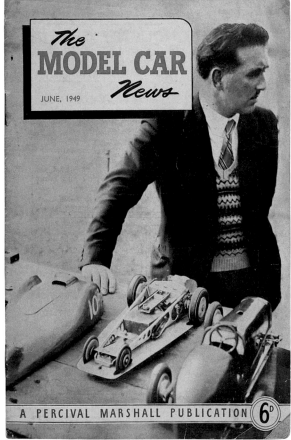

The Model Car News,
1949.

1972 Tamiya kit
catalogue.

Kong-based Dragon Models, founded in 1987, the brands featured herein are either long gone, or have been with us for decades.

Space prevents mention of many of the recent additions to the plastic kit firmament, whose introduction tends to contradict those 'wise counsels' who claimed the day of the polystyrene construction kit had passed. So, to all those newcomers: a big well done and please forgive the omission of your products in a survey of 'classic' kits. Who knows, one day in the future an enthusiast like me will write a book concentrating on all those firms from Eastern Europe such as Zvesda, AML, Eduard, Mirage Hobby, ICM, Lotnia and Roden; the newer Chinese manufacturers, most notably Trumpeter; Canada's Modelcraft; North America's MRC; Korean brand leaders Academy as well as Japanese new kids on the block like AFV Club and Tasca.

Neither is this book the place for stories about vacuum-form kit manufacturers such as Airmodel, Aeroform, Formaplane and Rareplanes or those firms who produce resin models. Of the latter the biggest and best is certainly VLS, established by master modellers Francois Verlinden and Bob Letterman in the 1980s. I well remember Mr Verlinden's superb dioramas gracing the pages of *Military Modelling Magazine* in the 1970s. Accurate Miniatures, Cromwell Models, CMK (Czechmasters), Resicast and others, are creditable manufacturers in this field.

Dating from April 1962 this edition of the ever popular *Hobbies Weekly* was the usual collection of "Up-to-the-minute ideas, practical designs and pleasing and profitable things to make." Subjects ranged from making model miniatures to building full size divans!

The Model Engineer, July 1950.

1. History and Development of Scale Models

***Thrilling Stories* – full of the sort of ripping yarns which captivated pre-war aero enthusiasts.**

Since time immemorial man has made miniature replicas of his world. The ancient Egyptians placed tiny models of the kind of worldly possessions the deceased would find indispensable in the afterlife (one 11th dynasty prince was entombed with an entire miniature imperial guard for protection). Tiny clay models of war chariots, dating back to 2800 BC, have been discovered at the site of the ancient Sumerian city of Ur and some 5,000 years later the Romans are known to have mass-produced cast lead 'flat' miniature soldiers – possibly the first commercially available scale models. Many cultures made similar offerings to the gods in an effort to thank them for the annual harvest or, with rather less benevolence, for victory in battle against an enemy.

Indeed, it was the increasing sophistication in warfare that proved the real stimulus to scale models, as we know them today. As England, Spain, Italy, France and the Netherlands – Europe's principal maritime trading nations – expanded their overseas dominions, the huge burden of policing trade routes was placed upon their navies. Expanding dramatically, their fleets devoured acres and acres of oak woodland as merchant vessels and fighting ships were built to protect the new territories.

Mass production of these rival armadas required shipwrights to be sure they could manufacture ship after ship to the same pattern in a consistent and accurate manner. In the days before computers and calculators, when many skilled craftsmen were illiterate and, anyway, incapable of reading complex plans, the best method of explaining the complexities of design and

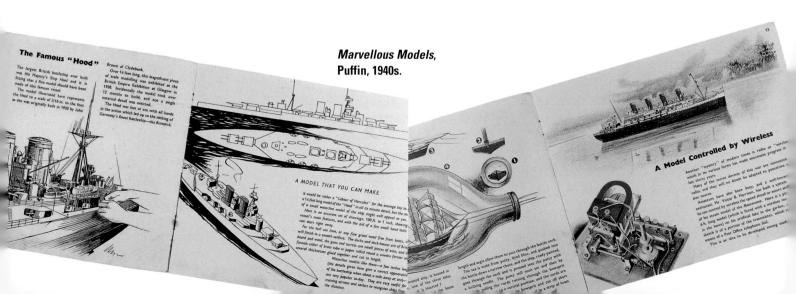

***Marvellous Models,*
Puffin, 1940s.**

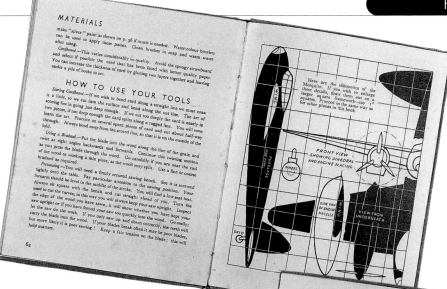

describing precisely how components fitted together, was to build an accurately reduced-scale replica of the intended vessel.

The fabulous Admiralty models prepared in England and those created in the support of competing maritime powers, were the first truly accurate scale models produced. Their construction required the development of techniques of modelling and finishing familiar today and encouraged the introduction of many tools and materials still in use. Many of these fine models survive in museums today.

Being largely landlocked and surrounded by potential enemies, it comes as little surprise to learn that Bismarck's newly unified Germany focused more on martial prowess. Consequently Bavaria, notably, became the centre of a burgeoning model soldier industry first manufacturing flats and later producing solid metal figures from famous manufacturers such as Heyde and Llegeyer. Similarly, Napoleonic France placed great emphasis on the achievements of its land forces and shortly after the demise of Bonaparte's First Empire, the French firms of Lucotte and, later the more famous Parisian firm of Mignot, established a pattern of scale model soldiers which survives to this day.

Together with items of cast and extruded metal, and long before the advent of polystyrene, Edwardian toy and model manufacturers experimented with a whole range of man-made plastics. These were mostly derivatives of nitro cellulose materials. In 1870 the Hyatt brothers invented 'Celluloid' in the United States as a suitable material for billiard balls. Shortly afterwards, in 1872, the Smith & Lock company patented the very first

Spreads from Richard Chick's *First Book of Model Aircraft*, 1944.

War shortages dictated a more modest treatment for Bassett-Lowke's Economy Catalogue.

1950s English-made ¹⁄₁₂th scale 'Do It Yourself' bedroom suite.

Dinky Builder, 1950's.

injection-moulding machine in an attempt to hasten the manufacture of such items. Unfortunately the new plastic proved unsuitable for the new process and Smith & Lock's revolutionary new machine would have to wait until some new raw material was synthesised.

Germany, rapidly becoming a major player in the chemical and dyestuffs arena, also had a fledgling toy industry. This had a facility with tin-plate and, using a spin-off of the burgeoning canning industry, quickly learnt how to print designs on this thin metal. German toy makers also turned to new methods in synthetic and composite production that were a by-product of their chemical industry.

In 1919, German scientists had at last produced a thermally stable cellulose plastic – cellulose acetate. A revised injection-moulding process was invented – the most famous system being that patented by the American Leo Baekeland, inventor of the famous phenol-formaldehyde resin/plastic 'Bakelite'. Although, today's polystyrene injection moulding machines are far more sophisticated, their principal mechanisms would not be unfamiliar to the early American and German pioneers of such technology.

Early 20th-century German production seriously challenged established British manufacturers like William Britain, who was then largely employing traditional hollow casting techniques using lead or an assortment of equally malleable alloys. Interestingly, just as Britain and Germany were vying for economic and military supremacy, their rival toy industries were fighting their own battles for dominance in the field of 'war toys' with each producing a profusion of soldiers, artillery and 'dreadnought' battleships!

During that time there were not really any model kits of the type we take for granted today. However, young and old were adept at assembling scale model locomotives and the myriad buildings required to complete a train layout (W. Britain's 54mm lead toy soldiers were originally designed to people toy railway layouts). An early example of the kind of business partnerships taken for granted in the modern kit industry occurred in

1900 at the Paris Exhibition when British model locomotive manufacturer Wenman Bassett-Lowke met Stefan Bing, the German owner of expensive top-quality toys and trains. Thus began an enduring relationship, which resulted in the production of some classic model locos and culminated in the Trix range of construction sets in the 1960s.

Prior to the Second World War the majority of scale model construction required a fair degree of craftsmanship and an understanding of basic metal or wood working techniques. Even the fuselages of early aircraft miniatures came partly formed from a solid block of wood and needed considerable working before they remotely looked like the illustration on the box lid.

A partly shaped wooden 'Skycraft' kit from the 1950s, typical of models available before polystyrene took hold.

Before Hamleys there was Gamages – 1961 Model Book.

Some manufacturers, however, embraced the new synthetics. They soon provided easier-to-assemble scale replicas, taking the labour out of the hobby and paving the way for the modern toy and hobby industry.

Principal amongst these was the brand Bayko, which utilised the revolutionary properties of Bakelite to make an assortment of miniature building blocks and James Hay Stevens' Skybirds.

Skybirds, a range of wood and mixed-media model aircraft, are justly famous for establishing the scale of ½nd – or 6ft to 1 inch. FROG, another British manufacturer, who had branched out from rubber-powered flying scale models to a new range of static display models, Penguins, immediately adopted this scale. FROG's Penguins were manufactured from cellulose acetate butyrate, but because of the material's fugitive nature, few examples survive today. More about Skybird and FROG later.

Embracing a range of traditional and modern construction skills, the growing scale models hobby evolved to generate a thriving support industry of publications, tools, adhesives and paints. However, although principally aimed at schoolboys, the name of London's annual Model

Wartime catalogue of a popular exhibition revealing German aviation developments – well, it was one use for all those wrecked enemy airframes!

Engineering Exhibition reveals the rather purist nature of the hobby at this time.

The Second World War proved the real catalyst for the growth of the modern kit industry which millions of us take for granted today. The loss of traditional sources of raw materials – notably rubber as the Japanese conquered British colonies in the Far East – forced the further exploration of techniques for synthetic production and plastic moulding. Developments in electronics, especially in aviation where numerous moulded components were required, created an enormous demand for plastics manufacture. Ironically, the discovery and capture of German manufacturing plant at the war's end turned out to be a further encouragement.

Even more starved of raw materials than Britain, Nazi Germany was forced to accelerate the development of the manufacture of plastics. With a tradition of inventiveness and having perfected some leading-edge production processes, the Third Reich was also in the van of injection moulding.

As the conscripted allied armies advanced on the shattered country, many over-curious former engineers took advantage of the opportunities presented by so much abandoned plant. Rather unscrupulously perhaps, details of German innovation and, allegedly complete injection-moulding machines, found their way back to Britain and America, forming the basis of both nations' post-war plastics industry.

The Second World War was a catalyst for the modern kit industry in another way, too. The rapid developments in military technology, especially in aviation – the modern jet engine came of age during the 1939–1945 conflict – provided a huge range of new subjects for kit manufacturers. Dozens of blockbuster war films, books and magazines provided all the raw material required to stimulate fertile young imaginations. Also stories of real-life heroes like Audie Murphy, Douglas Bader and Adolph Galland encouraged the demand for specific representations of vehicles and fighter planes. Further accelerated by the cold war and the space race, which each spawned dozens of new inventions, the post-war kit industry developed into a boom time for manufacturers worldwide.

As mentioned previously, the earliest construction kits of the type we take for granted today were manufactured by the British firm of Skybirds which was founded by James Hay Stevens, a well-known aviation writer and illustrator of the 1930s and 1940s. Stevens' replicas certainly established the internationally standard ½nd scale and the Skybirds range numbered more than 20 models by 1935. However, they were not really plastic kits, being constructed from mixed media, with wood, acetate and metal components.

Being highly unstable and inconsistent, the first commercially available plastics were unsuitable for the earliest injection-moulding machines.

The Micromodels range of card models extended to ships, trains and historic buildings.

Interior Details of War Planes **from 1942. Notice the fighter's Ring-Sight, a long-obsolete instrument. RAF reflector sights were still a state secret.**

Although the most famous surviving early plastic is Bakelite, an American invention, the credit for production of the first true plastic construction kit, made entirely from a synthetic cellulose acetate, must go to Britain.

In 1932, two brothers, Charles and John Wilmot, founded International Model Aircraft Ltd (IMA). IMA produced a range of rubber band-powered flying model aircraft under the brand name F.R.O.G. (**F**lies **R**ight **O**ff the **G**round). Each model aircraft, constructed from a combination of pressed pre-painted tin with delicately formed pre-stressed paper wings, could be trimmed to perform countless feats of scale acrobatics. Indeed at the time, 'FROG' competitions were very popular. Youngsters vied for superiority as they held their fully wound models on the ground and watched them accelerate and climb skyward as the rubber unwound and the propeller began to spin. Peter, a friend of mine who remembers flying such models, told me that enthusiasts generally replaced the supplied dowel rod, against which the elastic 'motor' was tensioned inside the fuselage, for a substitute of greater diameter. Apparently, the thinner material often broke if the rubber was over-taut, causing enormous torque which

In the early-1970s, pen maker Platignum produced a range of card models in an attempt to revive the craze of pre-war years.

Flying Review, **January 1961.**

***U.S. Army Aircraft** published in 1942. Written and illustrated by aircraft enthusiast Roy Cross. Twenty-five years later he would be painting similar machines on Airfix box tops.*

***Aero Modeller Annual,** 1961-2. On the cover is 'P11.27' – the 'Harrier' prototype.*

collapsed the lightweight fuselage.

Although they were essentially toys, FROG aircraft, especially their high-speed 'Interceptor' monoplane, were an immediate success and IMA prospered. In 1936 it introduced a range of accurate ½nd scale model aircraft. IMA had decided to exploit the growing 'air-mindedness' which prevailed amongst men and young boys whilst the growing diplomatic tensions in Europe encouraged an arms race with numerous new aircraft designs abounding.

Delightfully evocative and eminently collectable 'Skybirds' packaging for their pre-war ½nd scale Hawker Hurricane multi-media kit.

Scale-line Constructional Plan of 'Albemarle Glider Tug', ½nd scale, 1942.

Being non-flying the new range of IMA aircraft were branded 'Penguins'. The first three Penguins were accurate scale replicas of some of Britain's contemporary (but, compared with the designs emanating from Hitler's Germany, still woefully inadequate) front-line aircraft – the Hawker 'Fury', Gloster 'Gladiator' and Blackburn 'Shark'.

As mentioned above, being constructed from somewhat unstable cellulose acetate, the various parts of FROG Penguin kits were often subject to twisting and

warping in the box prior to assembly by the purchaser's eager hands. Apparently, the main reason for this inconsistency was caused by IMA's practice of paying piecework wages to its moulding-machine operators. These early machines were hand-operated and the acetate material feeding needed time to cool sufficiently before it was released from the mould tool. Not surprisingly, operators, concerned with increasing their take-home pay, frequently failed to pause the process sufficiently for things to cool down. Consequently, parts sprang from the mould with an inherent 'memory', which led to warping. IMA were aware of this problem and did their

Veron 'SAAB J.29', typical of the solid wooden kits of the 1950s.

level best to prevent it, even resorting to cementing together larger pieces, such as fuselage halves, and packing them, suitably braced, into the kit boxes. Celluloid was also used for the smaller transparent canopy parts. Whilst not prone to as much distortion as the larger pieces, these had a tendency to yellow after a short time.

Despite shortages, IMA continued producing their Penguin range throughout wartime and had added replica ships, racing cars and modern saloons to the range.

Finding a better plastic material more suitable to the new science of injection moulding became a priority.

Change, however, was in the air. The exigencies of total war encouraged the manufacture of myriad items from synthetic materials including control switches, goggles and oxygen masks, pistol grips and transparent map overlays. The scarcity of sources of natural raw materials further accelerated technological development. By the war's end, techniques of injection-moulding polyvinyl chloride (PVC), and the rigid and stable plastic polystyrene, were finally perfected. PVC was a material that dated back to the mid-19th century,

Hobbies Weekly,
May 1948.

Hobbies Weekly,
July 1946.

Aeromodels ¼₄th
Scale 'Comper Swift',
1940.

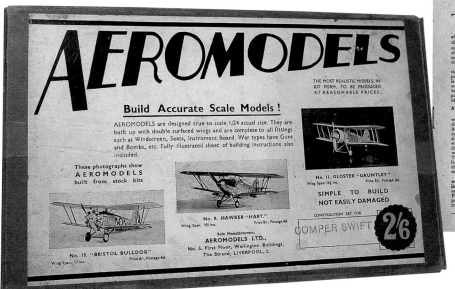

The Adventure Annual adding robots and spaceships to the lexicon of 1950s youth.

but which had traditionally been laboriously slow-cured in single moulds. Actually, it was only after suitable plasticisers had been added to PVC in the 1930s that this new material became useful at all.

As developers tried various formulas, one of them, America's Du Pont, launched the world's first polyamide – better known as Nylon. Among other things, Nylon was essential to the mass-production of reliable military parachutes. The previous silk ones, made from a material minutely studied by Du Pont chemist Wallace Carothers to point the way to his new synthetic, had a tendency towards static causing the silk parachute to fail and 'corkscrew'.

In Britain two major developments were of equal value in wartime. ICI's Alkali Division synthesised polyethylene, a material essential to the production of radar. Later, the same company developed polymethyl methacrylate, or 'Perspex', a material whose shatterproof qualities made it perfect for aircraft canopies.

Polystyrene as such was first discovered by the German apothecary Simon in 1839 but it was not until another German, Staudinger, had more carefully studied its molecular structure that its true potential was realised. As late as 1937 ICI were involved in standardising an economical method of stabilising polystyrene during storage – essential if the limitations exhibited by acetate were to be avoided.

By the early 1940s most of the uncertainties of injection-moulding polystyrene had been overcome and this

'Sky Devils Air Circus' – a typical entertainment for Britain's air-mad aircraft buffs.

Lincoln International
'Bristol Britannia', 1963.

method became the principal way of forming thermo-plastic materials.

Basically, injection moulding works like this: plastic material (usually in granulated form) is put into a hopper, which feeds the heated injection unit. The plastic is pushed through a heating unit by a recip-rocating screw and is softened to a fluid state. At the end of this unit a nozzle directs the fluid poly-styrene into a cold mould. Clamps hold the mould halves (or multi-sections) securely together. As soon as the plastic cools to a solid state the mould opens automatically and a series of ejec-tor pins push the moulded pieces attached to a frame or 'runner' (usually incorrectly called the 'sprue') out on to an automated production line. Here they are bagged, which is espe-cially important for transparent parts to prevent scratches, and boxed. Incidentally poor design of ejector pin location some-times leaves raised unsightly disks on visible parts of the model, requiring lots of tedious work to remove them.

With polystyrene the perfect raw material and injec-tion thermo-moulding the ideal process to shape its temporarily pliable form, the scene was at last set for the revolution in the toy and hobby industry which reverberates to this day.

Modern Wonder, 1938.

All-electric Erector set, 1940s, invented in 1913 by American manufacturer Gilbert. Very similar to Frank Hornby's Meccano, Gibert's Erector quickly became the dominant brand in the US and actually forced Meccano to close its fledgling factory situated in New Jersey. Incidentally, in 1990 the independent French Meccano bought the US Erector trademark and began marketing sets branded Erector Meccano in North America!

2. Going the Distance – the Classic Brands

Original artwork for the WWII 'Classic Fighters' set that Airfix packaged exclusively for British retailer Marks & Spencer in the late 1970s.

As with other products, differing brand names of kit manufacturers appear and disappear. However, due to the massive initial financial outlay required to enter the kit-manufacturing business in the first place, generally only those firms prepared to wait some time for a profitable return on investment – those in for the long haul – decide to enter the fray in the first place.

Fortunately, some of today's names would be familiar to modellers of many years ago. It's with these famous brands, principally Airfix, Revell-Monogram, Tamiya, Hasegawa, Italeri, ESCI, Bandai and Heller, that we shall begin. However, before we do, it would be unreasonable and alphabetically incorrect not to mention Accurate Miniatures in a book titled *Classic Kits*!

ACCURATE MINIATURES

I first became aware of the name Bill Bosworth whilst leafing through US publisher Schiffer's excellent tome, *The Master Scratchbuilder.* There, in the company of other modelling heroes such as Alan Clark and John Alcorn, a photograph of the genial founder of America's Accurate Miniatures depicted him proudly displaying his beautiful scratch-built Japanese WWII Mitsubishi 'G4M' 'Betty' which Bill built to an enormous ½2nd scale with a wingspan of 31 inches.

Shortly after seeing Bill's talents for myself and learning all about his fastidious attention to detail, I purchased one of Accurate Miniature's earlier kits, an excellent ¼8th scale replica of a personal favourite, Grumman's barrel-chested 'TBM Avenger' torpedo dive bomber. Like all other Accurate Miniature kits, the attention to detail and finesse of the parts in the thoughtfully packed box were remarkable and to my mind have never really been bettered.

I was fortunate to actually meet Bill during the IPMS Nationals in Telford in 1999. I was attending because my commemorative history of Airfix was being simultaneously launched on Dave Hatheral's Aviation Bookshop stand and on Humbrol/Airfix's stand. We shared the train journey back from Shropshire to London before parting company and heading for home – Bill had further to go – he lives in North Carolina, USA. We discovered we had a lot in common; a love for models and both our professional careers began in the advertising industry.

In their short life (Accurate Miniatures were incorporated in 1993 and ceased production in 2001), the company released models of more than 20 different types of aircraft, fixed wing and helicopters, and they produced numerous variants of many of their chosen subjects.

Each kit displayed the uncompromising attention to detail and accuracy that had previously characterised Bill's scratch building and had quickly established Accurate Miniatures as being quite different from the norm.

One of Accurate Miniatures' last kits, which I'm sure is going to be destined to become a modern classic, is their substantial ¼8th scale 'B-25B Mitchell'. This aircraft was immortalised when it mounted the audacious long-distance raid on the Japanese mainland shortly after Pearl Harbor. This version and its standard Army Air Force counterpart (Doolittle's raiders were stripped of all non-essential weight to enable them to complete their one-way journey) serve as a fitting testament to Bill's efforts.

In his *Plastic Aircraft Kits of the Twentieth Century (and Beyond)*, 'Guru of glue' John Burns says that following its demise, some Accurate Miniatures moulds were sold to Italeri. Apparently a new company entitled Accurate Hobby Kits might rise phoenix-like from the ashes. Let's hope so.

Accurate Miniatures' superb 'TBM-3 Avenger'.

AIRFIX

Fittingly perhaps, Airfix, the subject of my last book and a lifelong passion, is almost at the head of the list of enduring giants (if its position hadn't been usurped by Bill Bosworth's Accurate Miniatures it would have been precisely where Mr Kove, who founded the company in 1939, would have wanted). Kove came up with the name 'Airfix' – suggesting 'Fixed with Air' – so that his firm would appear at the front of trade directories. He founded the company in 1939 but it entered the model kit business in 1949.

As the original definition of the name suggests (many still believe it is derived from 'fixing' aircraft), Airfix originally made air-filled toys and novelties. These were mostly made of rubber, a commodity that became increasingly scarce following Japan's military conquest of British plantations in the Far East, forcing the firm to adopt synthetics.

Struggling to keep in business, Airfix was often forced to use myriad acetate scrap bits and pieces and even strip the insulation coatings off unwanted electrical flex in order to feed its hungry moulding machines. Fortunately, by producing acetate lighters and at one point actually cornering the home market for moulded plastic combs, Airfix survived the war years and the immediate period of austerity that followed. However, almost by accident, the firm took the first step on the construction-kit ladder.

Having acquired some injection-moulding machines – the latest in high technology – Airfix was commissioned by British tractor manufacturer, Ferguson, to produce a number of ready-assembled scale replicas of their newest tractor for use as a sales promotion piece. When Nicholas Kove, a wily opportunist adept at profiting from circumstance, was invited to provide a further quantity of these miniatures, boxed as unassembled pieces, he asked Ferguson if he could offer them for retail sale. Not surprisingly the tractor manufacturer jumped at the chance for such free 'PR'.

Where it all began, the 1949 'Ferguson Tractor'.

Airfix Toy Catalogue, early-1960s.

Unlike all Airfix kits that followed, the Ferguson tractor was moulded in acetate, which was a difficult material to work with and subject to distortion, encouraging frequent customer returns. Nevertheless, the tractor sold very well.

Encouraged by energetic young executive Ralph Ehrmann, who had brokered the deal with Woolworth and later rose to become Chairman of the entire Airfix group, Kove agreed to further pursue kit production by branching out into the production of new and different replicas. What seemed like an initial setback when Woolworth demanded a better wholesale price forced Airfix to abandon the use of boxes as packaging and supply unassembled pieces in simple plastic bags attached to paper headers; this proved a successful expedient. The classic Airfix plastic kit in its polythene bag was born!

The adoption of clear plastic bags meant that customers could see the contents of each kit without opening the package and risking either damaging or losing the tiny parts. A combination of Ehrmann's astute commercial activities, and the shrewd buying practices of the late John Gray, pointed the way to a future in kit production. Gray began his career at Airfix as a buyer

Examples of the toy range. Notice the charming innocence of juxtaposing the Tea Set and the Sand Moulds with the F. N. Rifle.

The Airfix F.N. Rifle in all its glory!

and profited from an extended supplier base and the dramatic reduction in the cost of polystyrene – a far better material than acetate as a substance from which to mould kits aimed at youngsters.

Airfix's first 'own brand' construction kit proper was the release of a tiny miniature of Francis Drake's *Golden Hind* in 1952. Moulded in polystyrene 'DS' – a new formulation that included a rubber component and was ideal for kit manufacture – the *Golden Hind* far exceeded sales forecasts.

Kove was reluctant to move away from a winning formula and thought Airfix should simply continue with model sailing ships. However, although the tiny 'Classic Ships' range was to grow and include numerous other vessels including *HMS Victory*, *The Great Western* and the *Santa Maria*, Ehrmann encouraged the firm's diversification. Soon a replica *Spitfire* was added to the range – almost an inevitability in post-war Britain – and the first in a long line of such aircraft, considered 'bankers' by most model manufacturers.

However, 1953's 'Spitfire BTK' was of doubtful authenticity and provenance, bearing a curious similarity to American firm Aurora's larger quarter-scale 'Spitfire' – even down to the erroneous decals! The 'new' 'Spitfire' was so bad that it encouraged a young modeller called John Edwards to write to Airfix suggesting that he could do better.

Hopefully, readers will allow me to spend a little time recounting details of John's short life (he died in 1970 aged only 38) which came to light following the publication of my last history of Airfix. His brother Peter told me about John's life before Airfix and it read like a thriller – I was only sorry that I hadn't been able to include it in the earlier book. Every Airfix veteran has told me that John was a charming, talented and very engaging chap but what I discovered reads more like a novel by John Le Carré or Len Deighton than anything to do with the gentle hobby of plastic modelling.

According to Peter, after John left school at Braintree, "graduating with 'flying colours' and passing matriculation with credits without even bothering with homework", he joined his uncle's photography business in Bayeux, Normandy. Although he "slogged away" in his uncle's darkroom for months, learning the tricks of the photographer's trade and perfecting his French to boot, he later nevertheless decided to return to Braintree. There he joined the Crittall Metal Window Company as a 'Window Design Draughtsman' and learnt the finer points of engineering draughtsmanship.

However, the story of precisely what John did when National Service beckoned immediately afterwards is even more enlightening and especially relevant to his later employment at Airfix.

Following his experiences in

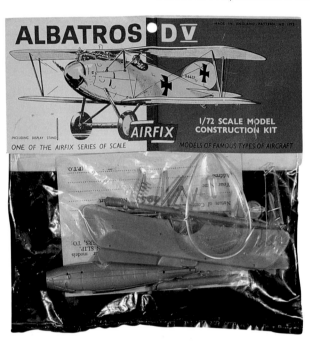

Original 'Albatros DV', 1957.

1960s Press Advertisement

France, John had demonstrated a particular facility with languages. He was as comfortable with German as French. Posted into the Royal Artillery he found gun laying somewhat boring and his new-found proficiency as a linguist little used.

John was asked if he could cope with learning another language – Russian. He said he thought it would be straightforward (his brother told me that John soaked up knowledge "like a sponge") and with his usual aplomb mastered the language in weeks. He was posted to the Intelligence Corps (I Corps) and soon found himself garrisoned behind the Iron Curtain in Berlin, a city then divided equally between the Soviet, American, French and British occupying powers.

John's first job with I Corps was to monitor Russian radio traffic. After a while he was involved with the interrogation of 'cross overs', those emigrants from East Berlin who sought asylum in the west – the Berlin Wall was yet to be built. Peter Edwards told me that John's role at this time was to try to help build a complete dossier of Soviet strength in personnel and equipment. Eventually, John and his colleagues noticed that a squad of Soviet conscript soldiers were quartered close by and, tasked with manning a mobile rocket-launcher kept secured in a commandeered barn, were in the habit

of abandoning their charge and nipping into the local town for a bit of rest and recuperation.

The opportunity to study this hitherto secret Russian weapon proved too much of a lure. When they were sure the Russian soldiers had left, John and his colleagues began their covert reconnaissance and broke into the Soviet arsenal hidden within the barn to record every detail of the armaments they found.

Being a keen modeller, it simply wasn't enough for John to photograph, measure and analyse every detail of the Russian missile system – he prepared plans and decided to build a scale replica of what he saw. Stealthily, he sneaked back to the British sector to begin planning this.

John then commenced scratch building a model of the new multi-barrelled rocket launcher. "Which was appreciated by all and sundry," said Peter. "I think he got his sergeant's tapes for that one," he laughed.

Now, with "the bit between his teeth", John proceeded to secretly build a collection of models of *all* the Soviet equipment in the Berlin theatre. His clandestine museum was exhibited on a trailer as a part of a travelling road-show which toured each quarter of the allied

½th scale Lifeguard Trumpeter, 1959.

Airfix/Bachmann Mini Planes.

First edition 'OO and HO' 'Farmstock'.

command, all this activity under the Soviet's nose whilst the Cold War was at its height.

Offered a commission to officer rank if he stayed in the army, John, by now married, declined and decided to return to 'civvy street'. Whilst back at Crittalls, in his spare time he built the first of the then brand new 2/- Airfix aircraft kits – the venerable 'Spitfire BTK' which was first available in 1953. Not surprisingly, Airfix's early and distinctly dodgy 'Spitfire' didn't much impress John Edwards. However, another kit purchase, a ½nd scale 'B25 Mitchell', by new US manufacturer Monogram, was a revelation.

Determined that British kits could be as good as those made in America, John answered an Airfix press-ad offering the position of design draughtsman. To boost his chances during the interview, John not only took references and details of all his qualifications and experience, he brought suggestions for the improvement of Airfix's fledgling 'Spitfire'. Armed with his own technical drawings, an improved version of the Airfix 'Spitfire' he had built himself and an example of Monogram's ground-breaking 'Mitchell', "which he revealed with a flourish, if I know my brother" said Peter, he warned the South London firm not to be too complacent.

"This is what you will soon be up against,"

he cautioned. As the interview drew to a close "the Airfix people went into a huddle," recalled Peter. Quickly they asked John when he could join. Without hesitation John told them he could start the next morning! The rest, as Airfix tyros will know, is history and as Peter said proudly: "The good old die was cast!"

Two years following the release of 'BTK', Airfix released a version of Johnny Johnson's 'MKIX Spitfire' ('JEJ'). Designed by John Edwards, this much-improved version of Mitchell's famous fighter was enhanced and retooled in 1960. Fittingly, this fine replica remained in the Airfix range for nearly 50 years and is a tribute to Edwards' skill.

Following his death, magazines heaped praise upon John Edwards. *Aircraft Illustrated* wrote: "John had been at Airfix for 15 years, almost from the beginning of the company, and was personally responsible for directing the design of all Airfix construction kits. It is only necessary to compare the early Airfix kits with such models as the Boeing 'B-29', 'HP O/400', 'He 177', 'Bulldog' or 'Sea King' to see what vast improvements were made. John's latest venture was the introduction of the new range of ¼th scale kits, but he has sadly only lived long enough to see the first, the magnificent 'Spitfire' I, put on to the market."

Perhaps May 1971's *Airfix Magazine* obituary says it all: "Mr Edwards leaves a fine memorial in the big range of kits he has designed and which continue to give pleasure to millions of modellers throughout the world."

First edition Airfix catalogue, 1962.

Veteran ½nd scale Messerschmitt Bf109G-6 (1965)

HO/OO scale 'Chieftain' tank, 1971.

⅓₂nd scale ready-made German half track.

kit collectors worldwide.

During the 1950s Airfix went from strength to strength and by 1960 was a big enough brand to warrant its own monthly consumer magazine. The inaugural edition of *Airfix Magazine* appeared in June of that year and was so successful it was to survive on and off until 1993. In 1962 Airfix published its first kit catalogue, the beginning of a tradition that has continued into the 21st Century, and now numbers more than 40 editions.

One of the secrets to Airfix success is the fact that it has employed so many gifted artists and illustrators to create its famous box art. Beginning with Charles Oates, Airfix went on to commission the talents of great artists like Roy Cross, a successful aviation artist who worked exclusively for Airfix for about ten years from late 1963. Still painting, for the last 30 years Roy has built an enviable reputation as a prominent marine artist. I was lucky

It is generally accepted that John's involvement with Airfix raised the bar in kit design, introducing innovations such as movable control surfaces and internal detail. Not surprisingly his criticisms of the appropriately short-lived 'Spitfire BTK' (recently re-released in bagged format on its 50th anniversary but using the mould of Airfix's seminal 'Mk1a' from the late seventies, the original tool having been revised to produce the first edition of Johnny Johnson's 'MkIX') means that original examples are 'rarer than hens teeth' and sought after by

A pocket money purchase dating from 1959, the year of the author's birth, Airfix's delightfully simple ½nd scale Hawker Typhoon.

Allegedly one of the rarest Airfix kits –
'Avro 504K', limited edition produced for
Quantas Airways' Golden Jubilee, 1970.

Definitely rare – *SS France* from
1963. The mould no longer exists.

Trio of ¹⁄₃₂nd scale old timers,
1962–1964.

enough to be introduced to Roy Cross whilst I was writing my last book about Airfix. I concentrated on his career in that book and touched on his time at Airfix in *Celebration of Flight*, his illustrated biography that I co-authored and which focuses on his aviation art. Roy's story is well documented and this isn't the place to repeat it. Other 'Airfix artists' include the chap who introduced the airbrush to Airfix box art in a big way.

However, readers might like to learn more about another famous Airfix artist, Brian Knight, who like Pete Edwards above, contacted me following the publication of my history of Airfix.

Like Roy Cross, Brian is one of the artists who add value to Airfix packaging with the addition of their wonderfully evocative illustrations. Equally, Brian also paints as actively today.

Brian was born in Reading in 1926 but is as bright and enthusiastic as a man half his age. Roy Cross, two years Brian's senior, also seems to defy the years – maybe there is a secret ingredient in Gouache paint which beauticians have overlooked!

Like many a youngster of his generation, Brian aspired to becoming an airman and hoped one day to join the RAF. He made model aircraft but although he enjoyed Penguins and Skybirds kits (when he could afford them) his favourite pursuit was scratch-building. Apparently, he used to fashion replicas from hard woods – his favourite was Sycamore because of its close grain.

"I have been drawing since the age of about four or five," Brian told me. "I guess most kids start then, but I was able to develop it more." As the Second World War

'Sheriff of Nottingham' Figures.

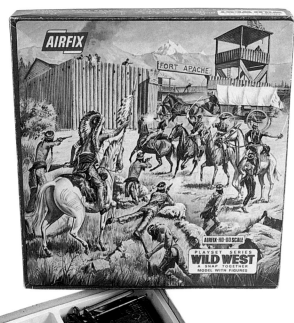

'Wild West' Playset, 1960s.

Airfix box top rough for Lockheed 'P-38J Lightning'.

Airfix box top rough for *HMS Hotspur* (1964).

Airfix box top rough for ½nd scale Grumman 'Widgeon'.

Airfix pencil rough for *HMS Cossack* box.

Pretty exciting promotional photograph of the Airfix 'Sherwood Castle' Playset. One can understand why, in the 1960s, the company relied on artists' skills to fire young imaginations.

Roy Cross artwork for 'Sherwood Castle Set'.

'Sunderland III' in Roy Cross box artwork.

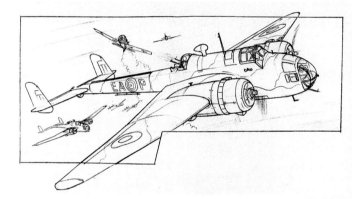

dawned and "the idea of doing anything artistic became out of the question", Brian joined Miles Aircraft as an apprentice draughtsman. He soon graduated into their design section. An early project Brian drafted was Miles's 'M52' supersonic aircraft. After this he joined an agricultural manufacturer and designed combine harvesters and associated agricultural machinery. Such subject matter hardly inspired Brian and very soon he moved on again.

His next move was to join the fledgling Atomic Energy Authority at Harwell. They had recently established a brand new studio and soon Brian rose to the position of studio manager there. "We did what politicians couldn't do for themselves," he told me. "They knew that the tax-payer was paying out all this money towards atomic energy research and that the only way it could be explained was by clear diagrams. So, I now became a technical illustrator – no longer a draughtsman." Employed at Harwell between 1947 and 1957, Brian developed a valuable facility for accurately describing the features and mechanisms of complex systems and structures. An essential ingredient for accurate depiction or aircraft or military vehicles.

At this period of his early career Brian said he "went into the technical illustration business with a vengeance." Better qualified to direct a variety of studio

H.P. HAMPDEN

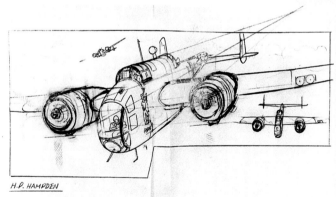

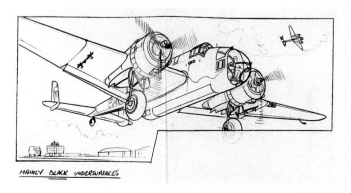

MAINLY BLACK UNDERSURFACES

procedures, Brian next became advertising manager for a small studio in Bromley High Street. Despite early enthusiasm for his new job, Brian soon discovered that few of his new colleagues were anywhere near his standard. Apparently the firm was simply unable to recruit staff of the standard blue-chip clients demanded and which the talented Brian aspired to. Disinclined to be held back, Brian decided to strike out as a freelance and he has been self-employed ever since.

At about the same time that Brian decided to go it alone, the US construction kit company established a British subsidiary, Revell (GB). With manufacturing capacity north of London at Potters Bar, the company was headquartered in the capital's Berners Street.

With his interest in aircraft and his facility for technical illustration, Brian decided that Revell, busy introducing a range of aircraft and ship kits into Britain, would make ideal clients. He pestered them relentlessly and

Surviving examples of early box top roughs are exceedingly scarce. Here, artist Brian Knight roughs out the box art for Airfix's HO/OO Arabs.

And here's the final result in colour! The release of this mid-'sixties set was no doubt inspired by the enormous success earlier in the decade of David Lean's 'Lawrence of Arabia'.

was eventually given a commission. He had fallen on his feet and a client–supplier relationship ensued which lasted a dozen years.

At this time Brian began to attend a great many toy and hobby industry trade fairs. Not surprisingly he made contact with Revell's competitors and soon came to the attention of one of the fastest-growing companies – Airfix. However, Brian had more than enough work from Revell, so wasn't desperate for new business. It wasn't until one Eric Robertson, Revell's new

Another Brian Knight box top rough. This time for the Airfix ½nd scale polypropylene 'Russian Infantry' set.

Final box art for the ½nd scale infantry set. Like other Airfix 'soft plastic' figures they aren't strictly kits of course. Nevertheless modellers used these cheap and plentiful figures as an ideal accompaniment in dioramas.

studio manager who had recently joined from Airfix told him of their interest, that he was encouraged to contact the famous British manufacturer. Brian was told that Airfix had a requirement for more artists – especially for their new larger-scale 'Classic Ships' range. Brian's first commission for them was *HMS Endeavour*. Soon, vessels from the age of sail became Brian's speciality. He progressed to produce the stunning artwork for the entire series, including such masterpieces as *Victory*, *Wasa*, *Prince* and *Royal Sovereign*. His last large-scale 'Classic Ship' was the *St. Louis*. Brian told me that he is somewhat disappointed by Airfix's current decision to cut out each ship as a vignette and discard some of the background detail of the original paintings.

As he was getting his teeth into sailing vessels for Airfix, Charlie Smith, the firm's then studio manager

Artist Brian Knight with two of his illustrations. He is standing alongside the Supermarine 'SE.6B' in Southampton's Hall of Aviation.

Original Brian Knight art for the Airfix HO/OO 'Astronaut' set. Dating from 1969, the release was timed to coincide with the 'Apollo' moon-launch.

said, "Brian, we are thinking about a new series. What are you like at figures?" Thus began another strand in Brian's career with Airfix and he began to prepare each and every piece of artwork for the entire HO-OO polythene figure range. Actually one of the factors that encouraged Airfix to ask Brian to switch to figures was because the firm had run out of subjects for sailing ships! Such was the success of these little and very inexpensive figures that Airfix could barely keep up with the demand. Brian recalls that each artwork was required "Yesterday"!

In fact, such was the pressure generated by the need to feed Airfix with illustration after illustration whilst the company expanded during the 1960s, that even senior Airfix management had to adopt a hands-on role to be sure that every new kit was released on schedule

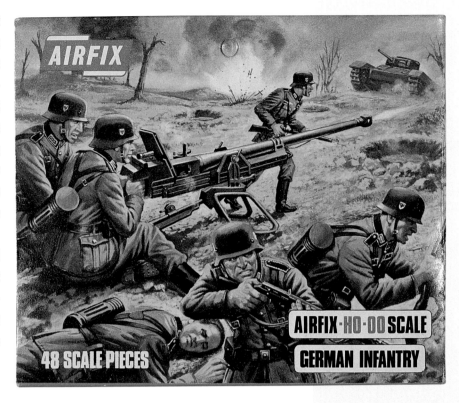

HO/OO German Infantry (First tooling) in revised box.

Brian Knight's art for the above prior to graphics.

Anonymous artwork for 'Caesar's Gate' Playset.

(remember the days when each month, at least three or four new kits appeared?) Indeed, even the late John Gray, when MD of the kits division, felt inclined to regularly mount dawn raids on his suppliers to check they were working to schedule.

"For example, early in the morning as he made his way to Airfix's Wandsworth offices, John Gray used to knock on the door of my Kent studio to enquire about the progress of *HMS Victory*," Brian recalled. "I said: 'For God's sake, I am working up until 10 o'clock on your work and you are on my doorstep at 7 o'clock the following morning. I need sleep!' Though in a rush, John respected me and left me alone." Such was the pace at Airfix nearly 40 years ago.

Both Roy Cross and Brian Knight regularly travelled by train to present their latest masterpieces to the Airfix management. Brian travelled from Petts Wood in Kent, Roy from Tunbridge Wells. Apparently they often

bumped into each other as they passed through London railway stations; one on their way to – the other returning from – a presentation at Airfix! "I knew Roy Cross very well. We passed each other like ships in the night. He was on the aviation side for Airfix and I was involved with ships and did some figure work," Brian said. When Brian joined Airfix, Roy Cross was already well established with the firm.

Brian was in the enviable position of working for three kit manufacturers at the same time (he clearly didn't need to sleep!) Together with Revell and Airfix, he also worked for Rovex (FROG) based in Margate. In fact he started with FROG on the same day as he secured his first commission from Revell. "I was so excited," recalled Brian. Cruelly, on the same day as he learnt that he had 'won' FROG, his father was diagnosed with cancer.

With business booming, Brian found it hard to keep

up with the demand generated by all three kit companies. "On one occasion, I had so much work on, I simply couldn't sleep for three days if I was to fulfil all the contracts," he told me. Once, on his way back home from a visit to FROG in Margate he was so exhausted that he fell asleep on the train, missed his stop and didn't awake until the train came to a halt in Charing Cross!

Brian told me that a good friend, the late Frank Wooton, was probably his greatest artistic influence. It was Frank Wooton who actually recommended Brian to Colport China and encouraged the artist to pursue a lucrative career undertaking commissions for collectible china.

Brian used to prepare monochrome gouache preliminary 'sketches' for each of his kit box tops. He found that the simple expedient of mixing black and white paint to create a range of tonal values produced illustrations that "enabled me to 'mentally' establish the

Detail from original art for ⅓₂nd scale 'Combat Pack'.

Detail from Stalingrad 'Battlefront' Set.

final colour concept of the finished illustration". He also prepared pencil sketches on tracing paper. He preferred working on this substrate because though it enabled sharp lines to be drawn it was equally capable of reproducing subtle shading and a range of tonal values. Brian used the full range of pencils – from HB to 6B.

I think the most memorable work that Brian ever did for Airfix was for the ½nd scale figure range. Here, he truly developed a unique style. Each of these boxes has an illustration of almost cinema poster impact which leads the viewer's eye from two or three figures interacting in the foreground leading back to a dramatic scene that extends beyond the middle distance to a panoramic background. I think these paintings, for which he was paid £125 per box top (they often took a fortnight to complete) were and are very different from the norm. They present a very imaginative way of using the limited space available and are, to my mind, Brian's

signature works.

Together with excellent box art, Airfix are justly recognised for the diversity of their subject matter. The following short selection of classic kits gives an idea of the firm's diversity. In 1965 Airfix secured the licence to produce replicas based on the successful 007 films. Their James Bond & Odd Job diorama from 'Goldfinger' was the initial result. Together with the Wallis Autogiro *Little Nellie* from 'Thunderball' that followed soon after, these kits commanded enormous sums on the 'collectors' market until they were re-released in the 1990s by Humbrol for a fraction of the dealers' price. Speculators beware – as long as they posses the original mould tools, kit manufacturers have an almost infinite capability to release supposedly rare kits. In 1967 Airfix added another 007 classic to their range with the release of James Bond's ejector seat-equipped Aston Martin 'DB5'. To my knowledge, this kit and James Bond's

Original art 54mm 'British Guardsman', 1971.

Original art 54mm 'French Imperial Guard', 1973.

Toyota '2000 GT' have yet to reappear.

Airfix are principally famous for their aircraft kits. The successes of the 1950s meant that the firm could afford to invest in larger injection-moulding machines. The consequence of this was that Airfix were able to produce larger and more complex kits. Even in ½nd – really the smallest 'universal' scale – many bomber and commercial aircraft with large wingspans required substantial tools. With the increased capacity, Airfix was able to meet the demands of eager younger schoolboys with the introduction of RAF Bomber Command's WWII 'Lancaster', 'Halifax' and 'Wellington' bombers. These kits were joined in 1966 by other 'heavies' – the RAF's Short 'Stirling' and the USAAF's 'B-29 Super Fortress' that had a truly awesome wingspan, even in ½nd scale.

The largest Airfix kits appeared in 1970 with the introduction of the massive ¼th scale 'Superkits' range of scale model aircraft. First in the range was a 'Spitfire

Revised HO/OO W.W.II German Infantry.

Detail from German W.W.II Polythene figures box.

Detail of W.W.II 'British Commandos' Box.

Mk 1'. This kit set new standards for worldwide kit production. It featured removable access panels, which revealed the fighter's eight machine-gun armament and detachable engine cowlings concealing an accurately scaled miniature of the 'Spitfire's' famous Rolls-Royce Merlin engine. For those who wanted more authenticity the model's propeller could be made to turn by the addition of an Airfix 'Spin-a-Prop' electric motor.

Incidentally, at the time of writing, the status of Airfix's legendary association

James Bond Toyota '2000 GT', 1968.

with model aircraft was again confirmed. This time by a letter that Ray, a keen-eyed pal of mine, spotted in *Private Eye*, the popular British satirical magazine. The letter concerned the accuracy of an Airfix 'Spitfire' that former Conservative leader Iain Duncan Smith was 'allegedly' constructing and had mentioned in 'his' diary. There's no escaping such a famous name!

Together with a demand for bigger and better kits, consumer trends in the 1970s also encouraged a big growth in military modelling – especially in the field of model soldiers. To satisfy this demand, in 1971 Airfix introduced the first of a new range of 54mm 'Collectors' model soldiers, a British Guardsman from the Napoleonic period.

Testament to Airfix's commitment to military modelling in the 1970s and especially to the 'traditional' British model soldier scale of 54mm was the

Airfix working 'Super Hovercraft' from the late 1970s – testament to the firm's confidence and diversity by this time.

Lotus 'Cortina', 1969.

VW 'Beetle', 1964.

Airfix 'Data Car', 1980. Complete 'with built-in electronic memory' – but how much? Certainly a fraction of what today's computer-literate youngsters enjoy on even the simplest PC game!

Spitfire

Classic Aircraft No.1
Their history and how to model them

by **Roy Cross** and Gerald Scarborough

The first in the *Classic Aircraft* range written by Roy Cross and Gerald Scarborough.

introduction of a fairly highly detailed 'toy' range of ready-assembled military vehicles. These series included the British army's then new Alvis 'Stalwart' amphibious vehicle and the artillery's powerful 'Abbot' SP gun along with some rather curiously chosen German 'adversaries' from WWII! The scale chosen for these miniatures was the direct equivalent of 54mm – $\frac{1}{32}$nd scale. At around the time of the introduction of their ready-assembled tank and vehicle range, Airfix introduced a series of construction kits in the same scale. They already had a well-established range of 00/H0 military vehicles, mostly tanks, introduced in the 1960s to accompany their famous polythene soldier sets. First in this excellent range was Airfix's finely detailed replica of General Montgomery's 'Snipe' staff car – 'Monty's Humber' – that appeared in 1972.

In the same scale, Airfix added other superb replicas to the range. These included a model of the half-

$\frac{1}{72}$nd scale 'Dambusting' Avro Lancaster from 617 Sq.

$\frac{1}{72}$nd scale Harrier GR-7

tracked personal vehicle used by Rommel, Monty's famous German opposite number in the western desert, and representations of Britain's 'Crusader' and 'M3 Grant' tanks, also from the El Alamein period. Unfortunately, $\frac{1}{32}$ scale was rather the odd-man-out in the field of military modelling, a genre which was rapidly being dominated by Japanese manufacturers, principally Tamiya. Airfix's competitors had adopted $\frac{1}{35}$th scale, which was also more popular in the USA. The incompatibility between scales, which prevented modellers from converting or adapting spare parts between kits from different manufacturers meant that $\frac{1}{32}$nd scale – for tanks and vehicles at least – was destined to fail. If you can't beat them join them, and ultimately Airfix were forced to chose $\frac{1}{35}$th. However, because they had to do so in a hurry, or risk losing market share, they were forced to purchase some mould tools from Japanese manufacturer Max and re-badge them as Airfix products.

By the mid-1970s Airfix had more or less conquered every area of plastic kit construction from aircraft to cars and ships through railways, model soldiers, military vehicles, large $\frac{1}{12}$th scale 'famous people' from history figures and numerous science fact and fiction models. On top of this, of course, Airfix Plastics had a large toy and craft range. The Airfix Group itself comprised a roll call of the most famous names in the British toy and model industry, including the famous model brand itself,

which like 'Hoover' had actually become synonymous with any product from its own industry, and equally respected names like Meccano, Dinky, Triang, and Pedigree.

Confident enough in 1975 to take a full-page advertisement in the *Financial Times*, under the heading 'Another Record Year', Chairman Ralph Ehrmann said "Never has such a short period of time so enhanced our potential." In the 1974/75 financial year Airfix Industries turnover was up 38 per cent and profits had leapt a staggering 30 per cent.

It seemed that nothing could stop Airfix, but little did Ralph Ehrmann and his MD know, trouble was looming.

The Airfix group of companies entered the 1980s with gradually accumulating problems. Although the kit division was still profitable, Meccano and Dinky were in trouble. Because of the cross-guarantee nature of the group structure, trouble within individual divisions quickly reverberated around the entire group. The knock-on effect of problems to the complex financial interlacing, essential to funding investment and providing cash-flow, was a cumulative disaster. Exports were down, which further limited cash.

Airfix products ceased trading in January 1981. Cruel irony dictated that the announcement of this sudden misfortune was made at the 1981 Earls Court Toy Fair.

Titled "Airfix Mirrors Depression", an article in the *Financial Times* from 30 January 1981, written by journalist David Churchill, read: "On the eve of the toy industry's annual

$\frac{1}{72}$nd scale North American P-51 D/K Mustang in Swedish markings

45

**Airfix HO/OO scale
'Jungle Headquarters'.**

trade fair, which opens at London's Earls Court tomorrow, Airfix Industries was yesterday finally forced to call in receivers."

His article, some of which I've reproduced below, gives the reader a very good impression of the tumult through which Airfix was trying to navigate.

"The development has been likely for the past 12 months as Airfix has struggled to stay solvent in a notoriously fickle business. Pre-Christmas toy spending — traditionally the industry's most important time — was unimpressive, even though low stockholdings by many retailers gave the impression that sales were good."

"With the recession continuing, and unemployment increasing, the outlook for toy spending this year is already gloomy. Exhibition space at tomorrow's fair is down by some 10 per cent and few exhibitors can feel at all buoyant about the prospects for 1981."

"Airfix, however, has been fairly bullish in recent weeks about its prospects, pointing to a revamped

**Airfix HO/OO scale
'Forward Command Post'.**

product range and claiming that its December sales were a record for the company."

The article went on to suggest that because wholesalers had let their stock of kits dwindle, the company might soon expect some hefty orders, but it was pessimistic about the future:

"In November, Airfix published its much-delayed financial results for 1979–80. These showed a pre-tax loss of £2.1m even before factory closures. These were followed in December by the interim figures showing a loss of £2.35m for the six months leading to end September on a decline in turnover from £11.8m to £11.3m."

"These results came after a year in which the company had struggled to reduce its bank borrowings. Just before Christmas 1979, Airfix closed its Liverpool-based Meccano factory with the loss of 900 jobs."

"The closure, a severe blow in an area of high unemployment, was contested by trade unions and MPs and managed to absorb much of the company's management time. Stockbrokers, Grieveson Grant, suggest that, 'had the Meccano closure proceeded smoothly the group would be in a stronger position'. In a further move to raise money to reduce its borrowings, Airfix sold its

profitable Crayonne and Declon plastics companies last November for £4.7m."

The day before the article appeared, Airfix issued a statement saying that it had "put forward proposals to its UK bankers for a financial reconstruction of the group", but unfortunately these had been unsuccessful. Ralph Ehrmann, Airfix's chairman, said that Airfix was "very surprised the banks were not prepared to accept the proposals as presented. They seemed very reasonable to us and our advisers." Consequently, Airfix had no option but to request a share suspension and to call in receivers.

The receivers continued to administer Airfix group businesses while they reviewed operations and sought buyers for the various Airfix divisions. "They aim to sell the various businesses as going concerns," said the *Financial Times.*

The 'Airfield Control Tower' originated in 1959 as a railway accessory. In the 1970s it reappeared for use in aircraft dioramas.

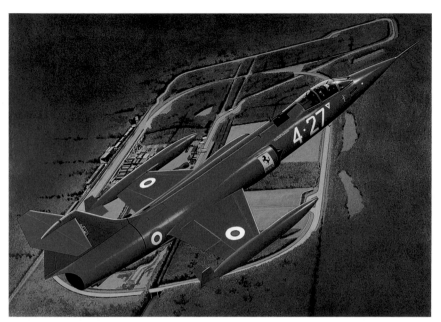

**Fine Gavin Macleod
artwork for the Airfix
¹⁄₁₄₄th 'F-104 Starfighter'.**

As the article made clear, Airfix wasn't the sole casualty of negative market pressures in the British toy industry. It reminded readers that only the previous year the famous British firms, Dunbee-Combex-Marx and Lesney were in trouble – the former calling in the receiver like Airfix and Lesney, the originators of 'Matchbox' cars, being forced to shed some 1,300 jobs. "Pressures on the industry face British industry in general. These include out-dated products, soaring sterling, rising imports, and a foreign stranglehold on vital new technology," wrote Mr Churchill.

The rather gloomy *Financial Times* article did end on a high note as far as Airfix is concerned: "However, Airfix has some bright spots since there is wide acceptance of the quality of its products," concluded the

**Gavin Macleod's
interpretation of Airfix's
¹⁄₇₂nd scale Junkers 'Ju-
87B Stuka'.**

Airfix BAe Red Arrows 'Hawks' (¹⁄₄₈th). Gavin Macleod.

feature. "But whether they can be produced cheaply enough to compete with overseas competition is a question that any potential buyer will have to consider."

Fortunately all was not lost and the famous Airfix brand was destined for survival. In 1981, outbidding Britain's Humbrol, who had long coveted Airfix, Palitoy, part of US Giant General Mills and famous as the British manufacturer of 'Action Man', the British equivalent of America's 'GI-Joe', plucked them from the limbo of receivership.

Shipping surviving Airfix moulds to their production plant in Calais, Palitoy audited the entire range under the heading 'List of A.F.T.O. (Airfix Take Over) Moulds'. So, beginning on 22 April 1981, Airfix classics such as the 00/H0 'RAF Refuelling Set' (acquisition cost: £2,000) and the new ½nd scale 'MiG 23 Flogger' (acquisition cost: £11,800 which gives some idea of their relative importance to a new owner), began their journey to the continent, where ironically they remain today, but more of that later.

Airfix's transfer of ownership to Palitoy wasn't a bad fit. Two years previously Palitoy had celebrated their diamond jubilee. Established by Alfred Pallett as

¹⁄₄₈th scale BAe 'Harrier GR3'.

Cascelloid Ltd in 1919 to exploit the new market for celluloid, the company manufactured a dazzling array of household articles. After exploring the potential of toy manufacture Cascelloid began the manufacture of toy dolls in 1925 and began to expand their interests in the children's market, registering the trademark Palitoy in 1935. Immediately after the Second World War Palitoy were able to demonstrate the first vinyl injection moulding of toy cars – to King George VI and Queen Elizabeth no less. In 1968 one of Britain's major industrial concerns, British Xylonite Company Ltd (BXL), who had

Airfix ¼₈th scale Supermarine 'Spitfire MkVIIIc'.

bought Cascelloid in 1931, sold Palitoy to General Mills Inc. By 1979 General Mills had grown into the world's No. 1 toy conglomerate. Airfix appeared to be in good company indeed.

In the early 1980s, whilst American-owned, decisions about forthcoming kit releases were shared with Airfix's North American sister company, M.P.C., also owned by General Mills. This explains why so many Airfix releases from the 1980s, such as the 'Star Wars' series of models, were also separately available as M.P.C. kits. Today Britain's Humbrol, who finally acquired Airfix in 1986, having earlier been outbid by General Mills and buying French kit manufacturer Heller in an effort to complete their hobby supplies portfolio, have only themselves to please.

As soon as a subject for a new model has been agreed, some three to four months of intensive product design work begins. Then, another three months are scheduled

for pattern making and as much as ten months allocated for tool making. Packaging design and commissioning the box top artist, designing and writing the instruction leaflet and production of the all-important decals (if included) runs concurrently with the tool-making phase. Combined, it takes at least a year and as much as 18 months before a kit idea actually reaches the shops.

Today the pace of kit release at Airfix is a fraction of what it once was. With tooling costs so fabulously expensive, like some other manufacturers the trend at Airfix is for mould-share – re-boxing kits which have appeared in other ranges (such as many of Airfix's more recent ¼₈th releases which were tooled by Japanese manufacturer Otaki). Fortunately, however, the famous Airfix logo can still be found aplenty in model shops and, as the kit brand enters its sixth decade, it remains Britain's greatest name in plastic construction kits. The story moves on.

Sadly, since publication of my 50th anniversary commemoration of Airfix in 1990, one of the major players from the 'old days' has left us.

John Gray, one of the prime movers behind Airfix kits, died in November 2000. He was 80 years old.

John will need little introduction to Airfix aficionados. Fans know that part of the company's initial success was down to his desire for scale accuracy and his love of aircraft – two passions he shared with Airfix's 'business brain', Ralph Ehrmann. However, I know Ralph would be the first to acknowledge John's particular role in encouraging Airfix to achieve new levels of excellence within the rapidly developing British injection-moulding industry.

John Gray involved himself in the minutiae of kit production and was as interested in box art as he was in mould tool design. Airfix artist Brian Knight told me that whilst on his way to work, John frequently called into

Gavin Macleod's interpretation of Airfix's venerable ½nd scale Westland 'Sea King'.

½nd scale RAF Avro 'Vulcan B Mk2' in the South Atlantic, 1982.

Brian's Kent studio to enquire about the progress of a particular illustration. At times this interference irritated Brian, who, like most artists, wanted to be left to work in solitude. However, they soon became firm friends and Brian realised that John simply cared. Fellow artistic supremo Roy Cross showed me surviving examples of pencil 'box top roughs', each emblazoned with either a bold 'Yes!' or 'No!' in John's distinctive hand. Such recollections are testament to his involvement.

John Gray joined Airfix from Lines Bros, where he was a buyer. Initially he fulfilled a similar role at Airfix, but soon rose to be general manager of the firm. Ralph Ehrmann told me about the volatility of Airfix founder

Nicholas Kove and how in the early days he often undermined John Gray and other senior Airfix colleagues. "Very shortly John and I became very close," Ralph told me. "When I first joined Airfix, there were two or three times when I had to stop John resigning. I'm sure that having John there helped me to carry on too," he said.

Every year Airfix would introduce new features such as optional parts and alternative liveries. They generally led where others followed and Airfix quickly became synonymous with value for money. Many such innovations were initiated or encouraged by John Gray. Modellers owe him a round of thanks.

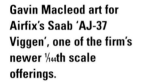

Gavin Macleod art for Airfix's Saab 'AJ-37 Viggen', one of the firm's newer ¹⁄₁₄₄th scale offerings.

Entire panorama of Gavin Macleod's art for the ¹⁄₇₂nd scale Westland 'Navy Lynx Mk8'.

Fortunately, Ralph Ehrmann is still very much with us. Though no longer involved with Airfix, typically Ralph is still involved with business and some very 21st-century ones at that. Despite his official retirement from industry, Ralph Ehrmann has become heavily involved with Cashbacs International, a leading-edge supplier of automated bank transfer systems established in 1987 and now sponsored by banking giant HSBC as an approved BACS bureau.

In January 1999, in the sumptuous surroundings of the Great Hall of Lincoln's Inn, shortly after the Toy Fair, Ralph Ehrmann was honoured for his outstanding contribution to the toy industry. At the British Toy & Hobby Association's fourth Roll of Honour Dinner, Ralph Ehrmann was presented with a specially commissioned bronze casting created by famous sculpture and figure modeller, Ron Cameron. As enthusiasts will know, coincidentally, Ron Cameron was one of the sculptors behind the master patterns of Airfix's model figure range.

This book is principally about the history and development of the plastic kit industry in general and the recent fashion in collecting old and out of production kits. An international market has developed with traders and dealers publishing lists of hundreds of mouth-watering rarities from yesteryear offered from a few pounds to many hundreds. A pristine Airfix Ferguson tractor might set you back a thousand pounds today and other rare Airfix kits are most collectible.

The fact that kit collecting has gained currency with experts is proved by recent media interest on the subject. Following publication of my aforementioned history of Airfix I was invited to present a section about collecting Airfix kits on British TV.

Recorded at Roy Cross's house in April 2000, the Airfix feature was actually broadcast on Channel 4's Collectors' Lot (a 'Two Four Production') in November the same year. Robert Smith was the presenter.

Despite having never seen it previously, I had some misgivings about the programme. I guess I was expecting a rather tongue-in-cheek satire along the lines of 'Here's Arthur – the test pilot for Airfix'. Robert's 'to camera' introduction, "Let's dive bomb into a subject dear to many men's hearts," didn't inspire much confidence either. I was, however, relieved when he confessed to being a collector himself – not of kits but of … chairs (and they say model fans are weird!) Apparently he buys classic furniture by designers like Charles Eames and Marcel Breuer. This revelation and the care with which the Production Company handled some of the more fragile examples from my collection quickly reassured me. I soon discovered that the programmers were sincere and not out for cheap laughs. Hopefully, the finished programme revealed their serious intent.

After turning a corner of poor Roy's studio into a 'shrine to Airfix' (lots of my kits piled atop a trestle table and flanked by Roy's original art and yet more kits) I was carefully positioned before the camera and encouraged to recall my fondest memories of Airfix. I was asked to explain precisely why and how I collect discontinued Airfix kits. Those lucky enough to see the programme might recall my somewhat disembodied head peering from behind a mound of classic old kits.

"Steady, steady …" Airfix 'Seafire' coming in to land. Another classic from the late Gavin Macleod.

Humbrol's Trevor Snowden had thoughtfully driven all the way down from Hull, bringing with him a bevy of current kits in varying states of assembly – thereby precisely demonstrating the kit construction process. Trevor was also able to unveil some Airfix newcomers which, as real enthusiasts will know, largely consist of licensed produced moulds like the ex-Otaki 1/48th scale aircraft (though these are very good indeed). He was able to show us early examples of the retooled 1/24th scale 'Harrier' now available in G3 guise.

Like me, Roy Cross was also put through the mill in front of the television camera. He was asked to explain how he brought the contents of the average Airfix box – some 40 or 50 small pieces of white, light grey or pale blue polystyrene – to life. He told viewers how he managed to create stunning artworks, which suggested infinite possibilities to the young imagination. He also described the process from box top rough to final artwork and took great pains to explain how he tackled the awkward 'letterbox' proportions of the average Airfix kit box – something I know Roy has always felt limited the

potential of his paintings. To be honest, Roy's performance suggested an entire programme dedicated to the box top artist's craft.

I have received a good few letters since my appearance on 'Collectors' Lot'. Some have come from unashamed enthusiasts and many from lapsed modellers who were spurred by the sight of so much 'Airfixania' into trotting to their local toyshop to buy an Airfix starter kit. Good for them! Many 40-something contemporaries of mine were relieved to come out of the closet in the happy realisation that they were in the company of lots of other over-grown schoolboys who couldn't escape all of their childhood passions.

What the programme managed to do, however briefly, was to transport sympathetic viewers back to an imagined halcyon time when, in exchange for 2/-, they could embark upon an exciting journey into an imaginary realm in which they controlled and led squadrons of fighter aircraft, flotillas of destroyers or troops of armoured fighting vehicles in pursuit of a vanquished enemy. To echo veteran enthusiast John Wells – Airfix

is after all "about childhood".

Finally, in this section about Airfix, enthusiasts might like to learn briefly some more information gleaned since the publication of my first book about the company. They relate to former Airfix factories and their survival and occupation today.

Haldane Place, the famous Airfix plant in Earlsfield, South London, survives today as a modern converted business complex. Previously, together with Airfix's design and manufacturing HQ, it was where all 'modellers of a certain age' posted complaint slips requesting the return of a missing or broken part.

Incidentally, today manufacturers have got wise to the fact that most of these requests are simply to help stock modellers, 'spare parts boxes'. Revell-Monogram for example minutely weigh each kit before despatch, so they know precisely if the contents is complete – be warned!

From 1949 to 1981, the products that filled the spare time of innumerable schoolboys (and their Dads) were made on the site of what is today landlord 'Workspace's'

Airfix ¹⁄₄₈th scale 'Buccaneer'.

JUST LIKE THE REAL THING!

The 66,000-ton "France" is the longest liner in the world, carries 2,000 passengers and a crew of 1,000. Launched in 1962, it cost almost £30,000,000 to build. This superb 1/600 scale model will make a wonderful companion to the Airfix "Queen Elizabeth" and "Canberra" 148-part kit—only 10/6. There are over 200 Airfix Kits covering 13 different series. And at 2/- to 17/6 you can well afford to make all your models *just like the real thing!*

AIRFIX CONSTANT SCALE
CONSTRUCTION KITS
Just like the real thing!
From model and hobby shops, toy shops and F. W. Woolworth

STOP PRESS

ROLAND C11
A realistic model of the World War 1 German fighter, known as 'the whale'. Complete with crew and swivelling guns, the kit includes special distinctive transfer markings. 31 part kit. 2/-

Also new Airacobra American Ground Attack fighter. 37 part kit. 2/-

Printed by Oxley & Son (Windsor) Ltd., 2-4 Victoria Street, Windsor

Press ad for Airfix's kit of the enormous liner, *S.S. France*. This is now one of the rarest Airfix kits as it is one of the few models for which the mould tool no longer exists.

previously occupied by Ediswan light bulbs. This building dated from about 1900 and had originally been an abattoir. Airfix then bought the building in about 1953, and subsequently acquired a laundry, a sweet factory, a Martini bottling plant and various other 'metal-bashing' concerns. The company's building (now demolished and replaced by a DIY store) that stood at the top of Haldane Place, at the junction with Garratt Lane, carried the Airfix name and logo on its roof.

Ralph Ehrmann recalled that "most of the workforce lived in the immediate vicinity of the factory – it was very much a local company, as were most of the many factories in Earlsfield and Wandsworth at that time. Some of the skilled tool-makers lived a little further afield in Earlsfield and towards Clapham."

Initially, all this, and the assembly and packaging as well, took place at Haldane Place. Subsequently Airfix set up a warehouse in nearby Ravensbury Road – one local resident remembers going there each week to collect a dozen or 20 models to make up for shop displays, a useful source of extra cash. In 1973 additional moulding and assembly facilities were established in a former tram depot in Charlton to meet increasing demand.

Interestingly, at the time of writing, a work colleague showed me an item on the internet which described the redevelopment of the Greenwich Peninsula Airfix site into a modern commercial retail park. "Redevelopment of this brown field old industrial site that was heavily polluted, required careful consideration," the article read. "Up to 4m of made ground contaminated with volatile organic chemicals and coal ash had been tipped on the Charlton Marshes early in the 20th century for a tram depot followed by an Airfix factory."

I find the phrase "an Airfix factory" rewarding. It suggests that, after all this time, in Britain at least, the brand name is still as synonymous with model kits as 'Hoover' is with vacuum cleaners.

Riverside Business Centre. Haldane Place and Bendon Valley, the next road to the north, were (and remain) narrow, unprepossessing streets of terraced housing and small factories and workshops terminating on the banks of the River Wandle.

Ralph Ehrmann, chairman of Airfix Industries throughout the Haldane Place years, remembers that, to begin with, the company rented a 14,000 square foot factory

Bringing the Airfix story as up to date as I can, I must mention the firm's recent change of ownership (Airfix fans are getting used to this!) In May 2003 a press release stated that: "Hobby Products Group (Holdings) Limited, the Holding Company for the Group including the famous names of Airfix, Humbrol, Joustra & Heller, has a new controlling stakeholder, Business Development Group ('BDG')."

BDG said that they had acquired the stake as part of a management review of the Group and foresaw the move would help it to further develop Airfix, *et al*, as a "major force in the hobby and leisure market." Humbrol's response was equally upbeat. They said they were "delighted to see such a major commitment from BDG in terms of their confidence in the future growth prospects of the Group" and looked forward to building on the success already achieved. Naturally, Airfix devotees worldwide would echo these sentiments.

The Airfix design office outing to Paris in 1964. It allegedly cost £14 10/- each. John Gray gave each employee an additional half-day holiday and said that he wished he was coming too. From left: Peter Allen, John Edwards and Mike Mason. Apparently, Mike was one of the product designers who had a penchant for mould design – Peter favoured component design, so they often swapped these elements with each other!

Upon his retirement from Airfix, John Gray (second from left) is presented with a travelling clock by Chairman Ralph Ehrmann. Fellow directors O.V. Hoare (left) and F.D.G. Norburn look on.

Titled Airfix 'Present ¼th scale Harrier', the original caption to this picture from May 1974 reads:
"During recent months Airfix have been working in close co-operation with the Royal Air Force and No.1 Fighter Squadron in particular to produce their latest ¼th scale Superkit – 'Harrier GR.1'. As soon as the first production model became available Airfix Technical Researcher, Barry Wheeler, got to work and built the first ¼th scale model of this famous aircraft."

Picture shows: Wing Commander P.P.W. Taylor, O/C No.1(F) Squadron, Royal Air Force Wittering being presented with the first 'Harrier' model by Barry Wheeler (right) while Airfix draughtsman Peter Allen (centre) looks on. The presentation took place on the airfield with one of the squadron's operational aircraft in the background.

AMT

I'm sure that most plastic kit enthusiasts know that 'AMT' – three letters that signify one of the greatest names in model car and truck construction kits – is derived from this American company's original name, 'Aluminum Model Toy Company'. Those who didn't know this have learnt something!

Although AMT, which began making construction kits shortly after the Second World War, released many aircraft kits in the late 1960s (mostly re-boxed FROG and Hasegawa originals), the company is justly famous for its automobile models. AMT's range is enormous and includes everything from their first ever all-plastic car kit, a 1953 convertible Ford 'Indy Pace Car' in ⅟₂₅th scale and the memorable 1960 'Edsel Ford' to more modern classics such as 1977's 'Kiss Custom Chevy Van' which came complete with decals of the US Glam Rockers clad in cat-suits, face-paint and outlandish platform-soled boots.

Like most other North American kit manufacturers who fuelled that nation's insatiable demand for models of the latest production coupés or show cars, AMT also caught the 'far-out' wave of Flower Power and produced many outlandish custom vehicles, characteristic of the late 1960s. Personal favourites include the 1960s ⅟₂₅th scale 'Lil Roamin' Chariot', which came complete with stylised bodywork which suggested it was Spartacus on wheels, and 'Royal Rail', a ⅟₂₅th scale dragster from 1970 which cocked a snook at supposed British pomposity by including a seat and cockpit arrangement shaped like a Monarch's crown!

In 1978 Britain's Lesney, owners of the 'Matchbox' brand, purchased AMT. A few years later AMT's tools were in turn acquired by the ERTL Corporation and most recently they have become the property of die-cast manufacturer, Racing Champions.

Snap-together AMT 'Batskiboat' from 'Batman Returns' movie.

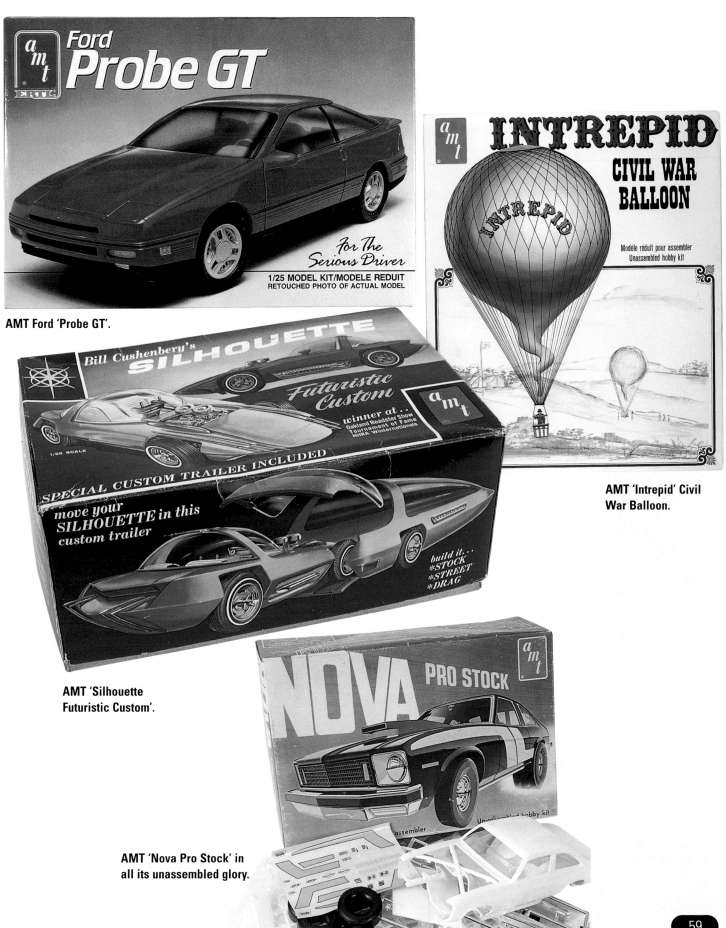

AMT Ford 'Probe GT'.

AMT 'Intrepid' Civil
War Balloon.

AMT 'Silhouette
Futuristic Custom'.

AMT 'Nova Pro Stock' in
all its unassembled glory.

AURORA PLASTICS
OF BROOKLYN, NEW YORK

Aurora began life in 1950 when Americans Abe Shikes, John Cuomo and Joe Giammarino rented small premises in Brooklyn, New York. Led by Shikes, a GI who had returned from active service and decided to invest his pre-war talents in sales into a new plastic manufacturing venture, the trio energetically exploited any opportunity to turn an honest profit.

An early success, which illustrates their imaginative spirit, occurred when Aurora purchased a job lot of failed coat hangers that were too narrow to securely support heavy garments. With the bravado that characterised its early days, Aurora simply converted the useless plastic items into inexpensive bow and arrow sets for kids! Production costs were diligently kept to a minimum. In return for crates of cold beer, off-duty firemen were employed to tie the bowstrings.

During its first two years, Aurora survived by making a disparate range of household goods and toys.

The breakthrough came in 1952 when Shikes was buying birdseed in a local general store. Noticing some new plastic kits, of the type Aurora were perfectly capable of producing, he was amazed to discover the apparently high price being charged for them. Returning to Aurora's offices, he convinced his colleagues that the kit business might be the way ahead.

So, reducing the scale and number of component parts, Aurora set about making models similar to the premium-priced ones Shikes had seen earlier.

Their first kit was a replica of a Grumman 'Panther' – one of the new breed of US jet fighters that had caught the mood of the times and about which no self-respecting American schoolboy was ignorant. It was 75 per cent cheaper than the larger model of the same machine with which Shikes had decided to compete head-on. Not surprisingly, Aurora's kit better appealed to the pockets of young consumers and the company immediately followed its first release with another jet fighter kit, this time a model of Lockheed's new 'F-90'.

Both kits were packaged in boxes which featured innovations. Firstly, the price (99 cents) was litho printed as an integral part of

⅛th scale 'US Sailor', 1957.

the box art and, secondly, each kit was shrink wrapped in transparent plastic. The former feature prevented wholesalers and retailers price setting, offering consumers an honest price, and the latter development meant that purchasers could take their new models home, secure in the knowledge that the contents hadn't been tampered with and that all the parts were included. Shrink-wrapping kits is now common practice.

Both kits sold extremely well and Aurora was forced to expand its operations and move to bigger premises in a re-developed bakery nearby.

In 1954 with a dozen items now in their catalogue and profits on the increase, Aurora moved yet again. This time, however, they enjoyed the luxury of a purpose-built facility housing 12 modern injection-moulding machines.

Aurora was a very pleasant working environment, and the management of Shikes as President and Vice Presidents Giammarino and Cuomo steered the company with a gentle benevolence, ensuring that staff enjoyed all modern benefits.

By the early 1960s Aurora had sales of around $20 million. Financial success could only be partly attributed to conventional plastic construction kits, however, because the company's revenues had been boosted by income

from slot car racing products, Aurora being one of the earliest American operators to invest in a popular craze that had developed in Britain. Aurora model kits, often marketed under the brand 'Playcraft Toys', did particularly well in Britain – it was definitely a reciprocal trade.

Another key to their rapid growth was Aurora's growing list of figure kits. Probably the most successful of these – which began with a small range of polystyrene figure models representing each of America's traditional fighting men – was Aurora's famous monster range. These ghoulish creations, each based on an infamous

½nd scale Ford 'T Dragster'.

Aurora Roman Bireme.

½th scale 'Mr Spock', 1972.

creature from movie history, had enormous appeal with young-sters. They are probably Aurora's most famous range and had enormous crossover appeal, and, being simple to construct, they were bought by enthusiasts and non-modellers. A 40-some-thing American friend of mine, Ed, grew up in Boston during the 1960s. Like most well-balanced characters he abandoned plastic kits when he entered his teens. However, as I was wittering on to him with stories about kit compa-nies, he suddenly perked up when I mentioned the name 'Aurora'.

Like thousands of American kids in the 60s, Ed remembered having many of Aurora's 'Famous Movie Monsters'. He remembered two kits in particular – 'The Witch', illustrated in Aurora's advertising stirring a boiling cauldron to which she was adding live rats, behind the slogan "Look what Aurora has cooked up now – Mrs Black Magic herself", and 'The Bride of

Frankenstein' ("Here comes the bride"). Each kit retailed for $1.49.

Together with Aurora's famous range of medieval knights like the well-known and very collectible 'Silver Knight of Augsburg', the manufacturers long association with D.C.Comics – on the pages of whose pulps Aurora booked regular press ads to promote model replicas of the very heroes shown on the covers – spawned the range of models for which the firm is most famous, Figure kits, which were really the high point of Aurora's success. Indeed, so popular are they that many of the kits are available today.

When Aurora ceased trading in 1978, Monogram pur-chased many of their moulds, reissuing them under their own banner. Figure kits such as 'King Kong', 'Batman', 'Superman', 'Frankenstein', 'Dracula', 'Wolf man' and 'Godzilla' enjoyed a new lease of life with Monogram, as did almost the entire range of 'Dinosaurs' – including the 'Giant Woolly Mammoth', which, in model form at least, shared the stage with pre-history's giant reptilians.

All collectors want to learn which kits from the famous manufacturers are the rarest and consequently most valuable. Well, during the transfer of mould tools westwards from New York to Monogram's home outside Chicago, certain Aurora moulds suffered irreparable

½th scale 'Centurion' tank, 1970s.

Fokker 'E.III'.

damage in a rail freight accident. The author has to thank John Burns of the Kit Collectors Clearing House, and possibly the world's most knowledgeable kit enthusiast, for supplying details of which kit moulds were trashed. They are the 'Aero Jet Commander', 'Albatros C.III', 'Halberstadt C.L.II', 'Brequet XIV' and 'Cessna Skymaster'. If you find these kits in their original packaging, think carefully before making them. Ironically, as with other collectible models, they are worth more unmade than assembled.

Collectors will be grateful for the activity of US toy company 'Playing Mantis', and specifically the actions of its cleverly named 'Polar Lights' kit brand (a play on 'Aurora Borealis' – geddit?), for they have taken it upon themselves to re-release many of Aurora's classic scale models. These include many of their figures from films and TV shows, such as 'James Bond', 'Lost In Space' and 'The Man from U.N.C.L.E.'

I understand that Polar Lights, who reproduce ex-Aurora models under an arrangement with Revell-Monogram who now own most of the tools, have perfected a process whereby they can actually recreate the original model without having to resort to the original heavy steel mould-tool. Apparently they use a process that reverses the original procedure and actual-

ly enables a new tool to be cut using surviving moulded parts from the original unassembled kit, as long as they remain in pristine condition. Who knows, perhaps they will furnish modellers with replicas of the 'missing' five aircraft mentioned above?

Mint and boxed Boeing 'F4B-4'.

Quarter scale 'DH10' Bomber by Aurora Playcraft.

Keen eyed readers will notice that the Nieuport cost 39p in Woolworth's in the mid-1970s.

BANDAI

Bandai 1974 catalogue.

Japanese and other Far-Eastern kit manufacturers have long recognised the commercial advantages of diversification. Although Tamiya is renowned as perhaps the best kit company in the world, it does not depend entirely on its plastic model business. Profits are evenly spread between model construction kits and radio control (RC) cars and, more recently, military vehicles. Indeed, relative newcomer Dragon produces parallel product lines with its substantial model kit operation operating alongside an increasingly successful range of ⅙th scale articulated military figures, designed in the Action Man/GI-Joe mould but aimed at collectors, not kids.

Bandai, like Tamiya, is a Japanese company that has also successfully built a business across a range of business areas. Today Bandai is the top-selling toy manufacturer in Japan with a range of market-leading products such as 'Gundam', 'Power Rangers' and 'Digimon'. Each has conspired to make it a global giant. More recently the company has diversified into the entertainment and leisure fields with operations ranging from confectionery and vending equipment to computer, video and DVD software and even children's toiletries!

Incidentally the original company name, 'Bandai-Ya', derives from a Chinese Zhou Dynasty manual of military strategy which, when translated into Japanese, means 'eternally unchanging', a concept the late Naoharu Yamashina, who founded the company, felt appropriate for an organisation intent on bringing joy to youngsters regardless of their nationality or circumstance.

Yamashina started Bandai in July 1950 and his company began life selling a range of celluloid and metal toys. It also did well with a range of rubber swimming rings aimed at the domestic market. However, within a few months Bandai was marketing its own products and by 1955 had expanded sufficiently to require new offices with in-house Research and Development, manufacturing and distribution operations.

Following the enormous success of its 'Cars of the World' range, own-brand slot racing systems (a craze which swept the world in the early 60s) and especially a particularly popular remote-control toy car product, Bandai had outgrown even these premises and was forced to move again. This time Bandai hit gold with its 'AstroBoy' product range — the company's first TV-Character

Delightfully 'deformed' McDonnel-Douglas F-15A Eagle by Bandai. Very similar to the bizarre 'Egg Craft' range of aircraft caricatures released by Hasegawa in the 1970s.

Some more great kits from the mid-1970s.

'RX-78' figure, one of the Mobile Suits (MS) developed by the rival forces of the 'Earth Federation' and its adversaries in the 'Principality of Zeon'. Actually 'Gundam', made a debut on Japanese TV in 1979. It was the idea of director Yoshiyuki Tomino and 'Hajime Yatate', the pen name of all those artists at Sunrise Studios, the animation studio Bandai bought outright in 1994. Since then, 'Gundam' has become one of Bandai's most significant product lines and by July 1999 the firm had sold an outstanding 300 million 'Gundams'!

With a name for producing a large and very successful toy range (many of them aimed at the lucrative pre-school and early teens market) and with numerous 'Power Ranger', 'Gundam', 'Tamagotchi' (how many other dads remember forking out for these 'cyber pets'?), 'Bratz', 'Betty Spaghetti' and, most recently, 'Digimon' toys to its credit, Bandai is a true giant.

However, other than for its earlier military miniatures range, today Bandai is perhaps best known with model enthusi-

Contrast in styles, Bandai's amazing ¹⁄₈₅₀th scale USS Enterprise NCC-1701 from Star Trek and the tiny ¹⁄₄₈th scale 'Panzer IV' from 1973.

Gone but not forgotten, Bandai's classic ¹⁄₄₈th scale 'Pin Point' series.

toy and the forerunner of many subsequent pan-media tie-ins.

Bandai Models was established in 1971 and very quickly caught the attention of modellers and hobbyists worldwide with a superb range of ¹⁄₄₈th scale military vehicles and accessories.

Very rapidly, Bandai exploited the enormous success of this range by producing accessory sets and various figures, enabling enthusiasts to complete realistic diorama settings to display their models.

Although Bandai's prolific range of military models is a landmark in the company's development for many modellers, the firm possesses a notable back catalogue of cars and commercial vehicles, some in very large scales, and has also produced a great number of aircraft kits. Many of the latter were made using other Japanese manufacturer's moulds – notably Imai and Kogure – and a great many were ex-Monogram (with whom Bandai had signed a co-operation agreement in 1976).

With many modellers, it has to be admitted that Bandai's high point was when it embraced the 'Patlabor' and 'Gundam' robot craze, producing dozens of these fantastic creations in a variety of scales and complexities.

Bandai introduced many modellers to the world of 'Gundam' in July 1980 with the advent of the classic

asts as a manufacturer of science-fiction kits. Recently, the company released a superb replica of the original TV version of Star Trek's *USS Enterprise* that was launched simultaneously in six countries including Japan, Korea and the United States. The mouldings of this all-singing-all-dancing kit are pre-coloured and, when assembled, enclose a complex range of fibre-optic filaments which enable purchasers to illuminate the finished model with an array of interior and navigation lights all to scale and guaranteed to make this, not inexpensive, masterpiece the talk of any collection.

Millions of Gundam owners can't be wrong.

DRAGON

Dragon ¹⁄₁₆th scale 'Warrior Series'. A figure modeller's dream.

won many awards – notably from enthusiast magazines and modelling societies throughout the world.

DML constantly re-invests its capital, procuring the latest tools and equipment required to maintain such high standards. Since it began, DML has produced more than 600 items, a prolific rate of new releases not seen since the heyday of Airfix in the early 1970s.

Recently DML's products have also been marketed under the 'Revell/Monogram' banner in the USA, 'Revell' and 'Italeri' in Europe, and 'Hasegawa' and 'Gunze' in Japan.

When DML's ¹⁄₃₅th scale military vehicle and figure range first appeared in the late 1980s, the quality and variety of the new kits were the first serious challenge to Tamiya's iron grip on this sector for nearly 20 years. These kits often feature box-top illustrations created by respected military artist Ron Volstad, familiar to readers of *Military Modelling Magazine* and Osprey's classic *Men-At-Arms* range of enthusiasts' books.

In 1997, DML diversified into the airliner model field, manufacturing models for airline promotional use and for collectors. The resultant 'Dragon Wings' line of 1:400 scale aircraft has since grown to become one of DML's most successful and diverse series, representing unique liveries from nearly 100 commercial and government air-lines. Maintaining strict standards to original aircraft specifications, working parts, accurate commercial markings and scale, Dragon Wings continues to hold a unique and respected position in the die-cast model aircraft industry.

The success of Dragon Wings encouraged DML to create an entirely new series of die-cast aircraft models – the 'Warbirds' – an ever-expanding line of 1:72 scale fighter aircraft ranging from WWII classics to the

President of Dragon Models Ltd (DML) Freddie Leung established the Hong Kong-based company in 1987 and created Dragon Shanghai as the company's mainland China operation prior to Britain returning Hong Kong to China when the 'lease' on the territory expired in 1997.

From the beginning DML designed and manufactured its own plastic model kits and exported them to all parts of the world via its agents in different countries. The high quality of DML products rapidly won the recogni-tion of international modellers and the new company cutting-edge machines of today.

In 1999, DML diversified further, using all the skill and knowledge acquired with kits and die-casts to extend its modelling activities to the much larger ⅙ scale with the introduction of its 'New Generation Life Action Figure' series. As Dragon themselves say, "By the following January, this series – fully poseable military and licensed 12-inch figures featuring meticulously researched cloth uniforms, detailed weapons and equipment – was universally recognised as the new benchmark in high-quality collectable action figures, winning several awards from industry magazines and building a strong and passionate base of Dragon action figure collectors. The series currently stands at some 250-plus individual releases, with subjects varying from World War II, Modern Special Operations and Law Enforcement to licensed character figures from film,

popular music, sports, electronic games and comics."

Buoyed by the success of its ⅙th scale figure range, DML has continued to expand its catalogue of figures aimed at collectors with a range of smaller items, the 'Dragon Minis' series of figures that are especially popular in Hong Kong and the 'Action18' series of ultra-realistic ⅟₁₈ scale fully poseable action figures. These figures, which Dragon claim feature "a unique composite of modelling and action figure philosophies", feature a comparable level of accuracy to Dragon's immensely popular ⅙ scale action figures, but are produced to a scale designed to appeal to modellers and diorama builders.

Currently, DML's wide-ranging business activities encompass everything from plastic model kits, action figures, die-cast collectables, to numerous resin, PVC and vinyl products.

Dragon's ⅟₃₅th scale military series range is superb.

EAGLEWALL

Eagle comic – what a brand!

The quiet Surrey town of Dorking seems an unlikely location for plastic kit manufacture, yet in the late 1950s its tiny West Street foundry was the birthplace of two classic brands.

After achieving some commercial success with a range of compact ⅟96th scale WWII warplane kits, moulded in grey polystyrene and packaged in inexpensive polythene bags as Airfix had, and marketed under the foundry's 'Vulcan' brand name, its foundry set its sights on a potentially more lucrative commercial arrangement.

Publisher Hulton Press's *Eagle* comic, which had been launched in 1950 supported by a massive £30,000 advertising campaign, had become an institution with British schoolboys. Illustrated by the legendary Frank Hampson, *Eagle* is most famous today as the home of space pilot Dan Dare and his faithful sidekick Digby. The weekly comic chronicled the duo's struggle against the evil Mekon, one of the first of numerous malevolent space aliens, which have since become a staple of science fiction.

Along with its flagship sci-fi series, *Eagle* also served up popular stories of allied derring-do from the recent world war. The war was still a vivid memory for many readers and their families. *Eagle* featured regular stories, which looked at the famous battles, campaigns, and assorted weapons, which contributed to the war effort.

The Dorking Foundry decided that reissuing the existing Vulcan model kit range under the *Eagle* banner might revitalise their products. Consequently the range was repackaged in stout boxes emblazoned with *Eagle's* masthead and accompanied by full-colour illustrations in

Vulcan 'FW190' bagged, prior to rebranding.

Vulcan ⅟96th 'Me109' boxed, prior to rebranding.

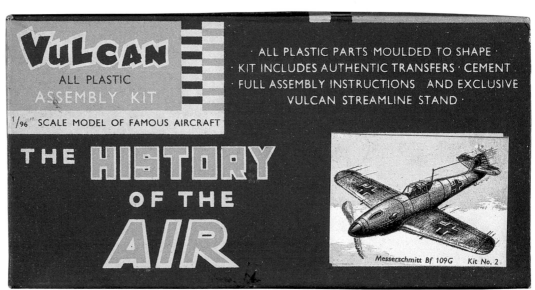

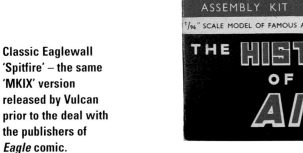

Vulcan boxed 'Spitfire'.

Classic Eaglewall 'Spitfire' – the same 'MKIX' version released by Vulcan prior to the deal with the publishers of *Eagle* comic.

Eaglewall *HMS Ajax*.

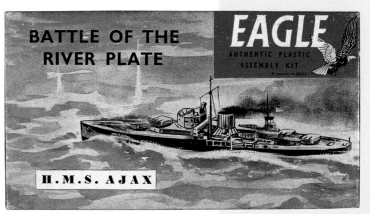

Eaglewall 'Battle of the River Plate' warship group.

Proprietor of 'Dorking Models', Anthony Lawrence, shows the author some of his large collection of Eaglewall classics.

Eagle's signature style (the bagged Vulcan range featured simple one-colour headers with dull illustrations, which doubled up as instruction leaflets). The new range was branded 'Eaglewall'.

Suitably born again, the 1/96th scale aircraft series was an immediate success with consumers and was soon supplemented with a range of WWII warships depicting incidents from famous naval battles. These included actions such as the 'Battle of the River Plate' and the famous *Altmark* incident, when British POWs were plucked from the eponymous German prison ship from the supposed security of a remote Norwegian fjord.

Enthusiasts will know that Eaglewall were adept at re-using supposedly identical sprues in an effort to release apparently identical sister ships like those in the Kriegsmarine's 'pocket' battle-ship class, for example. In reality the original ships differed considerably. This expedient enabled Eaglewall to rapidly increase their range at minimal expense!

Eaglewall produced models under license from other manufacturers. Notable amongst these were American

'Design-A-Car' instructions.

Eaglewall 'Design-A-Plane' packaging.

'Design-A-Plane' instructions.

manufacturer Pyro's 'antique' firearms and 'Design-A-Car' range. Despite such bold commercial initiatives, however, the firm ran into financial difficulties. Eaglewall was forced both to end its commercial relationship with Hulton's *Eagle Comic* and ultimately to cease all production in 1964. Consequently, Vulcan and Eaglewall kits are now sought-after collectors' items. For those keen to see how extensive the range is, I would recommend a visit to Anthony Lawrence's excellent shop, Dorking Models, where customers can examine probably the best display of such rarities in existence.

Eaglewall Royal Navy corvette and 'lend lease' US vessel.

Eaglewall Kreigsmarine auxiliaries.

Eaglewall ¹⁄₁₂₀₀th scale
'British Oil Tanker'.

Eaglewall *Altmark*.

Eaglewall *Tirpitz*.

Delightful (and very rare) Eaglewall 'U-38'.

HMS Prince of Wales battlegroup.

ESCI

1982 ESCI kit catalogue cover energetically illustrated by well-known Italian cartoonist Enzo Mario.

Italian company ESCI burst on to the international modelling scene in 1971 with the release of a stunning 1/9th scale replica of Germany's WWII 'BMW R-75' motorcycle/sidecar combination.

This huge model was so successful that it was soon joined by more 1/9th scale motorcycles: another German machine, a Zundapp 'Ks. 750', again with sidecar, a Moto Guzzi 'Alice' and an army Harley Davidson amongst them. The range even included a massive 1/9th scale replica of the Werhrmacht's 'Kettenkrad' motorcycle/half-track combination – one of the largest kits available.

Esci also produced a very nice range of 1/35th scale and 1/72nd scale military vehicles and in the early 1980s produced a range of aircraft, all 'DC-3 Dakota' derivatives, for the European market.

Famous toy firm ERTL purchased the ESCI moulds in 1987 and re-released many of the original kits under the ESCI/ERTL banner.

At the time of writing Revell-Monogram offer three of the best ESCI 1/9th scale originals: the BMW and Zundapp combinations, and, of particular interest because it has been unavailable for so long, the impressive 'Kettenkrad'.

The most collectible kits, however, are not surprisingly those in the original ESCI packaging dating from before 1987.

When first available in the mid-1970s, ESCI's range of massive 1/9th scale military vehicles and motorcycles were real head turners. This VW Kubelwagen was re-released shortly after the Ertl take-over in 1987. Today, Revell-Monogram are actively releasing many of Esci's earlier kits of 1/9th scale motorcycle and motorcycle/side-car combinations.

FALLER

Most famous for their enormous range of polystyrene kits of buildings and other accessories for model railway layouts, the German firm of Faller has none the less developed an enviable reputation for providing some interesting models based on other themes – I have a pretty rare Faller ⅟₉₉th 'Ju 52 tri-motor' from the 1960s in my collection.

Established by brothers Edwin and Hermann Faller in 1946, originally as 'Hermann Faller' but soon changed to Gebr Faller. Once the Stuttgart-based pair returned to their Black Forest home of Gutenbach, Faller started operations manufacturing wooden combs. Aspiring to make wooden buildings for train layouts, sales of the range of combs secured some financial stability whilst the brothers organised the tools and equipment necessary for the precise manufacture of construction kits. Having scoured the local whereabouts for equipment which could be fashioned into tools – at one point even assembling a saw table from the remnants of a nearby aircraft wreck – the brothers unveiled their first true classic, the famous 'Marathon-Kit' which enabled buildings to be constructed to a modular pattern. To make ends meet, at the same time, Faller also produced a range of wooden games and household accessories such as coasters.

It wasn't until 1950 that Faller released their first true HO-OO scale models designed to partner accurately the model trains that were gradually re-appearing in war-torn Germany – most notably those of German company Marklin. During this period, the buildings were constructed from a combination of paper, glue and fine plaster – not plastic.

A major breakthrough at this time was Faller's development of their famous 'scatter material'. It was originally only available in green, but nevertheless this grass effect accessory proved invaluable to those wanting to achieve a scale effect on railway layouts. Originally Faller employed local schoolboys to mix the colorants with the finely ground saw chips comprising the mixture. Apparently, the 'Faller boys' stuck out at school by virtue of their green dyed forearms! Today dozen of colours and hues of this material are featured in Faller's catalogue together with their famous range of scale trees, built from similar materials adhering to mouldings of various tree species.

Faller began the production of polystyrene components to enhance their buildings in 1953. Initially these were confined to elements more suitable to the precision achievable from injection moulding, such as window frames, doors, chimneys, gutters and the like.

Faller's first real plastic construction kit – a model of a 'stone viaduct' first appeared in 1954. Amazingly this replica is still in Faller's range.

Faller's classic kit No. B-246 is still in the range. This example dates from 1958. I recall my father assembling a pair of these houses for my brother and me in 1972. They were to be added to our new railway layout. It took Dad ages to rub the supplied 'mortar' in between the tiny brick courses – but the result was well worth his effort!

At the Nuremberg Toy Fair in 1956, along with their growing range of railway accessories, Faller exhibited their ⅟₁₀₀th plastic aircraft range. They also unveiled a fully functioning miniature electric motor that could be incorporated in other manufacturers' scale models, enabling propellers to revolve with life-like effect.

A year later, the makers of the film 'Bridge over the River Kwai' commissioned Faller to make a scale replica of the famous bamboo bridge that supported Burma's notorious death railway. Suitably assembled, the model was presented to the film's star, William Holden.

In 1964 Faller introduced smaller 'N' gauge models, scaled to ⅟₁₆₀ for use by model railway enthusiasts with limited space for their layouts.

By the late 1960s, Faller's models were available worldwide and the firm's reputation for quality was

lectors like me, whose upstairs ceilings are also sagging under the weight of so much hoarded 'loft insulation', will reckon this prudence is perfectly acceptable. Mint and boxed kits hold their value!

In 1992 Faller put its toe into waters traditionally the domain of American manufacturers with the introduction of its ⅟₄₃rd scale 'Memory Cars' range, these being lavishly produced replicas of classic Mercedes-Benz cabriolets and coupés.

Faller celebrated its 50th anniversary in 1996. The following year it acquired the trademark and mould tools of competitor Pola and began to produce this company's 'HO' and 'N' gauge railway models.

At the time of writing Faller's 2003 catalogue weighs in at a hefty 420 pages featuring kits, mostly associated with railway layouts (the days of Faller's extensive aircraft range being long gone), but also includes a range of figures and accessories which will be popular with modellers in other areas.

Military modellers, perhaps the main purchasers of this book, will be interested to learn of Faller's new ⅟₈₇th scale military programme, scaled as many enthusiasts will appreciate to the same size as the famous German ROCO 'minitank'

Faller's exquisite 'Ju52' kit.

firmly established. This reputation for excellence was further enhanced in 1984 with the introduction of Faller's 'Exclusive Models', a range of strictly limited-edition construction kits, the first of which 'Machine Factory' established the pattern of successive finely detailed replicas which came complete with a numbered certificate. Faller themselves say that "there are even collectors who buy these yearly appearing Exclusive Models only to put on their display shelf. The box probably never gets opened." I'm sure other kit col-

range ('HO' scale). Along with Faller's ubiquitous buildings, this exciting range includes fine replicas of military barrack blocks, assault courses, sand-bagged emplacements, guard houses and vehicle sheds suitable for housing three miniature 'Leopard' tanks side by side. The series is complemented by a large range of ⅟₈₇th scale soldiers in a variety of poses and, perhaps most useful to military modellers, a selection of figures designed to be placed in the cupolas and drivers' hatches of tanks and armoured fighting vehicles.

FROG

With £17,000 of share capital, in 1932 Charles and John Wilmot founded International Model Aircraft Ltd (IMA). Lancashire engineer Joseph Mansour quickly joined them. The brand name for IMA's products was 'FROG' and the honour of being the first manufacturer of scale model construction kits, entirely made from plastic, goes to them. Many will know that this curious brand name really relates to the period in the 1930s when the company produced delightful flying scale models. The firm claimed that each model **F**lies **R**ight **O**ff the **G**round!

Flying models such as the famous 'Interceptor' rode the wave of enthusiasm sweeping Britain at the time following the outright win in the Schneider Trophy seaplane race series in 1931. As the decade progressed and another war appeared imminent, Britain became 'air mad'. Aircraft, and aircraft models, drawings and storybooks with aviation themes were all the rage. IMA rode the crest of this unstoppable wave. Following the success of the ½nd scale mixed-media 'Skybirds' kits and with the introduction of new techniques of moulding new plastic acetates, IMA decided to manufacture a range of similarly scaled static model aircraft kits.

Consequently, FROG 'Penguins' (non-flying birds!), manufactured exclusively from cellulose acetate have the honour of being the first 'modern' plastic kits.

FROG Penguins first appeared in the shops during Christmas 1936. They were manufactured from cellulose acetate *butyrate,* one of the new thermoplastics that were

beginning to emerge from laboratories at the time. Cellulose acetate material possessed excellent moulding qualities and was far more stable than its sister material – the highly inflammable staple of the early film industry, cellulose nitrate. It was the numerous fires caused by cellulose nitrate stock that encouraged the photographic industry's urgent development of 'safety film'.

The first three Penguin kits were the 'Blackburn Shark MKII', 'Gloster Gladiator' and 'Hawker Fury'. They appeared in FROG's 1937/38 catalogue. Plastic model kits of a scale and type familiar to today's modellers date back to these first three Penguins. Despite wartime shortages, Penguins and Skybirds kits were manufactured throughout World War Two. The Penguin range increased substantially to include 'Spitfires', 'Hurricanes' and scale hangers, ambulances and antiaircraft guns, encouraging the diorama builder to create whole airfields. There were even Penguin 'Dorniers' and

FROG advertisement (1930s).

Ultra-rare FROG Penguin 'Hawker Fury' (1930s).

FROG flying 'Spitfire' monoplane (1940s).

'Heinkels' by the time of the Battle of Britain in 1940.

Eventually the Penguin range was extended to include racing cars and maritime vessels such as tugs and destroyers. However, cellulose acetate, from which Penguins were moulded, was far from being an ideal material. It was difficult to sand and shape with a knife and could suffer from fatigue; resulting in warping and the emergence of a powdery chemical 'bloom'.

FROG continued to support its enviable reputation with flying aircraft, even releasing minute petrol and diesel engines, which superseded their famous rubber band motors. By the early fifties their factories were manufacturing nearly 1,000 such engines every week.

Together with miniature combustion engines to further enhance their flying aircraft, IMA provided radio-control equipment. These sets weren't made at their own factory, but in part of Britain's famous Tri-ang Toys plant. Soon after IMA had been incorporated, Lines Brothers, owners of Tri-ang, had bought a controlling stake in the business.

Flying models were an important part of FROG's business but the firm never abandoned kit manufacture.

Penguin Plastic Racer.

FROG ½nd scale 'Spitfire II'.

Although the famous Penguin range had disappeared from catalogues, in 1955 a new range of plastic kits was announced. This time the famous FROG brand was chosen for these new, all-polystyrene, kits.

At last competing with Airfix head-on, FROG suffered the disadvantage of breaking into the polystyrene kit market after the former had established market dominance. Because of FROG's smaller volumes, they couldn't negotiate the best discounts. Their margins were tighter and consequently their models sold for a higher retail price. Nevertheless, FROG kits were presented in packaging superior to the flimsy plastic bags their British rival had been forced to adopt in order to secure Woolworth's patronage.

The first FROG ½nd scale models represented some of Britain's recent breakthroughs in aviation technology, delta aircraft like Gloster's sleek 'Javelin' and English Electric's impressive twin-engine jet bomber the 'Canberra'.

A range of military vehicles and state-of-the-art air defence and multi-barrelled weapon systems (Bristol 'Bloodhound', Nike 'Hercules' and 'Ontos' light tank, etc), produced from mould tools leased by North American model manufacturer Renwal, soon complemented the aircraft range.

By the early 1960s, sales of FROG's flying models and engines were beginning to decline. Deals were done within the Tri-ang organisation and with Britain's A.A. Hales and America's Cox Corporation, to divest the company of too much involvement within a sector it no longer dominated.

FROG's plastic kit range expanded rapidly. Soon models of ships and cars were added to the catalogue. IMA's parent, Tri-ang, manufactured a successful model railway

range and it was decided that FROG's designers should also produce a range of HO scale model buildings and accessories for use on miniature layouts.

Always with an eye on packaging innovation – their patented one-piece box was a significant development – the company consistently enhanced the presentation of its kits. FROG's 'Trail Blazers' and 'Inside Story' kits were object lessons in design. The Inside Story kits came complete with an integral booklet that revealed the complexities and structure of the full-size aircraft replicated within. FROG even released models that came complete with moulded picture frames enabling the purchaser to cut out and display the exciting box top illustration. Their collectible Battle of Britain 'Combat Pack', for example, featured a ½nd scale 'Spitfire' and 'Ju 88' bomber which could be displayed fixed to a framed illustration of the two 1940 adversaries in combat. With the introduction of 'Spin-a-prop' motor-packs to enhance the propellers of ½nd scale kits, the great days of IMA's heritage were recalled.

In 1964 Tri-ang bought Meccano Ltd. Meccano had long enjoyed a presence and reputation in France, having a factory in Paris since 1921 and more recently a large production facility at Calais. In 1965 a FROG executive was encouraged to discuss closer links with French polystyrene kit manufacturer Heller, who had by then established a reputation as continental Europe's leading manufacturer. As mentioned elsewhere in this book, the kit industry being what it is, these facts would later have an ironic link to Airfix. Firstly, in the early eighties during the 'Palitoy years' Airfix kits were manufactured in the Calais Miro-Meccano factory which was owned by Humbrol. Airfix was twinned with Heller (also part

FROG ½nd scale 'Curtiss Kittyhawk'.

FROG ½nd scale 'Spitfire' and 'Ju88' complete with 'Exclusive picture frame display'.

FROG ½nd scale 'Lancaster' bomber.

Very collectible ½nd scale FROG 'Avro Shackleton'.

America's AMT kit company enabled FROG to further penetrate the somewhat protected North American market.

Despite releasing some large and eagerly awaited kits such as their now very rare Avro 'Shackleton' and delightful boxed 'Spitfire XIV and Flying Bomb' combination, by the end of the 1960s, FROG was still chasing the elusive 'pocket-money' brigade – schoolboy modellers. So, reluctantly the company cut the cost of its smaller models by emulating Airfix and … putting them in a plastic bag!

of the Humbrol family), sharing the French kit manufacturer's production facilities in Normandy!

By the mid-1960s the sprawling Tri-ang group decided to shift FROG's production from Merton in South London to the factories of another subsidiary, Rovex Scale Models Ltd of Margate, Kent, it being decided that IMA and Rovex, both being model manufacturers, should share common operating practices.

By now FROG's kit range had expanded to more than 90 different models – which put great pressure on Rovex. The situation was eased by virtue of an agreement to share and repackage moulded parts with respected Japanese manufacturer Hasegawa. For FROG kits, Hasegawa were a way into the somewhat restricted Japanese market and Hasegawa's arrangement with

As the 1970s dawned, the British toy industry was enduring a very difficult time. One of the casualties of this recession was Tri-ang, who were forced into receivership in 1971. Bought by rival toy giant Dunbee-Combex-Marx Ltd and with a number of FROG models in advanced production, the remnants of Tri-ang's kit interests continued under the 'Rovex' banner.

The early 1970s brought competition in the UK not only from Airfix, but also from Matchbox, well established in the die-cast toy vehicle business but a newcomer to plastic construction kits. Their, cheap, multi-coloured kits, which could be assembled to reveal a colourful replica without the need to pick up a paint brush, proved enormously popular with youngsters and particularly threatened FROG's less secure

A real collector's item – FROG ½nd scale 'AW Whitley'.

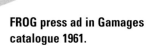

FROG press ad in Gamages catalogue 1961.

FROG ⅛th scale self-propelled 'Howitzer'.

FROG S.6B 'Trailblazer' in original box.

FROG's earlier 'Spitfire MkII', repackaged as part of the exciting 'Inside Story' range.

FROG ½nd scale 'Spitfire and Flying Bomb' – one of the firm's most successful kits.

market share. Airfix would simply have to produce even more new kits each month!

The final significant development in the FROG story relates to Dunbee-Combex-Marx's deal with the Soviet government during the mid-1970s. In order to secure lucrative trade agreements behind the iron curtain and hopefully obtain a slice of the huge Russian toy market - which the Kremlin had recently decreed should embark on a five-year modernisation plan which included the purchase of sophisticated toy-manufacturing processes and machinery from the west – DCM thought it might be a good idea to dangle the existing FROG tools as an incentive.

Consequently dozens of FROG's model tools – excluding any of Axis machinery – were shipped to DCM's Russian subsidiary NOVO. Mould tools, some which were so new they had not even appeared in FROG catalogues in the UK, continued to be sent to Russia at an alarming rate.

In 1977, when the tool-making and packaging of some great FROG kits, including 'Arado 234', 'Lancaster B Mk.1', 'B-17E' and 'Sea Vixen', had been completed, DCM decided to wind up the company. FROG packed and despatched its last moulds to Russia in November 1977.

An interesting postscript to the FROG story, as far as kit collectors are concerned, relates to the recent rise in values of NOVO/FROG kits. Regarded with derision when they first appeared, the products of the now-defunct NOVO operation have, ironically, achieved a collectible status all of their own. Apart from enabling British modellers to reintroduce themselves to old FROG tools which they thought would never be seen again – the company's venerable 'Shackleton' and 'Whitley' spring to mind – NOVO kits have preserved a kind of pre-glasnost charm which many enthusiasts find endearing.

As far as FROG and Penguin kits are concerned, virtually any of the latter range is highly collectible, especially pre-war ones. Regarding 'Flying FROGs', the company's 'Interceptors' appear for sale with surprising regularity, testament to their enormous popularity over half a century ago. The really rare kits include FROG's 'Light Ship', 'Lifeboat', Vickers 'Valiant V' bomber, DeHavilland 'Comet' and Bristol 'Britannia' (both ⅟₉₆th scale and in RAF markings) and their classic replica of the 'R-100 Airship'.

I'm unsure of the precise whereabouts of much of FROG's tool bank. Some kits that originated in the FROG drawing offices turn up re-branded on the pages of the mainstream manufacturers. Some appear in the Far East. I suppose many still languish in Eastern Europe. Who knows when we might see some FROG classics again?

FROG Penguin Armstrong-Siddeley 'Hurricane' – on four wheels and without wings!

FUJIMI

Japanese manufacturer Fujimi originated in the early 1960s. Starting with a range of 1/70th scale aircraft models of mostly indigenous Japanese machines from WWII – 'Zeros', 'Tonys' and 'Franks', but also including some very collectable American machines, especially two marks of Chance-Vought 'Corsairs' – Fujimi's kit list has grown and grown.

Apparently, during its early days, Fujimi also released a range of 1/50th scale aircraft kits. As the company developed, it soon realised that both its 1/70th and 1/50th range were fractionally out of synch with 1/72nd and 1/48th, the two internationally accepted standards. So, without further ado, the company repackaged the kits and miraculously they fitted the two regular scales – without the need even to change the size of the moulded pieces inside!

Today, the Fujimi range is vast and extends to military aircraft, civil airliners, ships, vehicles and a notable range of military vehicles in scales ranging from 1/76th to 1/30th. Allegedly, many of the 1/76th line were acquired from Nitto in the mid-1980s.

In the late 1970s, Fujimi's AFVs were readily available in Britain and made a useful supplement to the similarly scaled military vehicles available from Airfix and Matchbox.

Fujimi 1/48th scale 'Spitfire V' (1970s)

Marvellous Fujimi 'British Tank Commander'.

HASEGAWA

Hasegawa can trace its origins back to the early 1960s. Today it ranks with Tamiya as one of the greatest kit companies in the world and is ... Japanese to boot!

I understand that Hasegawa really entered the premier league of kit manufacturers following their purchase of a much smaller Japanese competitor, 'Mania', whose employees had demonstrated enormous proficiency in the kit design and tool-making field. This acquisition took place in the mid-1970s and certainly since around this time, Hasegawa's products have been second to none.

Apart from its curious range of 'Egg Craft' caricatures of famous aeroplanes, Hasegawa generally has a reputation for scrupulous accuracy, attention to detail and manufacturing finesse. The company has produced a vast range of kits of almost every subject and in all scales.

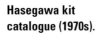

Hasegawa kit catalogue (1970s).

The company began with some ⅟₅₀th and ⅟₆₀th scaled gliders and a very desirable ½nd scale North American 'F-86F' issued in Blue Impulse livery in the 1960s. They then progressed to some truly massive ⅛th scale 'Museum Quality' WWI biplane fighters manufactured in wood, metal and plastic – Hasegawa has regularly demonstrated versatility and innovation. Indeed, the latter models are so good, I have often seen them in museums! Incidentally this impressive range spawned a series of separate models depicting each aircraft's power plant or machine-gun armament. I still have a complete 'SE.5A' in my collection, but I'm not sure I will ever be able to allocate the months and months needed to build it.

I understand that a very rare limited-edition model of a 'Disneyland Japan 747', manufactured for promotional use which dates from Hasegawa's earliest days, has become a Holy Grail for aircraft enthusiasts.

Military modellers revere Hasegawa as much as aircraft enthusiasts do. Indeed, at the time of writing Hasegawa has released an impressive ¼th scale Willys 'MB Jeep' complete with driver, apparently engineered from an entirely new tool. No doubt all those looking for a suitable vehicle to accompany their 70mm figures will snap this up.

Their current range comprises aircraft from ½nd through ⅟₄₈th to ⅟₃₂nd scales and a selection of ½nd scale military vehicles or, for those with a maritime bent, some ⅟₇₀₀th scale waterline models.

HAWK

Beginning with a range of balsa wood flying models in the 1920s to satisfy a craze that was all the rage with youngsters worldwide, Hawk began to focus more on scale accuracy and very soon developed a range of plastic (John Burns thinks Bakelite) accessories which could be attached to their balsa flyers. All-plastic construction kits naturally followed. In fact Hawk are a candidate for the title of earliest North American plastic kit manufacturer – the plans in their ⅟₄₈th scale 'Curtiss R3C-1' are dated 1946. After an initially lukewarm reception it appears to have been a couple of years before toy or hobby shops stocked the actual kit. By the late 1940s, however, moulded in black, the little model had found an audience. Buoyed by the success of the 'Curtiss' replica and the models that followed it (including a ⅟₄₈th scale 'Gee Bee' racer and a very collectible ⅟₁₄₀th scale Lockheed 'Constellation' airliner), by 1951 Hawk had ceased manufacturing wooden flying models.

Hawk produced their first ⅟₇₂nd scale replicas in the mid-1950s. These actually started life as identification tools ('ID' models) destined for the US military, origi-

nally appearing as pre-assembled solid replicas. They were soon re-engineered and released as kits. Anyone fortunate enough to have a surviving example of a 'Hawk Supermarine Swift' from this period, either in kit or solid ID 'recognition' form, is sitting on a gold mine as far as British collectors are concerned.

Of all Hawk's kits, the most famous are arguably their fantastic range of 'Weird-Oh's'. As the name suggests, these kits were pure fantasy and featured an assortment of manic characters in a variety of activities that generally included components from a traditional and existing Hawk kit.

Rare Hawk 'Spirit of St.Louis' monoplane.

Hawk ⅟₄₈th scale 'OV-10A' reconnaissance plane.

HISTOREX

Unbelievably precise ⅟₃₅th Armour Accessories W.W.II German infantryman – in association with America's famous 'Squadron' brand.

Great days – as good as bagged kits ever got.

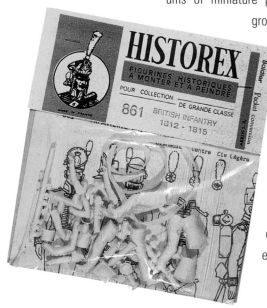

Modellers of my generation will remember opening the orange and white packets which contained Historex kits with fondness. For around 30 years this French manufacturer's range of 54mm Napoleonic soldiers set new standards for detail and accuracy. Historex's mouldings are still of unsurpassed quality. Towards the end of their reign the company released polystyrene miniature components of exquisite finesse. I remember their one-piece shakos or cornets with hollow bowls which seemingly defied the traditional restrictions inherent in 'under cutting' moulds. Historex appeared to produce the impossible.

It's probably no coincidence that the brand name 'Historex' sounds quite similar to 'Mokarex', because this French coffee brand was in fact key to the model manufacturers existence. Shortly after the Second-World War, the coffee supplier included 'free' premiums of miniature plastic soldiers with its popular ground coffee. These were based on the designs of Pierre-Albert Leroux and Lucien Rousselot, and tooled by master-engraver Jacques Fath. The resultant semi-round ('demi ronde bosse') polystyrene figures were enormously popular. Not surprisingly, a coffee brand that claimed its name was synonymous with 'quality' made great efforts to ensure that its 'Figurines

Historiques' series was also executed to the highest standard.

Variously scaled between 45 and 54mm, the Mokarex figures included foot and mounted subjects covering French military, royal and revolutionary subjects from the middle ages right up to the Great War. Soon the range had grown to over 400 figures, varying from a delightful 'Louis XI' period chess set (silver or gold plastic mouldings standing in for the traditional black and white pieces) which presumably required a lot of coffee drinking to collect, to my favourites, some 50mm mounted 'French 1914–18' troops released in 1959, each sculpted in the most naturally realistic poses imaginable.

However, over time, consumer tastes changed and eventually Mokarex became more associated with coffee makers rather than the ingredients of the drink itself. The figures ceased production. They had, however, proved so successful that in 1963, 'Atelier de Gravure' of Paris, the manufacturer of the premiums, decided to continue with model soldier production.

Under its 'Aeros' brand, the firm already produced plastic aeroplane kits, so, working with French artist and Napoleonic buff Eugene Leliepvre, they proceeded to produce their own 54mm model soldier kit. Branded 'Historex' the first release was a 40-part miniature of a French Revolutionary Wars 'Hussar'. It was warmly received and despite having no proper instruction leaflet and a length of paper tape that had to be cut to make belts and cross-straps, its manufacture established a pattern that was to continue for nearly 30 years.

Soon, Historex established an enormous range of foot and mounted figures all from the period of

Napoleon's 1st Empire. Early on they supplemented this range with exquisite replicas of period artillery, beginning with their '8pdr Gribeauval' field-piece in 1964. The field guns were also available with figures packaged in elaborate box sets. I well remember my father visiting London's 'Under Two Flags' and buying Historex's 'Friedland' artillery set for me. I ripped the shiny Cellophane from its stout crimson box at light speed!

One of the most significant developments in the Historex story was the establishment of Lyn Sangster's Historex Agents in 1967. Based in Dover, this distributor quickly forged an enduring bond with Historex. The British dimension also contributed to Historex's decision to expand its range to include soldiers from Napoleon's enemies and their allies and in 1970 Historex released the first of their famous 'Scots Greys' figures. The 'Scots Greys' were quickly followed by a series of 'Mamaluke Cavalry' that was received to huge critical acclaim when it first appeared in the shops.

In 1970, Historex Agents also published a stunning catalogue which, richly illustrated with wonderful colour photographs, introduced the work of master modellers Ray Lamb, Shep Paine and Pierre Conrad. An illustrated 'Spare Parts' catalogue that enabled modellers to pick and choose from Historex's enormous range of some 15,000 items accompanied this publication. Via their association with America's 'Squadron Shop' organisation, Historex agents also encouraged the Parisian firm to branch out into more modern figures with the release of the intricately detailed ⅓₅th 'Armour Accessories' range of WWII German soldiers and equipment.

In 1985 Historex Agents and Ray Lamb, who had now founded his seminal 'Poste Militaire' range of 75mm metal figures, established the annual 'Euro Militaire' event in Folkestone. This show became the forum for enthusiasts to see examples of the finest figure modelling, study the latest releases and meet their heroes.

Sadly, however, the gradual shift away from 19th- to 20th-century subjects and especially the huge growth in interest in WWII German armour, plus the burgeoning fashion in wartime dioramas, caused Historex's market share decline. Anyway, competition from other 54mm figures had intensified, especially with the appearance of a huge choice of Airfix's Napoleonic and W.II 'Multipose' range for example, and the rise of 'garage kit' short-run resin models. Apparently, all these developments conspired towards the decline of Historex.

By 1990 the Historex brand name had been sold and in 1991 the manufacturer ceased trading. Fortunately, all was not lost. The name survives and the independent Historex Agents continues to thrive.

In 1992 the new owners of the classic kit brand, Christian Sauve's company ADV, a manufacturer with an established reputation for excellent ⅓₅th scale figures and military vehicles, established NCO Historex. The abbreviation standing for 'Nouvelle Compagnie d'Origine', this new name enables a new generation of modellers to discover precisely why the name Historex is so revered.

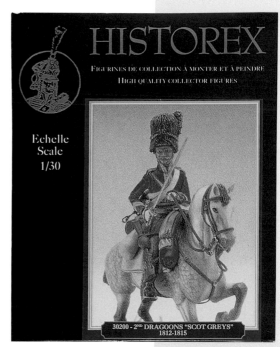

30200 - 2ⁿᵈ DRAGOONS "SCOT GREYS" 1812-1815

The great name lives on.

Nemrod figure by NCO Historex.

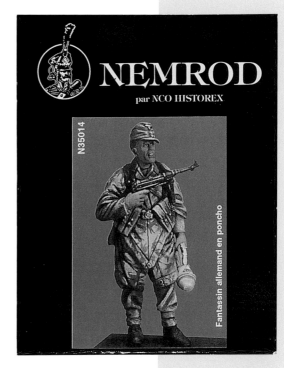

HELLER

Heller catalogue.

Heller has become better known to British modellers since partnering Airfix and Humbrol as part of the Hobby Products Group's business portfolio. Indeed, today all Airfix kits are manufactured at Heller's famous factory at Trun near Falaise in Normandy.

Although it shares the same initial capital letter as Gallic compatriots Historex, the firm of Heller predates the Parisian model soldier manufacturer and began trading in 1957. Its first kit was a ⅟₁₀₀th scale replica of the prototype 'Caravelle' airliner, naturally enough in Air France markings. This was an enormously popular model with Heller's home market and

some time later was re-released, updated and with new registration codes. Heller also produced a smaller, ⅟₂₀₀th scale replica of Sud-Aviation's famous aircraft.

Heller's range is wide and varied, as one would expect from a 'traditional' manufacturer. Whilst their catalogue has always included a good number of French machines, especially aircraft, ships and military vehicles, they have regularly featured mouldings with a more international appeal. Like many manufacturers they have acquired tools from long-defunct manufacturers. Many of these, such as their ⅟₄₈th scale Supermarine 'Walrus' and ⅟₄₈th scale Fairey 'Swordfish' replicas, originated from British firm Merit.

Heller introduced their extensive ⅟₁₀₀th scale 'Cadet' range in 1963, enabling modellers to build a pretty comprehensive, but nonetheless compact range of then modern military aircraft – notably front line fighters and helicopters – and their early Sepecat 'Jaguars' and Sud-Aviation 'Gazelles' are very collectable.

In 1966 Heller's 'Sprint' series included the novelty of motors and working lights.

Despite a range which includes car models ranging from classics such as Citroen's classic '15 CV' in ⅟₂₄th scale to the Subaru 'Impreza WRC '02' in ⅟₄₃rd scale and

Heller kit from the 1990s.

MESSERSCHMITT Bf 109 F

Vintage Heller 'MiG21'.

which includes replicas of ESA's 'Arianne 5' rocket and even a ⅟₄₃rd scale Peterbilt 'Conventional Wrecker Truck' of 1980 vintage, I guess Heller is most famous for its wonderful models of fully rigged sailing ships.

With the release of fine replicas of the 'Soleil Royal' and 'HMS Victory' in massive ⅟₁₀₀th scale (still in the range) Heller really joined the front rank of kit manufacturers. With such a rich tool bank to call on, and over 45 years of model manufacture to call on, I'm sure Heller will continue to achieve consistently high standards, and, with Airfix, fly the flag for European kit manufacture.

Collectable Heller ½nd scale 'Bataille de France' set from 1990 – produced for the 50th anniversary of the Battle of Britain, or France, depending on which side of the Channel (or la Manche) you hail from!

Chasseurs Alpines

Assortment of Heller kits from the 1970s.

INPACT

This short-lived British manufacturer first came to note in the mid-1960s with the release of a range of ¹⁄₄₈th scale kits designed to capitalise on the success of the movie 'Those Magnificent Men In Their Flying Machines'. Inpact's range of aircraft in this series included a 'Bleriot XI', Bristol 'Boxkite' and 'Martin-Handasyde'.

Some of Inpact's other ¹⁄₄₈th scale model aircraft, like their Fairy 'Flycatcher', Bristol 'Bulldog' and Hawker 'Fury', later cropped up in Pyro, Lindberg or Life-Like branding.

Inpact Martin-Handasyde from 'Those Magnificent Men …'.

Those Magnificent Flying Machines

MARTIN-HANDASYDE

An authentic reproduction of the 1911 monoplane of the Antoinette type, which is featured in the 20th Century Fox film production "Those Magnificent Men in their Flying Machines"—or how I flew from London to Paris in 25 hours and 11 minutes.

Veteran Aircraft Series   **INPACT** KITS

Scaled from actual plans. Scale ¼"—1' complete with full assembly instructions and stand.

Inpact ¹⁄₄₈th scale 'Bristol Bulldog'.

INPACT KITS

BRISTOL **BULLDOG**

CLASSIC FIGHTER SERIES

32 Squadron RAF

ITALAEREI

Testors ½nd scale 'Spitfire Mk22'.

⅓₅th scale Italaeri Jagdpanzer 38t 'Hetzer' from the mid-1970s – typical of the fine detail and first-rate moulding of this famous Italian manufacturer.

Perhaps because, other than for native Italians, this famous manufacturer's name was always a bit of a tongue twister, the company has now more or less adopted the easier pronunciation 'Italeri'.

Italians Gian Pietro Parmaggiani and Giuliano Malservisi began the company in the late 1960s, first trading as 'Aliplast'. The company went through some structural changes and re-emerged in 1971 with the current, or to be correct, more complex version of its well-known trademark.

Since then Italeri has established a reputation for moulding finesse and accuracy that few have managed to equal. Italeri kits of aircraft and military vehicles exhibit some of the most delicate mouldings available and the firm has a loyal fan base – notably in Britain – for the scale accuracy of its models.

From the early 1980s Italeri and American kit and hobby paint and accessories giant Testors began sharing mould tools. In 1990 Testors actually purchased the Italian company. Today, along with its extensive range of kits, Italeri's catalogue features Testor's ModelMaster range of enamel paints.

Happily, enthusiasts can purchase many Italeri classics. The firm's current catalogue runs to more than 100 pages and features kits of aircraft, motor vehicles, military figures and Italeri's respected range of diorama accessories. Amongst the many new models shown, enthusiasts will notice some old favourites like their

⅓₅th scale Opel 'Blitz' truck and 'Einheitskoffer' field command conversion and ½nd scale 'Waco' 'CG4' glider. Each of these kits, depicting machines from WWII, caused an enormous stir in the British modelling press when originally released in the mid-1970s.

Italeri ⅓₅th scale 'US Rangers'.

JO-HAN

Famous North American model car manufacturer Jo-Han originates from the 1950s. The brand name is a contraction of 'John Haenle', the founder. Following a temporary pause in the early eighties the company was re-financed following an agreement with SeVille Enterprises and many rare and original car kits from Jo-Han's huge range soon reappeared.

Jo-Han ¹⁄₂₅th scale 'Turbine Car'.

Jo-Han's wonderful 'Heavenly Hearse'.

KLEEWARE

British company Kleeware is perhaps best known for being one of the first companies to engage in an enterprise which is commonplace with kit manufacturers today – namely sharing another's mould tool and re-branding a competitor's creation.

Along with an assortment of ships and vehicles, from 1956, Kleeware produced a variety of aircraft kits across the entire spectrum of scales. Get this: their model of America's famous Goodyear 'Blimp' came in ⅓₃₆th scale whilst their Stinson 'Trimotor' aircraft was moulded in ⅙₁st scale – two hardly very common ratios!

Comet Series Piper 'Apache' by Kleeware.

1960s kit assortment – the Kleeware US Navy 'Blimp' is especially collectable.

LIFE-LIKE

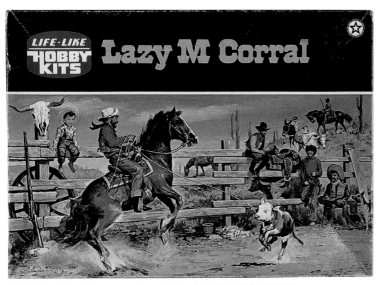

The 'Lazy M Corral'.

American predecessors like Adams, Pyro and Inpact originated many of the collectible kits from this US manufacturer. Consequently, these models, which date from the mid-1970s, include a real mixed bag of subjects.

In their patriotic 'American Wildlife' series, enthusiasts could opt for rather dull models of a Mallard Duck and Ring-Necked Pheasant or a spectacular Bald Eagle, wings vertical and claws outstretched as it prepares to strike its earthbound prey.

I have an elaborate 'Lazy M Corral' diorama in my collection, but despite searching high and low, I have never managed to trace surviving examples of Life-Like's ⅙th scale 'Cro-Magnon' or 'Neanderthal' figures. These models were first released in 1974 and show, respectively, our prehistoric ancestors, hunting or seated, surrounded by the impedimenta of such ancient daily life.

Following the success of films like 'Those Magnificent Men in their Flying Machines', everyone wanted a piece of the action.

Life-Like kit assortment.

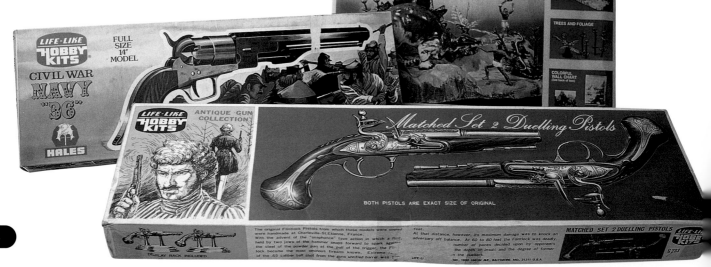

LINDBERG

Founded by Paul Lindberg in 1933, like many of its contemporaries this new company began its commercial activities by manufacturing balsa flying models. It wasn't until the late 1940s that his company, then trading as 'O-Lin', made polystyrene construction kits. These, a series of delightful ¼₈th scale aircraft models of American machines, included Lockheed's 'Shooting Star' jet-fighter and North American's 'Sabre' – the aircraft which was soon to earn its laurels in Korea.

By 1950 the company adopted the more familiar 'Lindberg' brand and released a series of inexpensive models ranging from cars to ships and aircraft.

During the late 1950s Lindberg models were often sold under the 'Boycraft' brand. Many of the early O-Lin kits were repackaged this way, together with a very collectable 'Spitfire MkII' replica, in the usual American standard 'quarter-scale' (¼₈th).

In his seminal *Plastic Aircraft Kits of the Twentieth Century and Beyond*, John Burns claims that Lindberg's 1996 re-release of a 1950s gift set, entitled 'Past-Present-Future' and including a pre-WWII 'Curtiss', a Douglas 'Stilleto' and a 'Flying Saucer', is a 'must have' for US collectors.

At the time of writing an interesting article by Tom Graham published in the March 2004 edition of *Fine Scale Modeler*, argues that Varney, a brand taken over by Lindberg's 'O-Lin' brand in 1951, might have claim to be North America's first polystyrene kit manufacturer, their 'PT boat', 'LST' and 'Fleet Submarine' kits apparently being available from early 1945!

Despite several 'brand evolutions' and consequent logo changes, and despite being taken over a couple of times since the late 1980s, Lindberg is still very much with us. Though never a manufacturer of the first order, Lindberg endures as one of those very few brand names that can trace its story back more than half a century.

Rare model of America's 1950/60s period aircraft carrier – *USS Valley Forge*.

Lindberg's version of the famous 'Spitfire IX'.

Great box art!

MATCHBOX

The 'Matchbox' brand originates from 1947 when two unrelated friends, Londoners Leslie and Rodney Smith, started the business they had long dreamt of. Their new company was called Lesney Products, a name that combined syllables from each of their Christian names. Almost right from the start the pair were joined by engineering designer John ('Jack') Odell who quickly became Lesney's pattern and die maker and was made a full partner in the new business.

Lesney are most famous for their 'Matchbox' range of die-casts. Made of 'mazac', a robust zinc alloy, Matchbox toys were virtually indestructible. Their classic '1-75 Series' cars packaged in their striking – almost literally, because the yellow and blue design was based on a matchbox – yellow and blue boxes, sold by the

million. Today, mint and boxed examples from the early years of Lesney's production command a king's ransom at auction – but die casts are another story…

By the late 1960s, 'Matchbox' had become one of the biggest toy brands in the world. The company's products included cars of all sizes and Lesney also produced a range of toy motorways and accessories, examples of which could be found in almost every boy's bedroom.

Ironically, as the 1970 edition of the Matchbox die-cast catalogue speculated about future car design, it mused: "Plastic will be used increasingly for body shells…" Although speaking of car design, the company seemed to be considering plastic manufacture in a very uncharacteristic way. So, in 1971, the company took the decision to enter the very lucrative plastic construction kit business. By then the Matchbox brand was as well known as Airfix and FROG and the decision to compete in this vibrant sector made sound commercial sense.

Matchbox began its classic ½nd scale model aircraft series in 1973. The first in this initial range of ten models, PK-1 was a replica of the RAF's inter-war 'Hawker Fury' biplane. Fittingly, PK-2 was a 'banker', a model of a 'Spitfire MkIX'.

When they first appeared, these models, though crude by today's standards (remember the trench-like engraving on the panel lines?), caused a bit of a stir. They were cheap and because they came with separate sprues moulded in approximations of the finished machine's colours, they could be acceptably completed without the need

1980/81 Kit catalogue.

to resort to paint. Not surprisingly, it appealed to young boys, impatient to finish their pocket-money purchase. Matchbox kits caused quite a stir with their competitors. Airfix were forced to accelerate production of new releases, bludgeoning Matchbox who couldn't hope to compete with the South London manufacturer's variety and market presence. FROG, much smaller and always a relatively expensive brand, was given a nasty shock by the market acceptance of Matchbox's innovative approach in their sector.

Together with a growing range of ½nd scale aircraft, Matchbox added a creditable range of ⅟₇₆th scale military vehicles. Again, contrary to the practice of the growing range of Japanese manufacturers like Fujimi and Hasegawa who opted for the larger scale familiar to aircraft modellers, Matchbox chose the smaller scale adopted years before by Airfix and designed to complement HO/OO railway layouts. Matchbox military models had one major difference to the Airfix offerings. Each of Lesney's kits came complete with an easy-to-assemble scale diorama in which to display the model. Again, Matchbox strove to go one better than its direct competition. Matchbox designers were very imaginative in their choice of diorama settings. These ranged from shell-pocked, cobbled European streets to the sands of North Africa. Matchbox also produced a series of soft plastic ⅟₇₆th scale soldiers to complement their tanks and armoured vehicles and to directly challenge Airfix's long superiority in this cheap and popular field.

Not content with smaller models, Matchbox released some very large ½nd aircraft. Favourites of many others and mine were their RAF interwar Handley Page 'Heyford' and Supermarine 'Stranraer'. Very soon they ventured into the much larger scales of ⅟₃₂nd for cars and aircraft. Matchbox's releases of both a late war 'Spitfire' and post-war

DeHavilland 'Sea Venom' were welcomed, as they had long been on many a modeller's 'wants list'. Despite the somewhat heavy-handed detailing and their propensity for including multi-coloured parts, Matchbox regularly tackled subjects that had long been ignored.

In 1978 Lesney purchased most of American company AMT's tools and released many of these under the familiar brand name in the US and 'Matchbox' in the UK. In 1991, Odyssey Partners acquired Matchbox, adding it to its two other recent significant purchases – Revell and Monogram. Since then, many of Matchbox's earlier military models have reappeared in themed combinations of vehicles and soldiers.

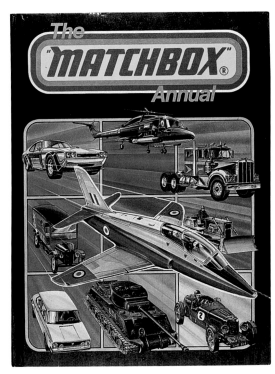

So confident, they even supported their kit and toy range with an annual.

Matchbox classics from the late 1970s.

MONOGRAM

Pooling their combined life savings of $5,000 Robert Reder and Jack Besser founded Monogram in December 1945.

As a youngster 'Bob' Reder was a very keen aero modeller who made flying model aircraft constructed from balsa wood and covered with doped tissue. These were powered by twisted rubber bands that, as they unwound, spun miniature propellers fast enough to pull the lightweight models skyward. He joined the local aero club and regularly

flew his creations in the fields surrounding his Chicago home. After high school Reder joined the staff of The Comet Model Airplane Company where he had previously worked part time on Saturdays.

The advent of war meant that balsa wood, which originated from Ecuador, was in short supply. In America, imported balsa was requisitioned by the military for the construction of floats. Across the Atlantic, the British used this lightweight material as a component of the laminate construction of de Havilland's 'Wooden Wonder'; the twin-engined 'Mosquito' fighter-bomber.

Adopting more readily available basswood, Comet switched production from flying scale models to recognition models which were then the easiest way for pilots, air-gunners and civil defence personnel to familiarise themselves with the silhouettes of enemy aircraft. Interestingly, Comet also made 'Target Kites',

November 1945 and Monogram's first kits are released. Among them are the destroyer *USS Hobby* and the aircraft carrier *USS Shangri-La*. Each wooden model came with a shaped wooden hull.

Cessna '180 Sport' plane complete with detailed engine.

Top marks to the kit designer – just look what happens when you turn the prop.

standard modellers take for granted today. For a while Monogram continued with model ships and a sprinkling of cars and aircraft. Gradually the Monogram range included more and more plastic components. Plastic was used for those pieces that were especially difficult to hand-craft, including engine cowlings, wing tips and, most tricky of all, propellers.

Monogram's 'Hot Shot' Jet Racer from 1946 was typical of the firm's construction style at the time. Consisting of a partly shaped wooden body, sheet balsa wood components and rubber wheels, it required hours of careful shaping and not inconsider-

large diamond-shaped kites with the silhouettes of Japanese fighters painted on them, hoisted skywards for gunnery practice.

Whilst at Comet, Reder met Jack Besser, the company's sales manager. Soon, the two colleagues began thinking about the opportunities an end to wartime hostilities might bring.

They concluded that the best plan was to form their own model company and at the war's end they established 'Monogram' in Chicago, Illinois.

As early as November 1945 their first three kits were released for sale. These true classics were a 'Landing Ship Tank' (LST), the destroyer *USS Hobby* and, appropriately, the cruiser *USS Chicago*. Each wooden model came with a 'shaped wooden hull' but required a great deal of extra labour to finish them to anywhere near the

⅟₃₂nd scale 'Blue Thunder' helicopter.

'Space Taxi' and contents.

Monogram Refueling Group duo.

¼th scale 'Hot Shot Racer' from 1967.

ing rather more precision-engineered moulded plastic components, which really paved the way for the company's future success in plastic construction kit manufacture. In 1952 Monogram's 'Super Kit' range finally put paid to the tiresome shaping required to realise accurate fuselage contours – 'Super Kits' came complete with perfectly preformed wooden parts.

Inevitably it wasn't long before Monogram abandoned wooden parts altogether. In 1954 the company released its first entirely synthetic model kit, the famous All Plastic Scale Model 'P-1 Midget Racer'. A 1932 Ford 'Roadster' and the 'Dipsy Doodle' speedboat immediately followed this. In their original packaging this trio of kits is highly sought after.

In 1957 Monogram's famous 'Snark Missile' appeared. Together with the aforementioned cars and aircraft, this example of space-age technology set the seal for the three types of model for which Monogram is now perhaps most famous.

able patience, before the streamlined vehicle on the box top could ever be realised. It did, however, feature an injection moulded transparent canopy!

It was, though, Monogram's famous 'Speedee-Bilt' flying model aircraft, incorporat-

In 1960, Monogram began to develop their famous ¼₈th scale or 'quarter scale' range of warplanes. At the time this went against the grain in the United States as modellers had happily adopted the far smaller ½nd scale, which had originated in England in the 1930s.

Revell-Monogram's late, great facility at Morten Grove, a suburb of Chicago.

Monogram's decision to adopt ¼₈th scale was prescient. Very quickly American modellers embraced this as the norm for model kits and today even in Europe ¼₈th has fast replaced ½nd.

After enjoying significant commercial success, in 1961 Monogram moved to a purpose-built 120,000 square feet plant at Morten Grove, a suburb northwest of Chicago.

In those days, like Revell, Monogram held up a mirror to US achievement, producing kits, which reflected the myriad inventions charting the nation's scientific progress. Whilst Revell had initially focused on the existing products of America's revolutionary motor industry, after the introduction of its 'Hot Shot Racer', Monogram had long focused on the future.

Of all these areas of technological development it was the fields of ballistic missiles and space exploration which generated most subject matter. Fuelled by the urgent technological advances triggered by the Soviet Union's astonishing achievements following the launch of Sputnik in 1957, there was now an abundant supply of new and projected American rocket and spaceship developments for Monogram to model.

Monogram quickly released replicas of America's contributions to the 'space-race' and the manufacturer marked all of NASA's milestone inventions through the 'Gemini', 'Mercury' and 'Apollo' programmes. The company also immortalised many of the weird and wonderful hypothetical designs that abounded at the time, committing them to polystyrene kit form.

At the war's end, most of Germany's WWII 'V-weapon' rocket engineers were spirited away by American intelligence to work for the US Military. The most famous of these individuals was 'V2' designer Werner Von Braun. However, a colleague of his, Willy Ley, was probably a

more prolific, if fanciful, visionary. Monogram's extensive range of Willy Ley 'Signature Designs' depict many of his weird and wonderful proposals and have since become enormously collectible.

In 1968 Monogram was incorporated into Mattel Inc, the world's largest toy company and owner of 'Barbie' and the ever-popular 'Hot Wheels' range of die-cast cars.

In 1970 Monogram established the 'Snap Tite' range of kits. Requiring no gluing, these kits were particularly easy to assemble and consequently very popular with novices. It wasn't long before most of

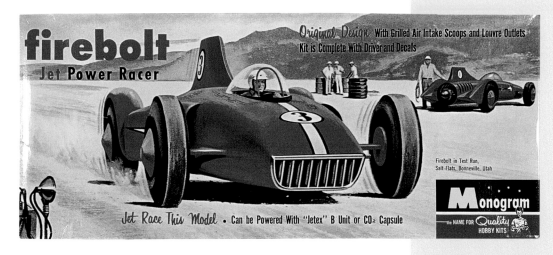

Monogram reissue of a 1950s classic, but where can you buy 'Jetex B units' these days?

Popular in the late 1950s and much sought after now, Monogram's 'Phantom Mustang' took kit manufacturing to new heights.

Monogram's Masters of the Universe 'Talon Fighter' and 'Attak Trak' from 1979.

Monogram's competitors released their own ranges of similar easy to assemble models. The Airfix range was called 'Snap Fix'!

In 1977 Monogram bought famous American kit manufacturer Aurora. Shortly after the deal had been completed many of Aurora's precious steel mould tools were badly damaged in a rail freight accident whilst *en route* to Morten Grove. Two years later, the ever-growing company opened up another facility, this time in Des Plaines.

In January 1984, Tom Gannon, Monogram's new Chairman, led a management buy-out, which purchased the company from Mattel. For two years, life at Monogram continued at a steady pace with the company introducing a new range of ⅛th scale cars and introducing the brand new ¹⁄₁₂th scale '57 Chevy' to all-round acclaim.

In 1986, it was New York company Odyssey's turn to buy Monogram; they also secured an option to buy Revell. Exercising this soon after, they decided to merge the company with Revell to complete their purchases in the plastic kit business. Revell's mould and equipment

Willy Ley's legendary 'TV Orbiter'.

SPACE BUGGY

Intraspace Cargo/Passenger Carrier

DESIGNED TO MOVE MEN AND MATERIAL BETWEEN SPACE CARGO SHIPS AND MANNED SPACE STATIONS. MODEL FEATURES OPERATING CARGO DOOR, 3 MEN IN CHROMED SPACE SUITS, SWIVEL-MOUNTED WORLD GLOBE BASE.

'Space Buggy' looking surprisingly similar to Willy Ley's 'Space Taxi' but … where's Willy?

was moved from its famous Venice, California facility to Monogram's Morten Grove HQ and so-called 'Plant II' at Des Plaines. Revell, Inc. was to be the parent company with Monogram its subsidiary.

Following the 1990 floatation of Revell AG in Bunde, West Germany, in July 1991 Revell-Monogram went public. In 1993 Revell-Monogram were merged into one company. However, all wasn't quiet for too long because in December 1994 Hallmark/Binney & Smith purchased them.

So, Revell-Monogram began the new year of 1995 as a wholly owned subsidiary of Binney & Smith, most famous as the owners of the 'Crayola' brand.

'The NAM Tour of Duty' TV series gives Monogram's ¹⁄₄₈th scale 'Skyraider' a new lease of life.

Kits of short-lived TV series quickly become collectable.

In September 2001, following five years of relative calm, Iowa-based Alpha International, best known for its 'Gearbox' brand of die-cast collectables and also the owner of Empire Stores, manufacturers of America's famous 'Buddy-L' and 'Big Wheel' brands, announced that now it had acquired Revell-Monogram. "We see the acquisition of Revell-Monogram and Revell AG as a strong complement to the existing Alpha structure," said Jody Keener, Director of Marketing and Production for Alpha International. "Jim Foster will remain as President and we see enormous potential from cross-selling product lines between Gearbox, Empire, Revell-Monogram and Revell AG. We also see opportunities to leverage our combined design, marketing and new product capabilities while increasing plant production capabilities in our Morton Grove facility," he added.

On 15 November 2002 RM Investments acquired Revell-Monogram and also Revell AG in Germany. They also established Revell-Monogram Asia Pacific with an office in Hong Kong to, as Chicago-based RM Investments' Chairman and CEO John Long said, "manage the development of distribution into areas not yet covered." Long also said plans were well under way to develop new product lines and further develop current ones "in order to further enhance Revell-Monogram's brand equity." Clearly model enthusiasts and especially those who, like me, adore Revell and Monogram's classic kits, can look forward to a very bright future.

A short post-script: Late in 2003, shortly after I visited Revell-Monogram's facility at Morten Grove and was able to study closely kit production, packaging and marketing (kindly arranged by the company's Ed Sexton), I learned that there had been another move. This time Revell-Monogram wasn't travelling far. Indeed the move to 725 Landwehr St. Northbrook is a number of blocks closer to Ed's home. So, I guess he has time for an extra cup of coffee before he leaves for work in the morning!

Joint promotion with Universal and the film 'Backdraft'.

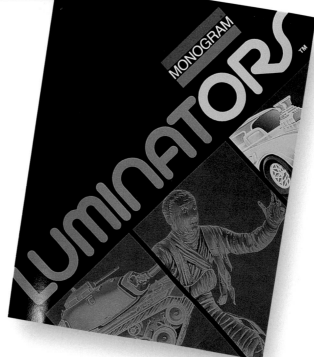

Gimmick. What gimmick?

Revell-Monogram's genial Ed Sexton outside his home, holding an ultra-rare 'Midget Racer'.

Bill Lastovich, Product Planning Manager, Revell-Monogram, selecting an early Ed Roth car kit from the hundreds of rarities in Revell-Monogram's archive.

Hundreds of classic Revell-Monogram mould ('mold') tools in store at Morten Grove.

Injection-moulding machine at Revel-Monogram's Morten Grove facility. Note the hopper feed and the massive hydraulic ram, capable of exacting tons of pressure on the enclosed tool.

NITTO

Nitto began life in Japan in 1962. Since then, this energetic company has produced a vast range of models of all types in a variety of scales. In the 1970s Nitto issued a model of a 'Gemini' astronaut charmingly classified as a 'Space Pilot'!

Military model makers welcomed its vast range of relatively inexpensive ⅟₇₆th and ⅟₃₅th scale tanks and AFVs, and its enormous range of model aircraft, ranging from a ⅟₆₀₀th scale 'Concorde' in JAL markings to a far larger ⅟₃₂ scale Japanese Yokosuka 'K5Y2 Willow' floatplane, are coveted by kit collectors. Many of Nitto's ⅟₁₀₀th scale airliner tools were acquired and re-issued by Japanese manufacturer Doyusha.

However, for me and many other enthusiasts the most sought-after Nitto originals belong to their short-lived 'SF3D' science fiction range.

SF3D was collaboration between the artist and model maker Kow Yokoyama, the writer Hiroshi Ichimura and the graphic designer Kunitaka Imai. The trio were greatly aided in their endeavours by the patronage of *Hobby Japan* the high-quality Japanese model magazine with a leaning towards science fiction and fantasy.

The pages of *Hobby Japan* gave birth to a unique experiment, a comic book style story series illustrated not with pen and ink drawings but photos of model miniatures. The stories followed the battles between colonists resettling a nuclear-devastated planet Earth and the incumbent military government – the so-called 'Shutoral Demokratische Republik'.

The combatants

Nitto ⅟₃₅th scale 'Sdkfz251/1' (1970s).

wore retro-styled faintly Germanic uniforms of 1939–45 vintage and did battle in a vast array of armoured suits, robot landers and armoured crawlers, each sprouting an assortment of weaponry which ranged from heavy-calibre machine guns to Nazi 'Panzerfaust' bazookas last carried by German soldiers defending the ruins of Berlin!

The various 'Maschinen Krieger' vehicles designed by Yokoyama, Ichimura and Imai had equally pastiche Wehrmacht names such as 'Neuspotter', 'Fledermaus' and 'Hornisse'.

Scaled to a very manageable ⅟₂₀th, these kits are very finely moulded and for my money are the best science fiction kits available. Nitto had thought carefully about every aspect of the presentation of these models – the boxes themselves were printed on buff-coloured board with subtle rust colours. Each looked very 'official' and came with a colour photo of a superbly assembled kit affixed to the box top for use as a colour guide.

The 'Patlabor' and 'Gundam' craze very quickly eclipsed SF3D. This robot fighting machine fantasy swept

Japan and the vast range of associated models, primarily by Bandai, were soon far more popular with consumers.

SF3D has its own distinct cadre of enthusiast, however, and today it is enjoying a resurgence of interest. Indeed, many of Nitto's original designs have re-appeared following an agreement with manufacturer 'Model Kasten' who are re-issuing some of the kits as limited-edition resin and plastic hybrids.

Nitto ended regular kit production in 1985. Doyusha acquired many of the moulds and re-issued several of the ⅟₁₀₀ airliner kits in the late 1980s and early 1990s. Some ex-Nitto kits were still available as of late 2002. Although kits have appeared with the Nitto logo in recent years, these are primarily for the Japanese market and are based on science fiction subjects from movies and TV programmes.

S.F.3.D. assortment.

PYRO

Originating from the early 1950s until 1972 when it was acquired first by US kit manufacturer Life-Like and then by Lindberg, Pyro produced a real variety of different kits.

Amongst an extensive range of kits of aircraft, ships and especially cars and motorcycles, the company is probably most famous for its ⅛ scale (life-size) series of antique weapons. This series included large replicas of rifles like Pyro's classic 'Moorish Rifle' and 'Western

Saddle Rifle' and side arms which included revolvers like a 'Western .44' and 'Civil War Navy .36' to an extensive range of older flintlocks and wheel locks.

When you consider the limitations of the injection-moulded polystyrene process, the fact that Pyro's 'Kentucky Rifle' was nearly four-and-a-half feet long is simply amazing. What's more, each replica came complete with a handy wall rack, enabling modellers to display their purchases in a most effective way.

From 1962, some of Pyro's replica weapons were produced under licence in the UK by Eaglewall (who also released some of Pyro's equally memorable 'Design-A …' range).

Pyro 1915 vintage 'Ford Pie Wagon'.

Pyro French 'Wheel Lock pistol'.

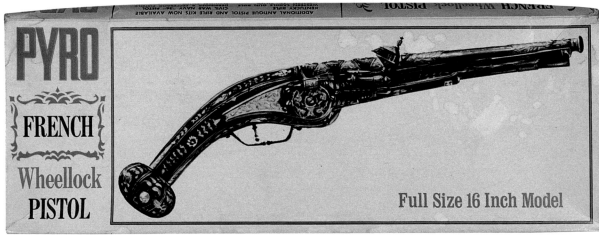

RENWAL

The revolutionary 'Aero-Skin'.

1957 Vintage catalogue.

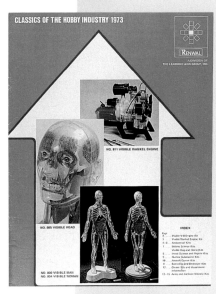

Renwal – 1973.

Though well known to modellers worldwide, New York's Renwal Toy Corporation was never a 'purist' kit manufacturer. Indeed, despite including kits of both a Martin 'Mars' and Boeing 'B-17' bomber in a toy compendium dating back to the late 1940s until the mid-1960s Renwal's catalogues were full of toys.

The only vaguely accurate aircraft miniatures in Renwal's 1956 catalogue are replicas of America's 'Panther' and 'Thunderstreak' jets – available in 'unbreakable polyethylene'. Even simpler were the bagged '3 Piece Plane' sets ("to hang on a rack … to sell from a counter") of which retailers could purchase four bags ("12 planes!") for the very reasonable sum of $6.00. However, what would current toy collectors pay for Product No. 273, an elaborate toy diorama of the 'Panama Canal' which filled with water and had working locks representing the entrance and egress of the Atlantic and Pacific oceans? The 'Renwal TV Mobile', "a new type of toy designed for the young technician to practice field telecasting of the big sports event, parade or news story…" is my favourite from the same catalogue.

Despite subsequent toy catalogues featuring wonderful products (to us military modellers) like Product No. 309 'Military Set' which included a jeep, ambulance, guided missile, armoured car, tank, howitzer with … 'cut-out soldiers', it wasn't until the 1960s that Renwal entered the construction kit business proper.

Beginning with a selection of educational models that revealed the internal anatomy of humans ('Visible Man' & 'Visible Woman'), Renwal produced an extensive range of 'see-though' replicas of objects as diverse as the human eye and the anatomy of a cow. However, the firm is best known amongst modellers for its intricate aircraft models that caused quite a stir when they first appeared.

In 1966 Renwal released the first of their famous 'Aero Skin' kits. These two model sets, entitled 'Fabulous Flying Machines', featured ½nd scale replicas of some of the earliest flying machines ever built. Not surprisingly, one of them was the 1903 'Wright Flyer' that was twinned with 'Bleriot's 1909 monoplane'. The extensive range also included a Curtiss 'Golden Flyer', an Avro 'Triplane', an 'Antoinette monoplane' and a Voisin 'Farman' biplane. All these were kits for which modellers had long waited.

The most remarkable component of these kits, however, was the inclusion of 'A Renwal Exclusive' called 'Aero Skin'. This consisted of delicate tissue paper, which had to be carefully cut and affixed to the wings and fuselage, moulded to represent only the skeletal framework of each aircraft's construction. Although the tissue was to be glued in place with the Testor's liquid cement supplied, the fact that the frameworks of each aircraft were moulded in black, rather than more accurate brown polystyrene, didn't really encourage scale realism.

Despite the fact that the kits were clearly marketed to capitalise on the success of the new cinema release, 'Those Magnificent Men In Their Flying Machines', around which, incidentally, British firm 'Inpact' had produced a range of ¹⁄₄₈th scale models based on the machines featured in the film and which they proudly exhibited at Brighton's 1966 Toy Fair, sales of Renwal's models were very poor.

Consequently, Renwal abandoned the very complex aircraft from the first generation of flight and released some simpler 'Aero Skin' clad machines dating from WWI. Amongst these were ¹⁄₃₂nd scale and ¹⁄₄₈th scale models including Camels, Spads, Nieuports and Fokkers.

By the mid-1970s Renwal had ceased trading and in 1979 US model giant Revell (now Revell-Monogram) acquired many old Renwal tools. If we will ever see any of Renwal's famous 'Aero Skin' range again is up to them. If the kits do reappear though, I'm not sure collectors will be too happy. Some of the earliest Renwal kits command premium prices!

What would the Valient (sic) kit command on the second-hand market today?

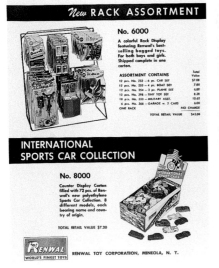

Far left: **1950s Dealer incentive.**

Left : **1956 Catalogue.**

REVELL

Revell 1962/63 catalogue. '3d' in 'old' money – equivalent to a bargain one and a quarter New Pence today!

Revell and Monogram are to America what Airfix and FROG are to the United Kingdom – household brands synonymous with model kits and one of youngsters' stepping-stones to adulthood.

Prior to their merger, Revell and Monogram were independently famous the world over. Revell can date its genesis to 1943.

Like Airfix, Revell really entered the construction kit business by accident. It was founded by Lew Glaser, who had previously set his heart on a radio sales and repair business in Hollywood. Unfortunately for Lew, the exigencies of America's war effort forced his wireless venture out of business – the supply of new valves and electronic components being prioritised for the exclusive use of the military. So, before the war's end, Lew was forced to look for new opportunities.

Revell can trace its origins to Precision Specialities Inc., a plastic injection-moulding business that Lew invested in following the demise of his earlier enterprise. The company's first really successful product was a ladies' compact mirror; the firm's brand name, Revell, sounded a bit like cosmetic giant 'Revlon' which Lew thought quite appropriate. Revell produced myriad inexpensive domestic items, such as picture frames and cigarette cases, demonstrating the practical qualities of plastic moulding throughout. Despite some success, however, Lew Glaser was forced to supplement Precision Specialities' income by accepting occasional contract jobs for the armed forces switching injection-moulding capacity to the temporary fabri-

cation of plastic components that were to be increasingly found in naval vessels and warplanes.

During the remainder of the 1940s following the advent of peace, Revell continued to manufacture toys and novelties which included collectible gems like the 'Toy Radar Radio' or the 'Toy Washing Machine', which claimed 'washes and wrings dolly's clothes'.

Although construction kits hadn't yet become a feature of Revell's catalogue the giant leap forward was around the corner. How it happened really echoes Airfix's entry into the kit business and, like the British firm, it was all down to a model vehicle!

In 1949 Revell was granted a licence to manufacture some of the toys designed by British ex-pat Jack Gowland. He was a former WWI balloon corps observer and had moved to California with his family shortly after the end of the Second World War.

Gowland Highway Pioneers 1951/52.

Highway Pioneers – 'The Gowland Connection', 1951/52.

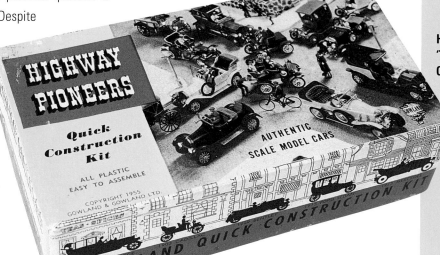

Revell's famous 911 'Maxwell'.

pioneers series' of kits was born. Without realising it, Revell's future success was assured.

The huge success of the 1911 Maxwell encouraged Revell to produce a sister model, a similarly scaled 'Back Firing Model-T Ford'. It also featured a pull cable; this time equipped with a trigger, which fired a hidden cap-gun mechanism – *voila* a backfire!

Although the pull-cord models, rather closer to toys than scale replicas', of course, were successful, it was the demand for the smaller ⅓₂nd scale 'Highway Pioneer' construction kits which encouraged Glaser to focus entirely on precision scale replicas. Goodbye to toys (by now surplus supplies of the ladies' compact had been sold to Mattel who found it an ideal accompaniment to dolls' accessories).

By July 1952 Revell, well into production of a second series of five additional 'Highway Pioneers', established a dealer promotion that heralded the 'car of the month' and encouraged retailers to purchase new models on a monthly basis.

Gowland's company also designed a range of ⅓₂nd scale cars which were marketed either as assembled 'pull-cord' toys, or available in parts, as construction kits.

A chance meeting at a trade show in New York with toy and hobby distributor Sol Kramer led to an enormous order for one of Gowland's designs (a ⅟₁₆th scale 1911 Maxwell auto) and encouraged Revell to extend its model car range. The famous Revell/Gowland 'Highway

The enormous success of Revell's car kits didn't go unnoticed by competitors. By the mid-1950s many potential rivals invested in polystyrene injection-moulding technology and regardless of imports from Britain's FROG and Airfix, California-based Revell's market share was being threatened by US manufacturers such as New York companies Aurora and Premier Plastics. Further afield, Chicago's Monogram was also proving a significant competitor.

Consequently Revell was encouraged to extend its range to include subjects from every sector. However, this had the happy result that by the late 'fifties Revell had once again achieved market supremacy. Now it was offering scale replicas of cars, aircraft, military vehicles, ships and, notably, models relating to

America's new frontier, the conquest of space.

By 1960 Revell's catalogue included perennially popular classics like the 'Robert E. Lee' riverboat, Boeing 'B-52 'Giant' Stratofortress', 'Flying Dragon' 'B-25', Douglas 'Skyrocket' and Sikorsky 'H-19' helicopter (which endured well into the 1980s). These ever-popular models were accompanied by rather more exotic and consequently far more collectible miniatures of US air defence missiles. These included the Northrop 'Snark', Bendix's 'Talos' and an elaborate diorama which featured Convair's 'IBM'. Scarcer-than-hen's-teeth replicas from the period include the Westinghouse sponsored 'Atomic Power Station' and a number of ⅟₃₂nd scale vignette gift sets featuring rival combatants from the Battle of Britain and subsequent Battle of Berlin. Revell even produced a range of cardboard 'Revell-O-Ramas' that provided ready-made dioramic settings in which to display their ⅟₇₂nd scale aircraft models.

However, I guess if there is one salient difference between British and American model kit tastes it is each market's demand for either automobiles or scale aircraft. Aviation modelling is a much smaller fraction of the hobby in America and, vise versa, car models have marginally less appeal to British modellers.

One type of model auto with international appeal with which Revell will be forever connected is the hot rod or dragster. These models date back to the 1950s when many customised 'funny cars' sprang from the beat generation. Lots more emerged during the early 'sixties and later 'flowered' during the summer of love.

One name of car designer above all others is inextricably linked with Revell: that of the late 'Big Daddy', Ed Roth.

Born in 1932, Ed Roth was the artistic son of an immigrant German cabinetmaker who, after a brief spell with the US Air Force, applied his more creative talents to the

Don Garlits' 'Dragster', 1974, 'JU88', 1975 and 'M56 SP Gun', 1958.

Bell's famous 'X-15' record breaker – a Revell kit dating from 1959, 'Martin Seamaster', 1956, 'Douglas Stiletto', 1957 and 'Phantom F4K', 1968.

art of 'striping'. This is an auto-painting technique from the 1930s, which was enjoying resurgence amongst California's hot rodders. He also applied his, not inconsiderable, mechanical talents to the art of customising and converting the many jalopies that the newly affluent American youth was buying and 'chopping' with abandon. Soon, in partnership with Bud 'The Baron' Crozier, a veteran of the original striping and hand lettering industry and Crozier's grandson Tom Kelly, the trio established their Californian business, 'The Crazy Painters'.

By the early 1960s, some of Roth's more elaborate custom jobs had caught the public's mood, notably 'The Outlaw', 'Tweedy Pie' and the 'Beatnik Bandit', and other memorable creations, each complete with elaborately painted fibre glass panels and fenders, futuristic dashboards and some even with one-piece moulded Perspex canopies.

Not surprisingly, Revell, depending on the whims and fancies of a largely youthful market, recognised that this new car craze was an ideal subject for new kits. They quickly realised that Ed Roth might be the ideal ambassador to front a new range.

Consequently, Roth was given a free hand to suggest the best subjects to turn into kits and very soon most of his creations were immortalised in scale plastic. However, Roth didn't stop at customising cars. His fertile mind and peculiar graphic style had invented a range of bizarre cartoon characters to inhabit his far-out world. Soon these too were moulded by Revell to occupy many of his car kits.

Gerry Humbert runs Revell-Monogram's photographic studio. He met Ed Roth on several occasions. He told me the old beatnik was "really out there!"

Once, during a visit to a customising show in Japan, a visitor saw Ed Roth changing out of his grubby, paint-splattered, work overalls as the event was winding down and Roth was preparing to leave for his famous trailer (apparently he rarely stayed in hotels and preferred to live in this temporary home nearby so that he could keep an eye on his precious creations). "Immediately the fan offered Roth $1,000 for his old bib – that was the man's allure!" said Gerry.

Ed Roth will forever be associated with one creation

¹⁄₃₂nd scale DH 'Mosquito IV', 1973.

1973/74 Kit catalogue.

'Huey' and 'Cobra' helicopters from 1967.

above all others – the crazed rodent Ratfink.

With his bulging, blood-shot eyes, manic toothsome gape and pastiche Mickey Mouse ears, Ratfink caught the beatnik mood. He was so successful that Revell quickly produced replicas of Ratfink and his vehicles. Seated in a custom car often adorned with an Iron Cross and or German WWII 'stahlhelm' (two emblems curiously popular with youths at the time) Ratfink became an icon for the alternative youth culture preceding the Punk rock generation.

Incidentally, Ed's 'Big Daddy' soubriquet was apparently invented in the early 1960s by Revell's then head of Public Relations, Henry Blankfurt – a former Hollywood scriptwriter who, like so many others, had fallen foul of the McCarthy blacklist.

Within no time at all Revell were selling millions of Roth's 'funny cars' and monster kits. Some caricatures of Ratfink featured illuminated eyes for added weirdness. The partnership conspired to create healthy profits for Revell and to make Ed Roth a very wealthy man.

I have spoken to many at Revell who had dealings with Roth. All testify to his definite talents and charisma and yes, he did live a very alternative life-style,

entirely living up to his beatnik image.

An uncompromising and very original showman. Roth's ability with pen and brush was held in such esteem that on many occasions when attending trade shows on Revell's behalf, he felt it prudent to accept part-payment in new kits which he would then either sign or decorate to sell to his huge fan base, all eager to own anything inscribed by the hand of the master.

Although he died in 2001, Ed Roth's creations can still be found in model shops and his legacy survives with frequent re-releases of his ideas in model form.

In 1986 Revell merged with that other US Model kit giant, Monogram, and moved from its base in Venice, California to Monogram's home at Morten Grove, a suburb of Chicago.

1976/77 Kit catalogue.

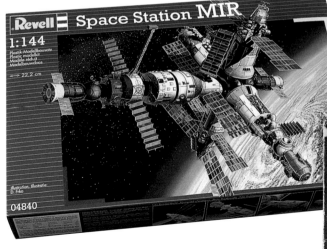

The ill-fated 'MIR'.

¹⁄₁₄₄th scale 007 'Moonraker' Shuttle, 1979.

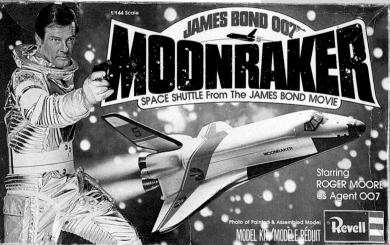

115

'Eurofighter' before it became a 'Typhoon'.

Ed Roth's 'Ratfink'.

Revell model kits produced to tie-in with the blockbuster release of 'The Hunt for Red October'.

On a recent visit to Revell-Monogram I was given a tour of the Morten Grove production facility and witnessed kit production and dispatch at the world-famous complex.

Kenneth Funk, Revell-Monogram's Production Manager, has worked at Morten Grove for 25 years. His career began when the facility served only Monogram. In those days he was employed mixing the raw materials – with his hands – which comprised the base ingredients for the particular colour and structural composition of polystyrene chosen for individual kits.

Ken told me that about 2 per cent of the base plastic comprises a colour concentrate and that when he joined Monogram, this colourant was in the form of a messy powder. Apparently, after climbing atop a ladder, this material had to be added in carefully measured handfuls to huge hoppers containing the raw plastic granules that sat above the injection-moulding

machines! Today the colourants come in the form of concentrates but, because model enthusiasts prefer to work with white or light grey uncoloured base material, very little is used.

At the time of my visit, in September 2003, to Revell-Monogram at Morten Grove the factory contained 16 state-of-the-art injection-moulding machines, which was far more than I have ever seen assembled on one production floor. Currently the machines operate three shifts and work on a 24-hour basis. Showing me a huge area, which is now used for warehousing and dispatch, Ken told me that this was nothing and that shortly after the merger, the factory contained 44 moulding machines all operating day and night. A sign of the times I suppose. The machines are still in operation around the clock because continuous production is conducive to consistent mould quality. The production facility comprises around 60 staff.

Revell-Monogram's moulding capacity ranges from machines with 75 tons' 'clamping force' to giants which can apply 500 tons' pressure on the enclosed mould tool. Enthusiasts might like to know that the moulded plastic parts, which are removed from one side of the mould as the two halves are separated, are known as a 'shot'. And, contrary to what a lot of 'kit bashers' reckon, 'sprue' is actually the short and thick plug of plastic at the junction of the input feed and the mould itself. This is connected to the 'runners' and their particular 'trees'.

Amazingly, Revell currently uses around 1,000,000 lbs of plastic each year. The Morten Grove facility is home to around 1,000, mostly active, mould tools each of which is carefully stored in an area adjacent to the production floor. Another 2,000 tools are stored ready for use in a nearby storage facility.

Today, a smaller market and fierce competition from overseas means that Revell-

Monogram now outsource much of their production capacity. In the old days Revell would produce as many as 200,000 new kits each month! China is the preferred location for high-volume items. The Chinese are able to provide pre-decorated mouldings and pro-finish pre-painted mouldings at the most competitive price.

The model kit business is an unpredictable animal. Judging forthcoming tastes accurately can be tricky. Like record companies, long-established model manufacturers have the advantage of an enormous back-catalogue of products. Steel mould tools are so substantial that if looked after, they will virtually last forever. Consequently, old models can be re-released with efficiency. The release of James Cameron's movie *Titanic* was a fillip for Revell-Monogram who quickly discovered that they possessed an excellent tool of *Titanic* that was stored amongst the 2,000 kept in reserve. Demand was such that for quite a while the factory was kept in full production churning out this veteran kit around the clock.

Made of machine steel, the original Revell tools are much harder than those made today. However, although they last longer, their toughness makes them very difficult to repair or convert. Many new tools include a beryllium (bronze alloy) component because it is easy to machine and consequently ideal as a base component for the moulding of fine detail and small parts.

Chrome plating is always done remotely from the company's production facility. Revell and Monogram are famous for including such parts in their kits. This specialist process is both messy and toxic. Not surprisingly, many of the firms contracted to do this work also serve the automobile industry – plating the insides of headlamps.

When I visited Morten Grove, two huge halls situated behind the administration, design and marketing offices were divided between moulding, packaging, storage (which includes picking and sorting direct-

ly on to pallets) and dispatch. The palleted cartons are loaded directly into the cavernous containers of articulated lorries that are backed up into loading bays, level with the factory floor, ready for delivery to wholesalers and distributors. The size of this operation is staggering. One can only wonder at what it must have been like at the height of the plastic kit boom in the 1960s and 1970s.

To help me learn more about the US plastic kit industry and Revell-Monogram in particular, I decided that I should make contact with the model giant. Revell's offices in the UK gave me the names of those they thought might be able to help, so I quickly fired off a couple of cries for assistance. Fortunately I didn't have to wait long and very soon arrangements were made for me to visit the home of Revell-Monogram in Chicago.

So, whilst preparing the manuscript for this book I had the great pleasure of being invited to stay at the home of Ed Sexton, Revell-Monogram's Senior Director of Product Development. Ed, his wife Ruan and their

1968 Kit catalogue.

Bell 'X-5', 1960.

Purdey's 'TR7', 1970s.

The Saints' Jaguar 'XJS', 1979.

sibility for assembling the product range each year, compiling the lists of new releases, vintage re-releases and, on occasions, deciding which models will be dropped from the catalogue. He is particularly involved with developing product themes when Revell-Monogram has identified a new category or forecast a fashionable trend.

"A large portion of my job involves licensing," said Ed. "This is intermixed amongst our model range. Basically, I go out and secure fresh licenses, identifying the ones with which we should be most closely involved, and pursuing those we wish to secure."

Ed told me that he is associated with each phase of the marketing cycle. "I am involved in areas such as advertising, creating catalogue entries and have responsibility for the information required on packaging." He is also intimately involved with license contracts. "The way just about all licenses are structured falls within a two to four year range. After the initial two years you may decide to sign a renewal should you wish to continue or, of course, you may decide to drop the new item after two years."

Ed explained the intricacies of the average license agreement: "A percentage royalty, based on the wholesale price is paid on every kit. In addition to this you make an advance payment before you even begin – this might be 24 per cent of what you anticipate the total length of the contract generating in royalties. You also sign a guarantee clause which, regardless of whether you get the product to market or not, commits to an agreed amount of license income." Clearly, Ed's remit is pretty wide ranging.

His earliest memories of plastic kits date from when, at the age of ten or twelve, he visited an older cousin who made WWI aircraft. Ed thinks that they were Aurora kits and particularly remembers 'Fokkers' and 'Sopwith Camels'.

As he grew older, and his cousin moved from the neighbourhood, Ed joined another group of modellers who introduced him to his enduring love –

young son Ted live in a large detached house in the Chicago suburb of Northbrook. This was a short drive from Revell's then HQ at Morten Grove but is even closer to the company's new home in Landwehr St. Ed's home is perfectly positioned from Revell and is a short distance to Chicago's O'Hare airport, which is really useful, as Ed spends time abroad at trade shows and at Revell AG, in Germany.

Although Ed's focus is on the product development side, Revell-Monogram also has a department tasked with evaluating the engineering requirements of each new model and he has to evaluate the budget implications of successive toolings. He also has respon-

Cadillac 'Eldorado', 1956.

'Cherry Pie', 1976.

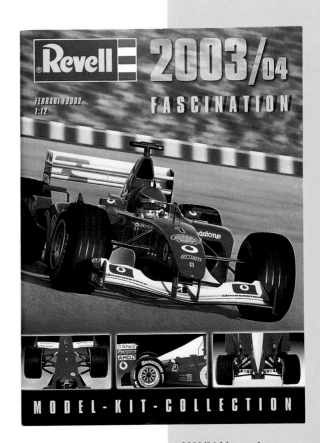

2003/04 kit catalogue, which at the time of writing had sold out.

Austin Powers' 'Corvette Convertible'.

'Bat Boat' from 'Batman Forever'.

The release of the movie 'Rambo' breaths new life into a couple of quite tired Revell kits.

commenced a period of aircraft modelling. This saw him concentrate on US carrier-borne aircraft, characterised by their folding wings and arrester hooks, equipping America's Pacific Fleet following Pearl Harbor. However, as soon as he graduated from college, Ed returned to his first love, automobiles and car models.

Ed told me that during the 1960s, Airfix kits weren't too well known in America. He said that until the early 1970s, the British brand wasn't really much in evidence. However, following a series of visits to the UK, he soon discovered that on this side of the pond 'Airfix' was the generic term for almost any model kit. "They say 'I'm going to build an Airfix. It's like Coke for us!" he laughed. "Although there is a reasonably strong ½nd scale contingent here (Airfix's core scale), America has always been dominated by ¼₈th scale."

Ed first learned of a possible job in the kit industry from Jay Adams, a friend he had first met in a local model shop. Jay worked for Monogram and had what Ed considered 'a really neat job'. After the merger of Revell and Monogram, new owners Odyssey brought the former from its Californian home to Morten Grove, Illinois. Initially, they were careful to maintain each brand's independence and set the two companies apart. Ed told me that the then head of Product Development at Monogram, Bob Johnston, "pretty much went over to the Revell side to manage product development there". Meanwhile Ed's friend Jay had been put in charge of Monogram's product development activities but soon found that the workload there had increased enormously.

Realising this, after about six months, Odyssey told Jay that they were going to recruit someone to help. Needing assistance, and knowing that Ed coveted a job with the famous kit manufacturer, Jay suggested that Ed "fitted the bill exactly" and asked him if he would come in and be interviewed for the new position. Keen modeller Ed jumped at the chance and was immediately hired. He

automobile models. All this occurred in the mid-1960s – the heyday of the North American plastic car model industry.

Whilst at college he dallied with making model aircraft and soon met a fellow student, residing in a nearby dorm, who also made such kits. Unlike Ed, however, this new acquaintance used an airbrush to achieve a superior paint finish. Adopting the instrument himself, Ed soon mastered the intricacies of the airbrush and

MESSERSCHMITT Bf 109E 1/72 SCALE

Revell

MESSERSCHMITT Bf 109E

'ME109E', 1963.

has worked there since 1989.

I asked Ed about the differences between Revell Inc. in the United Sates and Germany's Revell AG. He told me that although they are both part of the same American holding company, the European and American operations differ quite markedly. In the US, Revell-Monogram sells its products to model distributors and trade arrangements depend on major players buying bulk consignments. In Germany, on the other hand, the relationship is between Revell AG and independent model retailers. Another difference with the 'States is Revell AG's involvement with what is known as 'Pick & Pack' – the breaking of cases of one type of kit and tailoring mixed deliveries to suit a retailer's individual needs. In America this bespoke packing is the responsibility of distributors.

Ed told me that modellers' tastes also differ between Europe and the US. "The subject matter demands are totally different," he said. "Because of this, dating all the way back to the 1960s when Revell Germany was first established, the Continental Europeans have

M.R.C.A. 'Tornado', 1976.

Revell's tribute to the *Kursk*.

Rickenbacker's 'Spad' in ¹⁄₂₅th scale from 1976.

¹⁄₇₂nd scale Sopwith 'Triplane' from 1966.

¹⁄₃₂nd scale 'Typhoon' from 1973 and 'Stuka' in the same scale from 1972.

enjoyed their own product development, marketing and engineering structures. They function on their own and they decide upon their own range. Consequently, what we both do today is share our individual ranges as required."

Revell Inc. distributes the catalogue printed by Revell AG in Germany and offers its quite different products as a complement to the US range. Ed told me that there was once limited production in England at Potters Bar, but, because of modern communications and sophisticated operating procedures, Revell (GB) is now more involved with sales and administration. "A Revell (GB) salesman simply punches a specific order into a palm pilot and the order is efficiently fulfilled direct from Revell's base in Germany."

F4U-1D CORSAIR

Original Brian Knight box top rough for Revell's ½nd scale F4U-1D Corsair.

Like Airfix, Revell-Monogram regularly re-release vintage kits from yesteryear. Their Selected Subjects Program (SSP) has enabled modellers to rediscover some gems from the 'fifties and 'sixties without paying the high price such 'collectibles' often command. Competitively priced, SSP kits are bought to be constructed. Only the very brave (or fool-hardy) would risk assembling a pristine £300 rarity when there is no guarantee the kit could ever be located again!

Some SSPs are bought by parents who have fond memories of building the particular kit during their childhood and who are now keen for their children to share their warm memories.

Ed said that, initially, sales of SSP kits were very good. Recently, however, activity has slowed a bit. Ed reckons that this is down to the pent-up demand for the two or three hundred different kits re-released over the years being satisfied. As soon as the 'die-hard' enthusiasts had

bought the SSPs they had long coveted, demand tailed away sharply.

Traditionally, Revell's biggest competitor in its niche market of model cars is, and has always been, America's A.M.T., whose car kits have always given Revell's a run for their money.

Because success in car kits is key to the American market, Revell-Monogram take particular care to ensure that they produce models that will sell. Knowing what the market wants is important and Ed spends a great amount of time listening to the requests of modellers and distributors.

Ed told me that at the time of writing 'Tuners' were very popular – especially Hondas and Subarus into which "kids put ever bigger engines, affix chrome exhausts and add large fibre-glass spoilers on the front ends." Apparently this craze began on the West Coast but has now spread throughout the United States. Ed

GET YOUR EARS ON GOOD
BUDDY AND TUNE-IN TO...
REVELL'S VAN-TASTIC
SWEEPSTAKES!
IT'S A BIG 10-4 PROMOTION PLUS
17 NEW PRODUCTS!

AIN'T NOTHIN'
NEGATORY HERE!

**Dealer promotion
... "ten-four".**

sees it as part of his remit to reflect such interest with each new kit release and thereby satisfy the almost insatiable American demand for automobiles.

Together with Tuners, another popular category for which Revell-Monogram provides an assortment of kits, 'Low-Riders', is proving commercially successful. This fashion started amongst America's Mexican–American community where youngsters would put a set of hydraulics on a car's suspension so that the vehicle body could be raised and lowered – very low.

Low-Rider enthusiasts prefer a certain style of car, particularly old 'sixties Chevys and Bel-airs. The movement is popular enough to support its own magazine and Revell has endeavoured to produce model kits of the most popular Low-Riders seen cruising the streets or at shows and rallies.

Whilst trends such as the fashion for powerful Tuners and Low-Riders might go in and out of vogue, Revell-Monogram feels duty bound to provide replicas of many perennial favourites. Probably the

**⅟₁₆th scale 1910 'Maxwell',
the kit converted from a
pull-toy and first available
between 1951 and 1955.**

**Pontiac Club de Mer in ⅟₂₅th
scale dating from 1957.**

most popular of these car models is the 'Mustang'. This car, produced for years in a wide variety of versions, is to Revell-Monogram what the Supermarine 'Spitfire' is to Airfix – a 'banker'. Not content with simply re-releasing popular classics, Revell-Monogram also spends a good deal of its time producing improved versions of kits which have long been popular. A good example of this is Revell's re-tooled '32 Ford 'Hot Rod', an existing kit that sells well to a loyal fan base.

Revell-Monogram does listen to fans and endeavours to catch each successive new wave when it breaks. Indeed they can take pride in appreciating the growing interest in Tuners before their competitors.

They possess an almost unlimited tool bank of vintage kits. The fashion to tune, raise or lower classic American cars means it is relatively easy for the company to select an early tool and make the necessary amendments to the body shell or power plant and very quickly furnish car modellers with the flavour of the month. Only because it has such a rich heritage dating back more than 50 years, possessing dozens of high-quality, tough, machine steel moulds – which would be

virtually impossible to finance from scratch today – can Revell satisfy the changing demands so readily.

"Cars," as Ed told me, "are the core of Revell-Monogram's business." Because they employ real enthusiasts like him, auto fans can rest assured that the company will remain pre-eminent in this field for a long time to come.

When I visited Revell in September 2003, the company was preparing its move to Landwehr Rd. in Northbrook, so things were somewhat in a state of flux. Gerry Humbert, the head of Revell-Monogram's photographic department, has single-handedly managed the switch from film-based technology to digital photography. He prepares all of Revell-Monogram's catalogue and dealer promotion photos in-house using high-resolution studio cameras. Although the digital format has delivered numerous benefits, notably in the area of colour balancing and subject lighting, it has increased Gerry's workload somewhat. The author is partly to

Ed Roth's 1965 'Outlaw' with Robin Hood Fink, in ¹⁄₂₅th scale.

Ed Roth's 'Surfink' from 1964.

blame. Many of the images of Revell and Monogram kits, especially the earliest ones which I greedily selected from the Morten Grove archive, were photographed by Gerry. Sorry, Gerry, I guess you needed that request like a hole in the head!

Not surprisingly image manipulation has required him to get to grips with a range of computer software, most notably Adobe PhotoShop. Consequently he has also had to familiarise himself with a range of pre-press techniques, previously the province of repro graphics houses, to ensure images are reproduced correctly in print media.

At the time of writing, Revell AG have released their superb ½nd scale U-Boot 'VII C' – I had seen an assembled test shot some months earlier in Chicago. As fans eagerly awaited this enormous masterpiece, Revell AG's website claimed that although this kit had been "frantically awaited", their Junkers 'Ju 290 A-5' long-distance bomber in the same scale and the brand new 'legendary tri-plane' of 'Red Baron' Manfred von Richthofen were to be 'real eye-catchers'.

Like all the great brands, it seems, the secret of Revell's success is never standing still.

¹⁄₁₄₄th scale Laker 'Skytrain' from 1979.

Calypso – complete with miniature helicopter – c'est magnifique.

1932 'V-8 Hot Rod' dating from 1954.

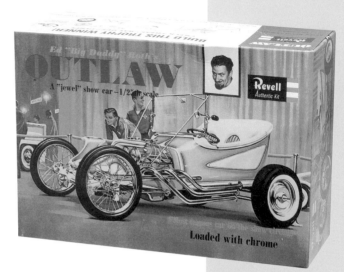

Original Ed Roth 'Outlaw' in ½₅th scale and dating from 1962.

1957 model Volkswagen 'Micro Bus' in ½₅th scale kit available between 1959 and 1963.

Revell's Douglas 'Thor' ICBM kit, unusual in ¹/₁₁₀th scale, dating from 1959.

ROSEBUD KITMASTER

Kitmaster's ¹⁄₁₆th scale 'Ariel Arrow' Motorcycle, 1961, soon to join the Airfix range after they acquired Kitmaster at the end of 1962.

Rosebud-Kitmaster is the name of another legendary and short-lived British manufacturer. Their models are high on the 'wants' lists of many collectors.

Founded in 1946 as Nene Plastics Ltd by Londoner Thomas Eric Smith, the son of an east-end toy maker, the new company quickly gained a reputation for the manufacture its high-quality plastic 'Starlight' dolls. Trading as Rosebud, the company gained a reputation for innovation – indeed in 1950 Smith registered two important patents for the manufacture of toy dolls.

In 1958 Rosebud entered the construction kit business. This was partly to utilise excess injection-moulding capacity and partly to jump on the construction kit bandwagon, which was encouraging a host of American manufacturers to flood a ready British market, challenged by only two indigenous manufacturers, Airfix and FROG.

The Rosebud 'Kitmaster' range of construction kits, mostly of locomotives and railway carriages, was of very high quality. The range included examples of some of the earliest railway engines, such as Stephenson's famous 'Rocket'. Miniatures were featured, all to the HO/OO scale established by Frank Hornby, of contemporary engines such as the Battle of Britain class locomotive 'Biggin Hill' and the new 'Deltic' Diesel class of high-speed engines.

Unfortunately for T.E. Smith, the success of the Kitmaster scale model range proved a double-edged sword. It stretched company resources because Kitmaster production drained capacity away from the doll range and also because the expense of running two quite separate types of businesses put an enormous strain on cash flow.

Late in 1962, to preserve the financial integrity of Rosebud, the Kitmaster range was sold to Airfix. Airfix

'Prairie Tank Engine', 1960.

**Kitmaster OO-HO gauge
'Evening Star' loco kit.**

were enjoying exponential growth and were eager to expand their range by acquisition of existing mould tools.

However, even without kit production, Rosebud's financial difficulties continued, and by 1964 the parent firm was forced into receivership.

The receivers administered the business until 1967 when American giant Mattel bought it. Overnight Rosebud-Mattel Ltd became the world's largest manufacturer of dolls. Incidentally, prior to this, during one of his many travels to North America, T.E. Smith had been offered and had *declined* the opportunity to manufacture G.I. Joe under license in the UK. General Mill's British subsidiary Palitoy ultimately became the lucky hosts of the British version ... Action Man.

The Rosebud brand name finally disappeared in 1971.

Because the Kitmaster range of model kits existed for only five years, surviving

models are scarce and highly sought after by collectors. Most, but not all, of Kitmaster's products were issued by Airfix and many collectors look for examples of identical models under each brand name. Despite being more than 40 years old, surviving examples of Kitmaster trains (they also originated Airfix's famous 'Ariel Arrow' motorcycle – a curious one-off) are of surprisingly high quality and are capable of giving some modern kits a real run for their money.

**Kitmaster rebuilt
'Royal Scot'.**

**Kitmaster '2nd Class
carriage'.**

**Kitmaster '1st Class
Restaurant car'.**

SKYBIRDS

Arguably the British firm of 'Skybirds', founded by one James Hay Stevens, manufactured the earliest construction kits of the format we take for granted today.

In the 1930s and 40s, Stevens was a celebrity author and illustrator amongst aviation enthusiasts. His drawings for George Newnes' magazine *Air Stories* had brought him to prominence amongst the 'air minded' youngsters who followed every development in Britain's rapidly expanding aircraft industry which was frantically re-arming as conflict with Hitler's Germany loomed.

Stevens is not only rightly famous as an illustrator and writer, amongst plastic modellers he is recognised as the founder

Press ad for Skybirds 'World-Famous Aeronautical Models' dating from 1938.

of ½nd scale. In this scale a miniature 1″ represents 6′ of the full-size object. Stevens' system was very quickly adopted by British aircraft modellers. At home, and internationally, it was also chosen as the scale for 'recognition models' used by civil defence forces and anti-aircraft gunners to learn the difference between the silhouettes of friend or foe.

Ironically, Stevens' art was to be a major influence on the young Roy Cross who was later to be famous as, perhaps, Airfix's premier box top artist. Fittingly, like Roy Cross, Stevens has also earned a place in the modellers' hall of fame.

Initially releasing a tiny replica of the RAF's 'Cierva Autogyro' – a kind of helicopter/aircraft hybrid – by 1935 the Skybirds range amounted to some 20 models. Amongst them was a DH 'Puss Moth', famous for its long-distance flights when piloted by Amy Johnson.

Skybirds' range also included the Hawker 'Hart' which, with the 'Hind' and 'Gladiator', comprised the trio of old-fashioned RAF biplanes expected to confront the might of the Luftwaffe immediately before the advent of the 'Spitfire' and 'Hurricane'.

In 'Series No 7' the Skybirds Fokker 'DVII' was typical of their products. It comprised a finely crafted, contoured fuselage and aerofoil-profiled wings with brass wheels and tailskid, acetate tail and elevator unit, and a sachet of glue in powder form – 'mix 1 part glue and 2 parts water and boil for 10 minutes'. Emery paper 'for wood work' was also included.

The exigencies of wartime production and his involvement in the war effort put paid to Stevens' model-manufacturing business. Anyway, by the late 1930s the cheaper and more accurate 'Penguin' kits from IMA were already challenging Skybirds' position.

Skybirds' delightful Fokker DVII kit from the mid-1930s. James Hay Stevens' 'Givjoy' brand is responsible for the established scale of ½nd and also for producing a range of multi-media (mixed materials not 'interactive'!) which top most collectors' 'wants' lists. They can be found but, not surprisingly, they are very, very expensive.

TAMIYA

Mr Shunsaku Tamiya.

Photo of the Tamiya Shoji & Co premises in September 1951. Standing in front of the recently rebuilt factory is Chairman Yoshio Tamiya, Shunsaku's father.

Before the introduction of plastic injection-moulding technology to Japan after the Second World War, Japanese craft toys and models had always been made from indigenous timbers like Japanese Cypress, Magnolia and Katsura.

Shizuoka-City, a suburb of Tokyo, had long been the centre for the manufacture of these artifacts. Along with numerous timber yards and finishing mills the area boasted the highest concentration of craftsmen skilled in the precision assembly of fine wooden products. Not surprisingly these skilled artisans were ideally suited to the switch in manufacturing techniques that was introduced during the mid-1950s to replace the smashed machinery of a defeated Japan. Consequently, Shizuoka-City became the location for the introduction of the latest injection-moulding technology, which transformed local industrial capacity as factories abandoned wood and began producing products made from plastic. Today, almost all of Japan's plastic construction kit manufac-

turers among them Aoshima, Hasegawa, Fujimi and Imai, are based in the area.

However, of them all, Tamiya is pre-eminent and today enjoys an unrivalled reputation as the finest firm of its kind anywhere in the world.

Like many of its competitors, Tamiya started life in the lumber business. In 1946 Mr Yoshio Tamiya founded a wood yard and saw mill in Shizuoka-City. Within a year his business had begun to exploit the market for high-quality wooden model kits. These construction kits were so successful that in 1953 the decision was made to close the timber yard and concentrate entirely on wooden kits.

Elsewhere though the trend was towards construction kits moulded from plastic. These proved enormously popular in Europe and especially the US. Here manufacturers like Revell and Monogram had discovered that consumers preferred to avoid a lot of the preparatory labour demanded by traditional wooden kits and eagerly snapped up the new plastic replicas which almost immediately resembled their intended subjects.

Yoshio Tamiya's son, Shunsaku, encountered his first plastic construction kit in 1958. It was a Revell import – a tank – and it was a revelation. Previously, Shunsaku, a keen scale modeller, had been forced to fashion tank wheels from miniature pulleys and to form gun barrels from aluminium tubing. In the ⅟₅₀th scale kit box before him, Shunsaku discovered finely moulded plastic pieces – wheels, gun barrel, turret and tracks of a far higher quality than any amount of woodcarving could hope to mimic. Although common today, in 1950s Japan polystyrene was a scarce and expensive commodity. Strictly controlled American imports were also an expensive luxury.

In his book *Master Modeller* Shunsaku Tamiya recalls the effort and financial outlay needed to acquire examples of foreign kits before Japan's prodigious plastics manufacturing revolution in the early sixties.

In 1959, convinced that the future of model manufacture lay in the production of plastic kits and with orders for their traditional wooden models falling away alarmingly, Shunsaku persuaded his father to take the bold step of switching to polystyrene injection-moulding.

A replica of the famous Japanese battleship *Musashi* was the subject chosen for the first Tamiya injection-moulded kit. Previously, when wooden models were all the rage in Japan, Tamiya was affectionately known as 'the warship company', so the choice of subject seemed appropriate.

Pre-production planning of a plastic kit required far more effort than was involved with simpler wooden

⅟₃₅th scale German Infantry from Tamiya's famous 'Military Miniatures' range.

Original Tamiya packaging for the cruiser *Atago*.

⅟₈₀₀th scale Yamato box art.

models. Fortunately, to help prepare the component drawings required to facilitate mould production, Tamiya secured the efforts of Hatsuji Shinomiya, a local warship enthusiast.

The painful learning curve required by the transition from wood to plastic meant adopting new techniques and out-sourcing a number of key processes that were then alien to Tamiya's traditional work force. The most conspicuously demanding service in terms of both money and effort was contracting a suitable moulding house. In the late 1950s, Japanese injection moulders had a surfeit of work and were in constant demand.

After imploring a suitable moulding house to accept the commission for the *Musashi* mould tool and agreeing to punitive payment terms and an unreasonable delivery schedule, Tamiya could do nothing but hope for the best. Anyway, in Japan at that time, moulding houses preferred simpler industrial contracts – Tamiya's request for so many finely detailed and fiddly pieces was hardly alluring. Tamiya even had to pay over the odds for imported raw plastic, Japanese material at the time being generally of poor quality.

In 1960 Tamiya's first plastic construction kit was at last ready. It was

in a box emblazoned with the company's new identity, designed by Shunsaku's art-student brother Masao.

Unfortunately rival Nichimo had made similar plans and had managed to get their model, also of the battleship *Musashi*, into the shops ahead of Tamiya's. It was also on sale for a lot less than Tamiya had planned to ask for their kit. Furthermore the rival's kit came with a pre-coloured hull that was red below the waterline. Although of a smaller scale, Nichimo's model outsold Tamiya's.

Forced to recycle their expensive mould and re-issue it as *Yamato*, the sister ship of *Musashi*, Tamiya braced themselves. This model fared little better and Tamiya sank further and further into debt.

After temporarily revisiting the wooden model business with almost inevitable futility, Tamiya considered releasing warships moulded from buoyant Styrofoam. This was viewed as too flimsy by Japanese enthusiasts and its lack of substance proved a non-starter.

Just as things looked desperate, Tamiya was saved by a happy accident. Shunsaku Tamiya was offered some second-hand moulds for a range of cheap toy cars and trucks – novelties of the kind given away as confectionery premiums in Japan.

Having agreed the purchase of the tools, Shunsaku called his new models 'Baby Racers' and packaged them in boxes decorated with illustrations he had scoured from coloured advertisements and

'M42 Duster' a ⅟₃₅th scale Tamiya classic dating from the early 1970s.

articles in American glossy magazines.

To everyone at Tamiya's surprise, the Baby Racers sold like hot cakes. These low cost mini-kits, which actually rolled along a flat or sloped surface, caught the attention of Japanese youth. Shunsaku decided it was time to return to the manufacture of plastic construction kits proper.

Boldly, this time Tamiya decided to move away from warships, the very subject that had made the company's name in its heyday. Shunsaku opted to produce a model tank.

The German WWII 'Panther' was the chosen subject, its angular lines and clean surfaces ideally lending themselves to injection moulding and featuring none of the myriad complexities of a warship. Shunsaku decided to add an electric motor, something rival American kits lacked at the time. However, his major coup was in securing the talents of the famous Japanese illustrator Shigeru Komatsuzaki to prepare the box top illustration.

Shunsaku Tamiya was determined that his new 'Panther' kit would restore the company's fortunes. No stone was left unturned to ensure perfection. At the time, Japanese instruction leaflets left a lot to be desired, being imprecise in almost every detail. With

Original packaging for the 'Panther Tank' kit which was available from New Year 1962. The stirring artwork is by the hand of Shigeru Komatsuzaki.

Exquisite ⅓₅th scale replica of the Wehrmacht's novel 'Schwimmwagen' amphibious vehicle. Released in the late nineteen-nineties this model was a great improvement on Tamiya's earlier kit from the 'seventies. It was soon supplemented by a great accessory set of figures based on the famous photo alleged to depict Joachim Peiper and members of his eponymous 'Kampfgruppe' in the Ardennes during the 'Battle of the Bulge' in 1944.

⅓₅th scale British WWII 'Cromwell MkIV'.

Inaugural edition of **Tamiya Model Magazine**.

100th edition of Tamiya Model Magazine.

the bit between his teeth, Shunsaku decided to prepare the new instructions in the American 'exploded view' style and draw them himself.

The model 'Panther' was finally ready for sale by New Year 1962. A great deal rested on its success.

Tamiya needn't have worried. It sold by the thousand and repeat orders flooded in. These were often difficult to fulfil on time – even with Shunsaku and his employees driving the delivery truck! An added bonus for purchasers was that the gearbox driven by the miniature electric motor had a higher gear ratio than rival kits and the Tamiya tank regularly won any neighbourhood challenges.

With the release of their 'Panther' kit, Tamiya established a reputation for top quality, exemplified by Komatsuzaki's superior box art. They also stole a march on competitors because of the quality of their motorisation. Although not the province of this book, remote and radio control-powered models are still a huge percentage of Tamiya's income. Enthusiasts will be familiar with the eternal success of Tamiya's miniature four-wheel drive models (the 'Mini 4WD Series') and their long involvement in larger ⅛th scale Radio Control (RC) vehicles. The combination of this long heritage in fine scale modelling and precision electronics and miniature motorisation has recently reached its peak with the release of Tamiya's superb ⅟₁₆th scale tanks. These motorised 'Tigers' and 'Shermans' even come complete with servo-controlled turrets, guns which recoil upon firing and sound boxes which mimic the distinctive steel roar and rattle of full-sized armoured leviathans.

The original 'Panther' kit also firmly established ⅟₃₅th as the standard scale for the majority of Tamiya's military vehicles and accessories. In fact the choice of this scale was almost accidental. It was adopted because it enabled the chosen electric motor to sit most comfortably within the 'Panther's' hull!

Tanks appeared to point the way forward. Very quickly the company produced more and more and is now probably most associated with this type of kit. Their classic 'World Tank' series of motorised WWII AFVs, from the 1960s and early-1970s, have now become collectors' items.

As they expanded Tamiya could no longer rely entirely on the output of free-lance artists like Komatsuzaki, so they decided to establish their own in-house training school and graphics facility. Together with Komatsuzaki, famous Tamiya artists such as Masami Onshi and Yoshiyuki Takani have conspired to create Tamiya's uniquely memorable style.

In 1963 Tamiya's first plastic aircraft kit, a ¹⁄₅₀th replica of Japan's famous 'Zero' fighter, was released. Apparently, for Japanese enthusiasts the design of its only real competitor, a 'quarter-scale' (¹⁄₄₈th) model by Chicago's Monogram, did not entirely capture the subtle lines of Mitsubishi's masterpiece.

Tamiya's Model 52 'Zero' Fighter, with box art again produced by the legendary Komatsuzaki, arrived in the shops in June 1963. It was received to wide acclaim and finally proved that homegrown Japanese product could compete head on with well-established manufacturers from overseas.

Tamiya's 'Zero' was the first scale replica to capture

faithfully the aircraft's shape and established firmly a tradition of accuracy and precision which is today second to none. Incidentally, upholding this tradition, enthusiasts will know that recently Tamiya have released another 'Zero' fighter. This one, a type 'A6M5' in large ¹⁄₃₂nd scale is surely the definitive injection-moulded kit of this machine.

Ships, tanks and aircraft – the definitive Tamiya combination. The great company was on course.

By the mid-1960s Tamiya began to investigate the possibility of bringing mould making – the one weak link in their

Tamiya catalogue 1984 edition.

¹⁄₂₀th scale 'Tyrrell P34' six-wheeled F1 racecar.

supply chain – in-house. Although contracting out for such specialist services was the norm, each time a new tool was required Tamiya were forced to endure a price rise and almost unbearable delivery terms.

Gradually the company established a cadre of young trainees who were each given plenty of time to learn the intricacies of this highly skilled business by enrolling on college courses or being apprenticed to master technicians at bespoke moulding houses. Shunsaku Tamiya convinced his somewhat sceptical father that the company should at least put its toes in the water of this complex process by investing in sufficient hardware to enable the company to at least repair and renovate its existing moulds.

Almost by a process of osmosis Tamiya developed the in-house skills and technological base to enable the establishment of its own Moulding Division. Quickly this

Tamiya diorama showing Famo, Kubelwagen and Wehrmacht soldiers.

department established standards to which other manufacturers could only aspire.

In 1968 Tamiya produced their first set of $\frac{1}{35}$th scale soldiers, a squad of German infantry, the ideal accompaniment for the growing range of predominantly German vehicles. Although not up to the standards of more modern releases, this set, and the box of US Troops that soon followed, sold tremendously well. Actually Tamiya subsequently perfected the anatomical poses of their figures by collaborating with the celebrated Japanese animator, Yasuo Otsuka, who had precisely studied the human form and especially how it moves as part of his particular art.

Tamiya kits became a huge success and before the decade was over the company had the honour of being the first Japanese model kit manufacturer to exhibit at the prestigious Nuremberg Toy Fair.

The success of Tamiya's military miniatures generated requests for the firm to produce a range of smaller vehicles and scale figures to accompany them. I well remember searching for the latest Tamiya kit at BMW Models, the famous Wimbledon model shop, or at Jones Bros of Turnham Green in Chiswick. These were two of the handful of 'real' model shops where, in the early days, one could be sure to find Tamiya's fine models. The advent of 'Beatties' made things even simpler.

Readers might recall that for most of this period Tamiya kits were imported and distributed by Richard Kohnstam (RIKO) whose David Binger enjoyed a close working relationship with Shunsaku Tamiya from 1966 until the latter retired

⅕th scale metal German 'Wehrmacht Squad Leader'.

Diorama featuring ⅟₃₅th scale 'M26 Pershings'.

It's a call for you.

30 years later. Incidentally, Richard Kohnstam could trace his family's origins in the toy business back to 1890. By the mid-fifties, amongst numerous other toy distribution agreements, Kohnstam was closely involved with Matchbox die-casts (see above), incorporating his own 'Moko' trade mark on Lesney packaging and at one point even owning the trademark registration of the 'Matchbox' brand!

Answering market demand in 1970 Tamiya produced a tiny 1/35th scale replica of Germany's wartime 'Schwimmwagen' amphibious patrol car. Today numerous 1/35th scale support vehicles, armoured and soft skinned, from every major international conflict since 1939 and dozens of figure and diorama accessories comprise Tamiya's huge military miniature range.

Since the early days, Tamiya has provided a host of

support services to modellers. The first edition of *Tamiya News,* the company's magazine for modellers, was a modest 16-page affair. Printed in Japanese, it was intended to provide modellers with articles, hints and tips about particular kits, supplementary to the information printed on the instruction leaflet.

Shunsaku Tamiya hoped to mirror the success of Britain's *Airfix Magazine,* which he considered an extremely valuable reference work and which particularly impressed him because of its impartiality and readiness to consider the merits of a rival manufacturer's products. Despite its small size Shunsaku considered *Airfix Magazine* an excellent publication and was confident that Tamiya should sponsor a publication of equally high standard.

Although, Shunsaku probably didn't know it at the

The groundbreaking 1/16th scale radio-controlled 'Tiger 1'.

time, the reason that *Airfix Magazine* pursued such an egalitarian course had little to do with benevolence. Ralph Ehrmann, Airfix Chairman during the company's 'glory years', told me recently that by the late sixties his financial advisers had told him that with 60 per cent of the home market and growing international sales, Airfix was in danger of monopolising the kit industry to an unhealthy extent which might lead to the demise of competitors and, ultimately, a decline of interest in the hobby as whole. For plastic modelling to keep growing there had to be a commercially viable industry in which others would trade.

Consequently, *Airfix Magazine* was encouraged to review the products of rival firms. I well remember the glowing reviews in the magazine for many of Tamiya's products (their celebration of the superb ⅟₂₅th scale

Centurion tank comes to mind) that began to appear with increasing regularity in the early 1970s.

Incidentally, enthusiasts might also be interested to learn that Ralph Ehrmann told me that Airfix's decision to begin their ⅟₃₂nd scale range of AFV models, beginning with the 'Crusader' tank, was a direct result of the impact of Tamiya's superbly detailed military models. However, after they commenced their new range, the sales volumes for the Airfix models were so low that they simply couldn't understand how Tamiya could make the formula work!

Airfix Magazine has long gone but the publication of *Tamiya Model Magazine*, which now appears in several international editions, has more than filled the void.

The inaugural edition of *Tamiya Model Magazine* was published in the UK early in 1985. On the cover it sported

German 18t 'Famo' half-track released in 1999.

a fine model of Tamiya's, then, new *USS Enterprise* aircraft carrier. This kit, in Tamiya's larger ⅟₃₅₀th scale (their 'waterline' vessels are in smaller ⅟₇₀₀th) was a revelation of super detail and moulding finesse. At over a metre in length the finished kit probably also required modellers who had chosen to build it to move house in order to find room to display it! At the time of writing (August 2003) *Tamiya Model Magazine* had just celebrated its 100th edition in the UK and has consistently upheld the tradition of excellence for which Tamiya is widely recognised.

Through the good offices of Mr Yasushi Sano I had the great pleasure of meeting Tamiya's President and Chairman, Mr Shunsaku Tamiya at Chicago's 2003 Model & Hobby Expo. This show takes place early in September. Mr Tamiya told me that when he and his colleagues left Chicago on September 11th, 2001, they were surprised when their Boeing '747' suddenly turned about and headed back towards O'Hare airport. Little did they know then that they were airborne at precisely the same moment that

the terrorist atrocity was occurring in New York.

After watching an exciting demonstration involving a radio-controlled duel between Tamiya's ⅟₁₆th scale 'Sherman' and 'Tiger' tanks — complete with sound effects — I was ushered into a meeting area on Tamiya's Expo stand. Plastic kit enthusiasts can take comfort in the fact that the gentleman is as enthusiastic about kits today as he ever was. Although reluctant to pick any favourites, when pressed Mr Tamiya chose one or two of his kits that he especially likes. Mr Tamiya is especially fond of his company's ⅟₃₅₀th scale *Prince of Wales* British battleship kit. Incidentally he told me that to ensure accuracy with their similarly scaled kit of the German pocket-battleship *Bismarck*, Tamiya had to refer to documents captured by the Soviets. Apparently the advancing Red armies overran much of the Third Reich's maritime administration and secured most of the Kriegsmarine's plans and archives. It was only glasnost and the thaw in east–west relations, which enabled Tamiya's designers to study the

Superlative ⅟₄₈th scale 'Fairey Swordfish' torpedo bomber from 1999.

original shipwright drawings – such is Tamiya's quest for accuracy.

Amongst other personal favourites, which include many armoured fighting vehicles – notably Tamiya's larger scale 'Tiger' tanks and especially the famous 'King Tiger' – Shunsaku Tamiya naturally has a soft spot for one kit in particular. Fittingly perhaps this is a replica of a Japanese classic, Tamiya's superb ⅓2nd scale 'A6M5 Zero' Fighter that comes with full internal detail

and many multi-media parts to help achieve the definitive model of such a great fighter plane. Fans will know that Tamiya sponsor a tank hall at England's famous museum at Bovington.

I have followed the, at times, stunning progress of Tamiya since I bought my first Tamiya kits in the early 1970s. I remember that they were boxes of 'Military Miniatures' Afrika Korps, US Infantry and three British Tommies laying the venerable 6-pounder anti-tank gun.

The memorable ⅟₄₈th scale 'Lancaster BI/BIII' from 1975.

Doing justice to Mitsubishi's classic at last – ⅟₃₂nd scale 'Zero A6M4'.

Tamiya's awesome ⅟₃₅₀th scale carrier **USS Enterprise.**

Famous artist Shigeru Komatsuzaki during the early years.

A while later I bought Tamiya's lovely ⅟₃₅th scale Kettenkraftrad — the ingenious motorcycle/half track combination Wehrmacht soldiers used to good effect on the snow-covered steppes of Russia. I recalled that when originally issued it came with an engine cast in white metal. "Indeed you are correct," said my mentor at Tamiya, the ever-helpful Yasushi Sano. "At the time of first release (August 1973), the model had a metal engine, but later switched to a plastic engine. I am not quite sure what was the real reason for the switch, but as an average modeller, I guess that back then many of us lacked the proper glue (instant cement, epoxy, etc.) to bond these (additional) parts together." Mr Sano told me that these metal castings were made in Hong Kong, and not in Japan.

Tamiya's memorable ⅟₂₅th German Metal Figures were

An assortment of Tamiya's famous ¹⁄₇₀₀th scale 'Waterline' warships.

Computer-aided design (CAD) in Tamiya's design division.

Tamiya injection-moulding machine in operation.

NC milling machine in Tamiya's tooling division.

Overview of tooling division.

also produced by their Hong Kong manufacturer. These figures were excellent and belied some of the criticism at the time about the lack of anatomical finesse in many of Tamiya's accessory figures.

"I think there are several reasons for discontinuing this series," said Yasushi Sano. "Firstly a similar reason to the above item, which is the lack of good cement. The lack of good primer for metal parts could also be a reason. Secondly, many modellers back then were a little discouraged to find that it was just a blown-up version from a ⅟₃₅th scale figure. Thirdly, building just the figures was not that popular back then with our Japanese audiences. They could be used for accompanying our ⅟₂₅th

tanks, but that is about it."

Yasushi Sano pointed out that at the time Tamiya, and Japanese modellers in general, were into motorising their kits rather than incorporating them into diorama settings – accessories like figures were somewhat superfluous. "You may remember that we re-released all the four figures plus six more in a plastic version in the early eighties," he added. These plastic miniatures were far cheaper than their metal predecessors and sold rather better which "indicated the difficulty of selling metal figures back then," he told me. The earlier cost hike for metal models made "a big price difference for kids," he said.

However, collectors haven't been forgotten. In November 2003 Yasushi Sano told me that because they retain the original tooling, Tamiya intend re-issuing those four metal figures again "this winter" in the original boxes.

By a combination of long-term planning, investment in the latest technology, innovative employee training schemes and, of course, legendary attention to detail and scale accuracy, Shunsaku Tamiya has built a company that has become the watchword for excellence in the kit industry. I'm sure his father would be very proud.

⅟₃₅th German 'Army Tank' crew set dating from 1968.

3. Genres

Some plastic modellers make miniature replicas of anything that takes their fancy, choosing subjects which include aircraft, military vehicles, figures, ships, cars, railways or space and fantasy vehicles.

However most enthusiasts specialise in one particular field. To be any good takes an awful lot of practice and the techniques required to make the best of a particular model can vary radically from genre to genre. For example, military modellers expend enormous energy 'weathering' tanks and lorries; adding rust streaks, paint chips or exhaust stains and often dusting the lower bodies of vehicles with powders to simulate the wear and tear of war machines in the action.

Car modellers, on the other hand, work hard to achieve the smoothest paint finishes, spraying and rubbing down only to re-spray and repeat the process in an effort to capture that elusive high gloss finish on a showroom vehicle.

Aircraft modellers will airbrush complicated matt camouflage schemes only to cover them with gloss varnish to ensure the adhesion of water-slide decals and then finally apply a matt coat.

For a long time in the figure modelling area there has been a healthy debate about the merits of enamel and oil-based paints. And now, acrylics have migrated from aircraft modellers and they have entered the fray. Regardless, most figure modellers generally agree that artist's oil paint is best for skin tones, despite the much longer drying times.

Different kinds of models require a great deal of very particular technical application. Little wonder then, that generally, modellers stick to type.

I thought that one of the best people to ask about the current state of the hobby would be the affable Paul Regan, currently President of the International Plastic Modellers Society (IPMS) UK. The IPMS is a truly global phenomenon, a vibrant forum where like-minded plastic modellers can meet to compete and discuss the latest developments in the hobby. They might also learn one or two trade secrets from fellow members, many of whom are masters of their art.

Lindberg ½th scale 'Search & Rescue CB Patrol Vehicle'.

Airfix 'Old Bill' & '1910 London bus' (1966).

"I am a bit of a rarity in the modelling world as I started when I was six (Airfix series one 'Typhoon', bought at Woolworth's in Sandbach on a rainy Thursday – I still have the model!), and have never stopped, managing to continue for the last 34 years without any breaks," Paul told me. "I joined IPMS in 1983, joined the National Committee in 1993 and was elected as President at the AGM in April 2002.

"I do not consider myself a collector as I fully intend to build the kits that I buy. However, when I moved into my current house, I took the opportunity to count the boxes as they were located into the loft, and the figure (adjusted for those bought since) means that I have approx 4,500 'kits' of one form or another in the loft as of December 2003.

"I have never really specialised in a single area of modelling, and thus although aircraft undoubtedly predominate, there are significant quantities of military vehicles, cars, some ships, and a considerable quantity of Science Fiction and Fantasy amongst them. Similarly, although most are straight injection-moulded plastic, there are (very) many vac forms, resin and metal items amongst the piles."

Hubley Mercedes '300 SL' (1960s).

MPC Camaro 'Z28'.

Airfix motor vehicle assortment.

Snap Fit 'Flintmobile'
from the 'Flintstone's'
movie (1994).

**¼th Revell Charlie's
Angels 'Mobile Unit Van'
(1977).**

Scale Models
magazine's "Power
Crisis' edition (March
1974). How many readers
remember the coal
shortages, power cuts
and the three-day week?

Paul works as a Commercial Manager for a packaging organisation, a vocation that he says has enabled him both to indulge his hobby and let him achieve a 'lifelong ambition' of securing a Private Pilot's Licence.

"The International Plastic Modellers Society was formed in late 1963 in the United Kingdom, and the UK organisation is still seen both as the founding father of the organisation worldwide and the body to which the overseas Branches look for leadership," he told me. "Despite the vagaries of the hobby, it is quite surprising that the membership of the Society has remained fairly constant for many years now, at between 1,500 and 2,000 here in the UK.

"We have a Branch network covering the UK consisting of some 55 Branches with 50 Special Interest Groups (SIGs – groupings of modellers who have an interest in certain types of modelling – civil airliners, warships, etc). There are around 45 International Groups around the world, which in turn have their own Branches and SIGs. It is definitely true that IPMS is the home of the true model enthusiast."

"The kit industry in the 21st Century has changed considerably from what was probably its heyday in the 1960s and 1970s, when it briefly had something of a mass-market appeal. In those days (when, I must add, I was a child so some memories are maybe a little 'rose-tinted'), it was possible to buy kits pretty well anywhere – the local paper shop, Post Office, hardware shop (before the modern DIY depots of course!) and sports shops all had limited displays of kits, and there was of course Woolworth's which seemed to have a new Airfix item each week.

"Even my relatively small town had 'The Model and Toy Shop' (note the sequence in the title), which held what would be regarded as a pretty good stock even with today's fragmented market, with kits from all the then important manufacturers – Airfix, FROG, Tamiya, Matchbox, Hasegawa and Monogram (strangely, I don't recall Revell much in those days), plus a complete range of paints, books, tools, scenic materials and some transfers.

"Nowadays, I live in the somewhat larger city of Leeds, within which kits can be obtained from perhaps a dozen outlets in total, with only a small handful who stock more than 'starter sets' and the basic ranges. Most will sell you some glue, and some may even have some paints … but certainly not very many. Sadly, as with most modern retailing, even in so-called toy shops, kits are sold as 'S.K.U.' (Stock Keeping Units for those not familiar with retail speak) by staff who know nothing of their product and, being honest, have no interest in them – indeed, this may be true of some of the members of the kit industry itself.

"This move has mirrored changes within the manufacturers of kits themselves, with the collapse of many of the original founding fathers of the hobby and with some of the names simply dropping out of sight altogether. Others have disappeared and reappeared, and a small number have apparently prospered. At the same time a huge explosion of smaller manufacturers, in particular from the ex-Eastern Bloc countries, has occurred, although the availability and longevity of some of these is questionable.

"However, what has happened has been a radical and rapid growth in the so-called 'cottage industry', which originally appeared back in the 1980s, initially concentrating on providing the modeller with options for markings and some small detail parts. Gradually, these small producers have increased their products and have also moved into producing their own complete kits, many of them being of subjects which the 'mainstream' producers would never contemplate, and produced to standards which could never be commercially viable."

I asked Paul to tell me how all of these moves have been echoed by the hobby and the modellers who follow it. "I suspect that the reduced sales of kits are reflected by the fact that even the enthusiasts are producing fewer finished models themselves nowadays," he said. "For instance, where modellers used to produce models almost on a production-line basis – more or less straight out of the box – nowadays, they seem to be spending increasing amounts of time and money on conversion parts, decals, etc., to produce a master-piece. In many cases, they do not even use kits as the starting point, with competitions usually being dominated by scratch-built master-pieces. The industry reflects this in the growth of the cottage industry, and in the rise of the super kit, with mainstream manufacturers putting etched metal, resin and metal parts into their kits in the pursuit of ever more highly detailed results – at a price.

"Fortunately for the industry most modellers are very unrealistic as to their actual building capabilities, which has resulted in virtually all of them moving into the kit collector category over the years. This seems to sneak up on people, usually beginning with just buying new products as they are released. The intent is always to

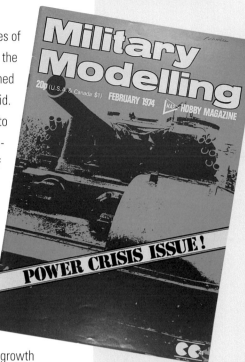

Military Modelling magazine's crisis issue (February 1974).

Selection of Merit railway accessories.

Matchbox challenge Airfix's market in soft plastic soldiers.

build the models purchased, then it becomes a case of buying them in case they disappear again quickly – perhaps enhanced by the way that quite a few products are limited editions, specifically to appeal to this instinct."

Paul told me that different modellers buy kits for very personal reasons. Some, because they are committed to completing a variety of aircraft or vehicles within a particular series or depicting a period within a famous military campaign. Others, rather aimlessly, just because the new model is the 'latest'.

Paul, however, is pretty focused. "I will continue to buy every aeroplane kit which Airfix release regardless of subject … but I still intend to get around to building them all, eventually."

As one might expect, many prominent plastic modellers are proficient in more than one category, happily building a military vehicle one week and following this with an aircraft model the next. However, it is generally the case that individual modellers choose a par-

Nichimo 'Spitfire' – *the* **Royal Air Force Fighter!**

ticular theme and stick with it. One of the by-products of making construction kits is discovering more about the subject you have chosen to model. Learning more about specific operational details encourages a more accurate build. It often surprises non-modellers to discover that far from sitting alone for hours on end, achieving little more than a completed model and a pallid complexion, many enthusiasts involve themselves in a wide range of research activities, some of which include visits to far-flung battlefields, museums or airfields.

Whilst briefly studying the broadly separate themes modellers choose to pursue, I've linked the following well-known modellers with the subject area they are most closely associated with.

I've decided to begin with military modelling, my preferred theme (son of a soldier and all that).

When, in 1970 I began to take scale modelling more seriously, the same names featured time and again in Britain's three main plastic modelling titles, *Airfix*

Magazine, *Military Modelling* and *Scale Models*.

In those days the names of John Sandars, Chris Ellis, Ken Jones and Roy Dilley were frequently associated with articles about armoured fighting vehicles or utility 'soft skin' lorries and 'Jeeps'. These gentlemen showed readers how to convert commercially available models of military vehicles, almost always based on the ubiquitous and cheap Airfix HO/OO range, or for the more adventurous amongst us, how to 'scratch build' from scale plans.

Scratch building consumed sheets of thin plastic card, which could be purchased in a variety of thicknesses and were measured in thousandths of an inch. With the advent of the early liquid cements such as 'Mek Pak', modellers were at last able to assemble models constructed of the most delicate polystyrene components. Their patience was rewarded with true scale appearance, something that even the best efforts of kit designers and toolmakers could rarely achieve with injection moulding.

Following the revolution in precision and scale heralded by the arrival of Tamiya's larger ⅛th models in the early 1970s, other military modellers came to prominence. Foremost amongst them were 'Mac' Kennaugh, Bill Evans and, of course, Francois Verlinden. Although modellers like Roy Dilley had long espoused the advantages of displaying figures or vehicles in a suitable diorama setting – showing tyros how to make terrain from 'Plaster of Paris' and fashion flock grass, so often the province of railway modellers, to create miniature landscapes – the honour of elevating the craft to an art really goes to Mr Verlinden.

In the mid-seventies, from his Belgian home, models by Verlinden regularly graced the pages of the British modelling press. He won award after award for his imaginative set pieces, each of which featured his unique approach to weathering and animation. Francois owned a successful hobby shop in Belgium, from where his 'VP' range of plaster accessories were received to wide acclaim, and had already started publishing a series of books illustrating his very

AIRFIX - 72 DOG FIGHT DOUBLES
BEAUFIGHTER & ME 109 G.6

accomplished techniques. In the early 1980s, award-winning American modeller Bob Letterman and Dutch investor Jos Stok joined forces with Verlinden. In 1985 the trio combined their talents and founded the VLS Corporation in Missouri, USA. It has developed into one of the biggest model and hobby operations worldwide, nurturing many successful offshoots and a thriving e-commerce business, modelmecca.com.

Francois Verlinden was one of the first proponents of

Starting with the release of their ½th scale Coldstream Guardsman figure in 1959 right up to their superb rendition of a Napoleonic Imperial Guard in 1976, Airfix have produced an enviable back catalogue of military figures in this large scale. The figure of the Emperor himself, seen here assembled, courtesy of John Wells, dates from 1959.

One of the popular range of 'Dog Fight Doubles'.

'Blue Box' HO/OO W.W.I. 'British Infantry'.

resin manufacturers are strictly outside the remit of this book about classic 'plastic', but his influence in the kit world is significant.

Together with Francois Verlinden and Bob Letterman, two other names, which absolutely must be featured in a list of contemporary military modelling maestros, are Steven Zaloga and Tony Greenland.

Between them, these gentlemen have rewritten the rulebook for the construction of model tanks and armoured fighting vehicles. With an unequalled ability to achieve a true scale effect, Steve and Tony have shown others how to work in etched brass; bending, snapping, braising and soldering side skirts, spaced armour and distressing fenders and gun-shields, from the metal, to achieve super realism. Steven Zaloga is one of those multi-talented modellers, adept in more than one area. He usually accompanies his vehicles with exquisitely painted and animated figures – proving his versatility with both paint and airbrush.

Mention of Mr Zaloga's artistry with figures leads us neatly on to that other military modelling sector – figure modelling.

working with resin, a material that delivered scale accuracy beyond the wildest dreams of modellers, previously used to the limitations of injection-moulded polystyrene.

As more and more modellers opted for the 'Verlinden Way', they sought to emulate his approach. Soon, his artistry was copied and his ever-growing range of products, which had now extended to vehicle and aircraft 'super-detailing' conversion sets, were released to coincide with the new offerings from mainstream giants like Tamiya, Italeri or ESCI. As I mentioned in the introduction, Verlinden kits and those of other

When I realised that models of soldiers could be found other than in boxes of Airfix's 2/- HO/OO soft polythene soldiers, I discovered a whole world of talent that had previously eluded me. The name of Roy Dilley was

¹⁄₇₂nd scale Vulcan B2 bomber – a Peter Allen classic from 1983

already familiar to me from the pages of *Airfix Magazine*. Roy's versatility revealed to me the dozens of manufacturers who cast 54, 70 (not forgetting 'Series 77') and 90mm model soldiers in lead alloy. Great names such as Hinchcliffe, Imrey-Risley, Mignot, Greenwood & Ball, Hinton Hunt, Tradition, Phoenix, and of course Stadden (Chas Stadden also being an accomplished figure painter). With the growing popularity of model soldiers, it wasn't long before mainstream manufacturers like Airfix, ESCI and Tamiya began making models especially aimed at figure modellers who had traditionally pooh-poohed polystyrene (France's Historex had shown unique faith in 54mm plastic figures since the early 1960s),

Consequently, it wasn't long before kit enthusiasts were encouraged to embellish the offerings of those mainstream manufacturers venturing into the previously haloed ground of military miniatures. And, surprise, surprise, chief amongst these were Airfix, who not only commenced a series of creditable 54mm cavalrymen and foot soldiers but also released numerous boxes of WWII 'Multi-pose' figures (to 54mm or ⅓₂nd scale) which, as their name suggests, were capable of being built into an almost infinite variety of configurations.

Soon, the pages of enthusiast magazines featured the work of modellers like Norman Abbey, Nick Larkin, Sid Horten, Graham Bickerton and Max Longhurst who combined Historex components with those of Airfix or manufacturers of metal figures and created works of bespoke genius.

Together with his ground-breaking work with Poste Militaire, who showed precisely how metal figures should be designed and cast, Ray Lamb also exhibited his mastery with Historex models. As did, of course, artists such as Pierre Conrad and Josaine Desfontaine. No list of military figures is complete without mention of the talents of Peter Gilder, Shep Paine, Ray Anderson, Philip O. Stearns or David Catley, each of whom had an inspirational role in the development of figure modelling.

Today, figure modellers like Mike Blank, Bill Horan, Mike Good, Andrei Koribanics, Peter Twist, Derek Hansen, Adrian Bay and many of those mentioned above are raising the bar even higher – just when most of us had thought that every model-making possibility had been exhausted!

Arguably the biggest single category is aircraft modelling and 'building plastic planes' is anyway how most non-modellers characterise the hobby. Making aircraft models was certainly how I discovered the fun to be had building kits. As a youngster I would rush home from the local toy or model shop – or, if on a trip into town with my parents, the Woolworth's store in the high street – and tear open my new purchase. In those days my chosen model was almost always Airfix, a brand which seemed to be available anywhere. Woolworth's always carried virtually the entire range, a legacy of a close commercial relationship dating back to the 1940s. If I fancied a change, I was

FROG catalogue (1960s).

Magnificent ¼₄th scale BAe Sea Harrier FRS-1

confident that the nearest newsagent would also stock FROG kits – brand owner Lines Brothers having explored all channels to circumnavigate Airfix's apparent retail monopoly.

Initially my purchases were assembled and painted at a frantic rate. Undercarriage legs and tail planes would frequently wobble and lean precariously before falling off the model dripping in strings of pungently sticky polystyrene cement. Dissatisfied with my crude and hurried attempts, I would invariably consign my recent purchase to target practice with an air rifle or the hungry lick of a flaming match. Didn't plastic fighters and bombers burn well then?

As my abilities improved I discovered that Humbrol's old marketing strap line of "Skill and patience …" really did pay dividends. As I took more care, my finished models began to pay more than a passing resemblance to the aircraft they were supposed to mimic.

It wasn't long before I heeded the advice of experts such as Alan Hall, Michael Bowyer and Chris Ellis, learning the importance of accurate camouflage colours and discovering how to cement crystal-clear cockpit transparencies to fuselages without causing them to mist up from the effects of polystyrene cement dissolving adjacent plastic.

One of the biggest influences on me in my twenties was Ray Rimmel, the aviation buff who seemed to contribute to every modelling magazine and actually became *Airfix Magazine's* editor for a while.

An expert on WWI avia-

tion, Ray now runs the perennially successful *Windsock* imprint and, as far as I know, still employs the talents of one-time Airfix artist, Brian Knight, to illustrate the covers of successive volumes.

After a while I became aware of the amazing talents of master aircraft modellers such as George Lee, Peter Cooke and Alan Clarke. These gentlemen showed precisely what could be achieved by scratch-building, although, if I'm honest, their dexterity with metal work and bespoke vacuum forming was always beyond me.

More recently I became aware of some of the work of Bill Bosworth (see Accurate Miniatures) and had the distinct pleasure of meeting someone who had turned his passion into a career.

At the time of writing I have just become aware of the model creations of Zdenek Sebesta – now one of Europe's foremost aircraft modellers whose work has recently been exhibited in print.

Like military modelling, the field of aircraft modelling appears to offer unlimited potential. These opportunities are no doubt greatly aided by the huge range of aftermarket tools, accessories and conversion packs which enable the keen modeller to achieve near 100 per cent scale accuracy. With the application of photo-etched seat harnesses and tiny cockpit instruments reproduced as decals and then sandwiched behind ultra-thin transparent plastic and etched brass bezels, the realism achieved by some 21st-century modellers would astound pioneers like James Hay Stevens.

Though never a model railway enthusiast, I would occasionally buy one of Airfix's 'Line-side' kits. These were usually of either buildings or trackside accessories like fences or telegraph poles. Though scaled to HO/OO (which is really 1/16th scale) they were ideal accompaniments for dioramas in the more common 1/2nd scale. Indeed Airfix rebranded their RAF Control Tower, originally a railway layout accessory in HO/OO, as a 1/2nd scale airfield accessory designed for display with the firm's enormous range of 1/2nd scale RAF aircraft. No one seemed to notice the

Addar 'Planet of the Apes Treehouse' in … a bottle! (1975) Established by ex-Aurora employees, Addar began life in 1972 and released lots of ships in bottles too. They were mostly ex-Gowland & Gowland or Aurora moulds. Sadly, the company ceased trading in 1977.

discrepancy in size.

Whilst I was never lured by the appeal of the working model trains of Hornby, Marklin, Fleischmann or Arnold – and reserved my modelling mainly to military vehicles and aircraft – I did keep a weather-eye on the work of modellers like Michael Andress and Bert Lamkin. These enthusiasts used the products of Airfix, Faller and Merit (with enormous dexterity) plus a range of craft material, to design and populate layouts of the most intricate complexity.

Like model railways, car kits never really caught my attention. Occasionally of course, one of Airfix's more ambitious models, notably Peter Allen's magnificent ½th scale 'Bentley Blower', would tease hard-earned cash from my pocket. I was also sometimes tempted to purchase one of Revell's outrageous street machines. I remember buying their outlandish 'Street L'eagle' trike in 1972. Of course, today I wish I had purchased one or two of Revell's early car kits and especially some of 'Big Daddy' Ed Roth's customised creations. Look at the values these achieve today!

Two of the biggest names in car modelling were Gerald Scarborough and Mat Irvine – the latter produced regular articles about what was new and exciting in the world of car kits.

Mat is also well known for his love of space and science fiction models and thus we neatly segue into the final major genre in the plastic construction kit world – space and sci-fi.

Mat Irvine will need little introduction to British modellers. During a reception for model collectors and car enthusiasts at Dean Milano's excellent Chicago Toy and Model Museum in September 2003, I had the chance to interview briefly fellow Brit Mat who, during one of his regular visits to the 'states, was staying with Dean.

In fact Mat and I had met before. At the 2002 British IPMS extravaganza at Telford, we exchanged our latest books: Mat's *Creating Space*, an illustrated history of space kits, and my work, *Celebration of Flight* – the illustrated history of Roy Cross's career in aviation art which I co-authored with the artist. Coincidentally we were both in attendance signing our respective works for those kind souls ready to part with their hard-earned!

At the Chicago party I was able to ask Mat about his long involvement with model kits.

June 1990 a collecting special from *Scale Models* magazine.

Denys Fisher 'Six Million Dollar Man' kit.

Tony James' Comet Miniatures ⅛th scale 'Mk1 TV Dalek'.

"As a youngster, I started buying 'two bob' Airfix kits from Woolworth's, spreading glue all over the kitchen table much to Mum's disgust," he said. Later as he entered his teens, although he discovered the charms of cars and girls (not necessarily in that order) he decided not to abandon modelling.

After he left school he joined the BBC, not initially in SFX, which is his current metier, but in the newsroom. "It was the time of Apollo 11 and although BBC 2 was broadcasting in colour, and BBC 1 was about to embrace the new medium, there was a lack of original colour film to broadcast," he said. Being a keen modeller and basically using Airfix kits and assorted bits and pieces, new boy Mat was able to put his hobby talents to good use and furnished 'Auntie Beeb' with a range of three-dimensional replicas, in colour of course, which proved

MPC's snap-together 'The Bionic Woman' repair laboratory.

a very valuable supplement to the broadcaster's programmes.

"It was a very crude set-up by today's standard," smiled Mat, "but it was all achieved very quickly. Remember, the whole thing had to be done within 24 hours. There was no time to waste." It was these early experiences of model making which encouraged Mat's abiding love of space travel and exploration. It also taught him the rigours of working under pressure, within a tight schedule and to a budget. Invaluable lessons for a features contributor in the unforgiving world of specialist publications.

At around the time Mat was producing his space models for BBC news, he developed his interest in American cars. "I have to admit a fondness for American machinery – mainly as these were the first

model cars to be made in the larger scales," he told me.

"At this time Airfix car kits, nice as they were, were manufactured in ½₂nd scale, which was smaller than American kits (generally in ¼th scale). Neither did they have rubber tyres or lots of chrome parts which were desirable features common to American kits."

Mat distinctly remembers encountering an impressive AMT kit of a 1962 Ford 'Fairlane', which was bigger and more impressive than anything he had seen in England. "In those days, if you wanted to build larger kits you had to opt for American models by AMT, Revell or Monogram," he recalled.

"Although I sometimes make aircraft kits, a long time ago I realised I had to specialise," he said. With experience of model making for TV under his belt, Mat soon transferred to the BBC effects department – usually working in the Space Studio. He worked on a wide vari-ety of programmes from Apollo, Soyuz and Skylab to unmanned missions like Mariner and Viking. Although his interest in models and specifically cars started as a hobby, it is ironic that Mat's long association with space started as part of his job.

As a BBC Visual Effects Designer, Mat is most famous for his creations on programmes such as 'Doctor Who', 'Blake's 7' and 'Tomorrow's World'. Working to an extremely tight budg-et and without the luxury of the sophisticated CGI techniques made famous today by Lucas Films and Pixar, Mat and his team had to think on their feet and be ready to assemble whatever the story required. "You get the script and then you basi-cally have to work out what is likely to be either a model or creature effect," he added.

AMT Star Trek (early version) *USS Enterprise*.

Airfix Series 10 'Snowspeeder' from 'The Empire Strikes Back'.

Pretty collectible Denys Fisher 'R2-D2' kit (1978).

Airfix 'Slave I' from 'The Empire Strikes Back'.

Mat left the BBC in 1993 and afterwards helped start the American import 'Robot Wars' in the UK. He was one of the main Technical Consultants on the first few series. Now he's now involved with the judging panel.

Together with his former regular monthly feature in *Scale Models International*, Mat has had many pieces published for journals that include *Airfix Magazine*, *Model Cars Plus*, *Model and Collectors Mart*, *Tamiya Model Magazine*, America's *Fine Scale Modeler* and even Britain's *New Scientist*. He is also a regular contributor to myriad sci-fi and car magazines. Although recognised as an expert about the history and development of plastic kits, he is not precious about kit collecting *per se*, preferring to see assembled models professionally displayed, rather than unassembled gathering dust in attic hoards. "It depends what you mean by collectible," he told me. "You can have a collection of boxes if you particularly covet the artwork."

His ambivalence to kits as investments might have something to do with his matter-of-fact relationship with them whilst preparing articles for specialist magazines or in advance of seeing them destroyed on a film set. He told me that he was forced to construct kits at such a furious rate, people were amazed that he could finish and photograph them so rapidly. But, as he says, he is in control of the actual image, "so if I screwed up one side of a model I would simply photograph it from the opposite side!"

In 'Creating Space', Mat says: "Not that long ago, second-hand kits were not worth more than a fraction of their retail price – and in fact most still are not. Like the majority of objects now deemed 'collectible', just because they are old (or perhaps to be more accurate, 'not brand new'), this doesn't mean that they are worth anything more than a second-hand price, and certainly no more than face value." However, even Mat has to concede that there are exceptions and that some old kits are worth their weight in gold. He cited rarities such as American manufacturer Hawk's 'Martin Matador' missile on its transporter and Lindberg's 'Five Space Ships of the Future' set, both from the 1950s, as eminently desirable finds for collectors.

Tony James needs little introduction to space and science fiction modellers. His Lavender Hill shop, Comet Models, is a Mecca for those visiting London, keen to discover the latest kit or collectible associated with science fiction or man's exploration of space. However, I first met Tony many years ago when he dealt in old and rare kits from much smaller premises nearby. This operation, 'Tee-Jay

Lincoln's 'FAB 1' car from TV's 'Thunderbirds'.

Models', was launched in 1986 after Tony attended the Biggin Hill Air Fair.

"I took along my collection to sell and returned on the Sunday with three times as many kits, a van and £3,000," Tony told me. "All weekend I was offered second-hand kits including many out-of-production types, so I decided to start a business specialising in these and other hard-to-find kits."

Incidentally, Tony recently told me that as far as nostalgia is concerned "time plays many tricks. Who ever thought the three-colour 'trench panel' kits from Matchbox would become collectible!"

Initially, Tony's new business, situated in one room under the present shop, was open by appointment only. "One of our Japanese customers offered some 'Thunderbirds' kits in exchange for some stock. This highlighted a gap in the market and I immediately began to offer Science Fiction kits as part of the business."

As things developed, Tony launched Comet Miniatures in 1989 and since then it has expanded on the same site. "We produced our first model (CM001) which was a vacform and white metal kit of the 'Nautilus Submarine' from '20,000 Leagues Under The Sea' and followed this with models of 'Stingray' and 'Fireball XL5'," he continued. "We then launched this country's first plastic kits of the TV and movie version 'Daleks'. Our final in-house model was the 'Blake's Seven' spaceship, 'Liberator'. All these kits are now discontinued and have since become sought-after collectors' pieces."

Readers might be interested to learn that before branching out on his own, Tony was an RAF Air Traffic Controller. Significantly, he spent his last five years with the RAF as a model maker. "I was lucky to be involved with a specialist team building full-size replica aircraft – 'Hawks', including a Red Arrows version, and a 'Tornado'," he recalled. Tony's specialist area was painting cockpit instrumentation and finishing the pilot's 'office'.

Now 54 years of age, Tony tells me he built his very first model at the age of five. "It was an Airfix

'Skyhawk'! Airfix and FROG set the standards for other manufacturers to follow and it is a sad reflection to have to look to foreign companies for the future of our hobby," Tony reflected. "I will always remember that it was the exciting artwork on the box tops which set our imaginations racing and had us running home from Woolworth's with our latest purchase only to get scolded by Mum for leaving glue and paint stains on the kitchen table! Today's PC rules have removed part of the fun from the hobby and no matter how good the kit is, it is the artwork which sets the expectation of the contents."

Comet Miniatures now specialises in Limited Edition Resin Sci-Fi kits as well as Die-Casts. "I still have the enthusiasm and will continue to produce items that enthusiasts require and it is a pleasing thought that the RAF Museum at Hendon still has three of my models on permanent display," Tony concluded.

I can't really end this section without mention of ship modelling. Lots of modellers specialise in this area. Two who had an enormous influence on me were Chris Ellis and Roger Chesnau.

Every manufacturer has a number of either warships or civilian vessels in their ranges. Choice is pretty neatly polarised between those who favour ships from the age of sail and those preferring armoured, steel battleships, etc., from the 20th century. With the latter, scales vary from Tamiya's substantial $\frac{1}{350}$th scale mammoths to $\frac{1}{1,200}$th scale waterline vessels, popular with war gamers and also made in plastic, in 'waterline' versions, first by Eaglewall in the 1950s and by Airfix in the 1970s – in Britain at least.

Scale Models **magazine, November 1992.**

4. Kit Collecting

The Model Village – one of the dozens of wartime publications showing youngsters how to build models from scrap card and paper.

FROG Penguin 'DH 86A Diana' (1930s).

Like the models they covet, kit collectors come in all shapes and sizes. Some scale model enthusiasts buy kits purely to construct, perfecting authentic details in every way and then displaying them in the hope of receiving the plaudits of their peers. Others seek out long-lost kits lurking in the dustier recesses of retail stores or amidst the debris of jumble in a relative's loft. But whatever their game plan – to build or hoard for potential future investment – model fans like me regularly scour locations we think might reveal hidden gems from modelling's history.

Of course it doesn't really matter why we 'anoraks' search out discontinued kits. It's a harmless pursuit and as long as it brings some per-

sonal satisfaction and isn't inconveniencing anyone, it's as valid as any hobby. When I began to collect kits, shortly after I learnt of the possible demise of Airfix in 1981, I rather grandiosely thought that by collecting a few examples of their products, which I had so eagerly built in the 1960s, I was preserving an important part of our social history. Certainly, I began collecting old kits because they were affordable – even 20 years ago rare Dinky cars or Britain's lead soldiers were beyond my price range. Old kits were cheap. I also figured that because they were relatively inexpensive when originally retailed and they lacked any perceived financial worth, most models must have ended up in the bin. I figured that ironically, this would mean that unmade kits, in their original packaging, would consequently be quite rare and that maybe, just maybe, they would be a long-term investment which 'serious' collectors had overlooked.

Well, prices for old models have sky-rocketed since I wrote my first book about kit collecting (1984's *Model World of Airfix*) and the phrase 'no-pain, no-gain' certainly has a resonance with kit collectors. You could buy a second-hand car for the price of some of the scarcer FROG, Airfix or Aurora kits!

Commercial opportunity in the kit-collecting world has made it possible for some people to dedicate part or all of their time to trading in collectable kits. But, before we consider one or two collectors and their activities, I thought it worthwhile singling out a few traders, two from the UK one from the US, so that we can better understand the current passion for old kits and, especially, the price we are prepared to pay for the long-lost models that we can't do without.

Malcolm Rolling started Shropshire-based 'KingKit' from his spare bedroom in 1983. Then, he was turning over some £50 per week. He decided to trade in old and discontinued kits after he discovered that his interests had changed and he thought of selling his personal model collection. Fortunately, this decision coincided with the temporary demise of Airfix, which suddenly put a premium on the examples of their kits he had earmarked for sale.

After maintaining the business on a strictly part-time basis, in 1989 with the annual turnover growing to £20,000, Malcolm decided to bite the bullet and trade in kits full-time. His decision was encouraged when he discovered his children using parcels he had painstakingly packed full of fragile old kits, as the building blocks for a western fort playing cowboys and indians around the 'redoubt'.

Realising that he had reached a fork in the road – the business was too serious to run part time from home – and wanting to change direction anyway, he secured a 3,000-square foot warehouse and went full-time.

"It was a difficult decision but on the basis that you don't regret what you do in life, you regret what you don't do, I decided to give it a go," he said.

Fortunately, Malcolm has experienced a boom in the interest of old kits – which has not surprisingly coincided with the rapid decline of new kits appearing in the shops as manufacturers reduce production and concentrate on fewer new kits. Since it began, KingKit has become one of the largest old and rare kit traders in the business, now with an annual turnover of more than £250,000. KingKit stocks more than 100,000 kits and publishes a quarterly catalogue that has become an accepted 'value guide' to collectors everywhere.

Malcolm was keen that I understood all the type designation collectors use to distinguish earlier types of Airfix packaging from more recent ones. For example, the first types of bagged kit header are desig-

nated 'Type 1' and so on. "The Airfix Type designations ... how they came about," he began. "When I started in 1983 I got a letter from a Brian Bunce of Norwich who sent me a photocopied hand-drawn diagram of the various Airfix bag tops designating them type I, II and III. He was a novelty then – a collector of Airfix kits. These designations seemed so logical I took them up too and now everyone uses them. I think it's time he got recognition," Malcolm urged.

Malcolm also told me he could never understand why the Airfix blister packs aren't really collected. "You can see that all the kit is there and hasn't been opened or tampered with," he

Box Brownie snaps taken by a teenage modeller during wartime. The threads supporting the 'Heinkel' are almost invisible!

FROG advertisement (1930s).

Blister-packed 'MiG-15' from 1973 (kit dates to 1958).

said, bemused why they never feature in dealers' lists. I reckon that the very fact that this award-winning packaging, introduced by Airfix in 1973, required ripping off the vacuum-formed clear blister from its card header to inspect the moulded pieces, means that few remain intact. Consequently, in the decade before the advent of 'collectors' shows on TV, few thought about saving the cheaper products and I'm sure most of them were inadvertently damaged and therefore unsuitable for second-hand sale. Collectors know that bagged headers could be carefully separated from the poly bag containing the Airfix kit and could then stealthily be re-stapled. Boxed kits, on the other hand, simply required the sellotape securing lid to base to be cut with a sharp knife – without any damage to the overall presentation. Blister packed kits didn't stand a chance. So, they must be scarce. Right?

"The market has changed over the 20 years I have been in kits," said Malcolm. "There are now endless kit re-issues and whereas the price on a discontinued item used to be created by the builders, now they can be set by the collectors.

"I haven't got a favourite kit, but I especially like the box art I remember from when I was a child. Airfix 'Type 3' (dating from the late-1960s to very early-1970s, the

Two versions of the Beam Engine originating in 1966.

James Watt invented this type of engine, the first producing rotary movement from Steam Power, in 1782. It was continuously developed and improved, and this model will illustrate an early 19th Century version incorporating a sliding valve and Watts' parallel motion. A handle is included for manual operation and the model may be motorised.

COLLECTORS SERIES

AIRFIX *19th Century Beam Engine*

last type of packaging sporting the remnant of Airfix's original 'banner' logotype) brings back happy memories. I remember popping into the local model shop in Falmouth and seeing they had the new 'RAF Emergency Set' in stock – but I didn't have enough cash on me. I dashed home and got more money, but the shop had sold out by the time I got back. The next delivery wasn't until the following month ... an eternity for a 12 year old to wait!"

You see readers? Memories are made of this!

I first encountered the activities of Pat Lewarne in 1987 when I purchased his excellent *Enthusiasts Guide to Airfix Models*. Since then I have bought kits from his firm 'Collectakit' by mail order and on odd occasions from Collectakit stands at hobby fairs. Together with Malcolm Rollings' KingKit, Collectakit has more or less cornered the British second-hand kit market, offering a reliable and reasonably priced service to enthusiasts in desperate need for that long discontinued model.

"Many modellers view the collecting of un-built kits as a sad hobby worthy of anoraks," Pat told me. "However the majority of modellers will be the first to admit to purchasing more models than they can build. This over-purchasing varies from 20-plus 'in stock', to thousands in the loft. Surplus stock or collections, whatever you prefer to call them, of several hundred models are quite common. So why would anyone initially buy extra kits

– perhaps there was an offer at the model shop, perhaps the kit has been superseded by a better one or perhaps the modeller's tastes have changed. The latter has been the beginning of many a collection."

I asked Pat to expand on other reasons that encouraged kit collecting. "A second key driver is nostalgia," he answered. "Many models are still purchased on the basis of 'this was the first kit I built'. Most people will then want further examples of kits from that era of their life. Some people will be really selective about what they collect, whilst others will splurge and buy anything. The latter will normally be the shorter-term collector, returning their collection to the market within ten years. Others will be drawn into trading unwanted extra items either at shows or on line.

"The final category is the 'build it when

Original Saunders-Roe 'S-R53' header, 1958.

Airfix ¹/₇₂nd scale Boomerang fighter, 1965.

Just like the real thing!

Airfix kits are not just models—they're exact replicas, each series to a constant scale.

Copyright photograph by permission of Imperial War Museum.

Airfix 1/72nd scale Lancaster bomber, 17" wing span. 7/6d.

There are models galore in the Airfix range from Aircraft from fighters to bombers (*all* to the same 1/72nd scale), 00 gauge railway accessories, vintage cars, warships. Airfix value is unbeatable—ask your dealer for the latest list.

Nearly 100 kits from 2/- to 10/6.

AIRFIX
THE WORLD'S GREATEST VALUE IN CONSTRUCTION KITS

From Model and Hobby Shops, Toy Shops and F. W. Woolworth

TRACKSIDE SERIES (Level Crossing 2/-)

VINTAGE CARS 1930 Bentley 2/-

MODEL FIGURES Lifeguard 2/-

HISTORICAL SHIPS H.M.S. Victory 2/-

Airfix press ads from the mid-1960s.

The classic ships of history!

AIRFIX BRINGS THEM TO LIFE! Revenge! Cutty Sark! Victory! The finest ships under sail brought to life with Airfix—accurate in every detail!

The vast range of Airfix construction kits covers 19 different series, including planes, ships, cars, historical figures and trackside series—each model just like the real thing! Prices from only 2/3d to 28/6d.

ROYAL SOVEREIGN

REVENGE

H.M.S. VICTORY

CUTTY SARK

P.S. GREAT WESTERN

WARPLANES, CARS, ...

STOP PRESS

F111A. This kit of the swing-wing aircraft is over 1 ft. long complete with transfers. Wings and tailplane are actually variable. Price 7/11d.

AIRFIX MAGAZINE 2/- MONTHLY ASK FOR THE AIRFIX CATALOGUE FROM YOUR LOCAL STOCKIST.

Full-page advertisement for FROG flying and non-flying (Penguin) kits in a pre-war edition of *Meccano Magazine*.

THE MECCANO MAGAZINE   vii

FROG READY BUILT MODELS THAT REALLY FLY

FROG FLYING MODEL KITS — YOU CAN BUILD AND FLY THESE
No tools needed – all parts cut to shape

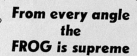

FROG PENGUIN NON-FLYING SCALE MODELS

HAWKER HURRICANE 2/-   HAWKER DEMON 4/6

AVENGER 1/-

From every angle the FROG is supreme

Every FROG model combines excellent appearance and design with accurate construction, while the flying models have an unequalled performance.

Whether scale or non-scale, flying or non-flying, ready-made or in kit form— each FROG model is supreme in its class. FROG ready to fly models are obtainable from 1/- to 42/-, flying construction kits from 1/6 to 21/- and Penguin non-flying scale models from 3/- to 21/-.

A new branch of the famous FROG Service is the introduction of comprehensive kits of material, including Balsa wood, fully-shaped airscrews, etc., details of which can be obtained from your local FROG stockist.

Many more models to choose from, including competition models to S.M.A.E. specification. See them at your local toyshop or fill in and post coupon below for the new FROG catalogue.

MAIL PLANE 10/6

SILVER ARROW 2/6

PV6 DIVE BOMBER 6/6

PERCIVAL GULL KIT 3/- MADE UP 5/-

FAIREY BATTLE KIT 5/- MADE UP 8/6

DE HAVILLAND DIANA KIT 7/6 MADE UP 15/-

ROTA AUTOGIRO KIT 3/6 MADE UP 6/6

VICKERS WELLESLEY KIT 7/6 MADE UP 15/-

FROG
MODEL AIRCRAFT

Covered by World Patents granted and pending. Made in England by International Model Aircraft Ltd.

OBTAINABLE AT ALL GOOD TOYSHOPS AND STORES   Sole Concessionaires:

LINES BROS. LTD., MORDEN ROAD, MERTON, S.W.19   TRADE MARK REGD.

COUPON Please send me your coloured leaflet with particulars of the "Frog" Flying Club and how to obtain handsome enamelled "Frog" Pilot badges.

To Lines Bros. Ltd. (Dept. 5), Morden Road, London, S.W.19

NAME..................
ADDRESS..................
1/36

FROG advertisement in *Meccano Magazine*, 1938.

THE MECCANO MAGAZINE   iii

VICKERS WELLESLEY CONSTRUCTION KIT **2/6**

...EAKERS

The Vickers Wellesley came into public favour by its wonderful Egypt-Australia non-stop flight.

Frog Aeroplanes have always been favourites of the air-minded youth of Britain.

The new FROG model of the record-breaking Vickers Wellesley is perhaps the most interesting of the FROG range of inexpensive constructor kits. It will give hours of pleasure to any amateur constructor, and, when it is completed, it really does fly.

Constructor kits from 1/6 to 21/-, including models to S.M.A.E. competition specifications.

USE THE BEST MATERIALS

Promising models sometimes give disappointing results, not because of errors in design, but through the use of inferior materials and inefficient airscrews. Do not make this mistake when building your new machine.

International Model Aircraft Ltd., so long famous for the excellent workmanship of the FROG models, are now supplying balsa wood, tissue, fully shaped airscrews and everything needed by the model aeroplane maker. These materials are of the same high standard as used in FROG models. Ask for them by name at your local FROG stockists.

FROG SERVICE IS ALWAYS AT YOUR SERVICE

ALWAYS ASK FOR

FROG AERO SUPPLIES

OBTAINABLE AT ALL GOOD DEALERS AND STORES.   Sole Concessionaires

LINES BROS. LTD., MORDEN RD., MERTON, S.W.19

COUPON Please send me your coloured leaflet with particulars of the "Frog" Flying Club and how to obtain handsome enamelled "Frog" Pilot badges.

To Lines Bros. Ltd. (Dept. 5), Morden Road, London S.W.19

NAME..................
ADDRESS..................
4/39

JUST LIKE THE REAL THING!

The magnificent V.C.10. This authentic 1/144 scale model of the powerful jet liner now in use with the leading air lines, is made from a superbly detailed 74 part kit costing 6/-. It's one of many exciting kits by Airfix. There are over 200 of them, covering 13 different series. And at 2/- to 17/6 you can well afford to make all your models *just like the real thing.*

AIRFIX CONSTANT SCALE
CONSTRUCTION KITS
Just like the real thing!

From model and hobby shops, toy shops and F. W. Woolworth

STOP PRESS WILDCAT VI

ALL THAT'S NEW IN MODELLING! Airfix Catalogue 9d. and Monthly Magazine 1/6.

Printed by Oxley and Son (Windsor) Ltd., 24 Victoria Street, Windsor

'Just Like The Real Thing!' advertisement in *Airfix Magazine* from 1964.

I retire' collector. This individual stores up large numbers of kits to build in a yet-to-be-achieved retirement. Whilst some do achieve this, many change their minds after filling the loft, or sadly do not make it to retirement."

However, like me, Pat recognises that there are often simpler, more emotionally subjective reasons for hunting down long-obsolete kits. "What all these people have in common, whether they regard themselves as modellers or collectors, is pleasure in owning the item," he said.

"Nowadays there are many kits that you would not build because that model has been replaced by a better one. In many of these cases, it is the box artwork that attracts the collector. Few people will dispute the fact that modern box art is inferior to older box art. Comparison of a Georgian carriage clock to a modern digital alarm clock springs to mind."

I asked Pat how he thought newcomers to kit collecting should begin. "Firstly do you have 'stock' in your loft? Is that what you want to expand on or can you use them for part exchange? Try to find old catalogues or reference books. Get sales lists from specialist second-hand kit dealers to find out what is available and at what prices. Do not get drawn into online or auction sales at this time – you do not yet have enough knowledge. Other sources that you can sample are car boot sales, toy fairs and specialist Kit Shows (mainly IPMS). Always bear in mind, the rarer the kit, the longer you may have to look for it.

"People will ask 'what should I collect?'" he continued. "Provided you are not collecting just to make money, it should be something that pleases you. It could be aircraft, airliners, vehicles, figures, ships or sci-fi, etc. Only the collector can determine what he wants to collect, but it is sometimes useful to find out what is available and how readily it can be obtained."

So how did Pat become a 'specialist kit dealer'? "As the quantity of kits coming on to the market as second-hand items increased beyond what the traditional model shop could handle, so specialists sprang up. Some can trace their history to meeting the market,

Matchbox kit catalogue, 1974/75.

whilst others had been long-term collectors and this was the next stage for them. Collectakit, based in Surrey, can trace its roots back to the 1950s, building Airfix tractors, aircraft, and tanks."

Pat had a 'major involvement' with model railways in the 1970s and then switched back to kits 20 years ago, which resulted in the emergence of Collectakit. Initially he focused on the ready market at Toy Shows, and then quickly followed this with a mail-order service. A natural development was Collectakit's subsequent attendance at IPMS (International Plastic Modellers Society) shows around the UK.

Pat told me that today Collectakit could be called a 'kit recycler'. With a smile he added that this gives it 'green' credentials: "Because not only is it a source of old kits, but it also repatriates quantities of relatively recent kits."

So how does someone like Collectakit price kits?

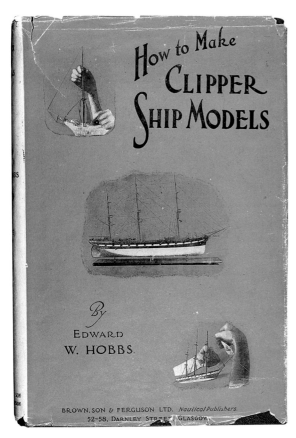

'How to make Clipper Ship Models', 1940s.

"Well of course it is based on the purchase price but also on availability. Something that only appears every five years is going to be more desirable than something that appears every day. The 'wants' of collectors are always a good barometer of demand – although this can change every time a specialist magazine prints an article on certain kits. Always beware the collector who says 'I remember those at 2/6 in Woolies' – cause that's all he wants to pay!"

Pat tells me that his favourite items are old gift sets. "Why gift sets? Well, mostly they were fairly short run productions, in specialist packing. These are not your modern gift sets – any three kits in a uniform sleeve – but kits that have been repackaged, usually in a unique box for a specific purpose. This could vary from

Christmas to an historic event." Because there are fewer gift sets than single kits issued, Pat told me that their rarity naturally adds to their collectors' value. Now there's a tip.

Revell-Monogram's Ed Sexton introduced me to Paul Milam, proprietor of the eponymous US kit dealership. Since then, I have added Milam Models to my small roster of reliable rare-kit suppliers. Indeed, some of the models shown on the pages of this book were bought from Paul.

"I began building plastic model kits when I was six years old," he told me. "I would put them together and my older sister would paint the wing or prop tips. As I recall these were Aurora kits. I have been in love with modelling ever since. From my earliest memories all I wanted to be was a fighter pilot, and modelling all of those hot jets of the early 1950s only strengthened that desire. As it turned out, my less than perfect eyesight prevented my being the next Steve Canon (an American comic hero – Aurora produced a kit of him in full flight gear standing in front of an 'F-102A'). But I did learn to fly and spent the next 40 years as a professional pilot.

"About 22 years ago I was introduced to John Burns' Kit Collector group. I have been a member since. The KCC (Kit Collectors Clearinghouse – see p. 181) opened a

1910 'B Type' Bus, 1966.

US Airfix 'Bronco'.

1/72 SCALE Unassembled Model Kit
Molded in Color
AGES 8 Years thru Adult

Photos of Actual Model

Quarter scale Aurora
'SNJ' trainer.

SNJ TRAINER 1/4" SCALE MODEL

.69

FAMOUS FIGHTERS

By Aurora

ALL PLASTIC ASSEMBLY KIT

MADE IN ENGLAND AIRFIX PATTERN No. 1384

SCALE MODEL

MESSERSCHMITT
Me 109 F
CONSTRUCTION KIT
HIGH IMPACT MATERIAL

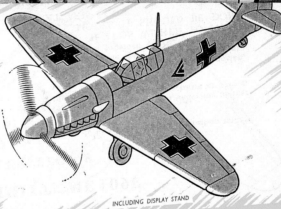

Original
'Me109F'
from 1956.

INCLUDING DISPLAY STAND

OF THE AIRFIX SERIES OF SCALE MODELS OF FAMOUS TYPES OF AIRCRAFT

FLYING WHITEHOUSE
E-4 BOEING 747

UNITED STATES OF AMERICA

1/144 Scale-Unassembled Model Kit
Modèle Réduit Pour Assembler

US-Airfix

USAirfix 1/144th scale,
Boeing 747 'Flying
Whitehouse' based on
the 1969 original.

169

AIRFIX-72 SCALE
FOLLAND GNAT

Folland 'Gnat', 1964.

whole new world to me - there were modellers looking for old and out-of-production kits, and willing to pay a handsome price."

At that time Paul had a small collection of maybe 400 kits: "Some of which were old and collectors' items, but I was not a collector. I was going to build every one of them," he added.

"Almost everyone that builds models has the same story. We all become collectors by default, buying far more kits than we can ever build. So I too am a collector. But that's good because you can't have too many kits.

"I accepted a position as a pilot flying for a major retailer and that took me to all 50 states and several countries. Every time I flew to a new city I would visit all of the hobby shops and toy stores, time permitting, looking for out-of-production kits. It was amazing how many I found. The profit paid for my hobby and then some," he recalled.

Paul soon had 1,000 kits, then 2,000, then 4,000. "Today the inventory is around 12,000," he said. "Becoming a business was an easy decision, and I have never looked back, this being my 20th year. We sell kits and a limited selection of decals and books worldwide. We publish five or six sales flyers per year and attend 10

to 15 model contests, shows or conventions per year."

Paul retired from commercial flying almost two years ago and now devotes all his time to the Milam Model business.

I asked Paul what collectors look for. "As to what is the most collectable kit? I don't think that there is a single kit at the top of most collectors' want list," he answered. "Having said that, I would put the ITC 'XF-108' kit in the top group, because it was only issued once and never will be again, and it is a kit of an aircraft that never was. North American Aviation did produce a wooden mock-up of the 'F-108' but the kit was almost a totally different aircraft, being launched like a 'Nike' missile. Others at the top of the list are first issues of many Aurora aircraft, such as their 'Me-109', 'P-40', 'B-29', 'B-25', 'Fw-190' and 'Zero'.

"I still get excited when a new kit comes out that I want to build and I am currently working on two. A dear friend in Seattle is building a paint booth for me, something I have wanted and needed for a long time. Now I should be able to complete my models with a better paint finish." As most readers will know, a paint, or spray, booth is invaluable for preventing surplus paint from an airbrush ruining adjacent furniture or fabrics!

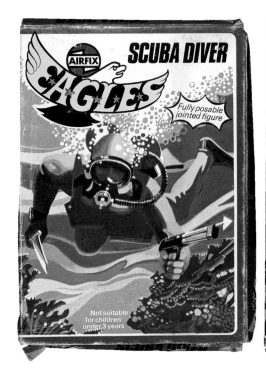

Airfix '*Eagles*' Adventure sets and individual figures – eminently collectable.

"I have always found modelling a relaxing pastime, an education on the history of aviation, people and places. I am convinced that modelling helped prepare me for my career as a pilot and helped me relax after a long day in the office at 43,000 feet. Fortunately I have been lucky enough to meet many who share my belief – that model miniatures are a satisfying and satisfactory way to spend what little free time we have today, enabling the curious to understand technological developments and milestones in aviation or military history in a way that studying archive footage or, worse still, the products of Hollywood studios can never do." Hear hear, Paul.

Where can you contact people like Milam Models, Collectakit and KingKit? Mostly they advertise in specialist modeling magazines or within the pages of newsletters published by enthusiasts groups such as the IPMS and Kit Collectors Clearinghouse. They have web sites and they appear at shows. Many will supply printed sales lists or email copies. Try to come to model shows and see the array of kits available and talk to like-minded people. The one common denominator amongst all those involved on the periphery of the plastic model industry is a love and interest in the history and development of plastic construction kits. You'll be amazed at what you might learn!

Ford '3 litre G.T.', 1969.

There isn't space here to mention all the enthusiastic

modellers and collectors that I have met and got to like. Anyway, many readers will know the likes of John Wells, Graham Short, Trevor Snowden, Anthony Lawrence, Bill Bosworth and Mark Stevens.

However, I feel that it's worthwhile singling out one or two enthusiasts with whom I have got more closely acquainted during the preparation of this book.

I asked Jeremy Brook, secretary of the Airfix Collectors' Club and publishing editor of its newsletter *Constant Scale,* about his particular passion for Airfix and how he finds the time to produce a regular, illustrated newsletter.

"I first started buying Airfix kits in the late 50s and had a racing set for Christmas shortly after it was first released. In 1963, when I was 13, I started buying *Airfix Magazine* and the catalogues, as well as collecting every leaflet or price list that came out. I had developed a strong interest for all things Airfix, although the kits always were my first love. Much as I enjoyed making models and playing with my hugely expanded racing set, I was probably more interested in the development of the ranges, the packaging and artwork, etc. With the brilliant Roy Cross and Brian Knight artwork and the logical development of the various ranges, Airfix seemed far ahead of its then competitors. During the 70s I kept careful records of all the kit releases, which has stood me in good stead when I took over the mantle of running the Airfix Collectors' Club.

"Following Airfix's bankruptcy in 1981, I lost some interest as it was no longer the 'Airfix' I'd known and was passionate about. Then, in the late 90s I joined FAMAS (the club dedicated to FROG and Airfix) and the Airfix Collectors' Club and was delighted to find that there were clubs and organisations that were devoted to the study of Airfix.

"Having written some articles for the Club magazine *Constant Scale*, things went quiet! One day I 'phoned up the founder of the club, John Wells, who informed me that he was inundated with work and asked would I like to take on the running of the club. I couldn't refuse! So I produced a magazine and sent it out to all the existing

'HP O/400', 1968.

'Craft Master' (USA) version of Airfix 'Fairey Swordfish'.

⅑₆th scale Triang Air France 'Caravelle'.

members, most of whom rejoined and were delighted that the club was active again.

"I now produce four magazines a year as well as a calendar, both of which are now commercially printed and include colour on a regular basis. Club members such as Arthur Ward supply me with articles and photographs; the remaining content comes from my records and collection. With well over 600 models produced by Airfix over the last 50 years, I should have more than enough information to keep going for the next 150 years or so!"

Airfix 'Dragster' originating from MPC in the United States.

The author of this book has a special reason for being grateful for Jeremy's efforts. Together with continuing my 'honorary membership' of the club, originally conferred on me by the inimitable John Wells, Jeremy has also revived my *nom de plume* from the old *Airfix Magazine* days and now as 'Tailgunner Ward' of old, I write occasional articles for *Constant Scale*!

Long-time Airfix fan David James runs one of the best enthusiasts' websites available. Certainly, if you want to better understand the variations in packaging or learn more about some of the British firm's earliest releases in construction kits, games or toy, his site is a must.

Married with four children (home is in Hampshire), David is an IT manager for IBM. Working from offices in Belgium he runs their project management education organisation for Europe.

David tells me he has been "mad about kits from the earliest age", and has made literally hundreds, mostly Airfix. He remembers that he used to cycle to Woolworth's every week to get another one. "Now, how many times must you have heard that! What would we have done without 'Woolies'?"

David, who was born in Bristol, tells me

that his favourite model shop was in nearby Weston-Super-Mare. "Whenever my parents took us to the seaside I always used to drag them to this shop just to look in the window ... full of unobtainable American Monogram and Lindberg kits which being larger scale than Airfix or FROG always appeared massive and mouth-watering."

He doesn't remember his first kit but recalls with amusement taking an Airfix kit to 'show and tell' at the end of term at junior school. "I took in the 'SRN-1' hovercraft to make. In my normal manner I couldn't be bothered to wait for the glue to dry so it wouldn't stand on its little wheels!

"I started as a modeller – a fanatic," he said. "I think that as a teenage boy I must have purchased and assembled nearly the whole Airfix range, plus many more from FROG and Revell. I still make the occasional model, but in adulthood my desire for modelling perfection far outstrips my abilities."

So why start collecting?

"For me the reason was that I saved most of the instruction sheets from the models that I made. Why? I have no idea! I just kept them. As I grew up, married, moved house several times, my

1970s Fantasy Kits.

cherished box of kit instruction sheets came with me. Then, a couple of years ago, I opened this box and realised two things – firstly that some of what I was looking at was old and perhaps rare and secondly that I possessed quite a lot of it!"

Rather than consigning his bounty to the loft "to lay unloved for another ten years", he decided to do something with the instruction sheets and turned them into a collection.

What is the appeal of Airfix I asked? "Simply, that during my modelling years the kits most freely available in England were the Airfix range," David said. "FROG didn't seem to be on as many shop shelves, Tamiya didn't exist and the American kit ranges (Monogram, etc.) were simply too scarce, too big and too expensive for a small boy. So my box of instruction sheets were 80 per cent Airfix. I had mostly Airfix, I had made mostly Airfix and through making the models, I felt I 'knew' Airfix."

Before embarking on a part-time career as an authority on Airfix, David had to be sure he knew enough about the firm. "You can't start collecting antique furniture just because you have one old bookshelf in the living room. I sensed also that Airfix kits were collectors' items, having seen some old plastic bag models on sale at what seemed very unlikely prices. If I was going to collect, and especially buy, I needed to know some more. I started by buying a few old catalogues. Just seeing the pictures of old favourites really got my interest going again, after all those years since making my 'SRN-1' hovercraft and Auster 'Antarctic'. Then I had a bright idea! I'd produce a catalogue! Of course, nobody had done this before, and of course I was the world's expert! Full of enthusiasm for this project I put an entry in an internet newsgroup announcing to hundreds of millions of people that they should soon expect the *Dave James Complete Airfix Kit Catalogue*. And on CD-ROM too!"

David says he "was soon put right". Discovering that he "wasn't an expert", and neither was he "doing something new". He says he was pointed towards my early *Model World of Airfix* and P.A. Lewarne's *Enthusiasts Guide To Airfix Models*, both of which I bought quickly. I can't better these reference works, nor do I now intend to," he added. The cheque's in the post David.

David's favourite Airfix kits are the 'Catalina', 'Evening Star' and 'Freddy Flameout'. His most wanted is Airfix's promotional 'Fireball XL5' model – so that's you and 20,000 others then, David! Most modelers of our generation either built dozens of Airfix 'Spitfires' or 'Messerschmitts'. David built the latter: "Lots of ½nd 'Bf109G-6's in all different colour schemes and markings," he remembered proudly.

His ambition? "To complete my 'Header Card' collection. I have most of the planes, all the AFVs, most of the trackside stuff, but I'm still looking for many of the cars and ½th figures."

Summarising, David says: "I'm content collecting what I can find, buying and selling a little bit to make it

'F-4B Phantom II', 1971.

Before they were bought by Humbrol, Airfix had their own paint brand.

more interesting, and generally finding out more and more things about Airfix that were unknown to that small boy making models so many years ago."

Dean Milano was born in Milwaukee in 1951. Since then, he has packed the experiences of a dozen lifetimes into little more than 50 years. Dean is musician, traveller, 'Americas Cup' crewman, Toy & Model Museum proprietor, model car enthusiast (America's *Scale Auto Enthusiast* magazine named him one of the Top 20 'most memorable characters' in the model car hobby) and for a decade, one of Revell-Monogram's Consumer Services and Product Development executives. Phew!

A keen plastic modeller since childhood, in 1965 Dean won his first model contest trophy at a local hobby shop. After graduating from college and with modelling still little more than a hobby, Dean's chosen vocation was music. His first band, the 'Casulaires', were very popular in Illinois and actually cut a single in the Chicago studios which Bob Dylan was to hire some years later. Dean joined the 'New Seekers' as bass player in 1980 and for the next four years he toured all over the USA with them. His career in music and entertainment saw him share the stage with the likes of Bo Diddley,

Chubby Checker, The Spencer Davis Group, Jim Belushi and Joan Rivers. However, by the early 1990s he foresaw the end of his live touring days and returned to the world of models.

When he first joined the recently merged Revell-Monogram, Dean initially worked in an office at the so-called 'Plant II' at Des Plaines but soon moved to their more famous location at Morten Grove, purpose-built for Monogram in 1961.

At Revell-Monogram, Dean is involved with the production progress of new models throughout their entire journey from concept to manufacture. His duties range from researching and writing the descriptive copy on the side of boxes to detailing product codes and skill levels. Much of his time is involved in liaising with the company's graphics department and telling them what information needs to be communicated to the consumer on box tops and instruction leaflets. An important part of this process involves deciding upon the size and format of the actual box, dictated to a large extent by the size

Beautiful replica of a '1931 Bugatti'.

Another American import.

and shape of the moulded frames within. He is involved with pre-production test shots at a very early stage. He also fields consumer calls on Revell-Monogram's free phone number, helping explain construction procedures to modellers who might be experiencing difficulty with their new purchase.

Readers might think Dean would have his fill of model kits; working with one of the world's leading manufacturers all day – they would be forgiven for assuming that he might fill his leisure hours with a very different pursuit. Not a bit of it! After work, he heads for the famous Toy & Model Museum he founded and has now franchised (a Milano museum recently opened in Mexico), busying himself with a thousand jobs there.

"The museum was a dream I'd had for 25 years," said Dean. It was an idea that stemmed from his love of model cars. In fact it was only when the friend who had actually introduced him to car modelling in the first place and always talked about the model car museum he planned to establish passed away without ever realising his ambition, that Dean was prompted to act.

Originally he intended a museum dedicated to model cars only, but after some thought he realised that this might not be attraction enough for wives and youngsters. Being also an enthusiast of old toys and automated storefront window displays, he decided to combine his model car displays with an exhibition dedicated to the history and development of children's toys. He figured that then, fathers could scrutinise Dean's huge collection of vintage roadsters and modern indi-cars whilst mom and the kids were free to marvel at more than 100 years of child's play or peruse the assorted toys available in the museum shop. "This way I could cover all the bases," Dean smiled.

People from both US coasts and the mid-west visit Dean's museum, usually combining it with a planned visit to Chicago. The content has to be seen to be believed. It is kit collectors' heaven, full of everything to do with the history of plastic modelling – not just kits but accessories, catalogues and promotional exhibits aimed at the trade. Not wanting to hurry their visit to the shrine, some visitors book local motel rooms nearby and study Dean's exhibits without a rush. On average, the museum, which is open from 6–9 o'clock each

Dean Milano's wonderful museum.

The inimitable Dean Milano in front of some classic kits in his eponymous Toy and Model Museum.

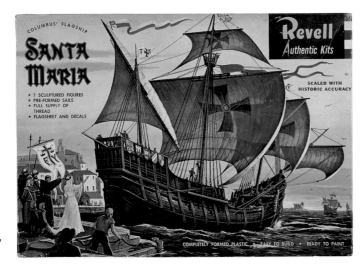

'Santa Maria',
1957.

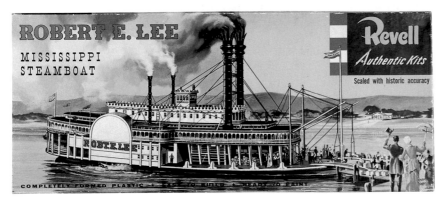

Robert E. Lee riverboat model
first released in 1956.

evening and from 11am until 5pm at weekends, attracts around 100 visitors per month. The opening hours are restricted because of the requirements of Dean's full-time job at Revell. How he generates the energy to work in the museum for hours after he has completed a full day's work at Revell-Monogram is beyond me. Together with the 2,000 different kits not on display – "not duplicates" he urged – Dean also has enough spare vintage toys in storage to fill a building half the size of the existing museum over again.

Dean has been a modeller since childhood, when he used to build anything from a variety of manufacturers, as long as it caught his eye. "I didn't build much Airfix though, because until the 1970s they weren't very common here," he said. Together with the hundreds of models on display in the museum, Dean has another 2,000 kits in his personal collection. He bemoans the fact that today models don't have the appeal they did. "Kids don't build model kits any more. They come in to the museum simply to look at the model cars and trucks." Dean's favourite models are still cars, prop-airliners, civilian cabin cruisers and space models – especially rockets. He is also a great fan of HO scale carnival rides.

Dean told me that the US Vintage monster kit enthu-

HMS Bounty released to
coincide with MGM's
blockbuster movie
starring Marlon Brando,
1956.

siasts dominate kit collectors' markets. "Just watch e-bay," he said. "On average we have swap meets every three months in this area." The location of Dean's Museum is a stone's throw from a well-established Chicago model shop, so it's an area targeted by enthusiasts. However, he reckoned that although prices for vintage kits weren't rising as fast as they had, because of their increasing scarcity they were unlikely to fall. This is partly down to what Dean calls 'attrition' – the fact that many old kits are built and because some actually fall foul of natural disasters such as house fires or even earthquakes.

Dean is not precious about old kits. He's not a speculator and prefers to see them well assembled and put on display. The supply of vintage models is sometimes reduced because their whereabouts are unrecorded. "There's the guy with a trailer full of old kits in Wyoming who dies and no one knows anything about them."

I was surprised to learn that the kit that started it all for Revell, the 1911 'Maxwell', isn't too difficult to come by and consequently not at all expensive. I guess this is due in part to its massive success and high production numbers. There are many Revell, and Monogram, models that are sought after. Revell's 1950s vintage 'XSL-01

Manned Space Ship' – the two-stage rocket to the moon is certainly one of them. It's apparently the Holy Grail of American kit collectors. Incidentally this space model is rivalled only by another Revell classic, their complex multi-coloured 'Space Station' kit from 1959.

Monogram's gigantic ⅛th scale car kits – 'Big Tub', 'Big Rod' and 'Big Drag' – from the early 1960s are also sought-after models that originated in Chicago. Their series of ¼th scale 'Classic Car Kits' (1934 Duesenberg SJ 'Torpedo Phaeton', Mercedes 1939 '540K Cabriolet' among them) dating from 1963 were produced to the highest standards and are on most car collectors' wish lists. Indeed, so high was the quality of these kits that Monogram were confident enough to promote them in auto enthusiasts' magazines as "being recognised everywhere as the finest car models ever produced".

Dean mentioned numerous classic collectors' items that originated during the heyday of either Revell or Monogram. Famous kits like the 'Autorama Modern Car' gift set from 1956 which included ⅟₃₂nd scale replicas of a Chrysler 'New Yorker', Ford 'Fairlane Sunliner', Buick 'Century' and Continental 'Mk II' – all in one box. The ultra-rare ⅟₂₂nd scale Pan Am 'Super 7 Clipper' Airport Scene complete with boarding ramp, baggage trailer

Revell 'American Firefighters', 1953.

and towing tractor dating from 1955 is "one of the rarest Revell kits in existence and probably built for Pan Am to sell directly to passengers".

Some early examples of Revell-Monogram kits will never be available again, the moulds having been damaged or, far more likely, permanently modified to produce a subsequent mark of the basic car. Monogram's 1969 Dodge 'Dart' is one such example – since its release it has been re-tooled to produce a 1968 'Dart'. So, keep an eye out for the '69!

Model kit firms regularly face the dilemma of irreversibly altering moulds. "It's just business," said Dean. "Making a permanent change to a mould is much more inexpensive than producing a new one. But because that change can't be reversed, the decision is a risky one. You never really know if you've made the right choice and might discover that in future, the unmodified version achieves really high sales. Trends change. You don't know what the fashion might be in 20 years."

Because the quickest that model kit firms can bring a new product to market is about one year, manufacturers have to tread with caution.

Dean pointed out that Revell-Monogram is in business to fulfill a forecastable demand – they are not speculators. Film tie-ins can be unprofitable, especially if the film flops and you factor in the cost and effort involved in securing licences. However, considering America's enduring love affair with the automobile, it's not surprising that re-issuing kits associated with movies such as 'Bullitt' or 'American Graffiti' that prominently feature cars, often bucks the trend and is very profitable.

Fortunately, like all manufacturers, Revell-Monogram have their 'banker' kits that sell and sell. These generally need little or no work to the mould tools, which being made of machine steel are tough as old boots and capable of virtually endless use.

Enough of cars for the moment. Many at Revell-Monogram today are certainly grateful for the sterling

VW 'Street Machine'.

An American classic.

business generated year in and year out by two ⅟₄₈th scale aircraft moulds which date to the early 1970s. Their 'B-17 Flying Fortress' and 'P-51 Mustang' kits have the same appeal today with countless American boys as they did over a quarter of a century ago.

Our final kit collector, another American and … well, all-round expert about the plastic kit industry, is that walking cornucopia of knowledge the internationally respected John Burns.

John is the founder of the 'Kit Collectors Clearinghouse' (KCC) and publishes a series of *Collectors Value Guides* for scale model plastic kits. I have the sixth edition of his guide and recently he kindly sent me his mammoth 'PAK-20' – a comprehensive guide to literally every plastic aircraft kit manufactured in the 20th century.

The KCC also publishes a monthly bulletin, which serves as a forum for kit collectors and model enthusiasts everywhere and is a mechanism for those searching for a particular kit to advertise their requirement.

"I celebrated my seventh birthday on December 7, 1941, but my modelling urges were already growing

'Saturn 1 B', 1971.

'Mercury' and 'Gemini' capsules, 1964.

John W. Burns: Font of knowledge and founder of the Kit Collector's Clearinghouse. Sketch prepared by modeller Eddy Waas after an original drawn some years ago by a Parisian street artist.

½nd scale 'Spitfire', 1963.

fast," John told me. "My first kit was the wooden Strombecker Northrop 'P-61', which survived hundreds of play-time deaths before I was bold and old enough to play with firecrackers! Lots of Monogram Speedee-bilt kits went down in flames as they were launched from the roof of our back porch! Then, I discovered girls and my simple, uncomplicated life was changed forever!

"After one year in college which was a wasted year in terms of learning and maturing, the North Koreans moved quickly to the negotiating table because the word got out that I was in the US Army Engineers and coming to get them! However, I only got as far as Japan, where I served for over two years in a Topographic unit stationed in Tokyo. We made new maps of the entire Far East to replace the very old ones of the early 1900s."

"I resumed my college career, intending to become an Industrial Engineer but two things changed everything. First, I found the right girl and married her a year later. She has put up with me for more than 46 years thus far. Second, I encountered God and His plan for my life

which was not my plan at all. I wisely chose His way and have been a minister of the gospel ever since.

"I retired from full-time service at the end of 1996. Six months later, the Child Bride said, with toe a-tapping and hand on hip, 'get out of this house and get a day job!' And so, 'She, who must be obeyed' had spoken and like my good TV friend, 'Rumpole of the Bailey', I did what she said. I now am the part-time pastor of a small Baptist church about six miles from my house but the big 70 is rapidly approaching, so who knows what will come next."

Most enthusiasts know that John is a man of the cloth but are unaware of the details; I think the previous words are enlightening. But, as John said "Back to the plastic parts of my life."

"In 1971, we were shopping in a nearby mall and I wandered into a hobby shop, got to talking with the owner and said, 'I used to build and blow up models when I was a kid.' He replied, 'big kids still do that.'

"He told me about a group of guys who were meeting that night. I went, got hooked on IPMS (USA) and plastic kits have been a major recreational part of my

SUPERMARINE **SPITFIRE** 1/72 SCALE Revell

SPITFIRE Mk II

life ever since.

"My first interest was in machines of the Korean War (WWII was my childhood war, but the Korean War was my personal war) but they were 'thin on the ground' (obviously, I have been to the Mother Country several times!) so I had to search for them. That search, obviously, took me into foreign territory again, kit collecting, and I've been wandering in that jungle ever since.

"I also built kits into models and even won a few awards locally, regionally and twice at IPMS (USA) annual conventions (Dallas, TX and Phoenix, AZ) but my heart and hands were not destined to produce masterpieces of modeling art. I discovered that I had more fun researching and reporting on old kits than I did building new ones and the Kit Collectors Clearinghouse was born."

John told me that after a while the KCC was not enough to keep him occupied, so he soon began producing books on plastic kits. Three different series have been published: the *In Plastic* series (five books), the *Collectors Value Guide For Scale Model Plastic Kits* series (seven volumes) and now, the *Plastic Aircraft Kits of the 20th Century and Beyond* with its annual updates.

"Of course, much of the fun along this way has been the folk I've met and admired," mused John. "What a different and delightful bunch we are and there seems to be no end to it all. KCC has reached out to men, women, boys and girls all over the world. There are now or have been KCC'ers in these countries: Canada, Mexico, Netherlands Antilles, Argentina, Brazil, Colombia, England, Scotland, Wales, Australia, New Zealand, Austria, France, The Netherlands, Slovakia, South Africa, Belgium, Norway, Switzerland, Sweden, Denmark, Italy, Greece, Czech Republic, Czechoslovakia, Poland, Russia, Japan, Germany, West Germany, East Germany and a few others I'm sure I have forgotten. Plastic has brought us together and courtesy and common interests are keeping us together.

"My goodness, this thing could go on and on!" John exclaimed. I'm sure many who know him, sincerely hope it does!

Veteran 'Jeep'.

1/144th scale Soviet 'Badger'.

5. The Future

Well, the hobby has survived for more than 70 years and has entered the 21st Century in pretty good shape. It's true that manufacturers can't expect the volume sales they enjoyed some 30 years ago, but indications suggest that any decline has been reversed.

Commercial stability has partly been achieved by the adoption of more 'mould sharing' than ever before. This enables existing manufacturers to package and market another's original – saving a fortune in pattern-making and tooling costs and often breathing new life into a kit that has been absent for years.

Another factor, which gives encouragement to the kit industry, is the fact that for many youngsters and their parents, building a plastic kit is often a new and creative diversion from television or computer games. Ironically, the hobby often derided as the province of 'anoraks' is a truly interactive hobby. Modelling teaches youngsters hand-to-eye co-ordination and a modicum of history – certainly more valuable than the passive pastime of progressing to the next level of a computer 'shoot-em-up' programme?

HO/OO 'Evening Star' Loco.

Like everything in our crowded multi-channel environment, the world of plastic modelling has now developed niche markets. So, manufacturers either focus on the mass youth market or project lower returns aiming at the serious enthusiast. I suppose the so-called 'garage kit' manufacturers who produced short-run injection-moulded or vacuum-formed replicas really led the way here.

New technology and the emergence of service operations in the Far East means that it is now possible for kit manufacturers to re-release a classic kit from the past without requiring the original pattern or mould tool. All they need is a reasonable unassembled kit and, as if by magic, they can clone the original. Often, when the original mould tool has been lost or damaged beyond repair, this is the only way an old kit can be reborn.

There is no doubt, however, that the traditional medium of polystyrene has been dramatically challenged by the emergence of resin casting. When opened, more and more models are revealed as resin. Not a problem, if you don't mind paring away the often-unsightly excess resin attached to the moulded part as a residue from the pouring gates. And we plastic modellers used to moan about flash …

With such a huge archive of surviving tools in existence – especially those of Airfix, Aurora, Revell and Monogram – it is my guess that the future probably lies in much closer partnership between traditional manufacturers and the new kids on the block who are adept at short run resin. Surely it makes sense for the 'old

FROG English Electric 'Lightning' prototype, the 'P.1'.

FROG ⅟₃₂nd scale 'FW190 A'.

'Dime store' kits from
Italy's CCGC.

guard' to join forces with some of the newer companies, releasing past classics complete with additional resin and etched brass components that can be combined to enhance or correct a kit that really needs improving?

My other forecast? I am sure that with the huge advances in moulding and painting technologies, notably abounding in China and Korea, many more manufacturers will release pre-coloured kits finished to the highest standards. These will enable novices to assemble very realistic models without enduring some of the frustrations we older modellers suffered. After all, often it was these early problems that prematurely convinced tyros to abandon the hobby. Revell-Monogram is to be congratulated for showing what can be achieved in this area. Some of their pre-coloured kits are stunning. They are also relatively cheap, which makes them enormously attractive, and

¹⁄₂₄th scale 'Lago-Talbot' Grand Prix racer by Merit.

within the range of youngster's pockets. Anyway, wasn't it the inexpensive lure of 2/- Airfix flights of fancy which took the British plastic kit hobby to new heights 40 years ago?

Surely all the kit industry has to do is provide a range of cheaper items, which are really different and get talked about at school, to encourage the resurgence it has coveted for so long? New, younger modellers are the life-blood of the hobby. Here's to a bright future!

At last, courtesy of 'Mirage Hobby', enthusiasts can assemble a decent ⅟₃₅th scale polystyrene Vickers 'E MkB' tank of pre-WWII vintage.

Two FROG originals which mysteriously re-appeared from behind the 'Iron Curtain' in the late 1980s.

Bibliography

FROG Model Aircraft 1932-1976,
Richard Lines and Leif Hellstrom
New Cavendish Books, 1989

Creating Space, Mat Irvine
Apogee Books, 2002

Collecting Model Car and Truck Kits, Tim Boyd
MBI Publishing, 2001

Aurora Histroy & Price Guide, Bill Bruegman
Cap'n Penny Productions, 1994

Classic Plastic Model Kits, Rick Polizzi
Schroeder Publishing Co, 1996

Remembering Revell Model Kits, Thomas Graham
Schiffer, 2002

Let's Stick Together, Stephen Knight, 1999

Figurines Publicitaires, Jeane-Claude Piffret
Histoire & Collections, 1997

Encyclopaedia of Military Models,
Boileau/Khuong/Young
Airlife, 1988

Plastic Aircraft Kits of the 20th Century (and Beyond),
John W. Burns Kit Collectors Clearinghouse, 2003

Ed 'Big Daddy' Roth. His life, times, cars and art,
Pat Ganahl CarTech, 2003

Master Modeler – Creating the Tamiya style,
Shunsaku Tamiya Kodansha, 2001

The Enthusiasts Guide to Airfix Models,
P.A. Lewarne, 1987

The Model World of Airfix, Arthur Ward
Bellew, 1984

Airfix – Celebrating 50 Years of the Greatest Kits in the World, Arthur Ward
Collins, 1999

Acknowledgements

Special thanks to Ed, Ruan and Ted Sexton for their hospitality when I visited Illinois in 2003. Not forgetting all at Revell-Monogram Inc. who tolerated my intrusion at possibly the worst time (they were in the process of relocating their business from Morten Grove to Northbrook).

I must also single out Mr. Shunsaku Tamiya and the ever-helpful Mr. Yasushi Sano, who promptly supplied me with whatever photographs I desired.

I have tried to acknowledge all those to whom I owe a debt of gratitude. Forgive my ineptitude if I have unwittingly omitted someone!

Bandai: Lynne Roberson (PA to MD Bandai UK) & Tammy Kobayashi. Global Business Dept. Bandai Co., Ltd.

Revell: Edward Sexton Sr. Director of Product Development, Bill Lastovich Product Planning Manager, Thomas Ramdrup Marketing Manager Revell AG, Gerry Humbert Photographic Services Administrator, Jonathan Tinio Graphic Designer, Gary Brown Sr. Engineering Graphics Design Administrator, Kenneth L. Funk Jr. Manager – Molding/Packaging, Angeline L. Pannarale Marketing Administrative Assistant.

Humbrol/Airfix: Trevor Snowden Research & Development Engineer, Michael J. Phillips Export Sales Manager.

Tamiya: Mr. Shunsaku Tamiya President & Chairman, Mr. Nobuo Yoshioka, Mr. Yasushi Sano, Sam Wright.

Marcus Nichols Editor Tamiya Model Magazine, Alan Harman Publisher Tamiya Model Magazine (ADH Publishing).

Ralph Ehrmann

Mat Irvine

Dean Milano

Jeremy Brook – Airfix Collectors' Club

David James

Peter Allen

Brian Knight

Anthony Lawrence – Dorking Models

Paul Emery

Ray Piggott

Malcolm Rolling – Kingkit

Ken Jones

Pat Lewarne – Collectakit

Paul Milam – Milam Models

Paul Regan – President, IPMS (UK)

John Burns – Kit Collectors Clearing House

Tony James – Comet Miniatures

Roy Cross

Claudius Eberl – Gebr. Faller GmbH

The author would also like to thank all those unacknowledged individuals from companies big and small who have been involved in the construction kit industry down the years. I apologise for any omissions and will make every effort to recognise them in future editions.

Index

The majority of illustrations appear on the same or facing page as the text covering the manufacturer or subject and, accordingly, are not indexed separately. Significant captions and illustrations that are not so closely linked to text pages are included in the index and are shown with the page number references in *italics*.

AFTERGLOW

SJ CAVALETTI

PAIDEIA PUBLISHING

1

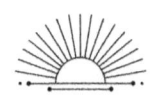

Drake

"I WON'T TAKE the clamps off till you tell me."

She squirmed underneath me, tied naked to the bed with a set of nipple clamps and as vulnerable as Maeve would ever let herself be. Nipple play was the only time where she'd let down her guard, but I had to tie her down to make that happen. But today, she teased me the whole time, taunting me with some information she held tight-lipped, rather than keep to her typical moans and groans.

This was my Achilles heel. Not knowing what someone else knows. There was a fine line between a surprise and a

secret. A surprise was when someone didn't tell you they were keeping something from you, and in one fell swoop of a moment, you found it all out. A secret was when someone kept something from you, and somewhere along the way you felt it on your fingertips or the hairs on the back of your neck stood up and told you something was amiss. Her teasing me with information was something in between, and it made me uncomfortable.

I could only handle being out of control if I was blissfully ignorant.

She smirked at my trivial threat.

I threw her a better one. "Okay. You love the clamps? Want to wear them for the rest of your life? That's cool. But I'm sure you don't want to be tied to a bed for the rest of your life."

Just so she knew I wasn't fucking around, I got up and walked toward the door, dick swinging between my legs. "I'll just be in the living room…"

"Oh, stop pretending you'll leave me here." She wasn't buying it. "And Alex won't appreciate your foot long dragging on his nice clean floor." She tried to look serious, but a smile wobbled on her lips.

"We both know he's not home." I grabbed my boxers from the floor and pulled them on, giving more weight to my threat. "You don't know this side of me. I *will* torture it out of you. Don't make me turn to Google for new ways to do that. I don't like secrets, Maeve. Surprises, yes. Secrets, no. You know that."

"This isn't a secret!" She laughed. "But I'm not supposed to tell you…yet… Come back. Please… Drake, I'm cold and dirty."

Worse than the nipple clamps was her lying on our wet spot. *Gotcha now, lady. Spill it.*

"Okay, you win. Come back and untie me. My hand is numb."

Frozen to the spot, I lifted an eyebrow and put a hand to my ear as if straining to hear her.

"Wow. Didn't know you could be so dramatic... A contract came across my desk this morning."

I sashayed over to the bed, sat next to her face, and the old spring mattress gave way so she rolled toward me as far as she could with her hands secured. I began to undo one of the knots I'd tied. My fingers loosened the fabric slowly as I eyed her. "Keep talking. I won't be done till you are."

"You have to promise not to say anything to anyone."

"I thought you said it wasn't a secret."

"It won't be for long. Plus, it's not a secret to anyone but you, which it won't be in a minute when you promise."

"Fine." I released one hand. "Promise."

"Go on," I said.

"They're already negotiating terms for tours." She bit her lip.

"Seriously?"

She nodded quickly then dipped her head to her other knotted hand, indicating for me to loosen the grip. I straddled myself over her chest to reach the other side, her little hummingbird heart pounding against my thigh.

"Looks like they're releasing some pretty big funds." Her voice was melancholy, coated in a veneer of excitement. "I'm pretty sure you're going international."

International? Shit. This had all happened so quickly. Within three weeks of my call to Reckless Integrity, I was recording. Months later, I'd played some support gigs and then some of my own shows, all local, but it had hardly seemed on a trajectory to going on tour already. Didn't I just landed in the City of Angels? It felt like only a couple of

days ago, not a couple of months, that I'd kissed my mom goodbye.

Maeve crossed her arms over her porcelain breasts and rubbed one of her wrists like a ghost breathing back to life. My beautiful dark fairy had done all of this for me.

Without that business card at Uyu, I wouldn't be here right now. And, it was likely a hell of a lot more than that card. When I'd called Reckless Integrity, they'd asked how I got the number. I didn't want to name-drop, but that meant I didn't get a call back. I was a nobody. So I'd mentioned Maeve, and when someone gave me a buzz, it was Gina. No doubt Maeve tipped her off to the identity of the mystery caller to Mitch's private number.

Maeve had orchestrated this all. I owed her everything. In my eyes, her skin glowed as brightly as my heart did for her. She looked ethereal in this moment. She was an angel —my angel.

"Are you going to say something?" She pulled at my arm, tugging me downward to join her in bed.

I snuggled down alongside her.

"Thank you." I kissed her like it was a prayer of gratitude.

"Thank you? You don't owe me..."

"Bullshit. I know you pulled strings. I'm okay with that. I'm not one of these pigheaded men who want to do it all themselves. I know it takes a village, and you're the high priestess of mine."

She kissed me hard and inhaled me in. When she let go, she asked, "So, you're happy?"

"Happy is just one thing I'm feeling."

For once in my life, I didn't want to say what was going on in my head. I wasn't quite ready to leave Maeve but I knew this particular train wasn't one that actually stopped

at the platform. When your one shot came, you needed to take a leap of faith, jump with all you had, and hold on for dear life.

I caressed Maeve's arm. We took a moment to just think and process. This was unexpected for sure. I'd had full belief that this day would come but I'd hoped Maeve and I would be more settled. Trust didn't form in a tornado. We had love, no doubt about it, but trust had yet to armor us up enough to face everything the outside world had to throw at us.

On the other side of the coin, one thing I'd loved the most about music was performing. I loved the yeasty smell of the bar when you first walked in, before anyone arrived. I loved the feeling of being backstage as the crowd buzzed outside and the pit of my stomach clenched with energy. I loved looking at all the faces in a crowd and connecting with strangers through music. My body always felt so alive at gigs.

But since meeting Maeve, I didn't crave that quite as much. Sure, I'd had a good time at gigs since meeting Maeve but I'd also found that I no longer wanted to leave every-thing on the stage. I wanted to take some of that back home to her. I even considered perhaps to stop performing alto-gether and be a songwriter at one point. She was doing crazy things to my soul, this girl.

But as much as I wanted to be with her, I wanted to support her. Songwriters didn't make as much as front men of huge bands, the revenue streams just weren't as plentiful. I needed to show Maeve's mom, Dixie, that I'd look after her daughter. Dixie was an old-fashioned woman in many ways, and so far, she wasn't impressed with me.

Even though her husband, Mitch, had started Reckless Integrity with Dixie's inheritance money, she was the type

who was happy to provide the pig but wanted the man to bring home the bacon. She'd expect the same here. Maeve had set me up, but it was up to me to turn this water into wine. Still, was this the way to do it? Was I to provide for Maeve by leaving her behind? Was I to take care of her by leaving her alone?

"Don't overthink it," Maeve said.

I gave a light chuckle. "Hey, that's my line."

"You have to do this, Drake. You really do. You'll regret it if you don't give it a go. *I* know this. *You* know this. We'll have to just be strong and be grown up about it."

She did that thing with her voice again. Whenever Maeve was about to shut down, her words came out almost monotone. Now wasn't the time to talk about it. Frankly, this time, I didn't want to talk straight away either. The terms hadn't even been pitched to me yet, and I really didn't know what I was getting into. What *we* were getting into.

I was sure I'd have at least a few months to court the hell out of my fairy. We had time to develop and blossom, and that's what I needed to focus on in the upcoming weeks. Wasting time on hypothetical conversation wasn't the way to build trust and connection. I needed to make Maeve see that my love for her was unbreakable, and perhaps, more importantly, that my fidelity was just as invincible.

Nothing would be more important to her than that. I knew women, and they lived for the three Ls—love, loyalty, and longevity.

Maeve

MY DAD HAD BEEN A REALLY busy man, but no matter what, we always had a sit-down dinner on Sundays as a family. This was when my mom would make a California-fied version of some Southern delight—healthy Georgia shrimp and grits or barbecue with sugar-free sauce.

Even as adults, Tyran and I were there pretty much every Sunday, and three months after my dad died, we still gathered around the table, but my mom never let anyone sit in my dad's chair. It was a wonder she never set him out a plate.

We sat around the living room, my mom with a bourbon old fashioned, while Tyran and I talked about the vacation our mom wanted to take with us to Europe.

"I just can't get a hell of a lot of time off, so we need to work around my schedule a bit, Tyran."

"You can take off whenever you want. You're just a workaholic. Who's your boss? Gina? She'd let you leave whenever..."

"Gina's not my boss..."

"Well, she's the big boss now, so pull some strings because I literally can't take days off as easily as you can."

DING-DONG.

My mom pushed herself up from her corner spot in the sofa, and her indent remained on the cushion. She didn't used to sit there that much but she did now. "I'll get it. Must be *that boy* of yours. Maeve."

Tyran came to my aid. "You mean Drake, Mom. What you mean is, it must be Drake."

I mouthed *thank you* behind Mom's back.

I'd stop mentioning her rude "nickname" when she dropped the other part. "That boy" was a level up from "that boy who made you do it". It was exhausting that Mom had displaced her anger over Dad's ashes from me to Drake. And frankly, I would have rather she be mad at me. I wanted her to love Drake.

It would have been easier for me to deal with her angst than to have it linger as gossip behind Drake's back. He was totally aware of the negativity, but because it never came out in the open, he couldn't address it. Dixie would always spray perfume over the stench of her gripe before he walked through the door. But the world could still smell sweat even through rosewater.

Thank God Tyran liked him as much as he did. A combi-

nation of Drake being the coolest guy in the world that even men crush on and Tyran wanting new energy around made them good buddies right from the start. Tyran wanted him there as much as I did. Drake breathed life into a house where grief still hung in the air like a stale mist.

"I'll get it, Mom," I said. "We'll meet you in the dining room."

"I'll get the wine poured," Tyran said, his eyes widening as if to say we're going to need it.

He took my mom by the arm, like a total gentleman, and ushered her toward the dining room. My chest warmed seeing my younger brother so chivalrous and manly. He'd stepped it up since Dad died or maybe he got pulled into the patriarch position through suction now that there was a vacuum. Either way, pride swelled in my chest, and somehow, seeing him with Mom made me know that eventually everything would be okay. We'd do this together.

Rushing to the front door, I smoothed my hair along the way. I took a calming breath, grabbed the enormous handle and tried to look cool pulling open the heavy, oversized door. Drake's eyes swept the room behind me, and then he pulled me up and into his chest, his forearm cradling my butt as we shoved our tongues into each other faces like we'd not seen each other in years. I craved his taste twenty-four seven. He tasted like spearmint, and cigars before they were smoked. Delicious. Moreish... I always wanted more even when I had him.

"Mmmm," he moaned into my mouth then set me down. "I skipped straight to dessert."

"Good thing because the main course is bitter."

"Shhh," he whispered, "your mom is just as I'd expect her to be. She'll come around but not if she thinks I talk badly about her, so mind your tongue, woman."

I kissed his cheek and hugged his rock-hard torso. He was so fucking good. Thank God he knew how to impress women. His charm would tame Dixie eventually, but I was so eager to let go of her grip on me. She held me back; her words pinched my heart like a vice. I wanted to give myself completely to Drake, but in doing so, it felt like I might have to let go of my mother, and I wanted to be there for her, too. I shouldn't have to make a choice between my mom and my lover.

"You're a kiss-ass," I joked.

He cupped my butt cheek, pressing his fingers right up into the crack, and I felt a finger flash across my pussy through my thin leggings.

"I kiss *your* ass. Why do you make it sound like a bad thing?"

WE'D MADE small talk through mouthfuls of sweet potato, and my mom had been mostly silent. She didn't talk as much as we used to, so mostly Tyran talked as he'd been excited about a site he'd acquired for a mansion.

"It's the last big site ever in the Hollywood Hills. Ten thousand square feet, and there's literally nothing like it. Honestly, the views are insane, but more importantly, with the hills almost completely gobbled up, ordinances in play and all that..." He took a bite of fried chicken. "... this place is going to be exclusive with a capital E."

Drake swallowed then asked, "Where does all the water come from nowadays? The drought won't be stopping, and I looked at the spec of your last build. All these places have pools, lawns, and more bathrooms than bedrooms."

"We can't get away with not having a pool at our builds, but all of them have Astroturf instead of lawn, drought-resistant plants, low-flush toilets, eco showers. This latest one, we're installing some new technology that pulls moisture from the air and cools it to create up to a hundred gallons of water a day. We also have rainwater capture, but as there's not much rain. Who knows..."

As if she hadn't heard a word of the previous conversation, my mom piped up. "Drake, have you managed to buy a car yet?"

She slurred, and even though I knew people weren't themselves when they were drinking, I didn't excuse her lack of manners. My mom's question came out not with concern but with accusation. I'd only discovered what a snob my mom was when I'd brought Drake home.

Drake turned from Tyran to my mom without any sort of reaction to her rude interruption. "Yes, I did. I bought a Ford Focus. Trusty, reliable."

"We do like trusty and reliable in this house. Hard to come by," she replied.

Tyran looked to the sky and stopped short of an eye roll. We all knew what she'd meant. She implied constantly that Drake was some deadbeat musician even though he was being backed my one of the world's biggest production companies. He had RI's best manager and the hottest up-and-coming marketing people on his team. Gina would have told my mom all of this, but my mom chose to act like he was no better than a busker with an empty hat.

It was all because she blamed him.

How on earth she was able to rationalize that Drake was in any way responsible for what had happened with my dad's ashes was still beyond me. We'd argued for hours about it in that first week back from Uyu. She'd said if he'd

been worth anything, if he'd been decent, Drake would have talked me out of it, not into it.

Now, he was a double whammy in her eyes. He was a starving artist *and* untrustworthy. What kind of guy she thought I'd meet in Los Angeles if not that was beyond me. I'd still be a virgin if I'd saved myself for the sake of those standards.

Of course, Drake had never done anything to betray my trust. Not that I gave it freely, I was the type to sleep with one eye open, but all I'd seen in the past months was someone who had my back.

The other part, Drake being from the wrong side of the tracks, was something I couldn't fix. It didn't help one iota that his monetary potential lay in being a musician, which we all knew was something of a long shot if you wanted to earn more than minimum wage. Even though the entire Lewis existence was built off people just like Drake.

I'd pointed this out anytime she'd said, "*Why can't you just find someone you have something in common with? Like another lawyer? A professional who'll share your schedule?*"

Drake, true, didn't have money, but his potential was as big as anyone's. It was as big as my father's had been. But when I'd brought this up, that was when she'd refused to discuss Drake any further.

She'd settled for nonstop drops of acid into every conversation we had until Drake and I were burned out and excused our tattered egos from the table.

I hoped like hell this tour worked out, we stayed together through the distance, and my mom would eat her words. Though I suspected she'd find new problems. She was determined if not anything.

I reminded her that Drake had actually been doing well

since arriving in LA. "Drake's streaming has been doing great. Bought you that car, didn't it, babe?"

He chewed and nodded but didn't look up from his plate. I could tell he didn't like it when I justified his worthiness with his earnings, but it was the only language my mom really understood.

"Well, anyway... Gina told me about the tour plans," my mom slurred, that last glass of wine shattering her annunciation.

I nearly spat out my drink. "Mom! It's still confidential."

She turned on me with heavy lids. "Oh, don't give me that hogwash, young lady. I know you told him."

"I don't know the details yet," Drake said, sitting back looking as relaxed as ever.

How did he do it? Even when I'd told him about the tour, he hadn't flinched or tensed with excitement, dread, imposter syndrome, or joy... something... he always seemed so chilled. He was chilled when something great happened, chilled when something bad happened. I loved that about him. I *needed* that about him.

"Well," my mom raised her glass, full of sloshing wine, of which she needed not another drop, "congrats. You're officially a rock star."

She drank before the rest of us had raised our glasses, which was so unlike her. Was it another effort to knock Drake down a peg or was it that she'd let herself slip? The old Dixie would have never slurred before midnight or missed the clink of a toast. As annoyed as I was with her behavior toward Drake, it was also sad watching her like this, and moreover, I was full of worry.

I'd heard more than one story of people turning into alcoholics after losing a spouse. My mom seemed well on her way. We needed to keep an eye on her.

"I appreciate the gesture, Mrs. Lewis..."

Mrs. Lewis... ugh. Nobody called her Mrs. Lewis but the gardener, housekeeper, and pool boy.

"Guess I won't be getting any granbabies anytime soon. Ya'll won't be able to see each other so much as to make that happen."

Fuck me. She wasn't swimming in her wine glass now she was drowning in it, and I wished I could, too. Embarrassing with a capital E.

"Mom," Tyran saved the day again, "let's just stay present and be happy for Drake, yeah? They're only in their twenties."

"I had both of ya'll by the time I was thirty."

"Well, it's not like that these days. It's normal to wait longer and have kids in your thirties. Not that we're..." I looked at Drake and scrunched my nose, this awkward conversation contorting my face with apologies and questions. "...like, we're just enjoying each other."

Drake wrapped his hand around my thigh and squeezed it. I could hear his voice in my head, he'd said it so many times before. "*Don't worry, babe.*"

He looked at my mom who tried to maintain eye contact with him. "We'll see. I'm trying to stay focused on my songs at the moment and not get too big for my britches. It's a lot more pressure now without any bandmates. I don't actually even know what the contract is yet either, so for me today is the same as yesterday."

I was happy to change the subject. "Not that Jay helped you much anyway. You'll be more than fine without him."

"No, I'm not even saying that. It's just the moral support. Having a band is that safety-net feeling."

He had me now, though. I supported him morally and immorally, too. Surely that had to be better than any bandmate?

Tyran got up to clear the plates, and Drake followed suit. Who knew what they talked about in the kitchen, but they didn't delay bringing in the peach cobbler, which was great because I really wanted to lay into my mom about her behavior, but it would have resulted in a conversation for one.

I'd hoped she would lose track of where we'd been and could talk about eco solutions in the building industry again. I was wrong. She was right back at it.

"I'm sure they'll have you set up with a band in no time," my mom said, spooning out some peach cobbler onto each of our plates. "It's not like you're Ed Sheeran or something."

"Mom, that's rude," Tyran said.

"I am *not* being rude. Reality is that Ed can pull it off with all his loop pedals and thingies. Drake is a front man."

"He's not *just* a front man, Mom. He writes his own songs and plays guitar," Tyran added. "He's produced entire tracks and is a musician. Drake doesn't need a band to justify himself in this industry. You should come to one of his shows. Hop on YouTube. Come on, Mom, you're normally a music aficionado, and this is the first time I don't agree with your assessment."

I thanked my brother for joining the battle. Why did she try to make Drake feel so small? It wasn't the right thing to do, but it also made me realize just how mad she was with me stealing Dad like I had. If several months later there was still residue, this shit might never get clean. But I'd lost him, too, and her not being happy for me and making things so uncomfortable when Drake was around was something I didn't have the daily strength to face.

I'd have to talk to her more one day. And I would, as soon as I knew a thousand percent that Drake was here to stay. I didn't want to go through hell and back with my mom

right now with it all being so new. I didn't want to make her think she and I had a deep-seated problem. She needed stability, so although I always stood up for Drake, just so he knew that I didn't condone her sharp tongue, and I was definitely his ally, I wasn't about to napalm the lady. She'd been through too much.

Drake had said this much himself. He got it all and told me not to worry about it. He'd said he was a big boy, which of course I believed because everything I'd ever seen, inside and out, proved it to be true.

"Tyran, being a front man isn't an insult," my mom continued, then she turned to Drake. "Anyway, I'm sure Gina will make sure it all turns out in your favor."

Favor. Drake's jaw clenched at that word. He pulled his lips into a thin line, and his nostrils flared ever so slightly as he looked down at his dessert instead of into my mom's eyes. I wish he had, though, because when I did, I didn't see the nasty expression of a controlling mom. I just saw a drunk woman who needed to go to bed. Only slightly comforting that she may not have meant everything she'd said.

Nevertheless, the table went silent for a beat, and we all took a bite of cobbler. There was no use talking to Dixie now. There was no use in being defensive. We all just had to wait it out.

I glanced next to me, and Drake caught my eye. I smiled but not a happy smile, a smile that said, *thanks for continuing to come to family dinner and put up with our bullshit* smile. He pursed his lips, popping a mini kiss in my direction. He didn't seem fazed but more likely he just didn't want to bother me with it.

Though Drake was resilient, there was no way my mom hadn't gotten into his head with all this negativity. I worried at times that he would find this all too much. Being poked

and prodded wasn't something any beast could take forever. But I guessed he'd be on tour soon enough and he'd get out of these Sunday night dinners for a while.

Shit... Drake would be leaving soon. I didn't know exactly when, but anytime was definitely too soon. He'd been such a distraction and a wonderful escape from it all. Drake gave me a reason to leave the house and be young and free. Under the weight of his fine abs and clenching pecs, I was protected from melancholy and this depression that eased its way into our home. I'd put down my shield but had been using him as my armor instead.

It scared me how much I loved him and needed him now. But if you love something, you have to let it be free. I could never nail Drake down and think he'd be the same man I fell in love with pinned to the bed. Wonderful as that image was.

Tyran finished licking his spoon and changed the subject. "Mmm. Very nice cobbler tonight, Mom. Something special in it?"

"Cointreau."

"Well, it was beautiful, thanks..." He turned to us. "I meant to ask if you guys want to go to a party in Topanga Canyon this weekend. It's a coworker's housewarming, but I don't really know anyone. Maybe I can third wheel."

"That would be us inviting you," I said.

"Whatever. It'll be fun. Drake, I need you to make me look cooler."

That wasn't true. Tyran didn't need anyone to make him look cooler. As much as I'd despised him most of my teen years, one thing that was clear was that he'd been plenty "cool." Girls in high school had practically lined up to fuck him, no strings attached.

He grew up rich and blessed with my mom's piercing

blue eyes and my dad's black hair. He'd never been short of friends either. Tyran had said this to remind my mom that he liked Drake. The more the pair of us enforced our fondness for him, the more quickly my mom would get over her grudge. She wanted us to both be happy after all. Well, she would do when she emerged from her own haze.

"Don't flatter me," Drake said. "I'm only cool with this one on my arm." He gave me a wink. "Wanna go? I'm working day shift Saturday so I'm off at night."

I looked at Tyran. "We're in."

When I glanced back at my mom again to see what she'd thought of our triple date, I'd half expected her have an air of ease and contentment. She'd always wanted Tyran and I to be pals in high school, and now here we were, being buddy-buddy going to parties together. But when my eyes met her face, she just stared off into space as if in a lucid dream. Her hand rubbed the seat of the chair where her husband used to sit once upon a time and whisper Topanga Canyon invitations and tell her how she was his best accessory.

Lying awake in my room that night, the moonlight poured in, and though it was beautiful, I wished for the sun. I couldn't get back to sleep. I hadn't been able to get back to sleep for days on end now.

Being a junior lawyer at Reckless Integrity, I'd had to do my time in each area of entertainment law. I was to spend a month minimum in each area and I'd started with intellectual property and had only just moved on to merchandising. I was happy when I had because I was certain that Drake's name wouldn't come across my desk. Not this soon. He'd

just finished contracts around brand, publishing, and demos, and this was the stage where the team (and Drake) would be working hard to build a fan base.

Touring was absolutely not where I thought he'd be at. So when a first-draft contract came across my desk with Drake's name on it discussing preliminary merch rights, my chin could have hit the desk. I didn't let it, but instead my eyebrows all but hit the ceiling. How could he already be at this point? How could they already be scheduling tours and with dates and venues abroad, no less?

But the question that had kept me up at night the past few days was: why didn't Drake tell me this was imminent?

I felt as though he'd been keeping a secret. It was true we didn't always have a ton of time to talk. Well, we did, but we often spent much of it doing other things instead. I'd never been so horny since meeting Drake. It wasn't easy having such limited time in a new relationship.

I lived in Malibu, which shouldn't have been far from him, but in LA traffic to his place in North Hollywood was forty-two minutes on the satnav but an hour and a half in real time. I worked my tush off because even though I knew my job was safe, as Mitch's daughter and Gina's close friend, I wanted to prove myself worthy and not a silver spoon. I wanted to one day boss that department and have everyone feel I'd earned it. The hours were long because everyone wanted that same thing as much as I did. The kind of person wanting to be a lawyer tends to be ambitious, and that added to sitting on tremendous debt creates a necessary grit.

Drake had grit, too. He'd waited tables any chance he could get, and RI owned his time in between. We both had the workaholic gene.

We'd started off meeting every night, no matter the time our workday ended, but making love and not sleeping,

going until midnight and getting back up again at half five, had me lacking concentration and Drake's voice fragile. We needed sleep to succeed so we were only able to stay over with each other a few times a week.

Still, Drake had certainly had ample time to tell me things were ramping up quickly at RI Surely it was impossible for him to be blind to such rapid success?

Why wouldn't he have told me? The question echoed through me on repeat when I closed my eyes and tried to concentrate on my breathing. I needed to get some more rest. I needed at least a few hours, especially as this was one of our "off" nights, so I should be getting a full seven hours. But I hated surprises. I liked to orchestrate and curate my life as carefully as possible. This had crept up on me like Hugh Jackman turning fifty.

I didn't know what was worse—the fact that Drake was leaving in a month or two or the fact that he hadn't told me this was coming.

The creepy little fingers of betrayal tapped me in the back, urging me to turn around and acknowledge her. She wanted me to come back to her because she and her gang, loner and suspicion, had once been my best friends. I'd been convinced by their friendship for so long that if I never trusted anyone, I'd never get hurt.

Of course, I should have known this wasn't true since my very first breakup with a boy. I'd never trusted that first motorcycle-driving, tattooed dickhead in high school, but he'd still broken my heart anyway.

Now I had Drake, and there was no way he'd want to be with me in the long-term if I didn't open up.

Open up.

He talked about it all the time. He reminded me that he wouldn't run no matter what I said and that we'd in time

learn how to talk about everything. He'd said I'd get used to the uncomfortable tinny tingle in my chest that happened every time I was about to be vulnerable.

Breathe, Maeve. Breathe. Deep breath in. Hold. Deep breath out.

I tried to exhale the need to just get mad at him. I had to release the lie that told me if I just let myself be angry I might like him less, and then it wouldn't hurt when I couldn't be in his arms three nights a week. His arms that I hated to admit gave me energy and strength and made me feel invincible when I was in them.

Being with Drake was like hiding behind the back of the biggest boy in school and sticking your tongue out at the bullies.

God, I loved being with him. Who was I kidding? I was so insanely into the guy. I loved him so much now I'd have settled for his shadow. Looked like that's all I'd get soon enough.

I WASN'T sure what was better, my house or Drake's. On the one hand, Drake's apartment was much smaller, and sound traveled right through the wafer-thin walls, but my house meant my mom was around. She usually stuck to specific places in the house, and thankfully, when we'd moved there, my parents had picked a place where my and Tyran's rooms were in a different wing.

But there was just something about having sex right down the hall from a parent who didn't like your boyfriend. It had totally lost the exhilaration I'd felt when I was younger.

We mostly settled for Drake's two-bedroom apartment because we felt young and free there, and his housemate, Alex, wasn't actually around that much anyway.

Before I even knocked, the door flew open with such gusto the breeze it created blew Drake's locks back a bit, and his brown skin glowed like the tropics in the soft light of the hall. He lifted my bag off my shoulder, took me by the hand, and guided me inside where it was dark apart from a single lamp and a lot of candles.

He breathed me in with a dramatic kiss, and when I pulled back slightly, still held firmly in his grip, I looked around. "This feels special."

He kissed my upper lip. "You're special." I melted in his arms as he speared me with his brown, hooded eyes. "I got us a carpet picnic if you're down? Alex will be late tonight. He got that part in that huge Valenti film."

I took off my jacket and threw it on the back of his couch. "Wow, he did? That's a big move."

"Yeah." Drake headed to the kitchen and poured out a bottle of wine he'd already uncorked. "He leaves in a month, I think, and he'll be gone for four to six. Filming mostly in Australia." He handed me a goblet of red wine. "So we'll have the place to ourselves."

I took a sip and arched my eyebrows at his comment. Drake would likely be gone most of that, too. Murphy's Law. He clearly didn't grasp the full weight of what it meant to be on tour. You didn't come home every fucking night. But I didn't want to bring this up. I'd told myself to keep it all in until it was an actual issue. Why ruin the time we had left?

I remember Drake once saying that worrying ahead of time didn't solve an inevitable problem. It only made you weaker to deal with it when the time came. Hope gave you strength. Why shouldn't I be hopeful anyway? My boyfriend

was about to become an international rock star. How could that be seen as anything but a positive?

"You okay?" he asked.

"Yeah. Course. Just thinking about a contract."

He gave me one of those looks like he didn't buy what I was saying but he didn't press. He took my hand and led me to the coffee table in the living room where he'd set out a carpet feast. We sat next to each other with our backs against the sofa. Taking a piece of sushi in a pair of chopsticks, he lifted it to my mouth.

"I got all your favorites…"

I took the sweet, umami tastes into my mouth and eased my jaws around the sushi gently. Dragon rolls were nearly a substitute for orgasms. "Mmmm. I'm so hungry."

"You need to stop skipping lunch."

"I have to if I want to get here with any evening ahead of us."

Drake had a bite of salmon roll and then reached over to the side where his guitar was propped up. He chewed as he plucked the strings. I was used to this now. In the desert, we'd been very distracted, but now that we were in normal, home settings, he played almost all the time. If we had a chat in the kitchen over coffee, he strummed. If we watched TV, he strummed. If we went to the beach or a party or anywhere but the movie theater, he would bring his guitar. It wasn't by accident that Drake was talented.

"You need to eat, too," I said, taking another sauce-smothered piece.

"I had some food before leaving work. I wanted to have a little time with this…" He played a succession of chords and closed his eyes. "I wrote you a song. It's going to be in the charts. I can feel it."

"The girls will love it, huh?"

"I only care if one girl loves it."

I took a sip of wine as the chords developed into a melody. Drake hummed, and the sound in his throat was full and rich like the warmth of a gong, and it wasn't any wonder that sound bathing was a thing. I'd have loved to shrink myself and snuggle into his vocal cords like some vibrating sleeping bag. It seemed such a comforting place to be.

His lips pursed, his full brows furrowed, and his nostrils flared slightly as the song developed behind his eyelids where he read his imagination. Watching this man unfurl a song was like watching a sunrise. You wanted it to be daytime but equally would give anything to pause the world spinning just for a moment longer in order to enjoy those fleeting hues that synced so perfectly with the feeling of anticipation in your veins.

"*PUT me back together*
  Take it all apart
  I lived without my edges
  Lived without a heart
  "*And they say, there's just one piece*
  To create the scene
  To bring it all together
  Make more sense of me
  "*So put me back together*
  Take me all apart
  I'll I've without my edges
  Live without my heart
  Until you place the piece
  Missing inside of me
  You complete the scene..."

His voice saturated the room, and it was so powerful I
swore it was visible. It swung elegantly through the air, a
samurai's sword piercing my heart. For once, instead of
being strong and trying to repair the hole he'd made, I let
him cut me, because even though it hurt, we bleed to
cleanse.

I swallowed hard, pushing down on the lump in my
throat when he looked up at me and crawled over next to
me. His hand cupped the back of my head, and his pillowy
lips kneaded mine with calm affection.

I kissed him back as relaxed as I could but I had to talk
to him tonight... but as he slid his tongue in my mouth, my
body responded with a desperation. It was the same last-
time desperation I'd felt at Uyu when I hadn't been sure I'd
ever see him again. The physical need and yearning that
reached a peak unlike any other when you thought you may
never see someone again.

It was crazy. He'd be here tomorrow. And the day after
that. Still, I felt like I was losing him.

My tongue tangoed with his, and my core grew heavy
and moist. Blood engorged everything, my skin so taut the
nerves sucked up every little flick and touch, and I held my
breath to handle the intensity. I wrapped my leg around
him, grinding myself into his hip bone, trying to release the
building pressure, even though in my mind I knew it was
about to get a whole lot heavier before it popped.

He whispered into my ear, lips grazing my earlobe,
"Take off your clothes."

He pulled back so we could stare each other in the eyes
while we undressed. The look in his eyes was wolf-like,
stalking, but somewhere within them was that usual
devilish smile his soul wore. God, I loved him. I loved how
he was the fucking alpha every day of the week but didn't

need to say it. Didn't need to show off or act tough or be a dick to make it known. You knew it when he ordered you to take your clothes off and you complied.

He undressed at the same time. It was all I could do not to attack him. When his top came over his head revealing those rock-hard abs and his pecs... fuck, I wanted to dig my nails right into him. But he was in the mood to take his time. He slid his pants off, his dick already hard but not as desperately so as my nipples. It was that firm kind of juicy that I loved during foreplay. I reached out to take it in my hand, and he leaned in.

I pumped, he pressed in, dancing into my hand with his dick, his ass flexing, he grew in my palm. I wrapped my hand around his cock nice and tight as the skin around it firmed up.

He bit his lower lip. "Put those ruby-red lips around me."

I opened wide and took him into my mouth, loving the smooth feeling of his cock. I loved circling his dick with my tongue and the taste of his salty pre-cum in my mouth. I sucked as hard as I could, my little mouth doing what it could around his thick cock. He pressed deeply into me, reaching right to my throat. He was so fucking delicious. I never thought I could want a man in my mouth so much.

He groaned and after one deep thrust pulled himself out, leveling his body with mine. He eased me down to the floor. His hands smoothed the hair back from my face to look into my eyes with desire that was almost scary. He made me scared every time we had sex. The level of ecstasy was something I could get lost in. The eye contact hypnotic.

His hand swept down the length of my side. He breathed the question he always asked, humid passion tumbling over my lips. "Who loves you?"

I closed my eyes and enjoyed his caress, delicate and perfect on my skin. "You do."

He sat up and flipped himself around. Facing my toes, he straddled my face. His balls hung down, and I grabbed the tops of his thighs and rubbed a thumb along them, making him squirm. Balancing on one hand, he reached down and eased his dick back toward my mouth, and I took him in eagerly.

The sensation of him filling my mouth was enough when his fingers found my clit and touched it gently. So gently he could have been breathing on it. He ran his fingers along my slit and inside me to wet them. Sliding them back up, moist and gentle, he made circles around my clit with my wetness, and my entire core opened up to him. I spread my legs further apart, willing him to have more of me. God, he made me feel so good.

He spread my folds open and placed his pouty, soft lips on my sex, and I could have died. My pussy was so hot with wanting it felt like it melted open for him. His tongue tenderly caressing my clit until it was ready to burst. His fingers made their way back inside, and he reached up toward the spot that seemed connected to my clit from the inside.

"Ahhh..." I moaned, his dick popping out of my mouth; I couldn't hang on anymore.

I clawed his leg to brace myself as he circled faster with his tongue. He pressed down harder, and when my core opened up to him, he eased a third finger inside, turning me inside out in every possible way. My whole body was on fire. My hips raised, I eased my sex into him for more.

He licked faster, harder, until everything gave way. I poured into him an orgasm that made me moan with pleasure. "I want you inside me now..."

"I haven't finished tasting you."

He lifted me off the floor and laid me out on the couch like I was made of nothing. He sat over my face again and entered my mouth as I palmed his strong ass in my hands.

When his hot, wet mouth licked my clit, I gasped. I was still so sensitive, but he whispered his tongue across it again like it was made of feathers.

I tried to keep his cock deep in my mouth while we fucked each other's faces, my core growing wetter, hotter, tighter, heavier... for the second time. Impatient for the ecstasy I knew he had in store for me. He licked me harder, just like I wanted him inside me.

He took his mouth off me only to say, "Now I know you want it."

Drake turned around so I could see the sultry, predatory look on his face. He wiped his lips with his forearm.

He quickly grabbed his jeans from the floor, found a condom, and watched. He didn't take his eyes off me while unfurling the sheath onto his fucking rock-hard dick. "Roll over."

I spun onto my tummy, glancing over my shoulder only until he tugged me upward, my ass now in the air, my cheek against the velvet fabric. His hands hung on to my hips when he plunged deep inside me. He filled every inch of me, I felt it right to the end of me. He thrusted in and out, every ripple and rib of his cock urged me to press against him, too.

"You feel so good, Fairy. Fuck, you feel good."

I loved it when he said I felt good. I always wanted to be the one to make him feel that way. I lifted my hips more, arching my back, allowing him in even deeper. His thumbs gravitated toward my tailbone and teased along either side

of it while his dick bore into me. I clenched around him, and he let out a groan.

He pumped faster, and his thumbs slid down from my tailbone, along the inside of my ass cheeks as his palm kneaded my ass. His dick filling every inch of me and his fingers so close to every entrance, making me wild. He forced my ass cheeks inward with his hands, squeezing my ass around his cock. I clenched as hard as I could, but everything inside me wanted to open up to him. Let him in. I wanted to make him feel the way I was feeling now. Wide open.

My desperation grew. His cock touched that place inside me that made me instantly wet. That opened me up to be taken and had and used if that's what he wanted. He felt it, too and thrust faster, harder. He braced my hip to get deeper inside me.

"I have to have you now..." he moaned.

His thumb grazed my asshole, and I went mad. I wanted him everywhere. I wanted him in everything I could open up to him. I thrust into him harder. Trying to take him even further inside. He thrust then strained and stopped when his dick pulsed inside me. My pussy released around him, soft and wet with soul-destroying desire pouring all over his pulsing cock.

I'd never wanted anything the way I wanted him. I'd give anything to him. Anything for him.

He pulled out, leaving me empty but satisfied. I lied down as he threw the condom onto the floor. He gathered me into him, his fingers trailing along my spine while we caught our breath.

Lying there in the candlelight, one of them flickered, clinging precariously to what little wick was left. Drake caressed my arm and my cheek felt the consistent gong

inside his chest like a grandfather clock sounding out midnight. I didn't know why his heart sounded sad. I was sure it wasn't.

But all the emotion and release of making love made me raw with feeling. I didn't want him to leave. I could have been thinking about a million other things right now. But I wasn't. I wanted him to stay, and it hurt.

I couldn't help a tiny tear escaping the corner of my eye. It rolled down, dripping right onto his chest. I didn't wipe it away and I wasn't sure he'd felt it. Either way, I left it right where it landed because I didn't want to draw attention to just how painful the thought of him leaving was.

Still, we had to talk.

"Drake?"

He inhaled slowly and answered with a hum through his nose. "Mmmm?"

"Why didn't you tell me that things were going so well for you? I didn't expect that contract to come across my desk at all. I thought you were still just recording."

"Shit. You hate surprises."

"Yeah."

His hand stroked my hair, and it calmed me, which was good because I'd started to sweat just a little, asking questions that I wasn't sure I wanted the answer to.

"I didn't actually have any idea myself," he said.

At that, I sat up and looked him in the eye. "How did you not?" I tried not to imply I didn't believe him, but it sounded ridiculous. To think he'd had no clue.

"It was TikTok. I went viral a few times. That's how I got the radio and streaming play in the past few weeks for 'Potions'. I have no clue what's going on there, but a few A-listers wrote me... it's super distracting and not my thing, so I wasn't really paying attention. I just made videos of

myself in the process of making songs and did a couple other trend videos Tayo told me I had to do. They uploaded and did all the admin, so I didn't realize this was a big deal at all."

Tayo was Drake's PR manager and the hottest ticket in the entire music industry right now. She was making lots of new artists hot on social media and she was only twentysomething.

"Wow. She's better than I thought," I said. "But you got radio play, and A-listers wrote to you. Anyway, you must have had an idea."

Drake ran his fingers through his hair. "Believe it or not, that's all happened to me. I've had radio play before to no avail in Seattle. I've even had some big-fish producers come to shows in shit bars in before, slumming it, and come backstage to say I'd done well. I've been at this awhile now, and those things promised progress but I ended up with lots of excitement and nothing tangible."

"Oh..."

"Actually, Tayo told me the same day you mentioned the contract about the viral videos and potential shows. It was *after* you mentioned the contract. Don't worry. I kept a straight face. The confidentiality runs both ways."

He flashed a row of pearly whites at me. He ran his fingers through his hair again, and for the first time, I stopped thinking about myself. It was pretty hard to believe that Drake didn't understand what was happening. But maybe he'd kept this to himself because he didn't want to jinx it. Or worse, he didn't think he deserved it. Was it possible, or was I projecting because that's what I'd do?

"It's not a lucky fluke, babe." I kissed his cheek and lay my head back down on his chest, trailing my fingers up and down the ravine in the center of his abs. "I'm not saying

social media can identify talent but... trust me. You're amazing."

"If this actually all goes through," he sat up and took my chin in his fingers, staring straight into my eyes, "I'll miss you. I feel like we're only getting started."

I nodded, but a lump clogged my throat again. I wasn't sure getting soppy was a great idea. I might break down in a full-on sob at this point. Drake had been my shield since Uyu, and when he left, it would be just me, my mom's depression, a mountain of work and jealousy. I knew myself. I knew I'd think the worst. I'd have to take this as a personal development challenge.

Drake pushed himself all the way up with his back against the sofa and pulled me onto his lap. "Come with me."

"What?" I laughed lightly. "What do you mean?"

"Just come with me. On tour. It's not forever. I'm not big enough to be gone for a year. It'll be a few months. Ask for a sabbatical and come with me on tour. You can be a groupie. It'll be fun. And sexy."

He kissed me, and I felt his fantasy of me on a tour bus right through his lips.

I wanted to. I really, really did. But I had a life to tend to. I had a duty to my mom. She really wasn't okay. "I can't, Drake. I can't just leave..."

He tilted his head and lifted a brow playfully. "You know you can, though."

I should have considered what I'd said more carefully. I should have said to let me think about it. Instead, what came out was the typical, childish defensive line that all entitled people said as a matter of habit. "I have to earn my keep just like everyone else."

When I realized how small that sounded, I added, "I

can't just ask for favors like this and then expect to get respect upon my return. What would it look like to other junior lawyers, Drake? Maeve Lewis gets to go off and party whenever she wants to and then come back and earn the same? Slot right back into jobs they might have sucked a dick to get? It's not cool."

I eased off the gas pedal and remembered he just wanted me with him. "I want to, babe. Trust me, I really, really want to with every fiber of my being."

"You care too much what other people think."

"And you don't?"

He didn't. He didn't really care what people thought. Or he did sometimes but he never let that change his direction or betray what his heart truly wanted. Unlike me. That's why he was so much cooler than I was.

"Maeve..." he took a deep breath, "it was just an idea. I'm not trying to interfere with your street cred. More than anything, you just need to know I want you there. It feels a bit empty without you around now. Even when I just sleep here at night without you, I ache."

Just like that, Drake's sincerity swam through the moat and battered right through my defenses. His eyes were sweet and warm as hot chocolate, and all you wanted to do was drink him in one go, knowing it would soothe your insides.

"I love you, Maeve. Distance can't change that."

It felt good when he said it. And God, I wanted to believe it.

But distance changed everything. Absence either made the heart grow fonder or it made it forgetful.

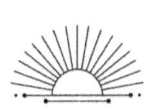

Drake

My small bedroom felt like an entire home when Maeve was in it. I loved when she stayed over. It was early morning now, and my room glowed with ambient light from the sunrise making its sparse, IKEA furniture look like a film set. Sometimes it had felt like exactly that—a film set. It didn't seem possible that this was my life yet. Even after a couple of months of living here.

When Maeve wasn't here, I'd sigh as I put down my stuff from a day at work. It was a big change from Seattle.

Sure, in Seattle, I was a fish slinger and only had a studio

apartment, but it was mine. It had my stamp on it. I'd taken the time to paint it as I'd liked. I had art on the walls, some rugs El had bought me in Morocco, and my mom's old kitchen things from when I was a kid. My plates had patterns on them that had started to fade with years of washing and reminded me of homemade pancakes and my grandma's lasagne.

This was a sublet. Not only was nothing in the room mine, but on top of it, I was borrowing it from a borrower. It was many times removed from being cared about by anybody, and when Maeve wasn't here, I thought constantly about how soulless it felt.

Maeve deserved more than this but loved me with only this. The thought of giving her something I'd earned, something we both deserved, gave me energy even through crushing rush-hour traffic.

LA kind of sucked.

Maeve's little white ass cheek stuck out from under my duvet as she slept, belly down, sprawled out. How I could have pinned her wide open again from behind, spread her open, and stuck three fingers right up inside her... such was the spontaneous desire I had rushing through my veins anytime I saw her naked.

But it felt such a rude awakening, so instead, I flicked the duvet aside a few more inches and ran a finger in a delicate circle over her soft booty.

She stirred, and her voice rose, reluctantly, muffled by the pillow. "You might have to do me asleep. I don't mind, you know. What's mine is yours."

I laughed. "Not my thing... but sex *is* better than coffee."

She finally lifted her head, and one of her tired brown eyes squinted. "Only just."

Her cell alarm went off, and she let her head plop face-

down back into the pillow. She had to get to work. I had to meet my manager. Even a quickie wasn't possible once that alarm went off because we always set it for the very last minute.

I lay down beside her, and she pulled her face out of the pillow enough for me to rub my finger over her pointy nose.

"Your finger smells like sex," she said without opening her eyes.

"My whole body probably smells like sex."

"Pzzt. It might. But you know the drill."

"No showers together. Boo."

We'd tried that a few times. We absolutely couldn't touch each other or do anything sexual once those digital wind chimes sounded out and told us to get on with it. I'd never been so addicted to anyone's skin before. The high I got when I ran my lips along it, inhaling her scent, was second to none.

I ran a finger along her spine and watched it rise and manipulate her gorgeous smooth back up to sitting, and eventually, her butt waved me goodbye as she headed into the bathroom.

Maeve had discipline. Good thing one of us did.

The room became brighter, and everything looked less appealing again. The one dresser drawer that didn't sit square anymore pissed me off, and the blemished wall stared at me with its previous owner's nail holes, like a teenage kid with pimples.

I didn't like this place.

One day, Maeve and I would have our own house. It wasn't long now. I'd get us some stylish Italian leather furniture, dig my rugs out of storage, and get one of those four-poster beds I'd always wanted. I'd tie Maeve to it every night

with silk, Gucci scarves, and we'd watch movies on the weekend in our cinema room.

I'd never cared before about having all of these things. And now that I knew Maeve better, I saw she didn't care either. But a hard-wired urge to provide like a boss came over me whenever I was with Maeve.

I let myself fall back into the duvet and stared at the ceiling as the sound of the shower came thundering through the thin walls. I closed my eyes and tried to image Maeve's hair, slick and black under a waterfall in Hawaii.

But I just thought again about the first home I'd buy her. And that I might keep my mom's old dishes no matter what I could afford.

When she emerged from the bathroom, smart enough to put her panties and bra on in there so I wouldn't be tempted by her nipples, sweet as candy, I couldn't help but feel a slightly melancholy. Though I knew it was extreme, it must have been what it felt like going off to war. You had to protect what you loved most by leaving it behind.

"THE MOMENT HAS COME." Jules, my manager, pushed a contract across the table at some swanky Hollywood Hills restaurant. Next to him, my PR chick, Tayo, beamed from ear to ear. "We're going on tour."

Tayo tapped her fingertips as she waited for me to look at the paper and probably say thank you. Her TikTok videos and "strategies" had been the gateway to this new opportunity, for sure, and at the same time I couldn't help but think we'd just found a lucky ride on the algorithm. I knew I deserved this but I wanted to deserve it another way.

I looked at the contract but didn't read it. "Do you two not think this is premature? It's like catching a wave your first time out and thinking you can ride Mavericks."

I glanced up at the pair, and their smiles faded. By now they'd probably have expected me to order the champagne.

"It's just that this isn't organic," I continued. "I mean, you do a smaller tour and you get the word out there, build diehard fans, not fleeting ones..."

"Drake," Jules peered over his thick, red square frames, "welcome to the twenty-first century. This is the digital age's answer to busking. *This* is the new old-fashioned way. TikTok, YouTube... social is the street. Take it and run. If you're worried about being a one-hit wonder, that's just down to you. We've given you the platform, but it's you who has to write the magic. And you're doing that a thousand times over. People need riffs, but when the lyrics back that up..."

Tayo leaned into the table a bit. A cocked smile told me she was joking. "You don't have imposter syndrome, do you?"

Tayo was beautiful in a way that was impossible not to notice. Dusky sepia skin and blue eyes with a mane of hair you couldn't ignore. But her beauty didn't make me like her. She was so... LA.

One thing I'd noticed here was so many people mistook being blessed with good genes for talent. On top of her not realizing that her beauty had a lot to do with her own success in PR, she was constantly diagnosing people with syndromes and mental illnesses, and it annoyed the fuck out of me.

Though I knew she'd said it in jest, my esophagus plugged with a mini rage. "I don't have imposter syndrome. I just want to be in it for the long haul. And I've always loved

the intimacy of face to face. This TikTok shit..." I reeled myself in, realizing I was biting the hand that had fed me. "...it's just all a bit quick. Just skeptical of the process."

And also, there was Maeve. Obviously, I wasn't about to bring her up here, in this setting, but I'd seen it in her eyes last night. It was going to take a lot for her to be okay when I left. She had a lot on her plate—her dad hadn't died that long ago, her mom was definitely in a depressive funk and becoming alcohol-dependent, and she was just starting out in a high-powered, intense career.

She needed me. She'd never admit to how vulnerable she really was right now. I didn't want to leave her and deepen her abandonment issues... shit, I sounded like Tayo now.

"Well," Jules said, taking off his glasses, wiping them with a little rag and putting them back on, "there won't be another opportunity. I came here to discuss the finer details not the bigger yes or no answer. Frankly, I'm surprised by your response to this. Most people would be thrilled."

"I'm stoked, of course. Don't get me wrong."

"I got you wrong," Tayo said.

I ignored her. She was the one-hit wonder if anything. Jules must be fucking her... "So what's the deal then with this tour? Paint the picture."

Jules tapped the papers in front of me. "You're mainly doing Europe. We have twenty US cities and fifteen European ones booked at the moment. The Brits love your kind of sound right now, so you'll spend a decent amount of time in the UK and then have five across mainland Europe."

"How long am I gone?"

"Eight weeks. These things have a way of extending a little sometimes, though."

"Will I be able to come back at all?"

"Maybe once." Jules sat back. "Drake, you're not asking the right questions. I only have an hour, fifty minutes now, so we need to talk money. Rights, brand... that kind of thing. RI want to sort you out a band, and you need a name."

"Fuck. I thought getting a band together again would be organ..."

"Organic," Tayo finished my sentence. "Drake, unless you're talking about avocados, nothing in LA is organic. And why would you want it to be? You have the pick of the litter. All the session musicians watch the social trends."

"Jesus. I'm getting hooked up with session musicians?"

"We audition tomorrow," Jules interrupted, urgently, as if he had only five minutes instead of fifty left. He wasn't happy with me.

"I'm waiting tables tomorrow." As soon as I'd said it, I knew it was a dumbass thing to say. But my body felt itchy and unfocused.

"Drake, you don't get it, do you?" Jules adjusted his glasses. "You're never waiting tables again if you pull your head out of your ass. What the hell is wrong with you? You haven't even asked what the contract is worth."

That's because all I could think about was Maeve. It was almost as if these words came out on their own. Self-sabotage, because the truth was, I didn't want to leave her.

But I had to remember, in order for me to take care of her, I needed to earn. That was the catch-22 of the whole situation. In order to have her, I had to leave her.

I took a drink of water, trying to soothe the arid cracks that had formed under my skin. "Tell me about it then. Hit me with the numbers."

"So obviously there's merchandise and other considerations, but the per-show rate is generous. They've offered fifty-five K per show. I think that's worth taking at this stage

since you've only had two singles out. It's pretty hot shit, given where we're at."

What. The. Fuck.

"Did you say thirty-five shows?" I asked as calmly as I could, because even one show would have been enough at that rate.

"Yeah. They wouldn't normally *ever* offer such a big fee this early on, but I'm good." He brushed imaginary dust off his shoulder. "I had the TikTok leverage, and of course, capitalized on the last-minute nature of it all. They need some hot fill-ins. You're opening for Stitch Fix in Europe. And for Filly on for your US dates."

These were big established acts. I wasn't really a fan of Filly but I knew plenty of people were. She seemed too contrived for my taste, but at a fifty-five thousand a show, it didn't matter anymore if I liked her. I'd learned in week one living in LA that you pick and choose who you work with like a doubles match, not like dating.

"*The* Stitch Fix? And Filly?" I glanced at Tayo, and her smug smile said it all.

She gobbled up every morsel of this win like she'd singlehandedly baked the cake. It annoyed me for some reason. I knew it would be like this if I left Seattle and got into a bigger pond. There would be sharks and people feeding off the actual talent all the time.

Jules was less mercenary than Tayo. He'd been around a lot longer and was in his early fifties. Though I made no mistake about it, he was one hundred percent out for commission, at least he seemed more keen on nurturing talent for longevity than Tayo who chased bright and shiny objects.

"Okay, so I'm confused about one thing," I said. "My album isn't finished."

"Doesn't matter, you were number one with 'Patient' for a day. We swooped in on a broken-up band and an unexpected pregnancy. A couple dropouts mean you drop in. The supporting acts for those two bands aren't available anymore, and you are. It all slotted together like fate, my friend."

"I don't know if I can rush the album..."

"Drake," Jules leaned on the table, "pardon my French, but what the fuck is wrong with you? Do you have a concussion or something?"

He was right. What the hell was wrong with me? If Maeve and I couldn't survive a mere eight weeks apart so I could make serious bank, then we had bigger problems than distance. Plus, that four-poster bed wasn't buying itself. Wouldn't I love to invite Dixie over to my own dining room in Hollywood Hills and make *her* grits one Sunday...

"Jules, I'm just in shock, you know? I only moved to LA a couple months ago."

"Look, you're almost as surprised as I am, but we need to get our heads down. Step one: call work and tell them you won't be in. Step two: you need to hunker down and finish the last two songs you've been working on so we can record this shit. Step three: we need to get a band together. Actually, all this needs to be happening at the same time. We hardly have enough time for you to get your head around it. The team sorted auditions for tomorrow. You better just pack a suitcase and stay in the studio. You won't be leaving there for a while."

"When do I leave on tour?"

He slid the contract closer to me again. "Gimme your John Hancock." He surveyed the room to call the server over then studied me. "Your first flight is in three weeks, but you'll feel like you're gone after lunch. Nothing will ever be

the same again, Drake. My advice? Go with the flow. Listen to the professionals. You could be the next Dave Grohl. Rock needs a new 'nice guy' face. Which reminds me... are you okay with the name Graphic Temple?"

The name made me chuckle because instantly, I was reminded of the Kink Dome at Uyu.

"I love it."

"Good. Tomorrow we put the band together."

5

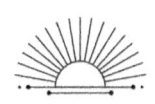

Drake

AFTER HAVING some celebratory drinks and lunch, Jules had left me with just one last piece of advice.

"Whatever it is that you're hanging on to, you can't take it with you if you want to survive."

He hadn't meant Maeve. He hadn't known my hesitation was about her, even though everyone and their dog at RI knew we were dating. He'd just meant I had to see this as being in survival mode. I needed to treat this like my sole focus. That was easier said than done, but he wasn't wrong.

As soon as I stepped out onto the sunny California pave-

ment after my lunch, I called up my manager at the restaurant and told him I couldn't come in because I was going on tour. It wasn't my style to leave people high and dry, and to my surprise, he just said, "Let me know if you ever need your job back," and hung up. This town was strange to say the least.

But I didn't expect the same laid-back reply from Maeve.

I headed back to my place to pack as Jules had said to do. I clasped together my suitcase and threw myself down on the bed, bouncing up and down because it was a spring mattress. Soon, I'd afford one of those luxury space memory foam mattresses that didn't make noise while you were fucking.

Taking in a deep breath, I took what I hoped would be one last look at the faded carpet and the ugly frosted-glass light fixture. This was one thing I was okay saying goodbye to.

Now it was time for the hard part. I grabbed my cell.

I texted Maeve: *Any chance you can get a few minutes to FaceTime me? I need to talk to you and don't want to do it by text.*

She'd shit herself when she saw that. She'd think I was in a car accident or something. I added another text: *Love you. And I'm okay, just want to see your face.*

Her: *I can call in two. Stand by. xo*

When her call came in, her little pixie face lit up the screen like she lived with a permanent ring of light around her. Man, there was something extraordinary about her. She was like an elf. Or like some *Game of Thrones* character. Her face was epic to say the least, and if one day she pulled up to my house on a dragon, it wouldn't look out of place.

"Hey, Mama... I met with Jules and Tayo and I finally saw the contract. It's all happening a lot more quickly than I

thought it would. I'm spending the next three weeks in the studio and then off on tour."

Her eyes widened. "What? Wow. That's so quick, though..."

"I know. But I'm joining some other acts as a last-minute opener. It's all surreal. But it pays well, and when the door opens..."

"... you gotta walk through. I get it. I'm really happy for you, babe. Congratulations."

I could tell that she'd tried to put an exclamation point at the end of her sentence, but she couldn't muster that level of enthusiasm, and it came out like an ordinary period. I didn't blame her. I'd acted much the same with Jules.

Maeve smiled with her mouth, but her eyes were busy holding on to the future; they grasped it tightly so at least one of us had a grip.

I remembered a couple in high school, when one of them decided to go to college and the other one went off traveling in Europe. They hadn't made it. I'd seen the one who'd stayed behind about a year later, he'd come to one of my and Jay's gigs, and when I'd asked him about the girl, she'd dumped him only a week into her trip.

It was hard to be present when you held on to the past. It was just as hard if you were holding on to the future.

Thankfully, I was the one going away. It was selfish of me to think that, yeah. But I thought it anyway.

Maeve walked as she talked, and she pushed open a door and the sun bathed her skin, illuminating her red lips, and I felt sad thinking all we'd have was a bunch of pixels to enjoy for eight weeks.

"So," she said, "tell me more. What's happening with the album? You're obviously finishing it before you leave."

"Before *we* leave."

"We?"

"Yeah, I have three weeks to finish an album and get some new bandmates. There are only a couple songs left to record, so it should be fine on that front, but I really don't like the idea of plucking two strangers off the street and expecting us to have chemistry. It's messed that I'm going on tour in such an artificial way..."

"It worked for One Direction."

"Do you think I'm reassured being compared to a now broken-up boy band?"

"You should be. They've done well and they're all still working. Depends what you want for yourself."

What did I want for myself? For the longest time I wanted to tour. Crowds were electric, and that feeling of being plugged in had always made me feel so alive. I couldn't even imagine what it would be like in much bigger venues with some of the anthems I had in my repertoire now.

Most of my songs were heartfelt, but Reckless Integrity had given me direction to write two "singalong" songs with memorable one-liners. They told me I needed a "We Will Rock You," "Sweet Caroline," or a "Piano Man." Anyway, the difference between poetry and a hit song was the hook, and that was something that I'd been missing. RI had amazing mentors, and in a short time, I'd come a long way.

RI had been right to guide me, and my two viral songs were the exact ones that bought me the Ford Fiesta in a short amount of time with almost one million downloads. If only it had been a million albums. It was shocking to think a million people streaming only bought me a Ford, but such was the nature of the business now. And I was grateful for that and for the education. I was enjoying songwriting more than ever now.

After meeting Maeve and working with RI, I'd started to think that being a songwriter alone might be enough. I could write songs for other people and just stay in LA with Maeve...

But then Dixie had come along. And I saw the property prices. I wasn't going to provide for Maeve the way her mom wanted, hell, the way I wanted, simply by being a songwriter. I needed to tour. I needed to be the face on the merchandise and the guy on the copyright.

There would be time to drop back, but it wasn't now when I was still young, had my looks, and more importantly, had an actual touring deal on the table worth over a million. Jules assured me this was the tip of the iceberg if I was well received live.

In particular, he'd said that Filly was a star that made stars. She had a way of catapulting people from D list to A list and that I was lucky to be paid to support her. Most people would pay *her* for the privilege. I wasn't sure if this was true. Jules really liked to remind me that he was earning his commission, so whether he really had negotiated this unprecedented deal or not, who knew.

I hated it when my brain reminded me that Gina might have something to do this, and at the same time, that very reminder kept me humble.

My mind spun with all the moving pieces. There were so many people counting on me now. Maeve. Jules. Tayo. My soon-to-be bandmates. And I never forgot that Dixie's last name was Lewis and Reckless Integrity owned my ass. If I messed up now, Dixie would never like me.

"I can't go to Tyran's party now." Just like at lunch, the dumbest things were coming to mind.

She puffed a laugh out of her nose. "I can't believe you're even thinking about that right now."

"I'm not. Just trying to keep talking... the mood has shifted. At least it has for me."

"What do you mean?"

"Just... this is as hard as it is amazing."

"Drake, I just want you to be happy."

"I appreciate the brave face, but it's okay for us to talk about this, Maeve. Don't think I don't have mixed emotions, too. Much as I didn't want to wait tables, I would have done it for us to have more time together before something like this happened."

"That's sweet..." She looked down at the phone. She'd found a bench or something to sit on, and her face peered down, her hair falling on either side of her face. She pushed a tuft behind her ear. "I don't want to say anything that'll sour this, though. It's only a short time. We'll both be so busy it will probably fly by."

"True. Will you come to the studio whenever you can? I don't think I'll be escaping much. I could probably make some dinners out but nothing crazy."

"Course I will. Can't tonight but I will tomorrow. I'll congratulate you in person. Properly. Well, maybe not as properly as I'd like..." She tried another smile, and this one succeeded. She was happy for me somewhere in there. She'd wanted my success more than anyone. Hell, she'd created this success.

"...nor as I'd like. I love you, Mama."

"I'm your biggest fan. Don't forget that. I don't care how big their titties are, no one loves you like I do."

I laughed. "I'm an ass man. Just bring yours by as soon as you can. I miss you."

I'd only just seen her that morning. But I meant it as deeply as if months had passed. That's how love worked.

"Miss you, too, babe. I'll text you later. I'll try for

tomorrow at the studio. Love you so much. So proud of you."

AUDITIONS WEREN'T what I'd expected. I didn't know why I'd thought it would be like *American Idol* or something with me sitting with a panel of Reckless Integrity judges while we watched prospective bandmates perform for thirty seconds. It was nothing like that. In fact, the word "audition" alone was the completely wrong choice.

By the time I got to the studio later that afternoon, there were only four people there: Jules, Maya (the RI producer I'd been working with on the album), and two strangers.

One was a guy, a few inches shorter than me, with hair that even I envied. It was thick and shaggy but in a planned, styled sort of way. He wore jeans, a tight t-shirt, and enough necklaces to let me know he cared about his image even though his understated jeans and t-shirt tried to exclaim otherwise.

Next to him was a woman, also tall, slender but with a huge rack of fake ones. More like a supermodel than a musician, she, unlike the dude, looked like she'd curated her appearance for the past several hours, if not weeks, such was the design she'd crafted.

As much as I liked effortless, I'd have been lying if I said that I didn't like her style. Insane ear cuffs, creamy-white hair, tied up tight into a fierce ponytail that fell right down to the small of her back. Tight black leather pants and black lace corset could only be daywear in LA, and that was one thing that did make this town more tolerable.

She smiled as I walked in, the kind of smile that was the

perfect opposite to the brooding, serious expression on the guy's face.

It didn't take me long to put two and two together. These were the only musicians I'd be meeting today. These were my new bandmates. It was a total head-fuck. At least they dressed the part. And lucky for them, I wasn't an asshole and had always wanted a brother. Or a sister. Now I'd have to work quickly to make us a dynamic trio because I sure as hell wasn't going to let Maeve down.

I'd told myself the best thing I could do was to leave for eight weeks and come back victorious.

Jules stepped toward the newbies. "This is Park Tae-Min," he pointed to the guy, "... and Quinn Hartley."

The chick raised her hand and waved like the Queen.

Quinn stepped toward me and put out her hand so I could shake it. "I heard you were a poet. Hope the rumors are true. I'm a lyrics kind of girl."

Just when I was about to think "at least the girl is pretty" my thought flipped to "at least this girl is smart." But people were good ass-kissers and bullshitters in this town. If it weren't for all the Chanel Mademoiselle, it would reek.

Still, there was no use testing her, being skeptical, or holding back now. We had recordings, practice, photos... and possibly quite a few TikToks if Tayo had her way. I decided to take the gracious approach.

"Nice to meet you," I said, taking her hand and noticing how soft it was. She must be the drummer, because no guitar player could be any good without a few calluses. "I take it you're the drummer?"

"Good call." She put her hand on her hip.

I walked over to Park and shook his hand. "That makes you the bassist?"

"Yeah. And I go by Tae." He pointed between himself and Quinn. "We both sing as well."

Quinn glanced at Tae. "I know it was weird that we were both in *Prep School Musical*. Right?"

I stared at them blankly.

Quinn continued. "It was a musical movie on Dis... with Tae... we just found out we were both in the same movie. Just as ensemble, though. Anyway... we're both trying to Miley..."

Another blank stare that I was sure would be met with an explanation. It was. This time by Tae.

"It's when you're trying to transition a kid career to an adult one."

"Oh. Sounds like you're both more experienced than I am."

Quinn was quick to make me comfortable. "Not really. I think Tae and I have both only ever done film and TV. You're the one with actual stage experience." She smiled eagerly and was a lot more down to earth than her image suggested.

"Well, I'm sure you both know we have very little time, so the best thing we can do is get started. Sorry if that seems abrupt, but it's my personal plan not to fuck this up."

"Less talk, more practice sounds fine to me," Tae said. "In fact, I think music is a good way to get to know each other."

I agreed. "True. And it's not like any of us have much choice in the matter, so let's just dive in the deep end, forget about pleasantries and be as tight as possible on this tour. I'm for it. My songs are your songs. Most of the time I've been a musician I've been in a band so I'm not about to be a prima donna. I just want us to get as much done in the next few weeks as possible and be hot when we hit the stage."

Tae and Quinn looked at each other and sharing a smile

as if they might have thought I'd be a dick and they were both relieved. They weren't as fierce as they appeared on the outside if they were scared of me.

Then again, people were often scared of me on first glance. It was something I'd learned to live with and appreciate. It meant people were often standoffish, and I learned to make the first move.

Being a leader suited me like a made-to-measure Armani three-piece. This was why my soul popped into action having a band again. It wasn't much fun being the boss of yourself. Okay, I wasn't the boss of these guys, but with them here only thanks to my merit, they were turning to me for guidance. And this was my sweet spot.

Maya walked in the direction of the instruments, already set up in the studio, and we instinctively followed her.

"Thanks for making this easy, guys. We don't have a second to spare for drama, so the more cohesive you are before going off on tour the better. If people can get married twenty-four hours after meeting each other, you can do this in a few weeks."

She was straight to the point. I liked that. We took our positions at our instruments.

"Drake," she turned to me, "Tae and Quinn brought their things here to stay as well. Quinn lives in Malibu and Tae in Venice Beach, so we thought you could all just stay at the hotel down the street for the next few weeks. Just charge food and drinks to your room and we'll sort it out." Maya pulled out her cell phone and held it up for a picture. "Wow. The very first photo of Graphic Temple. Smile like you're the next big thing."

Maeve

GETTING home from work that night, I didn't feel the same sense of relief I usually did when I opened the front door and kicked my shoes off. Normally, after a ten-hour day and a two-hour drive, the smell of the lavender diffusers my mom had going twenty-four seven worked like menthol vapor rub on a snotty nose. Everything just cleared away.

But today, I clung on to the mucus lining every inch of my being. It was quickly becoming a disease. Drake leaving was all I could think about. I'd had to reread so many clauses today I'd have to work the weekend at this rate to get

through the mound of work I couldn't focus on. Every cell in me ached thinking about him being gone and me being alone with my mom. Every. Single. Night.

Worse than that, because I could at least imagine an end to that misery, he'd come home eventually, was the jealousy that started to wind up within me, an evil hand on an even more sinister jack-in-the-box. My intestines twisted thinking about all the groupies and the fans and all the new people he'd be meeting and finding fabulous.

Drake loved throwing a few back, and people did stupid shit when they were happy and drunk. Hell, that's pretty much how we'd ended up together. Though fate made us see each other, Jägermeister made us touch each other. He'd be high on life and not getting laid. I knew how dicks worked. They got cold easily. They were cold-blooded and always searching for a heat source.

I wasn't ready to trust him. We'd only been together such a short while. A few months ago, he'd been a complete and total stranger. He'd never done anything to hurt me, but then we'd never had any challenges... for the past couple of days, since seeing that contract, it felt as though I had constant PMS.

My bare feet hit the fresh tiles, giving me fifty steps to cool off before I opened the fridge in the kitchen. I wanted a glass of wine so badly I could have pulled the cork out with my teeth. But staring at the bottle, I knew I'd have to settle for drinking it with my eyes because I told myself I wouldn't drink on weeknights and try to set a good example for my mom.

Fuck my life. I wasn't even thirty.

I took out a container of leftover Chinese and a bottle of fizzy water. The sun was setting, and the kitchen grew dim, but I stood in the light of the microwave, a zombie staring

blankly at its target. This was my life now. Day-old Chinese and sobriety. This would be my life for the next couple of months.

The microwave beeped and woke me from my daze. I took my food out, popped on the kitchen light, and pulled up a stool. When the sweet and sour hit my tongue, endorphins released within, soothing the dull ache just enough for me to think Drake might come back to a few more Maeves if I didn't shake myself out of this funk.

I needed to be happy for him. I needed to support him. And I needed to be the best version of myself if I wanted him to want me. I could not let this wave of nausea make a big smelly mess of this good thing we had going.

Live in the present. That's what my dad would have said. Right now, today, Drake loved me. A person I loved was having his biggest, most impossible dream come true. And if we were meant to be, we'd come out the other side in an even better place than we were in now.

No, Maeve... that's the future...

Now. I had to focus on the now. Drake had said to buzz him whenever I got off work and that no time was off-limits. He'd told me not to be "polite" and that if he was in the middle of something—sleep, practice, whatever—he'd simply call me back. He hadn't wanted me to "leave him alone" for the sake of it.

I finished my last bite of deep-fried gooey goodness, wiped the corners of my mouth, and grabbed my cell ready to FaceTime my man. My man. Today, right now, he was my man.

Two ringtones in, and his big brown eyes and beaming smile appeared on screen, instantly switching the lights back on in my dark chest.

"Babe!" he said, happily, eagerly, almost as if he was one beer deep at a party. "How was your day?"

"Same-same." I couldn't help but smile in return. It did feel so good to see him shine like this. "I'm much more interested in your day. Did you find any good people for the tour?"

"Well, the bad news is, I didn't get to choose... but the good news is..." he turned the phone on two people who sat eating food at a table in the background, "they chose two kickass ones for me!"

I couldn't make the figures out completely in the background, but it was a man and a woman, and they waved at me from several feet behind Drake and wiped their faces, presumably to come over and say hi.

Holy shit. He already had bandmates? And he liked them? Jesus, it might as well have been El and Jasmine at the table behind him, he talked about them like they'd already known each other for years. Suddenly, the stool I sat on seemed really hard, and I shifted on it, trying to get comfortable, but my leg was numb, and I shook it to bring it back to life.

This had moved so damn fast. I supposed it'd had to, but I'd had Drake almost exclusively to myself, and now only a day after he'd signed the contract, he had two new best friends to spend all his time with. Jealousy tapped my shoulder, and though I tried to ignore her, I could see her in my mind's eye, wiggling her fingers with an impudent hello and raising her eyebrows like a mischievous wedding crasher.

I hoped the blonde in the background was ugly. Who was I kidding? She wouldn't be. Nobody in LA was ugly.

Immediately, I wanted to be super-sexy hot girlfriend and make a good impression but I realized all my lipstick must have washed away on the greasy dinner I'd just eaten.

But there wasn't time to brush my hair, smooth my liner, or reapply my lipstick. Drake's insta-friends were now standing behind him, leaning over his back, and I swear the blonde's boob rested on his shoulder.

Why couldn't he have had two guys?

"Hey, guys..." I said, trying to sound enthusiastic, and more importantly, confident.

Drake introduced them. "Tae and Quinn..."

Quinn...?

Said Quinn leaned into the camera, again brushing Drake's shoulder with her tit, or at least it seemed like it, but then again, he didn't pull away, and I *know* he should have pulled away if she was touching him like that.

"Hi, Maeve! Drake's talked about you so much. Hope you're going to come to the studio sometime?"

Her voice sounded familiar, and there weren't many Quinns around... it couldn't be...

She continued, "Also, this is really weird, but it will be like a reunion because we went to high school together! Malibu Academy? Remember me?"

Oh shit... no... it can't be.

"It's Quinn Hartley. I used to have brown hair, so maybe you don't recognize me?"

Fuck. Fuck. Triple fuck.

Drake beamed as though this was a good thing. He probably thought because I "knew" Quinn that this was all going to be happy families. That we could all just form some new friendship circle and sing around the campfire like we did with the Uyu gang. All hunky-fucking-dory. It fucking wasn't. It really fucking wasn't.

Quinn Hartley had been a grade A bitch in high school. She'd tried at least a few times to steal my motorcycle-driving James Dean lookalike boyfriend at the time. She'd

only wanted him because he hadn't wanted her back. He'd said she was too mainstream, and that's when she'd decided to start calling me "emo" behind my back. She'd also resorted to "ugly Goth bitch" a few times when we'd both been drunk at parties. Again, only behind my back, but we all know when private conversation become public on purpose.

When my boyfriend had cheated on me and had left me in the dirt, the only thing I had to be grateful for was that he hadn't banged her next. Now here she was, all changed and no longer mainstream in the slightest. She didn't even sport a tan, which was saying a lot here in California, as I knew what an effort it was to repel one. I'd never envied her image nor her position in high school and had just put her down to being a spoiled brat. There had been so many of them.

I hadn't cared about being popular. But now, she had style to die for and was in with the exact crowd I cared about.

"You've changed," I said. "Sorry, I didn't recognize you at first."

I hoped she'd changed on the inside, too.

"I know! I went blonde."

"And other changes, too. Nice corset." I tried to play nice. I knew how important it was to Drake that I do that. He needed me to do that. At Uyu, me being friends with Jasmine had been a top priority for him. Drake wasn't going to be a boyfriend with only guy friends. He'd always be a part of mixed groups.

And also, just as good a reason, the best way to keep a girl off your man was to get her on a contract. Girl code. That meant being friends, or at least friendly.

She rubbed her hand along her breasts and down the

front of her corset. "Yeah. Less Lykke Wullf, more Chanel and Cavalli now."

Guess Daddy still bought her clothes, because we all knew she didn't make that much off that one kid movie. Now I was sounding bitter.

"So cool that you guys already know each other," Drake said.

I forced my face into agreement. One good thing, so far, was that if Drake was saying this, Quinn clearly hadn't told him much about high school. It was probably better that way. Definitely for her, since she'd been mean girl extraordinaire, and for me, too. I really didn't want Drake to see me as some dweeb with shoe prints on her face.

Tae pushed forward this time. "I don't know you but I want to. Does that count? I'm Tae."

I waved into my camera.

A genuine smile replaced the one I'd been wearing for Quinn. "Nice to meet you, Tae."

He seemed nice, and even though I didn't have any reason to, the juxtaposition of him against Quinn made me like him. At a minimum, he wasn't a woman with double-D implants.

Drake spoke again, "Babe, it's so cool you know Quinn. How crazy is that? Small world."

"Totally..." I waited for Tae and Quinn to shove off and leave us to a private conversation, but they lingered. I hoped this wasn't my new reality. Executive meetings with Drake and his team over Zoom.

Fortunately, Drake turned his head and excused himself, talking about what they'd done that day as he walked down a hallway. He found a quiet room and plopped down on what looked like a Chesterfield sofa.

"So how was your day?" he asked.

"Nothing compared to yours," I said, still feeling blinded by Quinn's creamy-blonde hair and former moral code. "So where are you staying tonight? At the studio?"

"No." He ran his fingers through his locks and then twisted the end of one of them.

Damn, I loved his hair, and it always smelled like coconuts, too.

"They're putting us all up next door at The Forge. We need real beds."

"Oh, Tae and Quinn, too?"

"Yes."

Nooooo.

"That's nice," I said, somehow preventing my voice from cracking. "Guess you guys will get a lot of work done that way. My dad slept at the office sometimes. Traffic kills deadlines."

"Can't say I'll miss driving. It's the only thing I hate about living here."

"Lies. You hate other things. Don't tell me you're a convert."

Funny how he suddenly loved LA now that he'd met Quinn. Drake wasn't one to be critical all the time. Overall, he was a very positive person with an optimistic outlook. But LA had things about it even Ned Flanders wouldn't love. And he'd voluntarily lived next to Homer Simpson.

"You're right," he conceded. "I don't love everything, but the number one pet peeve is definitely traffic. I swear I have asthma now."

"Don't we all?" I laughed lightly. "So are you happy with your bandmates? Seems like you're already becoming really close."

"Yeah, they're super cool. Tae is a mean bassist, and you already know Quinn plays drums."

"No, she played flute in high school."

I thought Drake might have thought that less cool, but instead, he said, "Oh wow. Might need to take advantage of that at some point. She never mentioned that, but that's sweet. Anyway, she plays drums now, and both of them can do background vocals. It works. Our voices sound great together, and neither of them seem to have giant egos."

"Too early to tell," I warned.

I hadn't wanted to sound like a doomsday prophecy, but it came out a bit like one. Thankfully, Drake was on a high, and with the detachment of a video call, he couldn't feel my vibe. I was the grumpy to his sunshine, but he didn't notice the weather.

He thought about my comment for only a millisecond before saying, "True. But first impressions are great. It's going better than I could have asked."

I didn't hear it clearly, but a snide comment mumbled inside my head. All my thoughts were filled with pejoratives. I couldn't think of one nice thing to say and for that I felt like such a shitty girlfriend. What was wrong with me? Why couldn't I be more selfless? This was the best possible outcome of the situation we'd put ourselves in, and here I was, about to cast a dark cloud over all of it.

When I'd left my dad's card in Drake's hand at Uyu and kissed him goodbye, making his dreams come true was what I'd focused on almost all of the time. It felt almost as if birthing his dream was like a phoenix rising. Something new was coming into the world, out of the ashes and out of the dust, my father still lived and could give something beautiful to a man who so deserved it.

Drake turned out to be just as great a guy as I'd hoped he'd be when I'd left the desert. He was good, like my dad. He was giving, generous, not needy, and when he looked at

me, he listened with every cell of his body. He would donate his last dime, sit with a homeless person who seemed lonely, and ask even a total stranger if they were okay when they were crying. Hell, just a couple of months ago that stranger was me.

Thing was, I was fully aware that, like myself, anyone touched by his special life force would probably fall in love, just as I had. Maybe it wasn't him I didn't trust but everyone else.

It wasn't every day a woman found a diamond like Drake, and we all knew how the song went. They were our best friends. Beyond that, we wanted to get them around our fingers and keep them there forever.

Would Drake really want me when he saw everything else out there? For God's sake, he was about to see a whole world of women. Who was I to think I was good enough to compete with that pool?

I needed to go. I needed to get my act together and put on my damn lipstick. I need to put on my big girl pants. I needed to channel my inner Dixie. Like she'd always said, "It's better to look good than to feel good, darlin'."

I would not be shedding a tear. I would not be catty, unfair, or let my fear guide me. I would show him nothing but joyful jubilation and be the ever-supportive girlfriend, stable and true, and something solid to come home to.

Maybe being a rock wasn't as sexy as being a diamond, but we didn't build homes out of gemstones. I'd be Drake's foundation.

"You should probably get back to work, babe," I said. "I'll pop over to the studio. Tomorrow, I hope, but might be next day, because someone put a late meeting into my schedule tomorrow. I'll try to shuffle it."

"You're so sexy when you talk all power woman." He licked his lips and bit his top one.

I laughed lightly and teased him with a breathless, sultry voice. "Arbitration... statute... jurisprudence."

He pulled at the collar of his shirt. "That legalese makes me hot, you know."

"Well, I can't wait to have you in an airtight contract."

He smiled without teeth, just his gorgeous full lips turning upward. "I signed that long ago, baby."

"Get back to work, Drake Jackson."

"Till we meet again, Miss Lewis."

I felt a little better when we hung up. *A little.* He still loved me, and maybe it was a good thing that Quinn and I had known each other. If she made a move, he might go off her completely.

Drake had no time for betrayal in friendship. Not after Jay. Probably not ever.

7

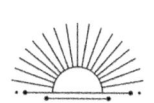

Drake

SOMETHING WAS OFF WITH MAEVE. She didn't think I knew but I did. Thing was, I had two problems. One was that I couldn't see her in person anytime soon, and the other was that she wouldn't tell me her problem until I coerced it out of her. Or screwed it out of her, because she had to take all her armor off in the bedroom.

I always tried to slide in the cracks and plant seeds while we were naked. The more I planted in there the more likely I was to grow roots and she'd never be able to untangle herself from me.

Trust was the issue. She didn't trust me. It was hard to make someone trust you in such a short amount of time. Anyway, trust wasn't something anyone could make happen. It happened invisibly over time. In a strange way, I was almost excited to prove to Maeve that she could have faith in me. If we stayed in LA for years and rolled along like we were now, she'd never have a chance to test my loyalty. Maeve was the kind of person who needed to do a whole lot of fact-checking before she made up her mind.

"Knock, knock," said a voice from the door I'd left ajar. It was Quinn.

I stood and slid my cell into my back pocket.

"I still can't believe you're dating Maeve. It was good to see her on the call. She hasn't changed much. Shorter hair, but she doesn't look like she aged a day."

I nodded but didn't want to encourage the small talk. We didn't have time for small talk.

"How long have you two been together?" Quinn continued. "Did you know her dad before he passed? He was such a cool guy."

This was hardly small talk. It was the kind of question that took at least a couple of cups of coffee to answer. It was a loaded question, though Quinn didn't know it.

I didn't know her father yet somehow felt like I had. I'd come into the picture on the cusp of this transition in Maeve's life and felt closer to him than Quinn might have been. Still, the only thing I could answer was, "Maeve and I have been together for a bit more than two months now. I moved down from Seattle almost two months ago. So I never met her dad. I didn't know him personally, but I think I do spiritually. Story for another day."

"Must be hard to leave her so soon into a relationship?"

Her eyes seemed sincere. I had to check because I'd

learned my lesson before about opening up to the wrong people. Telling everything to the wrong person didn't always go down well. People loved to twist words whether on purpose or simply by the inherent nature of seeing them with a different lens.

And with Quinn, I needed to be especially careful not to tell her anything that might get back to Maeve. I knew they hadn't seen each other in years, but that never stopped a girl from popping in out of the blue with a bottle of bubbly and a story. Nothing made two women better friends than shared gossip.

Not that Maeve was like that exactly. That was one of the benefits of her keeping her cards close to her chest. I believed that I'd always be the first to torture her true feelings out of her.

At first, it had been a game to me. To make her say how she felt, I'd tickle her and tease her until she'd talk to me. But now, I picked my battles. I only urged her on when I knew it was important for us to open up, and also, when she had fully formed things to say.

Just as bad as not talking at all was discussing a topic before you actually knew how you felt. Those conversations were often full of regret.

This was exactly why I changed the subject with Quinn. "Yeah, of course I don't want to leave Maeve. What about you? Got a special someone?"

"No, no, no. Hard to find good guys in this town, especially at our age. Everyone is still out to make it, and that's their top priority. Honestly, it's mine, too. And yours, apparently."

Was that the bitter truth? Maybe.

"I have the long game in mind," I said, trying not to sound as if I'd corrected her. "I don't actually give a shit

about the fame, though I do love performing and fans and making them happy. Really, I just want to get myself in a position to be in the music business for a really long time. I don't want to do anything else. But I don't want to be on the road forever."

Quinn grabbed my wrist and pulled me out of the room. "It's too soon to say that. We have places to go and people to please."

Her light-heartedness was exactly what I needed. Tae was more like me, I could see he was pensive and probably as happy to be alone as in someone else's company. Quinn was going to be the extrovert of the group, and anyone could see that she loved attention. Not that this was a bad thing. Maybe it was even a good thing in the business because we'd all be getting a lot of it.

I'd often been told I was charming, and I would have used the word to describe Quinn as well, though there was that feeling on the back of your neck that wondered about the charm's sincerity. There was a difference between lighting people up with your positivity and casting a spell on them. In any case, in order for me to get on with the task at hand, being in a good mood was a bonus.

But I did take my wrist back as subtly as I could. "Let's do it. Don't you worry about me, girl. I know how to work a crowd."

"Oh, do you now? I mean, you were okay on TikTok, but I don't know how many takes you did," she teased.

"Shit, you saw those?"

"A million times. I was in awe to be honest. Loved your stuff immediately, but it wasn't just the song. You do actually have that je ne sais quoi, my man."

I should have been flattered, but even though those videos had played a large part in getting me where I was

today, I still thought it ridiculous. I walked ahead of her. She followed, and I turned to say, "If you still play flute, we should try to incorporate that into some of the songs. Since Lizzo, it's not just for band camp anymore."

"So I see you and Maeve were talking about me? Hope she didn't tell you all my secrets." Her full lips cocked to the side in a smile. It was hard to tell if she played coy or was just smiling because her natural grin was sideways.

"We talk about everything."

As soon as I'd said it, I knew it wasn't true. Yeah, Maeve and I *could* talk about everything, but we didn't. We both hid things, but I wasn't sure why, because personally, I knew everything that was going on behind the mask anyway, so it was a little like playing hide-and-seek with a two-year-old under a table.

She didn't talk about the fact that her grief still ate away at her, nor did she really dive in to what was going on with her mom. Both of these things were heavy enough to have become a daily burden, and though her shoulders didn't slump, her soul did.

And I kept to myself just how badly I wanted to make this work so we could have a life together. One that was to the standard Maeve deserved. I didn't say anything because my inner macho man's mouth was still aghast that I wanted to impress Dixie. I usually didn't care what people thought, but then again, I'd never wanted something permanent with anyone before. And permanent meant playing nicely and even giving other people their way sometimes.

When we got back into the session room, Tae was plucking away with his hair over his face.

"Dude," I said, "are your fingers bleeding yet? You haven't stopped."

He barley raised his head. "My calluses are so thick I could probably play from across the room."

"I hope you don't use those in your girl," Quinn said.

Tae and I both turned our heads, surprised by the boyish banter.

"What? I'm dirty. Now you know I think about sex pretty much twenty-four seven. I can be the band member who cracks the pubescent teen boy jokes." She slid behind the drums, picked up her sticks, swirled one between her fingers, and lifted her eyebrows.

Tae strummed a chord. "Trust me, I'm okay with those. I laugh at anything. Even dad jokes."

"Can't offer you any of those," she said, tapping out a downbeat. "Just lots of double entendre."

Tae never stopped plucking his strings but said, "Okay. I got a game for us to play later. Heard it on British radio... Innuendo Bingo. Heard of it?"

"No," Quinn said, still drumming. "Sounds right up my alley, though. Actually, that's a good band name... Innuendo."

"Yeah. Would be," Tae said.

I loved talking as we strummed and tapped... this was my element. This was why I missed Jay even after he'd screwed me up the ass, stealing our material. Who wouldn't want to have a conversation over a constant backtrack? I wished my whole life had a backtrack.

It was pure relief for the mood to be so lifted. Though occasionally it took a bit of angst to write a song, band practice was one thing that needed everyone in a positive zone.

I slung my guitar over my shoulder and said, "Right, Innuendo Bingo over dinner in an hour. Let's do 'Distance' from the top and then slow it down over the chorus. Get those vocals sorted. Maybe Tae and I can harmonize and,

Quinn, you should maybe get something else going. Almost like a canon or echo? Or maybe a call and response type of thing? When I wrote this one, I'd seen this as a crowd anthem, participation kind of song, so maybe as the female vocal you should be the one acting as the audience would."

She hit her cymbal hard and clasped it immediately to stop it. "Yes, Daddy." She thumped the pedal of her bass drum and rattling out the bass line of the song.

"Slower. Just a few beats slower. Not much."

She slowed it, and after several bars, I strummed the melody over the bass line, and Tae quickly joined in, creating an epic new riff only good bassists could add to a song.

"That's hot, man," I said.

He flicked his hair up over his face and nodded. When we were in full tilt and had looped through the main melody a few times, I took to the mic and sang.

I had to admit the song came together magically, and the three of us seemed meant to be. Hats off to Reckless Integrity. Quinn was more technical than any drummer I'd ever had (and thanks to Jay's bullshit, I'd been through more than a few), and Tae added some serious spice and magic. He was a focused musician, or maybe a prodigy, because while I'd talked to Maeve for ten minutes, he'd taken this song from a seven to a ten.

As I sang my song of angst and wonder, I struggled to feel the undercurrent, because on the surface the words were melancholy, but I really felt like smiling from ear to ear.

This was all coming together so smoothly. We all got along and vibed together so instantaneously it was like my first time at Uyu with my crew. It just worked naturally.

All my dreams were coming true, and I was even being

offered dreams I hadn't been creative enough to invent myself.

We jammed and perfected the song, then had dinner at The Forge, being extremely rude, spitting out water at the table while playing Tae's game involving innocent comments gone dirty. I could have stayed up with these two all night, but we'd have plenty of those ahead of us.

When I curled up under my crisp, white hotel sheets, I looked at my cell clock. Nearly midnight. Maeve was asleep now, so I couldn't call, but I left her a voice note, trying not to sound as though I'd had one more shot than I should have.

"My dark fairy... just wanted you to wake up to the sound of someone loving you."

I PACKED UP MY LAPTOP, and my phone buzzed. It was Jasmine. We'd become close since Uyu and even closer since she'd moved temporarily to Orange County in order for her dad to get medical treatment. A few months ago, dancing in the desert, I'd never imagined we'd get so close. Then again, I never imagined she'd have so much in common with me. She was going through it with an ill dad, and we leaned on each other.

I always answered the phone for her. Even when I didn't want to. Like now. Firstly, I was going to meet Drake at his

hotel tonight and I didn't want to waste any of our precious time together. Secondly, I dreaded that she'd have bad news.

But I'd never let her down.

I wanted to be the person I never had to talk to about my dad. Not true. I'd had Peaches, my best friend, but where she'd never gone through anything traumatic, I found the conversations fell short of relevant with me doing all the talking and her doing all the sympathetic nodding. I never felt any better after.

I was determined to be a rock for Jasmine. Even sex with Drake wasn't going to stop me from making sure she felt supported.

"Hey, girl," I said, popping my wireless earphone in so the rest of the office didn't have to listen to us as I packed my things, getting ready to jet.

"Hi! Hope I caught you when you were done with work? Not in the middle of anything?"

Her beautiful, Polynesian face beamed brightly, and I knew she'd had a good day.

She didn't have that many of those anymore because she hated being out of Nakiki. She hated her job at the smoothie shop and resisted making friends, her psyche insisting that the whole thing with her dad was more temporary than it was.

"Whatcha doing?" she asked.

"Just packing up a few minutes early. I'm meeting Drake's new band tonight for dinner then staying at the hotel with him. I shouldn't but I think the next couple weeks will only get worse and worse schedule wise, and then he's off."

Jasmine knew the whole deal with Drake. All our crew did because we kept a WhatsApp group from Uyu. Drake hadn't made the announcement, I had. I'd wanted him to

feel like all the people he loved were rooting for him and behind him so I would have shouted it from the rooftops if I could have found a megaphone. And been able to yell that loudly.

"He must be getting busy. You'll have to keep yourself busy, too."

"That's not a problem. The junior lawyers always have a lot to do."

"So he does his European tour first and then the States, right? Leaves in a few weeks?"

I shoved a metal water bottle into my tote bag. "Mmm-hmmm."

"Maybe we could go to one of his dates in the US? You must be able to get VIP passes?"

"Really? Can you get away for a night?"

Clearly, I wanted to see one of Drake's shows, but I really didn't want to go alone. I would have felt like a nuisance. But going with Jasmine would be a lot more fun. Drake wouldn't feel like he had to babysit me then.

"Of course I can. Maybe we can get Liz and El... maybe even the boys over from Nakiki?"

For the first time in the past few days, I felt pure, untainted excitement for this tour. Drake would love to see all of us in the crowd. He'd feel so proud with all of us cheering him on. I knew that part of him now. Like he was a protective big brother, it would thrill him to no end to get us backstage passes and treat us all to a good time.

"Yeah. I'll talk to him tonight about it. I'd really love to see you. I need some sister time."

Jasmine scrunched her nose. "You're going to miss him, eh?"

"Yeah... not just that." I debated whether or not to tell Jasmine about Quinn. I wasn't entirely sure she'd keep it to

herself, and the last thing I wanted to do was drive a wedge between Drake and his new bandmate. He needed to make this work and not worry about me and my fragile feelings.

"Just..." I went for it and trusted Jas wouldn't want to bring drama upon Drake either. We could keep it between us. "His drummer is a girl I knew from high school, and she was a bit of a bitch back then. But time changes people."

"Whoa. That's a crazy coincidence."

"Not really. This is LA, and I do live in a gated community with a bunch of actor parents and performers of all sorts. A lot of the kids there are giving it a go in the biz now. Quinn, that's her name, was in a decent movie not that long ago."

"What was it called?" She put her cell on a phone stand and shifted her laptop in front of her as she sat at a table.

"*Prep School Musical.*"

"Oh, I know that one. I mean, the way lots of people know it." Jasmine typed, and within no time, the cast was in front of her. "Which one is she? Quinn Hartley?"

"Yup. That's her."

Jasmine found her cast photo and nodded, the corners of her mouth downturned, and I knew she was thinking Quinn was decent. With her darker hair she'd been at least an eight. But now, she was a solid ten.

"She doesn't look like that anymore, though," I said. "Google her."

Jasmine did, and when she clicked through a few images, finally said, "Whoa. She has the pearl hair now?"

"Yeah."

"Oh."

"Yeah."

"Hmmm."

The exchange was curt but telling. Jasmine thought

Quinn was as hot as I knew she was. It was like sending your guy into war with a very persuasive enemy. Men fell in love with their eyes, and Quinn was stunning.

"Well..." Jasmine closed her laptop and set her phone closer again so her eyes were on display. I could see every bit of sincerity in them. "Doesn't matter what she looks like or even if she tries anything sneaky. Drake isn't the cheating type."

"I didn't say I thought he'd cheat."

"You didn't have to. I know you're thinking it. And he wouldn't do that to you."

Her certainty took me by either side of the shoulders and shook the insanity away. She was right. It didn't matter if Quinn was still a total jerk. What mattered was Drake wasn't.

But just as much as I didn't want him leaving me in his wake, motoring off for a more rock-and-roll romance, I also didn't want Quinn to make things awkward and ruin his big chance. If she was smart, she'd keep it professional. It was her chance, too.

"I don't really want to think about it," I said. "The important thing is that Drake makes the most of these tours. I don't want him even thinking about me or worrying about what's going on here. I want him to enjoy it, savor every minute of the experience, and just go for it, you know? Just want the best for him."

"Yeah," she agreed. "He deserves it. He took care of his mom and even that crackhead, Jay. He's a good guy, and good things should happen to good guys."

She spoke about Drake, but her voice trailed off. It was wishful thinking for all the good guys in the world.

"How's your dad?" I asked.

"It's weird. He just seems the same as always apart from

feeling guilty we're all here with him. It's alright. But we can talk about that some other time. I don't want to keep you from hotel sex. It's the best."

"It is, though, right? I wonder why?"

"Dunno, but it totally is. Anyway, let me know how the band is. Hopefully, this Quinn will end up being cool and know she better not mess. I'll fuck her up."

I laughed and smiled deep inside my chest. It was everything to have someone who had your back. I was sure this future drama was all inside my head but I wouldn't have minded Jasmine throwing a punch for the past drama Quinn had created. Maybe just a little bitch slap would evaporate my grudge.

"Thanks, hon. In the meantime, let's assume all is fine. I'll see about the tickets to his show and see how many of the crew we can get. Should we keep it a surprise or tell him?"

"Surprise, of course! Drake loves surprises."

MY HEELS CLICKED on the pavement, and a heavy humidity clung in the air, threatening to melt my vicious cat eyeliner. I'd spent more time than I should have getting ready. A confident woman would have gone straight to see her man, without the primp and product, because the clock was ticking and because she knew that the most important thing was spending time together, not looking good.

Why had I wasted time putting makeup on when Drake was leaving in a few weeks and more or less unavailable between now and then? Why would I spend even a millisecond doing anything more than chewing a piece of

gum and spraying on some deodorant? That was enough, of course. Drake, in the past, sure as hell jumped my bones with doggy breath in the morning.

But, I didn't do it for him.

The psychology of appearance was far more important to apply in female relationships than male ones. Sure, it was nice when a guy thought you looked good, but let's face it, pheromones made a guy think you looked good, not the latest Balenciaga dress or perfectly arched eyebrows. The best outfit to a man was naked with your legs spread.

But a woman started her judgment from a distance when she saw your top was in last season's lilac hue rather than this one's lavender and the cut of your pants was off trend. There was no way in hell I was going to let Quinn think she could fuck with me ever again, so I dressed defensively. I dressed like a woman who had second-strike capability. After all, the only thing stopping World War Three was the knowledge that other countries had nukes.

My nuclear weapon was the latest pair of Louboutins money could buy. My mom might have been pushing sixty, but she still strutted like a debutante, and thankfully, she was my size, because I could never bring myself to spend such money on a pair of shoes I couldn't tolerate for more than a few hours.

But that's all I needed tonight. I needed to get from the valet to the table, let Quinn see that Drake and I were solid, and I wasn't the same girl she'd known in high school.

That's what I was going to try to pretend anyway. Because the truth was, in many ways, I hadn't changed at all. I still hated confrontation and the genetics of my laid-back dad and mom who insisted upon composure above everything else resulted in one hell of a flight mechanism. It was my only option. Fighting was violent. Freezing was uncouth.

The only thing I could do when I saw something I didn't like was run.

The psychology of fashion was my best option. If Quinn thought the only thing protecting her from a mega-bitch was a thin piece of vegan leather, she might not start any drama. Equally, the fact that I'd thought so much about this showed that I was both a lawyer and therefore determined to use the finer details to sway things in my direction. But it also meant that I didn't trust Drake enough to shoot down the advances of another woman.

Drawing that conclusion saddened me. Overthinking this whole thing came down to me not trusting Drake. I knew Jasmine had said I could. She'd known him for a pretty long time. But you couldn't pretend to trust someone, and my attempt at stealing the runway proved I wasn't there yet.

I actually needed to focus on that. I needed to focus on building the trust rather than keeping obstacles out. Drake was a gorgeous, compelling human being and would be for the rest of our lives. Even if we got to seventy together, I was pretty sure the LA widows would twerk with their hip replacements for him. And even if his hotness did fade, his charisma and beautiful soul created an aura better than the northern lights. Who wouldn't want to bask in him?

This was the thing driving me crazy. He was so special, I was now convinced that if it didn't work out, I would absolutely *never* find someone as good as him. When you got to that point in a relationship, things got scary, and the jealousy kicked in like a bull in Madrid. The need to keep him had become a force in and of itself, and sometimes, like now, it felt like I'd need an exorcism to get rid of it.

Or a ring on my finger.

Then again, we all knew that meant nothing in this town.

I entered the hotel restaurant, and the host led me to a table where I saw Drake's back, animated, and his arms were in motion as he told a story. Tae and Quinn stared at him, enraptured, and I wondered what his tale was about. They were so focused, I worried about ruining the punch-line, but then Quinn caught my eye and smiled. She tapped Drake's shoulder, and he turned.

I'd underestimated the effect of my outfit on Drake. His eyes grew wide and hungry like when you dangled a piece of bacon in front of a dog. He bit his lip, stood, and walked over to me. With my five-inch heels, we were closer in height, and he didn't have to bend down far to kiss my neck and whisper in my ear, "You little tease. How do you expect me to get through dinner with you dressed like this?"

When his eyes met mine, I fluttered my eyelashes. "This old thing?"

I gushed inside. And outside, because my panties went moist involuntarily when I was this close to Drake, and especially when he kissed my neck right under my ear and that hot breath trickled down like smoke between my breasts.

He kissed my lips gently, only slightly less polite than one would find acceptable while standing in the middle of a restaurant. "God, I missed you. Ridiculous really, because we've spent more time apart than this." He leaned in again tighter, his body pressed against mine. "You're killing me softly, Maeve Lewis."

My lips could reach his collarbone, so I kissed it and looked up. "Behave."

But the truth was, I didn't want him to behave. Drake had no idea how his desire and blatant PDA shored up my

eroding confidence in us. Just as soon as this war between me and Quinn had started, he'd come home as *my* solider.

He took my hand and led me to the table. "You know Quinn, and this is Tae."

Tae stood, almost as tall as Drake, and he shook my hand. "Nice to meet you."

Quinn shook my hand as well, and when Drake pulled out the chair next to him, I took it like the princess he wanted me to be. This was one of Drake's most attractive qualities. He was sincere and himself beyond society's rules. Where I'd been taught that a restaurant was a place where one limited physical affection, he did what came naturally.

So many people would have limited the way they touched their partner in front of two new people, thinking more about making the newbies comfortable than about where their arms really wanted to be.

Meanwhile, Drake had shifted his chair close in to mine, and his arm draped around me like a toga. *This* was the best accessory in the world. It transformed the way I felt about myself more than any expensive silk scarf could. My love for him roared inside me, a fire not even a whole ocean between us could put out.

"Aw. Lovebirds," Quinn commented.

"Drake, you are one lucky man," Tae said.

"I'm the one who's lucky," I said, kissing Drake's hand on my shoulder. I'd never been more grateful for his affection. Not even at my dad's ceremony. Call me shallow, but reassurance was better than sympathy. "Anyway, it seemed like I walked into the middle of a fabulous tale. What were you guys talking about?"

"I was just getting excited about a song and talking about how I'd see the video being if we ever made one," Drake said. "It's so nice to bounce ideas off people again."

"Which song?" I asked.

"'Afterglow.'"

It shouldn't have, but my heart sank a little because it only felt like yesterday that was my song and my song alone. But it was such a great one. I knew he'd always planned on it being his biggest hit, and seeing Drake be so happy was amazing. It was a joyful part of him that I'd never seen before.

We'd been quite serious when we'd met at the festival. Sure, we'd danced like total dust devils and drank and made plenty of merry, but it was a time of grief for me, and Drake had mirrored that with his own loss of Jay and all his songs.

It was his turn for redemption. Drake had been the biggest reason I was able to pass through the valley of grief and see a new horizon. Now, he was almost at the top of his mountain, too, and he was high in every way. He was even more beautiful this way. A smile full of hope was more beautiful than anything I could ever dream up, and I promised myself in that moment that I would do anything to support that smile being there every single day.

I had to get over myself. I would get over myself. I wanted him to think of me the same way I thought of him—an angel. Drake was my angel, and I wanted to be his.

The three of them resumed their conversation, and I watched Drake animate, some wild artist throwing paint at an enormous blank canvas. "Afterglow" was a song about new love. It was about our week at Uyu. Naturally, the video he described had a guy and a girl in it, and the premise was that they'd do the things we'd done. There was a giant slide, a shower for two, bikes, pastries, RVs... the lovers swirled around at this festival, but no one else was there. The wonderment of whether or not they'd last was the point of the song.

Drake had told me he'd written this song on the way home from Uyu. When he'd told me about it, I'd been speechless. The way he'd dreamed all the same things I had inspired a feeling like no other I'd had before. It'd felt private and intimate. Like a confession.

Now everyone in the world would know about it, but they wouldn't know it was about us. It would be about their own unrequited love. Their own summer fling.

Drake finished talking about how he wanted all the inanimate objects in the video to become real. He spoke about the elephant sculpture we'd sat on and wondered if they'd ever have budget for a real elephant and if animal protection groups would make a stink online.

Tae and Quinn had plenty of ideas as well. I saw very quickly that Quinn didn't want to coattail. Though it was a good thing, it didn't make me like her more. Drake needed real partners, and I should have wanted his bandmates to have opinions. Tae was happy to be a backup guy, but not to be confused with one lacking talent or vision, he contributed, proposing musical changes to the song itself.

When they'd mostly completed the vision for the video, Drake turned to me and asked, "What do you think, doll?"

It meant so much that he'd asked. I hadn't expected my opinion to matter. Hell, I didn't even think I had a relevant opinion, but to be asked, to be included, and to be relevant, made this all a hell of a lot more fun. But also, during this whole conversation, I dreaded the idea of Drake being in the video and kissing another girl. Acting or not.

"I love it, but not so sure about having the couple in it?" I said, hoping nobody realized what I was actually thinking. "Maybe it's nicer if that part isn't so literal and you just have the metaphorical representation of things coming to life and lasting?"

Drake cocked a brow. "So you're saying you don't want to be in the video?"

"Me? What are you talking about?"

It was incredibly rare for bands to use anything but actors in their videos. It would be some dramatized, idealized version of me, with very likely Drake as the main. I wondered if he'd have to kiss a bunch of girls in the casting process.

"Yeah, you..." he said, turning his body toward me as if the others weren't even there. "You don't think I'm ever going to kiss someone else's lips again, do you?" He flicked my nose. "There has to be a kiss at the end of the video."

The only thing better than public displays of affection were public words of affection. Not only did my heart belt a high C like a goddamn opera singer, I had kitty flutters, my pulse raced, and my cheeks prickled with joy.

It was time to get out of here.

Thankfully, great minds thought alike. Tae told us to get a room, and we did.

Drake

MAEVE AND I EXCUSED OURSELVES, leaving Tae and Quinn with most of the sushi, but I didn't give a fuck because I was only hungry for one thing right now. As much as I knew it would be good for Maeve to get to know the guys more before I left, it would have made her more comfortable with my entourage, I had to have her.

We got into the elevator, and immediately upon the doors closing, I cupped her core and brought her into me. "I thought that would never be over," I growled softly.

She giggled. "It wasn't over. We just left in the middle of it."

With my hands on either side of her face, her soft hair and delicate skin cradled in my palms, I eased her lips just shy of touching mine and breathed her in. "Mmm. Cherries. Seems to me it's dessert time."

I kissed her sticky, sweet lips, wanting to devour them. Maeve's lips were almost always glossed or painted. Red matte lipstick when we were out and about, but she used a shiny, cherry gloss at restaurants. She had a thing for her lips being perfect, and I had a thing for them, too.

I stared at her with predatory intent, and she played coy in that elevator. Maybe just to drive me mad. Or maybe it was for decorum's sake as it was quite possible anyone could enter as we rose up the shaft, and I was certain even the way I stared at her would be enough to make anyone uncomfortable.

"The band seems to work well together," she said, her head still held by my hands, pretending to ignore the way I bored right through her clothes with my eyes. "Is it as good in the studio as it was working out that video concept?"

My brain barely comprehended the meaning of her words.

"Mmm-hmm." I kissed her lips. Her head still in my hand, I moved one to the small of her back to bring her closer and moved one around to the nape of her neck where I couldn't help but grab a handful of her sexy bob. I gave it the slightest but most noticeable tug, her head tilted upward.

Decorum was for people who were boring. I purred, "Are you saying what you're thinking or what you're supposed to say to keep my hands from clawing off your clothes in a public space?"

I inched in on her, and she forced her head back against my hand, arching her back slightly, pretending she wanted to keep a polite distance between us, but I knew Maeve. This was cat-and-mouse foreplay.

"Wasn't this whole evening about me getting to know the band?" She lifted a corner of her mouth and tried to move an inch further, the arch deepening, almost into a dancer's dip. She may have moved her face further away, but the motion only pushed her hips deeper into me.

I pressed my hand hard into the small of her back and forced her sex into me, my growing cock brushing up against her hip bone. Her body, firm and hot on my dick made my heart race. "They were bait. I really wanted to lure you into the hotel and up to my hotel room. They made me seem like a nice, innocent rock star, but really, I have bad intentions."

Ding.

The bell of the elevator told us the doors would open, and in the moment before they did, I ripped open the buttons on Maeve's shirt and tugged her bra aside, exposing her breast. She fell into the back wall, a surprised but wanting expression meeting my eyes, and I quickly pressed the "doors closed" button.

I undid my belt with one hand, then my top button, and drew down my zipper. Still holding the closed button, I tugged aside the flap of my jeans. "You want to have a little feel? See what cherry lip gloss does to a man?"

She heaved off from the back of the elevator, approached me confidently, as if she'd always meant for her breast to be on display; in fact, she tipped her chin slightly and straightened her shoulders, drawing them back, exposing it just enough to make my temperature rise.

She didn't touch me at first, just urged her entire body

into my side. Slowly, she ran a hand down my chest, along my abs, tickling my navel, and then into my pants, where right through my boxers, she took me into her hand. She cupped my dick, bunched up and desperate behind the cotton prison, and rubbed it, gently at first, then squeezed and kneaded my cock.

Fuck, I was getting hard. And it was getting hard to hold on to that button, too. But I held on for dear life when she knelt in front of me. She lifted my shirt and kissed above my boxers then ran her wet tongue along the top of them and tugged them down. My dick sprang out, thick with desire, and she took me into her mouth.

With my free hand, I braced the back of her head and urged myself deeper inside her, the wetness and heat of her mouth a sweet relief on my stiff cock. She sucked a bit harder, and I could have fucked the shit out of her face. I didn't have to, though, because she smoothed her mouth back and forth along my shaft, taking me in and out, in and out, somehow holding on to me with her lips so tightly it was driving me mad.

I watched her hair sway back and forth. "You like that, Little Fairy?"

She looked up, my cock still in her mouth, her glistening cherry lips driving me mad. She didn't stop sucking, but her large doe eyes made me crazy when it was clear they said "Yes."

Suddenly, two voices spoke outside the metal doors. Muffled words of annoyance and wonder as to why the elevator wasn't working.

Maeve kept pleasuring me with her mouth, seemingly oblivious to the hotel guests. I grabbed a handful of hair to stop her mouth fucking my dick.

"I'll finish this off inside you."

I tugged softly at her hair until my dick popped out of her mouth. She helped me stuff it back into my pants and zipped me up so I could keep hold of the door button while she put her beautiful breast back in her bra. She didn't bother to redo the buttons, the lace of her bra, confidently but obediently, waiting for my next move.

When I let go of the "door closed" button, the door slid open, revealing two guys our age. One made eye contact with Maeve. They both knew exactly what had been going on within a millisecond. The one with eyes on Maeve dared to smile at her with a dirty little smirk. She glared at him with her perfected "fuck you" look while I put my arm around her, and as we walked past his ear, I whispered, "Mine."

The hallway felt longer than it had yesterday. Each step a practice in self-control and thank fuck for key cards. The beep of the door opening and the sound of it closely loudly behind us blurred into white noise, and we ravished each other instantly upon entering the room.

Tugging at clothes, easing toward the bed, she swept her shirt overhead. Our eyes were locked as I eased down my jeans and boxers. She reached around her back and unclipped her bra. It fell open, and when she threw it to the floor, I felt ravenous for the milky skin that smelled like vanilla and tasted like ecstasy. She undressed quickly but left her panties on.

I liked to take those off. I had a million ways to do it.

I tugged my shirt over my head, and the cool air rushing out of the vents made my skin tense and my body pause. Maeve stood at the edge of the bed with the eyes I imagine Cleopatra had used to tame men.

One step.

Two steps.

I swept her into me, and my body warmed again, my dick pressed against her, hard and unrelenting, like steel, it was a wonder it didn't pierce her delicate skin. We held each other while I felt our hearts pump desperately between us with anticipation.

With our shoes off, she was once again only up to my pecs, her cheek caressed my torso. Her nipples were tight on my chest when she floated her breasts lightly along my skin, from side to side, easing them with the contact she craved.

She wanted me to pinch them. Bite them. Ease the tension in those little nipples, because for Maeve, it was as delicious a feeling as me licking her clit. She loved nipple play. It was one of my favorite games, too.

I smoothed a hand along her head, grabbed some hair at the nape of her neck, and tugged her head back so I could see her eyes. "Tell me what you want."

Her eyes were heavy with lust. "You."

"Say my name."

"I want you, Drake Jackson."

The sound of my name on her lips drove me mad. I picked her up under her ass; she wrapped her legs around me, and we kissed madly, deeply. I wanted to lick my name right off her tongue.

Taking her to the bed, I eased her down gently. She held on tightly, and when her back hit the bed, she didn't let go. My cock was hard on her thigh, and I pressed into it, giving me a moment of relief.

I wasn't playing any more games. Not even nipple games. I had to have her. I reached over to the nightstand and found a condom, then held it between my fingers. "You do it?"

Slowly, like a stalking tigress, she took the condom from between my fingers, opened it, and I'd never seen someone

so seductively play with latex. Her painted nails delicately grabbed the tip of the sheath and unfurled it into form. She bit her bottom lip like I was the most delicious thing she'd ever seen.

Before putting it on, she slowed down our entire pace. She kissed my thick cock with those shiny lips of hers. First, little kisses. Then pulling the smallest amount of me carefully into her mouth. My head fell back, and I moaned.

When I looked down, her big brown eyes were on mine, connected, as she slid the condom over my dick. Every millimeter was ecstasy as she rolled slowly, gently, until the very end when I started to wonder if I'd even make it inside her. She was a siren and she was totally killing me.

I eased her back down on the bed. She opened her legs for me, and I reached my hand down to spread open her sex with two fingers, using a third to find that precious clit of hers.

She sucked air in through her teeth, threw her head back, and closed her eyes. In this moment, she gave herself to me fully. I played with her clit, tickling, tingling ever so gently until she lifted her hips into me, wanting it harder. Wanting more from me. She was wet, slippery, and glistening with her juices.

I held her hand and slid it down the length of her body, taking it right to her swollen clit, and she took over, circling herself with two fingers, in circles harder than I would have as she spread her legs wider for me. An invitation to enter her soaked core.

It was a torture I loved but I took my cock in my hand and eased it in circles around her entrance. Watching her play with herself; I played with her, too. My dick throbbed. It was so thick now I could feel the pulse right through the tight skin. I went in and out, little by little, allowing only the

smallest bit further while she rose into me, urging me deeper inside. But I loved to watch. I loved seeing her get off, take herself to that place where she'd moan and not even know it.

"Deeper..." she whispered.

She didn't have to ask twice. I thrust myself into her, enjoying the hotness of her core. She clenched around me when I pushed deep inside, my ass forced firmly toward her. She circled her clit faster now, and I thrusted in and out, thinking of how close she might be. She took her fingers out and lifted them to my mouth. They smelled of her, my favorite scent in the whole fucking world, and I took them into my mouth, soaking them with more wetness, licking her cum like it was fucking ice cream.

She brought them back down to her clit, one hand desperately stroking herself, the other reaching around to push me in harder. My cock was huge with wanting, holding back for only her to pulse around me. With one big *smack* on my ass, I went for it harder, plunging deeper, reaching the deepest parts of her, my cock full...

That's when I felt it. Her body tensed and quivered, then a rush of cum from her pussy wet us both right onto my balls. It made me crazy feeling my balls slap against her ass, and I thrust faster than ever, insane with desire, until my dick exploded inside her, the sound of us coming filled the room, our orgasms pulsing against each other.

I slowed my pace but still felt the cum beating slowly through the entire length of my cock, until all that was left was a tingle, warm, emotional, and fulfilled.

I lay down next to her. My dick finally stopped pulsing, and I stroked my fingers along the small of her back, over the delicate humps of her ass. Her cheek rested on my chest, and we settled into a relaxing rhythm, breathing in tandem.

I loved this girl. I loved her more than I loved anything. It was the kind of love that you knew would never leave your soul.

Maeve was complicated, and though it was difficult, I wanted that. I wanted someone I could help work through problems and grow with. I didn't want a fully formed person. I wanted to be a seed in the ground with another seed.

This was that. Maeve and I were just starting our lives in so many ways. She'd been through a serious coming of age with her dad passing and having to become lady of the manor with her mom the way she was.

I, too, felt like everything before this was just me being a boy. Sure, I'd paid rent, but that didn't make you a man. Taking care of a woman made you a man. That's what I was about to do, and as I felt her soft skin on my stomach, her goosebumps forming under my fingertips, I knew this was my coming of age. Maeve was a rite of passage into the life I'd always wanted.

She suddenly drew in a sharp breath. The skin where her cheek lay grew moist.

"Are you crying, Fairy?"

She wiped my chest, but instead of clearing her tears, she just spread them around. Shit. For the second time since hearing about the tour, she cried.

She hid her face, burrowing into my skin as far as she could, which wasn't far. "Maybe a little."

I pushed myself up against the bed board. "Come here..." I pulled her up with me; she shuffled alongside me, and that's when I saw her eyes. A subtle pink lined her bottom lids. "Come on, girl... tell me what's going on. Talk to me."

"You already know."

I did know. And if I didn't have to stay so strong for her, I might have wanted to cry, too. I stroked her hair. Her eyes softened further, and she lowered her eyes, not wanting me to look inside too deeply. Not wanting to be too vulnerable.

"I'm sad, too," I said, lifting her chin. "But this dream coming true for me is nothing compared with *our* dream coming true. That's what this is about for me. I used to want this for myself. Now I want it for us."

Her voice cracked a little as she began to speak, and she cleared her throat. "I don't want to cast a mood over your moment. Honestly, Drake, I promised myself I wouldn't cry and I don't want to show you this selfish little part of me that wants you to stay. You deserve this to be pure and amazing and... perfect."

"Sometimes doing the right thing has unpleasant consequences. Your tears aren't the reason I'm sad. I'll miss you. You're my inspiration. Every fucking word I write now is about you or about us. Every time I'm doing something that isn't with you, I'm in a hurry to get to you. This will be painful for me, make no mistake. But songwriting lets me feel like I'm still with you when I'm not. You'll be with me no matter how far apart we are."

She pressed herself into me and wrapped her lithe arm around my chest, settling into the nook under my arm. "Well... if that's the way it is, then I guess in some way, we'll still be together."

She said this, and it all came out so logically, but we both knew she didn't mean it. My gut told me she was trying really hard to stay strong for me, and her trying meant the world to me. I'd been making an effort to surround myself over the years with people who cared about me as much as I did about them, and I knew I had that in Maeve.

"It won't be the same, right?" I asked, urging an actual

cure rather than a bandage. "I'm saying it, and you're thinking it. It won't be the same."

She smoothed her hair. Whenever she did that, it was like she got some special power. It always had a calming effect on her. Her voice came out a lot more resolved and a lot less emotional. "There's no use bringing that up because it doesn't change anything. There's only one way for you to pursue your career, and this is it. As much as I do want to talk about it, I don't. You know? It is what it is."

Her matter-of-fact statement was true, but it unsettled me. Suddenly, I felt clammy and hot inside, so I got up, wrapped a nearby towel around my waist, and walked to the window, peeking out at the Hollywood skyline.

This didn't feel right. It didn't feel necessary. And I couldn't agree that this was the only way we could go about things. I turned abruptly. "Just come with me, Maeve. I get it... I get that you don't want to call in a favor, so just quit your job altogether. I'll take care of you from now on. This contract is worth enough for both of us. We could have an adventure of a lifetime. A story to tell the grandkids."

I walked to the edge of the bed and sat, admiring her nymph-like body and baby-powder skin. "Saying yes is step one. I don't want to do this without you."

She inched herself up the bed and against the head-board, pulling the sheets up over her stomach, but her beautiful little nipples still teased me and looked like they'd say yes. Then again. They said yes all the time.

Her eyes wandered the room. From me, to the TV, down at the sheets, up to me again. She started to say something a couple of times without a single word coming out. Then, she sat there silent for another moment. Probably only a total of sixty second passed, but it felt like sixty years.

"Were you planning on saying yes today?" I asked, stroking her from neck to navel.

Nothing but more silence. This wasn't good.

I handed her a drink of water. She took a sip and put it back on the bedside table. "I... you know I'd love to, babe."

Shit. It's a no...

"You know I would. But it's not just about pulling favors. *My* dream, I mean, work wise anyway, is to one day take over my dad's company. I can't just spend my twenties off on tour drinking every night and shopping by day. I need to cultivate my skills. I have to stay."

"It's only eight weeks..." I protested but quickly stopped myself.

Her dreams were important, too. They were as critical to my happiness as my own. I didn't know what it took to run a billion-dollar company so who was I to assure her that it would still be there even after only eight weeks had passed?

I was pretty sure that it already belonged to her in some way, but Maeve was a very proud woman. She'd want to be a great leader. She'd want to grow the company and disrupt the market. She'd want to do more than go to board meetings and whatever it was that music execs did.

Plus, neither of us said it, but there was also the issue of Dixie.

I lay down and pulled her on top of me, aligning her body over mine, and for a moment I felt so overcome by sadness, enjoying her ghost-white body on mine for one of the last times before the world between us changed so dramatically.

It was painful to hear her say no. It was painful to leave. It was painful that I'd celebrate one of the most exhilarating times of my life with two people I met twenty-four hours ago.

It hurt like hell to do something so monumental without her by my side. I didn't give a shit about celebrating a big show with Quinn and Tae. I wanted to see Maeve's bright face when I came off stage, gather her up in my arms, and twirl her around like a helicopter. Like we had at Uyu.

Life had been much simpler there. I guessed life couldn't be simple for more than a week.

But I had to believe. Instead of telling her it was only eight weeks, I had to tell myself those words.

And as masochistic as it seemed, hurting was a sign of something valuable between us. After all, infatuation was measured in pleasure. Love was measured in pain.

So MANY TIMES in the past two weeks, I wanted to change my mind. I wanted to throw my career determination out the window, tell my brother to look after my mom, and let Drake pop a collar and leash around my neck to follow him wherever he decided we should go. Hell, there were points where I was so desperate, staring at his bright eyes on a cell phone, him only an hour away, where an overwhelming sense of us against the world took over.

But I'd never been that kind of girl. Even when I'd fallen in love in the past, I'd never let the guy know it.

Neither of us ever peeped a word after that night at the hotel. It would have been too painful to continue resurrecting the same shit over and over.

It was only eight weeks. Nothing on my end would change much in eight weeks. I was all good.

On the contrary, everything was changing for Drake in this eight weeks. I saw it turning and churning already because we spoke every night, lunchtime... every morning, even though I had to wake up at five instead of six because he worked from dawn till dusk.

It was the morning now, four weeks after I'd told him I wouldn't go on tour, which was a thousand and one reconsiderations and about a thousand more second-guesses.

He was almost leaving. This was the last day. Tomorrow, he'd be gone, and we'd be in head deep.

My alarm went off, and for the first time in my life, I didn't struggle one little bit to feel awake. Adrenaline pumped my heart, brain, and body into action, and I reached over, turned off my alarm, and pressed the button next to my bed, sending the blinds up to half mast.

We kept bragging about which one of us called first in the morning, which was the cutest but also most ridiculous challenge. I'd set my alarm for four forty-eight a.m. There was no light to speak of coming in from the window, and the birds weren't even chirping much.

All at once, I remembered waking up at Uyu next to Drake, thinking about how the birds always sounded out their dawn chorus here at our home. Now, the only thing to greet me was the night's silence.

It was natural, and I should have expected it, but it still made me sad. Talking to Drake from my sterile, dark, soundless bedroom felt like a stark contrast to his life, full of spotlights, music, and people.

I picked up my cell, and just as I was about to press the icon for FaceTime, my phone buzzed.

"You beat me to it," I answered.

Drake's cheek was squashed against a black satin pillowcase. I'd always think of Drake now and forever more whenever I saw a silky pillowcase. He'd had one at Uyu, he had one at the hotel... I had one for him at my house. His hair was very important to him, and I'd never get between a man and his good hair.

"Why aren't you wearing the scarf I sent you?" I asked, referring to a personalized do-rag I'd ordered online from a company I'd read about making luxury headscarves. Like I said, I was a big supporter of men and good hair.

"I took it off before calling you. What am I without my hair? I'm still trying to impress you."

"Put it on. Trust me, you could be bald and still be hot."

He lifted his brows like he might not do it.

"What?" I asked. "I want to see it on you. Why won't you put it on?"

He licked his lips and raised a brow. "I will, it's just... you know... never mind."

"What? Say it."

"I know all white people think we look like thugs with them on."

I was taken aback. This was the first time he'd mentioned race since we'd chatted about him dealing with it as a kid at Uyu. I wasn't exactly sure what to say. Tell him he wouldn't look like a thug? Say looking like a thug wasn't a bad thing? Plus, was Drake actually being insecure?

Before I responded, he said, "Knee-jerk reaction. It's early, and I went to bed late."

He reached next to him in the bed, wrapped the scarf around, and tied it. "Thanks for thinking of something like

this. I actually do have a black one but don't wear it when we sleep together." He finished tying it and held the phone far enough away for me to see.

His face did change. With his hair off his face, all I saw were those deep, brown eyes and fierce cheekbones. Luscious lips. "All I see is perfection."

He smiled, a closed-lip grin that made his lips look even more pouty.

I laughed lightly into the blue light of my phone. "I didn't think you'd always be able to have your pillow. Thought it might be easier to have something like that shoved in a satchel or backpack. You'll probably sleep on buses and planes and stuff, and I want every curl coming back to me intact. Course, I didn't realize you had one..."

"I love it, babe. It'll remind me of you when I'm home-sick." He laughed, and a dry cough came out with it. Dark circles shaded his eyes. His voice was rough and raspy. We'd said goodnight at nearly midnight last night.

This was going to be his life for the next eight weeks. Zero sleep, demanding, high-energy performances in spite of jet lag.

"Are you drinking enough water?" I asked. "I sent you that coconut water, too, and the kombucha. Try the kombucha instead of coffee for energy. It's less dehydrating."

He chuckled. "You've gone all doting girlfriend on me."

"I know. Look what you've done. I'm dicklashed."

He laughed bigger this time and pushed himself up in bed. "You'll never be dicklashed. I tried to be your sugar daddy, and you dissed me."

I smiled, and my heart was like a hot cocoa bomb dipped in steaming milk. I melted, and sweet feelings exploded inside my core. Having lived so rigidly, protectively, it was nice to just feel... soft.

Maybe he really didn't realize just how much he had the upper hand in our relationship, but every woman liked to feel the power of being in charge of some guy's soul.

"What do you have on today before we meet?" he asked.

"The usual stuff." I knew it wasn't a very good answer. It was one of those answers that didn't help keep the conversation flowing, but really, how many times could a person say they were reading contracts and getting sign-offs before that was just as boring as not talking at all?

I dreaded how that was going to play out in our long-distance texting, sexting, FaceTime relationship. Drake would likely feel the conversation was one-sided. But maybe it would be nice for him to have someone so interested. As he'd once said himself before, all too often when people were "listening" they were actually thinking of the next thing to say. I had nothing to say, so that made me a good listener.

"What about you?" I turned it around as I had been doing a lot lately.

"Actually, I'm so happy to have an afternoon out of the studio. Since they never have windows, it's like it's night all the time. I'll evolve into a vampire doing this any longer."

"Promise you'll make me one, too, if it happens?"

"Oh hell yeah. My one and only victim." He lifted his eyebrows.

The thought of him biting into my neck and sucking my blood made my skin tingle. "Don't make promises you can't keep."

"Have I ever?"

I shook my head with a ridiculous grin on my face. "Do you have plans for the day before we meet up? If not, I'll try and see if I can get off early and meet you at the hotel before

we originally planned? If I can?" I ended that last little bit as coyly as possible.

"If you can do that, I'm all yours. In the meantime, I do have plans for the morning but I'm not going to talk about that. I'll show you later." He ran his fingers through his hair. I couldn't wait to do that myself. "You actually going to show me the goods or what?"

He joked but didn't. Often, I'd let my boobs answer the phone call for a laugh, but I'd gotten caught off guard today.

"Dirty boy..." I propped my phone on the nightstand and turned on a lamp. I got out of bed and stepped back until my entire body was naked and in full view.

"That's what I'm talking about. Turn around," he demanded.

I turned, looked over my shoulder, and wiggled my butt.

"Mmm. That reminds me of that shower we took at Uyu. Reach down and touch your toes."

I spread my legs ever so slightly, then bent myself over to reach the floor, exposing the view that I wanted him to see but was glad I couldn't. Almost as soon as my fingers hit the floor, I pulled myself back up, ran to the phone feeling silly, and hopped into my bed.

I snuggled back into the sheets and asked, "Now where's my dick pic?"

"I'll give you a live later. Here's a sneak peek..." He hovered the phone over his chest and slowly ran it down his torso, the shadows hiding the exact mystery I wanted to uncover. The cell reached his hip bones and pubic hair. He lifted the sheet and gave me a very dim view of his dick.

"You tease," I said. "It's too dark to see anything."

He put the phone back on his face. "Oh, you really want to see, do you? What are you going to do when I show you?"

"Depends what you're doing with it when I see."

His eyes narrowed devilishly, and he reached over to pop on some more bedside lighting. "That better?" He moved the phone again, this time where I could see his cock on full display with his beautiful fingers wrapped around it.

I heard his voice but saw nothing but his hand on his juicy cock.

"Touch yourself," he said. "Imagine it's my fingers easing up and down you." His dick grew quickly while I watched him pump it. Eager veins forced blood into the shaft as he ran his hand up and down.

We hadn't really had phone sex before. Up until now, it had never seemed like something I'd be into. But with the thought of him leaving tomorrow, knowing that this might just keep things fresh and together for us, I reached down and felt even before my mind had decided I wanted this, my core did. I rubbed eager, warm, wet juices in circles over my clit and nearly moaned.

His voiceover continued, "Are you playing with yourself, Fairy?"

"Mm-hm."

"Good. Keep moving those wet fingers over your hard little clit for me. Tell me how wet you are."

"You know how I drip for you."

His hand stroked faster along his thick shaft, and he stopped pumping to run his palm along the tip. "Put your fingers inside. I want you to feel what I feel every time I ease mine inside. Every time my fingers are enveloped by you... I want you to feel what I feel. Put them in and give them a squeeze."

I eased my fingers inside and clenched my core, feeling pressure against my fingers. My pussy was smooth but tight, and I pushed two fingers in and out. It'd been a wonder that

his enormous cock could be devoured by such a small person until now. My core felt like it'd been doused with lube and WD 40, my fingers slid in and out almost without me trying.

"I wish it was you inside me," I whispered.

"Close your eyes. I'm there."

"I want to watch you come first."

His hand wrapped around his dick, he slid it up and down vigorously, and I pulled my fingers out to circle my clit in the same rhythm he pumped. He urged his cock on with more aggressive strokes.

His voice groaned. "Fuuuuck."

The timbre of it made me weak, and I circled my sex faster, willing myself to hold on to the edge of this ecstasy without cutting it too fast. His dick grew ever thicker, and then he exploded. Cum squirted out onto his fingers, and he used it to wet himself more, slowing his action but instinctively raising his hips toward where my pussy should have been.

My clit grew hard, and I closed my eyes and willed for him to be touching me. My imagination complied, and there he was. Touching me with his fingers... the heat and tickle, the heaviness... I finally released and pulsed onto my fingers. "Mmmmm..." I moaned so he knew I was there with him.

I closed my eyes and let my head hit the pillow as my clit shivered under my fingers. I held them gently over it, not wanting to end, thinking it might never, but then I heard him.

"Babe...?"

I hadn't been paying attention to where the cell was and realized he'd probably had a view of my shoulder.

I lifted the screen. "Sorry. I'm a novice. First timer."

His phone was on his face now, too. "Oh. You've never had phone sex?"

God. Had he?

"Me neither," he said before I answered.

Phew.

He continued. "We'll have plenty of time to get good at it."

"Yeah, maybe if this lawyering thing doesn't work out, I can start a hotline."

"Diversify those income streams, baby."

I chuckled softly and was glad to shake off the surprising embarrassment I felt. What the hell? It made no sense really. This guy had seen me turned inside out. He'd seen me touch myself before. Maybe it was the thought of doing it right. Of not being able to cuddle after and make up for any inadequacies or less-than-attractive spontaneous moans, screams, or groans. Phone sex felt very full display in spite of it being the total opposite.

I'd better get used to it.

My second alarm sounded. The one that told me playtime was over and I needed to get my ass to work.

Drake grimaced. "Already?"

"Yeah. But think of what progress we've made so early in the morning. We've had orgasms and embarked on new careers."

"Ha. We're industrious. So you think you can meet me early?"

"Hope so."

He took a deep inhale then let it out slowly. "Hard not to start missing each other before I've even left. You know?"

I knew. Because I hadn't started today. I'd started to miss him the first time I'd laid eyes on his tour contract.

THAT MORNING MASTURBATION session had been less of a release and more of a wind up. I'd felt relentlessly horny all day long.

Finally on my way to see Drake; he'd picked out a sushi place. I valeted my car and stepped inside with my highest high heels and my shortest skirt, my flirtiest eyeliner flicks, and my glossiest hair. This was the last time I'd see him for eight weeks. Or at least until we sorted out tickets to one of his US shows. He'd leave at the crack of dawn tomorrow, and I wanted an image of his girlfriend etched deeply in his memory so that nothing could erase me as his muse.

The host led me to a private table in the back where Drake stood when he saw me coming his way. He bit his fist then shook it out, letting me know my choice of outfit hit the mark. A few steps closer, and he took me in his arms, picking me right up off the floor with the biggest bear hug in the world.

He carefully put me back down, balancing me on my pins. Sliding the chair on the opposite side of the table around to his side so we could sit next to each other.

Drake always did that. Contrary to belief, you didn't need to be two feet opposite a person to make eye contact. He made dates feel like a snuggle in bed with room service. They were always intimate and felt so incredibly private as he was the master of shutting everything out of his view but me.

I was the luckiest girl in the whole world. I was sure of it.

"You have no mercy tonight, my Dark Fairy. I love your legs..." He swept a hand up and down my bare thigh, and I

wondered for a moment why we weren't getting room service right now. Perhaps because I'd only seen Drake in his hotel for the past of couple weeks.

Yearning as I was, it was nice to be out on the town. It made everything seem normal again.

"This old thing?" I asked. "I save some things for best."

"Oh, I'm best, am I?" His lips met mine, warm and soft as ever, smelling like coconut lip balm and mints.

I'd dared myself tonight to be more verbal with my feelings. I needed to lay it all on the table. There was no use holding back, which probably came across as playing coy half the time. I had to let Drake know exactly where I stood.

It was scary. Scarier than letting him see me cry about my dad. Scarier than letting him see the tears over missing him. That was skydiving scary.

Telling someone you thought they were "The One" was next level. For me it was comet-heading-toward-Earth scary. Shark-attack scary. Hannibal-Lector scary.

But all of those things multiplied weren't as frightening as the possibility of losing Drake. And maybe even worse, him not thinking I loved the hell out of him before he left.

All day, I'd been distracted by thoughts of him being surrounded by beautiful women, and this all shifted into other things like plane and bus and car crashes. Anything could happen while he was gone, and I wasn't letting him walk out the door without knowing not only that I loved him but that he was my person.

I returned his kiss, kneading into him, then created just enough distance for him to see my eyes. "You know you're the best."

"But do you know that?" He cocked a sideways smile.

"Best implies there are others." I ran my fingers through his hair. "You're the only one for me. So that makes you gold,

silver, and bronze. You take the entire podium." I looked down then back at his eyes that concentrated, surely wondering where my gushing came from. But I went on. "In fact, I've called off the entire competition now."

"Oh, have you now?" He kissed my cheek.

"Yes."

It felt childish coming out of my mouth, but Drake embraced me and squashed me against him. "That's the nicest thing you've ever said to me." He let me go. "Going off to war has an effect on people, eh?"

"I know I don't say I love you enough. Or tell you how important you are to me."

"Wow." He nodded gently. Licked his lips. Squinted one eye while contemplating what to say next. "So you're saying I'm it then? You're gonna stick with me?"

I leaned in closer and placed a hand on his cheek. "Through thick and thin."

"I'm not the kind of man who needs a lot of reassurance, but it's still nice to hear it."

He bent down and picked through a shopping bag he had sitting next to him. "I got you a present."

He lifted a wrapped box, and I took it. It was dense, heavy, and not jewelry.

"You didn't have to get me anything."

"It's nothing big. But I think it will come in handy. For both of us."

The server came over, and Drake ordered a bottle of champagne and two chef's choices and rushed the server away.

"It's a bit of a nuisance being in public when I want to ravish you, but we need to celebrate."

"We do," I agreed.

He pointed at the gift. "Open it. Go on..."

I grinned as I picked at the edges of an abundant amount of sticky tape on the rough wrap job he'd obviously done by himself. Drake was such a man, one so large and in charge, oozing in self-confidence; seeing these childish creases and overuse of tape was that boyish part of him I adored just as much.

When I finally picked through it, it was a box of cards. I read the packaging. "'What's your love language?'..." I looked up, not understanding. He got a card game?

He tapped a finger on the box. "Maybe instead of thinking of this time apart as a bad thing, we can use it to get even closer. I want to know everything about you, Maeve. I was actually thinking that maybe by us talking, you know, not in person, maybe it would be easier for you to tell me those things you keep hidden but I know are there. Open it. Let's do one now."

I unwrapped the cellophane and opened the box of laminated cards with questions and flicked through to find one appropriate for the occasion.

"No!" He interrupted. "Cheating. Just take the top one. So I was thinking, you take half the deck and I take half. Every time we talk, while I'm away, we each draw the top one from our pile and just, you know, get to know each other better. The old-fashioned way. Talking."

My cheeks were starting to hurt. I hadn't realized just how hard I'd been smiling since I'd got here. Nobody wanted a goodbye date, but as far as they go, this was going better than I could ever have expected.

My lord, Drake was perfect. I didn't deserve him.

I pulled the top one from the deck and read it silently, then threw my forehead into my hand.

"What?" he asked. "Come on, read it out loud."

I straightened up. "Okay, our first love language question is: what memory makes you smile most?"

"Oooh. That's good," he said, his eyes moving away, him starting to think, but they soon snapped back. "No cheating and saying something that happened between us either. This is a getting-to-know-you thing. So it has to be like, lived experience, stuff before we happened, okay?"

"Okay. Fair enough." I thought for a moment. "I have to admit I'm a pretty lucky girl because quite a few have come to mind. But one that makes me really smile, I'm going to sound like a show-off now, but my dad started off as a manager and scout in the music industry before my mom got her inheritance, and he started Reckless Integrity.

"Anyway, he went back home to visit his family in Boston, he was from the East Coast, and he found a band on a night out with his brother. He got them some representation at the company he worked for, and I mean, I don't understand all the details, of course, I was like, twelve, I think? Yeah, twelve."

My body came alive as my nerves tapped into this magical experience, layers deep in my psyche. Drake propped his elbow on the table, his head in his hand, and listened, his pearly-white teeth shining on me like a spotlight for my moment.

"Anyway, the band, which ended up being 'Salem'..."

"Salem! Your dad discovered Salem?"

"Yeah, but that's not the point..."

"Of course. Sorry. Do go on..." he said, with a clipped British accent.

I laughed.

"Anyway, it was clear these guys were going to be big. My dad's first diamond find. So before everything went mental, before they had anything huge happen, my dad invited me,

my mom, and my brother to the studio to hear their new single come together. Our family listened on the other side of the glass as the band recorded, and we all burst out spontaneously in dance."

I stared away into the expanse of the restaurant but didn't see any of it. My memory brought visions of that day back like we were still in the studio.

"I waved my arms wildly, my dad did his digging, pointing-to-the-ground dance, my mom had her arms in the air. Tyran was only little, and he jumped up and down on a couch that was in the control room. We just all went crazy hearing this amazing sound, a song nobody had ever heard before."

I met Drake's gaze, and he soaked in my story with his warm eyes.

"I was young, but I remember that it felt like this life-changing moment in history. The song just felt special, you know? We all knew it, and in the middle of the song my mom grabbed all our hands, and we danced around in a circle like a crazy tribe. It was one of the most natural moments of happiness we'd ever shared as a family."

"Totally unexpected and not curated," Drake added.

"Yeah, exactly. Unlike Christmas, where my mom had made everything so perfect. Or a vacation where our itinerary was exciting but well researched... yeah... exactly that. It was a moment of pure, spontaneous joy. It might have been one of the last times I really, really felt like a kid, too."

Drake swept his thumb from the corner of my mouth across my cheek with such affection I leaned into it.

"This one really does make you smile. Not just any smile either. Seeing this one, Maeve? I want to make this happen for you every day."

"You do. You do make me smile every day."

"No... this is different. I won't belittle this smile by pretending it's the same as every other. One day, I'll make you smile like this, and you'll feel it. And you'll know. You'll think to yourself—Drake was right. This smile is different, and it's back again."

I looked down. A sudden urge to cry came over me. I needed him to say these things before leaving. I wanted him to offer me this security, but it made it so much harder, too. I took a deep breath and met his eyes.

"I fucking love you," I whispered then mustered a voice a bit louder. "I love you because I know you mean that."

He kissed me and whispered on my lips, "I do mean it."

I could have melted into a puddle of sweet, sticky love. How did I get here? How did I deserve him? Deserve this?

I kissed him. "So what's yours?"

He looked into his head, his eyes shifting from side to side. "One of my go-to memories that makes me smile? I do have a few because Mom loves to laugh... but first one that comes to mind?" He pondered.

I pointed at him. "You're smiling now. That's the one. Go..."

"Yeah..." He beamed from ear to ear now, in part from the memory, in part at me and my girlish excitement for his story. This was fun. It was light. It was the foundation that love could live on for a lifetime.

"So, it was Mother's Day coming up. And I'd felt kind of bad because they'd had a Mother's Day sale at school where you brought a few dollars and brought something home for Mom from like a PTA sale or whatever. I was nine and asked my mom for money because obviously I didn't have any of my own really. She told me, don't worry, you're the best present I could ever have."

"Sweet."

"Yeah, but I still felt bad when I saw the other kids taking home chocolates and 'Best Mom in the World' keychains and stuff. I actually remember feeling annoyed that their moms would have that keychain when mine was actually the best."

I giggled. "That's actually hilarious."

His face lit up. "I know... you really don't even know how annoyed I was." He laughed. "I nearly wanted to pop this kid named Toby in the face when he said I didn't bring anything home because I didn't love my mom."

"That's nasty."

"Kids are all sort of fucked-up nasty sometimes."

I nodded.

"Anyway, I vowed to make my mom's day special so, do you remember those cassette tapes? I'm sure your parents had some."

"Mm-hmm."

"My mom had some blank tapes and a stereo shoved under her bed, and I dug it out when she wasn't around and did a beatbox background and made up a song for her. On Mothers Day, I did the usual toast and stuff in bed for her and then performed this 'Best Mom in the World' song to my backtrack. She cried, but like, tears of joy, of course, and pulled me into bed with her, and we watched movies and ate junk food all day, and she didn't work once that day. We left all the dishes in the sink and just... relaxed. But you know, I look back on that and just smile and think we really don't need much to show a person we love them."

"I wouldn't call that nothing," I gushed. "Every woman wants a serenade."

"Hold up. I should correct the story. It wasn't some fully fleshed-out song. It was like ten lines of bad rhyming and beatboxing that sounded more like spitting. But my mom

just stayed in bed with me all day. I felt so good thinking I could take care of her, too. It made me feel like a man for the first time ever, and I always wanted that. Even from a super young age, like seven, I wanted to be in that role. And we watched some funny-ass movies, too. Just makes me smile thinking of that."

Our drinks came, followed by our sushi in quick succession.

We drank and laughed and cuddled loads and then went back to his hotel for epic sex. It wasn't easy to say goodnight, and neither of us slept a wink.

He left at four in the morning, kissing my shoulder and lips for the last time for weeks. He left the box of cards on the bed next to me, and when I picked it up and shook it, only half the deck sounded out into the emptiness of its missing half.

That was pretty much how my heart felt.

Half empty.

Drake

As I settled into my seat on the plane, I realized that just a little over two weeks ago, I'd never been out of the country and didn't even know about visas or the exact time zone difference between London and Munich. Not that I needed to know any of that now. My tour manager, Vanessa, was all over the details and told me I should get all the rest I could and just leave everything but the performing to her.

I wasn't used to letting other people be in charge of where I was when, what I ate... not that I was the most particular person. I was definitely one to go with the flow

most of the time, but even on day one I noticed my gut unsettled being so out of control. Though I'd been taught as a child to always be self-sufficient, Vanessa's huge, overflowing binder of paperwork was a heavy load, so I sat back and focused on the songs, some of which were new, and of course, getting closer to my bandmates.

Crowds could tell when a band wasn't gelled, and unlike some reality show where we were put together over an eight-week period where people rooted for us while a big-time producer forced us toward stardom, we were supposed to deliver on day one.

Tae and Quinn, coming from entertainer stock, got this, so they made massive efforts with me and were super-hard workers. None of us had taken our fingers off the pulse since we'd met.

Quinn raced onto the plane, into the aisle, flustered as if she'd thought she might not make it. She had shopping bags hanging off her shoulders and she brushed some hair off her forehand, read the numbers, and made her way toward me. We weren't big enough yet for RI to get us a private plane. At that, the rushed departure had us seated in economy. Not that I'd expected anything more.

Quinn had a lot more hold luggage than I'd ever been able to afford. She furrowed her brow, still searching for her seat, making her way further to the back. She had a glow about her, and it wasn't just the white halo of hair. Passengers watched her pass, one guy lifted an eyebrow and flared his nostrils, a young woman watched Quinn carefully when she passed, then nudged her friend to look, too.

Maybe they'd recognized her from somewhere. Whether they did or whether they didn't, Quinn was someone you'd either seen before or wanted to see again. She had "star" written all over her tall, skinny butt.

"Hey," she said, catching my eye. "Is this our row?" She flicked her head toward Tae in hello.

He sat in the other window seat of our aisle next to a crew member.

I nodded, and she shoved her things under seats and in the overhead, then plopped down in the aisle seat of my row. "Oof. Glad I made it. I'm a duty-free whore. I did actually miss a plane once."

Vanessa plopped down in the aisle and leaned over to Quinn. "Next time I'll pop you on a leash, Quinn Hartley." She spoke to me, pointing at the perpetrator. "It was like rounding up a piranha."

I chuckled.

"What?" Quinn challenged, one second away from a head wobble. "Don't tell me you don't like to shop. You *look* like you like to shop."

I blew air out of my nose. "I'm a binge shopper. Like, if there's a special occasion or a festival or something, I get everything I need then don't get anything for a long time. I've never had enough cash flow to do it otherwise."

"You needed a sugar mama," she joked.

"Is that who bought you all this? Your sugar daddy? Or mama? No judgment."

"No, just my real daddy. I'm a totally spoiled only child. Just laying it out there."

"Is that you being self-deprecating?"

Quinn smoothed her long blonde hair behind her and clicked on her seat belt. "Drake, this is the first time I've ever flown economy. Self-deprecation? Not in my vocabulary. It would make me an absolute prick, trying to be humble. I'm rich. Not a jerk. I understand what I've got and have always been appreciative."

I had to admit that I'd never have normally gravitated

toward someone like Quinn in real life. Yeah, she was funny, but she was super showy, and I didn't usually like people who needed all eyes on them.

But she had a huge likability factor somehow. And she'd hit that nail right on the head. She was rich, privileged, and spoiled, and she wore it on her sleeve like a glamorous Cartier bracelet that you were dying to admire. She owned that and everything about herself. She wouldn't apologize but didn't pretend to deserve it.

The juxtaposition of her glamour and gutter talk was fun, and I'd seen right away she wasn't one to be too serious.

"So this is your first time in economy?" I asked. "What do you think of the fact that this is my first time abroad?"

"Is it really?" She was slightly surprised.

"Yeah. The closest thing I've ever done to being out of the States was Nakiki. Little US territory by Hawaii."

"That does sort of feel like going abroad, though."

"It does. Especially since all my friends there are proper islanders. But I'm not kidding anyone. I'm an international virgin."

"Oh. Say that a little louder. That's the mating call for the elusive sugar mama."

"Good to know, but not my style."

"Course not. I didn't take you for a beta. You have alpha written all over you."

"I'll take that as a compliment."

The plane caught wheels on the runway and screamed forward. I watched out the window and watched the pavement go blurry, then felt that tingling sensation of rising off the ground. Just then, Quinn's hand was on my arm.

I turned to see her with her eyes closed. "I've flown a thousand times and I still hate this part."

I wanted to pull my arm away. That was Maeve's arm

only. But Quinn had genuine terror on her face, and she swallowed as if some bile had made its way up her throat, so I waited until we leveled out then subtly inched back by reaching down and adjusting a zipper on my backpack.

Quinn seemed like the kind of girl who flirted with everyone, and therefore, no one really mattered, which I was pretty sure included me. But I wasn't one to send mixed messages.

She wasn't Jasmine or Flick or Helena. One of my Uyu girls Maeve would have understood; they were just friends, and we'd been giving each other platonic hugs long before Maeve ever showed up. But this was new, and I didn't think letting Quinn be touchy-feely, even if it was just in her nature, would do anything for Maeve trusting me.

I had to be careful. I didn't think Maeve was the jealous type, but she was emotionally raw still. The dust hadn't really settled yet. I couldn't begin to imagine how long it would take to feel and function one hundred percent normally after losing a parent. I shuddered to think of it; my mom had been my everything.

Thank God I had Maeve now, too.

And Maeve had me. I'd be back before too long and I'd take care of her.

Quinn opened her eyes again, took some fizzy water out of a Gucci-branded shopping bag, and had a glug. "Shit. Sorry about that. You wouldn't believe I love roller coasters. Sometimes I wonder how this is any different... every time I take off, I pretend I'm on one. Doesn't work. How can you not feel nervous?"

"I just look out the window and get curious."

She smiled but with a curious sideways nod of her own. "And that works? Getting curious? Or do you just not have flight anxiety? It's one of the two, more likely the latter."

I shrugged. "Maybe. I feel it more when landing. That's when I think about the bad shit. Not going up."

"It's always coming down where it hurts like a bitch, eh?"

I caught her double entendre. "Ha. Exactly."

She bumped into my side with her arm. "Well, we can hang on to each other. I'm bad both ways."

She took some lip gloss out of her purse and smoothed it on slowly, still examining me. When she finished, her shiny lips smiled that crooked smile. "I'm really glad you ended up being so... nice?" She closed an eye and thought, then corrected herself. "No. Not nice, that's generic. You're an original... I'll think of something better."

"Don't worry. I don't survive on compliments. But it's a bonus your expectations were exceeded. Then again, sounds like they were pretty low."

She chuckled. "Not at all. How could I have low expectations of someone who became an overnight sensation? I couldn't do it. And I have a daddy who was a member at Mitch Lewis' golf club. So I've met a few overnight sensations if you know what I mean."

I stiffened. I got it. Quinn was a jokester and made clever quips, but at the mention of Maeve's dad... I didn't know what it was. Kind of like that feeling when your religious grandma tells you not to take the Lord's name in vain. Then you wonder if you should talk about Him at all.

So I didn't. But she noticed the shift in my body language.

"Sorry. I didn't mean to make light of Mitch or anything."

"I know."

She shifted subtly in her seat. I didn't know anything could make Quinn squirm. She came across so confident, but a short silence unhinged her. So I filled it.

"I can't explain it, but just felt a little weird to hear his name in such a casual way."

"Oh..." Quinn paused, and in that beat, I noticed she wasn't a total narcissist. Her face softened, and there was even a hint of awkward there. She changed the subject. Sort of. Unbeknownst to her, it wasn't the biggest segue. "How exactly did you meet Maeve? I mean, you're from Seattle, right?"

I threw my head back, and when I came back to level, I couldn't help but smile. I'd tell her the good part. "We met at Uyu. Know it?"

"Course. Everyone knows Uyu. Especially since celebrities started going."

I lifted my brows and tried not to roll my eyes. Celebrities had brought the gawkers to Uyu, ruining it just a margin from previous years. But then again, maybe I'd soon be one of those celebrities who "ruined" the anonymity of Uyu. Irony sucked. "Well, that's where I met her."

"Oh. Summer fling that actually lasted. Nice..."

"I can tell you it felt anything but a summer fling."

"They never do."

I wasn't giving her any more. "Right you are. They never do at the time."

Quinn studied my face carefully, and though she was a good listener, definitely considered her next word as I said mine. She was emotionally intelligent and socially adept. I didn't want to keep a distance from her. I wouldn't forever. I was sure we'd become good friends through this whole thing, but equally... I had to perfect the subtle art of "we're only friends and I can't let my girlfriend think anything's going on even though I want to be close to you—as a friend." It was a complicated thing to execute on.

It didn't matter if I knew we were only friends. Maeve

had to know it, too. And by the sassy smile on Quinn's face, that again I was sure she offered everyone, still, I had to make sure she knew it, too.

"You're right," I said. "Summer flings feel real at the time. This one made it through summer, and it still doesn't feel real sometimes. Not that I haven't made up my mind about her. Just that, it's still that good. You know?"

"So, Drake, are you one of those people who think a love affair can last forever?"

"You say it like you don't?"

"I dunno. Just watching my parents and the couples that lived around us in The Colony? Seemed like everyone was cheating or getting divorced. My parents were no different. I overheard my dad when I was younger, right before my parents split. He was talking to someone on the phone and told them his marriage counselor said when marriage began being a thing, people only lived for thirty years."

I scoffed. "What kind of fucked-up marriage counselor is that?"

"An honest one."

"Oh, so you don't believe people can stay together for like, fifty years? But we see it all the time."

"Yeah, and people stay alive for a while after having their heads cut off by a guillotine, too. We can survive anything, but being happy? I don't know. Anyway, I don't want to be too serious. We're off to rule the world. I'm sure Alexander the Great wasn't talking about this kind of shit before conquering."

I nodded but had actually been enjoying the conversation.

She lifted her eyebrows. "You're a serious kind of guy, huh?"

"Yeah. It's a comfort zone."

"I have to say, it's kind of refreshing. Men just aren't like that."

"The men I know are."

She smiled and smoothed the long ends of her hair with her fingers. "Greatness attracts greatness?"

"Pzzt. I wouldn't say that."

She had a glint in her eye that I wished I hadn't put there.

"I would definitely say that." She blinked, and thank fucking God, the glint was gone. "You'll have to introduce me to one of these serious men one day."

I tipped my head back then met her eyes with a smile. "Sure, how should I make the introduction? Here's Quinn. She doesn't believe in forever but she's good for a year or two?"

She laughed. "You're serious and 'nice' but you can be a little fucker, too, huh?"

I shrugged.

"You're not trying to make a romantic out of me, are you, Drake?"

"I take people as they come, Quinn. You said it. Not me."

She bumped into my arm again. "I'm sitting next to Tae next flight."

THAT DAY, I'd found myself hanging around the break room and making inconsequential small talk with my coworkers. That was the first sign.

I'd read the labels at the supermarket. The second sign.

At said supermarket, I'd asked the cashier if they'd tried the gluten-free donuts I was about to buy and did they like them... that was the third.

Only one week after Drake had left, it was official. I was in a hole of loneliness.

Before I'd gotten there, I'd thought it would be just me,

but I now knew there were a bunch of other people just like me who settled for idle chatter just to not think about something else.

I had so much going on in my life, it shouldn't have been like this. I wasn't some pathetic girl who waited and pined for a man. I was a determined career woman with a plan.

And an alcoholic mother. Which was making this all the more difficult.

I just wanted Drake, my security blanket and sweet relief back, and this was the first time in my life when I realized why, since the dawn of time, people partnered up. Whether it was two straight or gay people or a polyamorous family, we were creatures hardwired to want variety only while peeping out from the cradled arms of certainty.

We could handle waking up in a tornado only if our house hadn't blown away.

Thankfully, I had my brother now. It was weird now to think back on how my parents used to interrupt our torrid arguments and say how we'd love and need each other when they were gone. I thought it had been a dramatic attempt at conflict resolution, but it was the total and utter truth.

Tyran had sensed my sadness at our first Sunday dinner without Drake and told me he'd take me out for a siblings' date. I'd bitten his arm off. Tyran lived in Hollywood and had started dating vegan girls, so naturally, he'd asked me to a steak place. When I walked in, before I spoke to the host, he waved me over from a table.

I took off my jacket and placed it across the back of my chair. "So, you're a secret eater. Does Natasha know you've sacrificed a cow today?" I sat.

"Don't even go there. Nat is no longer. But I have been hanging with Sheetal, and she's Indian so... just as bad on

the cow situation. One day I'll get a mail-order bride from somewhere they eat real food."

"Or you could just convert. Go veggie. It's good for the environment."

He looked at the menu then up at me. "I've been saying this is my last steak for a long time, trust me. I'm a junkie who keeps saying it's the last hit."

I skimmed the menu but already knew I wanted ribs. While Drake was gone, I was going to eat all the disgusting, dirty foods that made you feel like a slob while eating them.

I sighed. "So speaking of junkies..."

"Don't..." Tyran put his menu down and stared at me with a parental disciplinary gaze. "Don't say that."

"Okay, not the nicest segue, but we do need to talk about Mom. She is *not* okay."

"Of course she's not. None of us are. We're all self-soothing the best we can."

"Tyran, she's an alcoholic. We need to talk about this at some point. You're captive for a five minutes, so I'm doing it now."

He put his menu back up but had trouble focusing and slapped it back down on the table. "I don't know what's worse. You ruining my first steak in a month or you calling our mom an alcoholic."

"She is, though."

"It takes years to become an alcoholic."

"It doesn't, you know. Have you researched this at all?"

Tyran inhaled deeply then let it out loudly. "No. But you did, so let me have it." A hint of his old, passive-aggressive eye roll threatened to take over, but he stopped himself.

"Okay, do you want to know why I actually looked into it? Why I even called Doctor Sobel?"

He slapped his menu down. "You called our family

doctor? Maeve, that's crossing the line. This is Mom's privacy here..."

"Hear me out. Things are not good, Tyran. They're really not good."

"You better not be overreacting." The eyeballs made it out for a jaunt around the block.

"You decide if I'm overreacting..." I pulled back from getting defensive and getting into a teenage tiff. We needed to talk about Mom, not compete for the upper hand.

I took a deep breath. "A few weeks ago, I asked Mom if she wanted to go for a long walk up the coast and get some lunch at Vito's. She was up for it. I could see she wasn't doing that great at one point in the walk, so we stopped to take in the sights and have a seat for a bit, have a drink. When she put her bottle down off her lips..."

It was hard for me to say the next part. It hurt to think this had happened. "She had vodka or something in her water bottle, Tyran. I smelled it on her breath... she was drinking *al-co-hol* on our fucking walk up the coast in the middle of the day."

The shock on Tyran's face was more than I'd thought it would be. It was soon replaced by defensive mechanism. "Are you sure?"

"I'm sure. Not a shadow of a doubt."

He ran his fingers through his hair and ruffled it with frustration. He closed his eyes and rubbed his fingers in the sockets in circles. Without opening them, he just let out a long, moan. "Fuuuuuuck."

"Fuck is right." I took a sip of water, trying to send the knot down my esophagus. "The longer we let this go on the worse it will be."

"Let it go on?" He now eyed me and smiled, but it wasn't

a friendly one. It was one of those cynical, *you're dumb as shit* ones. "You think we have control over this?"

He shook his head quickly, annoyed.

I remembered this wasn't the first time Tyran had seen addiction. His best friend in high school had been in and out of rehab a few times.

"No. I'm not saying we have control, but she will care what we have to say."

"Pzzzzt."

"Stop it, Tyran! She's not Luke."

His eyes met mine, and a storm of emotions passed like cloud over a clear-blue sky. For the first time ever, I saw in his face that he must have battled hard for Luke. I remembered his concern. He'd spoken to our parents about it. I eased off, knowing how hard it was for him to think this.

"Sorry, I didn't mean to be insensitive," I said.

"Being sensitive isn't something we can afford right now anyway."

I hadn't expected that comment, but he'd really grown up. What a fucking man he'd become. Almost overnight he was easy to talk to, strong, resilient, and considered. Maybe he'd been this way for a long time but just hadn't bothered to show this side to me. I was so happy to have this brother now. I needed this brother now.

"I know it's hard to talk about this, but don't you think there's something we can do?" I almost begged. "We have to be able to help her somehow. Maybe we should remind her that she's all we have..."

"You can't guilt someone with dependency. It makes the problem worse."

"That makes sense. What do we do then?"

My brother's handsome face was suddenly replaced by some fifty-year-old professional psychiatrist's as he walked

me through the plan. "First, we support her positively. Nonconfrontational conversations seeing if she'd like some help. Just telling her what we notice but be careful to stay positive. If that doesn't work, we'll have to do an intervention eventually. But let's hope it doesn't come to that. Ultimatums are hell."

In law school, I learned that the Latin word ultimatum meant "the last." It's the final proposition in negotiation that, if rejected, leads to a break off in negotiations.

I couldn't even begin to imagine breaking off communication with my mom. More so now than ever, but even before. Family was everything. I believed this right down to the very last nucleus of my innermost cell. "Surely we'd never have to go there with Mom."

"We would. Why the hell do you think I've not brought this up before, Maeve? This is not going to be fun. The best we can do is hope that she'll see for herself that she needs help. We're going to have to be careful. Dixie is dynamite in her best of times."

He thought to himself for a moment, and a server came over to take our order. When she walked away, he said, "Why don't we sign up for a charity walk or something?"

I shook my head, not seeing where he was going with this.

He continued, "Mom loves charity, right? We'll find one of those fifty-mile things and then we'll need to get miles in, right? So we'll both ask her to go on walks a lot. She went with you once, she'll go again. It's terrible to say, but if she's drinking this much, she's probably worried about her weight."

Fuck. That sounded bad, but it also sounded true. Dixie was vain.

"Eventually, the alcohol thing will come up again, but

we can frame it positively, encourage her to exercise, see how the conversations go like that. Keep it as light-hearted as possible in the early days, because I'm telling you, Maeve, if you use the A word with her, this is not going to go down well. I promise you."

"So our plan is to walk our mom?" I asked, doubtful. I had my mom's blood in my veins. I was one to blast a hole, not dig it. "Are you suggesting getting healthier will reduce her dependency? You did hear my story about the vodka Chilly's bottle, right?"

"She won't stop. But it will come up naturally. One of us can suggest she go see Doctor Sobel. She might do it. And that could be our saving grace. Or her saving grace. If we can get her to him..."

"She believes everything he says," I added wishfully.

Tyran nodded. He lifted two hopeful, glossy black eyebrows. "It's most likely going to be a process, Maeve. Don't expect anything to happen anytime soon. It's a good thing you live at home, too."

Until now, I hadn't thought about my needs one time in this conversation. Who would? This was about Mom and her health. But suddenly, Tyran mentioning me living at home made me think of Drake again. It made me think about living with him and adulting with my man.

In seven weeks, he'd be back, and he'd have a completely different financial situation... we'd have missed each other so much and hopefully grown closer. Those silly little questions at night were actually bringing us together like that strange love and marriage show where people didn't see each other before getting engaged but just talked through a wall.

This dashed every dream I'd been holding on to that had got me through this awful first week with him away.

I'd imagined Drake coming home and sweeping me off my feet, carrying me over a threshold of a new house, and giving me a key. This thing with my mom wasn't going to resolve between now and then.

I'd even changed my mind about going away with him if he asked again. It wouldn't ruin my career, just extend the path to where I wanted to go. I'd decided life was about detours, and sometimes, when you took them you actually ended up on the scenic route.

I wanted to take the scenic route with Drake. But now... I was stuck in a traffic jam. It felt impossible to move on with my life while all this was going on, and like Tyran had said, it was a good thing I was still living with Mom.

What would she be like when no one was watching?

Tyran changed the subject to the very one I was already on. "How's Graphic Temple doing? I'm following them on social. They look like they've been together for ages. Is it just for camera, or does he think it's going to stick?"

"Drake doesn't really think like that. He doesn't wait for things to work or not. He's the driver, not in the pit. Even if he hated these guys, he'd make them all come together as one big dysfunctional family."

"Yeah, he's a winner. But is that where he's at?"

"No... thankfully, he likes them both."

He searched around for the server, undoubtedly hungry after all this heavy talk. "Unreal that Quinn's in the band. Hope she's changed. She was a bit of a bitch in high school."

"I could hug you for saying that." I shouldn't have been so mean-spirited, but it felt good to know someone in the world knew where my apprehension came from.

"Why do you say that?" he asked. "You're not jealous, are you?"

"Have you seen her lately? She's changed, and most people would say for the better."

"Drake would never go there anyway, so it doesn't matter if she's hot or not. I know it's hard, but one piece of advice? Control that urge to talk shit about her."

"I don't want to talk shit about her..."

Tyran eyed me suspiciously. He didn't believe me for one second. Hell, I didn't believe me.

"I really don't actually... well, I *won't* anyway. I'm reminding myself Drake has been surrounded by beautiful women from the first day I've known him. I just don't trust her after all the shit in high school. She was a snake."

"Agreed."

The server approached, and he put his napkin over his lap.

"I'll talk shit about her for you if you want."

I tipped my head to the side and had that soppy feeling one gets when seeing a puppy dog. "This is the second time I could hug you."

"Ha. We gotta have each other's backs, sis."

"We do. I got yours, too. If you ever get stuck with a vegan despot, I'll sneak you bits of steak under the table."

He laughed. "That's a new kind of cheater."

A server passed us with someone else's dish, and the aroma of pink peppercorn filled my senses with savory happiness. Life wasn't perfect by any means, but I always had Tyran and steak salads.

My dad had always taught us to be present and grateful for the little things. Looking up at my beautiful brother, I was hit with the fact he was hardly a little thing in my life anymore. Somewhere in the past several months, he'd become my best friend.

13

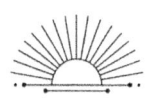

Drake

JESUS. I never thought I'd get to the day when I could be in my private room and make a private call my girl. I'd already bused through Germany without the chance at a hotel room, but for our first night in London, we posted up in a hotel you'd never get in the States. There was plaid furniture everywhere, and pictures of horses and hounds all over the walls. Didn't feel like a rock star abode, but I liked it anyway. It was comfortable and didn't smell the way it looked.

I took a quick, hot shower, with a massive amount of suds, swiping away the grime of a short practice session.

Even though Maeve couldn't smell me through the phone, for the past week I'd been spraying cologne before our calls or making sure my pits were all right. Being clean and smelling good helped me be more alert, when in reality, I was exhausted.

I'd been surrounded by people for over a week now. Not that I sat around pining away exactly. I was too busy to have time to think about it much, but when I did, it hit deep. Missing her cut like a knife. It wasn't about me, though. Yes, I wanted to feel her skin again and be soaked in warm spicy perfume, but mostly, I worried about her when I was away.

It wasn't that Maeve was the type who couldn't take care of herself. She'd gotten through law school, euro-railed across Europe on her own and, of course, did the unspeakable at Uyu. She was smart as shit and tough as nails. The problem with her was that she took the weight of the world onto her shoulders because she thought she could take it. She lived in a pressure cooker.

I turned off the shower and squeezed water from my hair. I wrapped a towel around my waist, threw myself down on the bed, and grabbed my phone.

Video call was the biggest tech gift of this millennia. At first it had connected me with Mom when I'd moved to LA and now, to my girl. I only had to tap my screen twice. It was as easy as rubbing a genie's lamp. In seconds she appeared, her hair perfectly sleek and her lipstick fresh after what I imagined was her first coffee. It was morning for her.

"Hello, my Dark Fairy," I growled as seductively as I possibly could at an inanimate object.

Maeve's face illuminated the dim dusk light in my room, and the blue light from my phone went from being toxic to ethereal as soon as she answered. I laid on my hotel bed,

relaxed and warm from the shower, staring at her with hungry eyes.

"Hi, handsome," she said. "Whatever you say, assume you're on speaker." She lifted the phone to show her background. The office was already booming and in full motion. "I can't afford to blush in front of my fellow soldiers."

"Damn. Can't you go off to the bathroom or something?"

She laughed. "I'm not sure I could, uh, perform in a toilet stall. They aren't that private."

"Well, my room is private, so don't mind if I do..." I reached downward and pretended to grab my nuts.

"Drake!"

"I'm kidding. Like you said, I'm on 'speaker.' My balls are so full I think I'd erupt as silently as a geyser if I did that."

She laughed again. I loved seeing her laugh. I loved it even more if I was the source.

"It's darker in London than I thought," she changed the subject. "Or do you not have any windows in your hotel room?"

I stood and walked her over to the window. "I do..." I turned the phone onto the twinkling London skyline. "It's four-thirty p.m. and practically pitch-black." I turned the camera back on me. "You don't really think of it, but I guess we're pretty far north. It wasn't like this in Germany."

"Mmm. You look a little tired, my love."

I let myself fall back into my plush bed. "Yeah, thankfully we have a night off tonight. I don't feel the tiredness too much, though. Everything is such an adrenaline rush, you know? The travel, the shows, meeting people from my favorite bands. It's impossible to feel too tired, but sometimes I think that's just because I'm dreaming. Like I'm actually just asleep right now."

Maeve's chin bobbed as she walked out of her office, and

I had a view of her nostrils on screen as she walked with her cell just a little too low. She sought privacy; but it was never private enough... there hadn't been any since I started this tour.

I'd thought that maybe we could have loads of phone sex while I was gone and expand our dirty talk horizons, but in reality, I was never available on weekends, and the time difference meant I mostly called Maeve while she was at work in the morning. It sucked. I kept reminding myself it was only eight weeks, actually six and a half more now. Time on my end was going pretty quickly. I barely had time to blink in a day.

She settled on a bench outside the offices, and the sun caught her lip gloss. Two tiny suns brightened her brown eyes like an anime character.

"So," she said, "what are you doing with your time off? It's your first day off since you left."

"I know. We didn't stay long enough in Germany to see anything really. But the architecture in and of itself made me know I was away. I wanted to hit up the British Museum this afternoon, but it closes at five. I'll try to get an early night and go there in the morning before practice."

"Look at you all cultured! Get me a magnet or something."

"Yeah. I can just see a collection of magnets on your kitchen fridge. Dixie would freak if they scratched the metal."

Maeve's smile faded, and a hollow expression gobbled up her face. She blinked quickly, like she always did when she tried to hide her true thoughts and manipulate the conversation. She tried on a little smile again. Something was up.

"What's wrong?"

"What do you mean? Nothing's wrong?" An empty smile tried to convince me.

"I saw you blip for a minute."

"Blip?" She laughed, and it genuinely felt like she was back with me again. "Everything's okay just... been slightly worried about my mom, that's all. So yeah, I definitely am not going to be putting your magnets on the fridge. Not going to wind her up in any way. But I don't want to talk about that. We only have a few minutes to talk every day and when we do it's happy o'clock. Okay?"

I didn't want her to feel like she couldn't talk about things while I was away. True, it was nice to keep things positive and light-hearted so we didn't sink into quicksand of lover's despair and stop breathing altogether.

Equally, I wanted to support her. But I knew Maeve. When she'd made up her mind not to talk about something, she meant it. Some other people would say they didn't want to talk when they really did, they just wanted you to ask again. Not Maeve. She either talked or she didn't, and the only coaxing mechanism I had was sex which I was unable to employ right now.

I knew Dixie wasn't right, but what did anyone expect? Hopefully, time would make the pain more tolerable, and she might even like me when she came out of her funk.

Maeve reached into a large purse she'd placed on the bench beside her and pulled out our cards. She wiggled them in front of the camera. "Shall we?"

"Aw, my little Fairy! You brought them to work? Melt my heart."

"I thought I'd better start carrying them around or we'll never use them. So, deal was, draw from the top. Do you have yours?"

"Gimme a sec." Before walking to my suitcase, I whipped

off my towel from around my waist, letting it drop to the floor, and placed my cell in front of me to let her see my family jewels dangle while I wandered across the room.

She giggled. "London really does have the best views."

I put the phone back to my face and rummaged through my suitcase. "Not as good as LA, my love. Nothing could be good as that... here we go."

I took the pack of cards out and went back over to my bed, sprawling out. "I'll draw first." I read the question aloud, "Your house catches fire. After saving your loved ones and pets, you have time to make one final dash and save one item. What would it be?"

She jumped at it. "I'll go first because it's so obvious you could guess. I'd have to get the urn with my dad's remaining ashes."

"No doubt," I agreed.

"What would you save?" she asked.

I rubbed my chin, scratchy with stubble. I knew as immediately as Maeve had what I'd save. It was obvious for me, too. But, it was opening a can of worms. Still, that's what the cards were about. "Before my grandma died, she wrote me a letter telling me how much she loved me and..."

I didn't necessarily want to continue. Not when Maeve was so far away. I'd never told anyone about the information my grandma's letter contained. I wasn't even sure my mom knew.

The seal on the envelope was untampered when my mom had handed it to me many moons, and I was pretty sure I'd buried it better than Atlantis.

"And..." Maeve urged me to complete my thought.

"And... it also had my dad's contact information in it."

"You never told me that!" Her eyes were wide with

genuine surprise. Shock more like it. "At Uyu, you said you didn't know where he was and you were okay with that."

"Yeah, and this is exactly why I don't divulge that information. Because it would turn into a conversation about do you or don't you go find him. But you know, these cards are about getting to know each other better, so there's no use hiding it. Sweet as my grandma's words were in the letter, it's all predictable, you could guess what she said. But now you know the saucy bit."

"Wow. So you actually know where your dad is?"

"Nah. Who knows. She wrote that letter a long time ago. He's probably moved on. The only thing that made me curious was why she would do that when he screwed over her daughter and grandson? I mean, it's strange, right?"

Maeve pushed some hair behind her ear, letting the sun shine on the apple of her cheek. "Yeah, that is strange... so she didn't say anything about him? Just his contact information?"

"Yeah... feels like..."

All of a sudden, my door flung open, and Quinn was there. "Drake we're goi..."

"Shit..." I grabbed the duvet and threw it over my dick.

"Oh, sorry..." she said but she was already tipsy so she didn't mean it. She also didn't leave and walked deeper into my room. "We're doing a historic pub crawl tonight. Leaving in fifteen. Though your birthday suit is gorgeous, you might want to get dressed."

I knew Quinn meant no harm, and to me, she really was becoming one of the boys. But I wasn't stupid. If Tae had been the one to walk in on me naked in bed chatting to my girlfriend it would have been fine... but it wasn't. It was Quinn. Fuck, this looked bad.

"Fine. Give me a minute. Close the door behind you."

Quinn left, leaving the door slightly ajar like a total dude. I turned back to Maeve's face onto which a Joker-like, very scary grin was plastered. Fake smiles were always creepy, but Maeve's was downright terrifying.

Her voice came out an octave higher than usual as she tried to act cool. "Does Quinn have a key to your room or do the doors not auto lock?"

"We're in a suite..."

"Oh..." Her voice went even higher.

I tried to reassure her. "Sorry, babe. My door was closed. She's not one for personal space and manners. Just one of the boys..."

Maeve said nothing, which indicated my reassurance had done nothing.

"Sounds like you need to get a move on," she said, standing from her spot on the bench.

"I don't have to go. I'm not as desperate for a pub crawl as I am for time with you. Plus, we haven't done your card."

She gave me a tight smile. "You need to take advantage of this experience. Trust me, I want to talk, too, I'd *love* to continue this conversation, and we will..." she waggled her pointed finger at me, "you're not off the hook. I will be addressing this Dad thing again in the future."

Maeve would be ruthless. Telling her this was like opening Pandora's box. But if I was going to hell, I'd be fucking Hades and she'd be my Persephone. "I expect a cross-examination. You know I do. I love you, Maeve. I love you more than seeing new sights. I love you more than pub crawls and new fans and fancy hotels... I love you more than all of this."

"And I love you enough to make you take advantage of all those things even if they're second best." She fluttered

her eyelashes, and though her comments were flirtatious, I knew she still wasn't a hundred percent.

"I'll let you know when I get in," I said, hoping she'd know she was my priority. "Pop you some photos, or we can call?"

"Seriously, Drake, it's okay. I have work anyway and I'm going for a walk with my mom tonight."

I tilted my head and bit my bottom lip.

"I'm fine!" she said. "Go have fun. I love you."

"K. Chat soon, love."

When we ended the call, the pit of my stomach was heavy. If I expected to prove my loyalty on this trip, a hot girl walking in acting as if seeing my dick was completely normal was not the way to do it.

A PUB CRAWL wouldn't have been my first choice of cultured activity in London, but when Quinn said it was historic, she'd certainly meant it. Having hardly left Seattle in my life, where things got replaced when they were old, drinking in the city's most ancient taverns was an experience to say the least.

From the bridge at Blackfriars to the "gentlemen only" signs to ending up at a pub named after Queen Victoria's daughter, I was in complete awe. London still made me think of soot on a chimney sweep's face and Oliver Twist, or at least these pubs did.

We sat at the bar in our last place with Quinn, Tae, and the rest of the crew, in no hurry to leave. I took it easy because before I'd left, I promised myself I'd leave Maeve a voice note and I didn't want to sound completely trashed.

All I could say for the others was it was a good thing that they were backup singers.

I sat on a stool at the far end of the glossy wood bar and leaned in to order a water. When I did, Quinn, on the other end, caught my eye.

"Water?" she mouthed, gesturing to the bartender who handed me a pint glass.

I nodded. She got up, with a martini glass in hand, and walked over to me in her impossibly high heels, not stumbling one little bit, even though in them she was tall enough to need extra oxygen.

When she reached me, she inserted herself between me and Vanessa, set her drink down, and placed an elbow on the bar. "Don't tell me you're tapping out? I've waited to get away from the beer and have something sophisticated all night. I need a drinking buddy."

"Sorry. Some of us have work tomorrow."

"Ha... stop bring grim."

"Is that grim?"

"No... I'm just trying to peer pressure you. It's actually admirable and makes me like you more because you're a better person than I am."

"Being the last man standing doesn't make you a bad person. That's normally me." I sipped my water and thought how it was actually unlike me to be this responsible. I usually sobered up while I was sleeping, not before.

"So..." She tilted a little closer. The pub was loud, and she had to raise her voice. "Do you plan on letting loose at all while on tour? I'd like to see that side of you."

Quinn's crooked grin threw me off for the millionth time. Thing was, it looked flirty, cocky, and coy all at once. But in reality, this was just her smile. It was her smile when she said thanks to the cashier at the coffee shop. It was her

smile for the crowd. It was her smile when she'd heard the good news from back home that her cousin had had a baby girl.

In any other situation, I wouldn't play with fire. I'd err on the side of caution and stay away from a girl like Quinn completely. Either she truly was trouble, or your girl would think she was, and both of those scenarios rendered the same result.

But I had no choice. I had to make this band work, make my money, and live happily ever after with Maeve. Quinn was somewhere in the messy ripples of life's butterfly effect, and without her, I wouldn't get where I was going.

She was good for the band. She lightened things up. Where Tae and I could be a bit too serious, she'd bring in a stupid joke. She had insane energy and was incredible with press and on social. And more than that, her musical skill was insane. I was part of a great trio and I planned to keep it that way.

This was why I struggled with how to bring up the fact that she couldn't be seeing my dick again.

"What are you thinking about?" she asked.

"Just that... you need to learn how to knock." I swirled the ice in my glass.

She slapped my arm, only it wasn't a slap it was more of a stroke. "Oh, that. Don't worry, nothing I haven't seen before."

I lifted my glass. "And nothing you'll see again if you learn how to knock," I joked and kept it as light as possible.

I didn't want her to think I was annoyed about it. I actually wasn't. I didn't really give a shit who saw me swinging, but Maeve's face told me she did. And fair enough. I wouldn't be happy if the tables were turned.

The saving grace was that Maeve knew Quinn. Hope-

fully, she knew her playful nature and understood how harmless she was.

But I'd never been one to put my chips on hope alone. You were about as likely to win on that as on a roll of roulette.

WHAT THE FUCK was she doing bursting into my boyfriend's room while he was naked? What the fuckety fuck!

Those words, or some version of them, had been running through my head all day. Quinn fucking Hartley had seen my boyfriend naked. And she'd acted completely natural as if she had done it before.

I wanted to ask. I wanted to see if this was the first time. After all, they'd pretty much lived on that tour bus and they probably had to share dressing rooms... I didn't want to know but I wanted to at the same time. Maybe I

needed to know because my imagination was driving me mad.

Ignorance was not bliss. I'd never believed that and I certainly didn't now.

Somehow, I'd made it through the day without any inappropriate expletives, but I did manage to mess up some the numbering of my clauses. I also forgot to call back a client today, and now she was out of the country again, so that was going to bite me in the ass.

How could I let this get the better of me? I kept telling myself this was nothing to worry about, but that logic had the power of a bandage on a severed head.

It felt like a big fucking something, and the more time I had to think about it, the worse it got. I wished I would have just told him that it had bothered me. I was trying so hard to not be *that* girl. To be cool. Not only for the sake of my own reputation but also for Drake. I truly wanted him to have fun and to make the most of this opportunity.

I'd pried online (as anyone would) and found out that both of his new bandmates had not only played in some bands previously but also had written songs for other pop stars. Not charted hits, mind you, but at least they actually wrote music. I wanted that for Drake. I wanted him to be with other musicians who wouldn't just drain him and ride his coattails. I wanted him to be part of the next Queen. Or U2, because they gave the entire band credit. I wanted Drake to really enjoy this and make some new lifelong friends, especially because he'd lost one in this very process.

Admittedly, not all of that went through my head the second after a girl I "used to" hate "accidentally" walked in on my boyfriend naked on the bed, interrupting our conversation.

She could have been up to her old ways. Or maybe not.

Those were my first thoughts. But after that, I did come around to thinking that me being a sane and supportive girlfriend would be best for both of us.

Sadly, supportive I was nailing. Sane, I was not. But I had to get sane quickly for more than just Drake. I was about to meet up with Mom for our next power-walk session. Tyran had signed the two of us up as a team to a fourteen-mile charity hike to Mount Wilson.

This should have been enough to distract me from my jealousy. Not only did I need to get fit enough to get up a 5712-foot peak, while walking fourteen miles, I also had to raise money for the privilege of doing it and convince my alcohol-dependent mom to help me train.

Tyran had asked her to join as well, but even if she wasn't where she was both physically and mentally, he'd gone and picked the Ironman of charity hikes. Most people would have declined and not even politely.

I walked through the front door, popped my shoes in the cupboard, and ran up to my room to change. I was exhausted having just had a ten-hour day and driven almost two hours on top of that but I looked myself in the mirror and reminded myself I could binge on takeout and watch reality TV later.

I ran to Mom's room first. Empty.

Down the stairs to the kitchen. Empty.

"Mom?" I said loudly. "Where are you?"

No reply. I chased around the house from room to room when finally, I noticed a shape at the far end on the backyard, sitting on a lounger by the pool. I went outside, and it didn't take me long to see she wasn't at all dressed for a hike.

Nothing about her was ready for a hike. She was sleeping in a bathing suit covered by a zebra-print kaftan, with an empty highball glass next to her on the ground.

There was no chance there'd been anything but a Manhattan or a whisky sour or something of the sort in there because my mom never misused glasses or tableware.

I sat on the lounger next to her and gently shook her arm. "Mom?"

She woke up immediately, not having been in a deep sleep. "Ooh. I must have dozed off."

"Yeah... you're not dressed for our walk."

"Oh, honey, can I take a rain check?" She pressed herself up further in the lounge chair and straightened her sunhat.

"No. I need a walking buddy, and this charity walk is just around the corner. I can't afford to skip training days."

"What were ya'll thinking signing up to an umpteen-mile hike with only a few weeks to train and this close to Christmas?"

"It's to raise money for a good cause... we can handle it."

She took in a deep breath then let out a sour sigh. Sometimes, I wondered if me merely mentioning how bad her breath was now would do the trick. She'd be mortified.

But I'd read that humiliation and guilt, or anything that made the person with the problem feel lower, was not a path toward sobriety.

"Tyran told me he asked you to do it, too," I said. "Lord knows you have enough friends who'd donate. It's a good cause, and it'll be a beautiful day. We've got twelve weeks to train..."

"I'm not ready to hoo-rah-rah for pancreatic cancer awareness yet. I don't want to be anybody's poster child or ask my friends for a pity donation."

I thought to myself that Dad was really the poster child, not her. Thank goodness I'd learned to hold my tongue. "What *do* you want? I get that you *don't* want that, but have you ever thought about what you *do* want, Mom? You can't

possibly want to take a nap every afternoon, watch TV, then go to bed. That's not the get-up-and-go Dixie I know."

She flopped her head to the side and peeped over the top of her sunglasses like a fifties movie star. "I'll make a hefty donation, Maeve Lewis. That's all you need to know."

"And all *you* need to know," I said as I stood and held out my hand to help her up, "is that a promise is a promise, and that means you're coming with me right now before it gets too dark."

"I never *promised*..." She put emphasis on the word we took very seriously in this household.

From the time when I was little, my parents instilled in me that I should be careful to say 'I'll try' instead of 'I promise' when I wasn't certain I could deliver.

Promises were sacred guarantees.

"Don't even try to say you didn't promise to walk with me tonight," I said when she didn't budge a millimeter from her sprawled-out position. "When I asked you to come, I also asked if you promise. And I happened to have my cell on to record it. I can play the evidence if you'd like."

She let out a rich laugh. Her Southern drawl came out warm, and for a moment I saw a glimpse of my old mom.

"You're lower than a snake's belly in a wagon rut."

I gave her a bit more of that good old Southern slang to make her feel like home. "You look rode hard and put up wet. I'm fixin' to walk you."

Her laughed rolled out, beautiful and young and genuine in a way I don't think I'd heard her laugh for over a year now. I smiled, and the feeling was so overwhelming that in an instant a film of tears coated my eyes. I blinked them back.

Her laugh calmed enough to say, "You do make me laugh, you little Yankee stinker."

She pushed herself up but lost her balance and fell back down. She laughed again, and it grew into a mighty fit. We both giggled in a fit that had us holding our tummies.

When Mom finally caught her breath, she said, "Now look at me! You're right... we need to walk this old dog."

I helped her to her feet and she started off to change.

"It's fine, honey. I'll be down lickety-split. You just wait out here in this beautiful sunshine. You've been in that office all day."

I DROVE Mom and I out to the trailhead of Escondido Falls. It was cooler on this trail, and the microclimate caught us off guard at first in our light hiking kit, but soon we warmed up, taking up as brisk a pace as my fifty-something mama could.

She'd never been big on exercise apart from a Peloton or two a week, just enough to stay a standard size ten, thus expanding her wardrobe consistently. She always told me to set my size at thirty and stick with it.

She certainly had. In fact, I had to admit that I'd almost never seen a hair out of place on her head. Even now, an hour after waking her up from passed out on a lounger after God knew how many drinks, she looked the part in her Lululemon Lycra getup.

We talked about work, and I told her about Rob from the office who thought he was God's gift to lawyering. We talked about what was happening on the latest episode of a reality show we both loved and about Tyran and how he was a vegan magnet.

It was light, fun, girlie chatter, the kind I hadn't realized

I'd missed so much until now it had happened, and my cheeks grew tight from smiling so much.

Hats off to Tyran. This was good for my mom, true, but it was also proving good for me. The endorphins helped sweep away the cobwebs, and I felt a little better about everything.

Until Mom brought up Drake. A subject I'd intended to avoid.

"Looks like Graphic Temple is in England now? Have you two been able to talk much? That time difference can be a killer."

"We're trying. He calls me at work in the morning. How did you know they were in England?"

"Gina."

"Gina keeps tabs on Drake? Surely she doesn't have time for that."

My mom adjusted her lightly-tinted sunglasses, and her eyes widened right through them. "Special interest."

"Oh..." I was going to see if silence would drop the subject, but maybe this was a chance to show my mom how close Drake and I were becoming. Had become.

"Before he left, he got me these getting-to-know-you type cards. So even though we can't talk much, it's really... I don't know. It's like at least we're have meaningful conversations with the time we have. It's hard, but that's been good. Maybe if he hadn't left we wouldn't have these deep-dive conversations."

"Mmm. And what does he think about Quinn?"

I nearly stopped walking. "Uuum... yeah, she's fine. Why?"

"Just that I wasn't so sure about that combo. It was between her and a guy from that little band that just broke

up." She paused to think. "Pope and other Idols? Was that the band? You know more about the scene than I do."

"Hold on." I stopped my mom from taking another step. Just how involved was she in all of this? It sounded like she'd been the one to choose Quinn over this other guy. This other *male*. "How do you know all this? Gina again?"

"No, this time it was someone else. Maeve, I've been on top of what happens at RI since the day your daddy started it. He used to say I was the mastermind, but I don't have any real power. Just nosy."

Only she did have power. Plenty of it. Not only was she highly persuasive but she had that thing about her where if you said no, she might put a pin in your doll.

Plus, she was Dixie *Lewis*. The Lewis name was everything at RI And now that my dad was gone, on top of her usual sway, she had the sympathy vote.

My heart raced knowing that my mom could have pushed for someone other than Quinn. It beat in that way it did where it felt like every seam was under pressure.

"So did you have something to do with picking Quinn? A girl you *know* I had problems with in high school and is just..."

I shook my head and didn't finish. I had to stay positive. Tyran had told me. Be optimistic. No problems...

"Honey, business is business. Don't take it personally. If Drake is trustworthy, you'll know soon."

"Mom!" I calmed myself. "Sorry... I'm just a bit sensitive about this. I don't really want to talk anymore about this but I do want to say that I already know Drake is trustworthy."

But I didn't. I didn't know and I didn't believe myself any more than the raised, drawn-in eyebrow on my mom's forehead did. My underarms prickled. What did all this mean?

Did my mom do this deliberately to try and break me and Drake up? Or was it really 'business is business?'

I couldn't help but wish that my mom had had my back. She could have swayed the vote. She could have thought back to high school when Quinn had been ruthlessly chasing my boyfriend that she might not be the best person to put next to my new one without me even being around.

But just as soon as I worried that my mom was a bad guy, she took my hand.

"When he shows you who he is, believe him."

The shock life quote stopped me from spinning. "Is that Oprah?"

"Maya Angelou via Oprah."

"Oh."

She took off her glasses and actually seemed caring and sincere. "Every relationship gets tested at some point, Maeve. There's no point in worrying about it or fearing the outcome because you really want to see who this man is and you want to know now. Not ten years and two kids down the road. This is a blessing." She headed for a nearby bench and sat. "Now, this washed-up old bird needs a breather."

She grabbed a bottle out of the running belt she wore and had a drink.

"Why do you have a running belt when you don't run?" I joked.

"Glasses make me look smarter. The gear makes me look fitter. It's all about the illusion."

I sat next to her and had a drink myself. I put my arm around her in an attempt to be present and tried to forget about the Drake thing the best I could. She was right after all. As much as I feared potentially being without him, I had to see him for who he was.

Thing was, I thought I'd already seen it, and I loved that guy. Hopefully, this wasn't a running belt situation.

Uyu wasn't a normal place to meet someone. It wasn't like meeting at a bar. I saw so much Drake there he'd practically been standing behind an x-ray curtain the entire time. In my heart, when I switched off all my crazy, jealous thoughts, I really felt he was the one. The one who would be loyal. The one who'd be my best friend forever. The one I'd never stop wanting to jump my bones and hold my hand.

Hope could be cruel.

Drake wasn't the only joke hope might be playing on me.

My mom took another swig from her bottle, and it smelled like vodka.

15

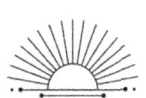

Drake

Oh, hell yes. I'd made it through the European stint of our touring. It was our last night in England, and tomorrow, I'd be in New York City. Almost halfway through the tour. I'd finally caress Maeve's silky smooth, Cleopatra ass' milk skin again.

She'd organized our little entourage, too. Koa and Jasmine were flying in now as well for our first New York show, and I really needed a dose of family. She'd told me a couple of weeks ago, saying it was supposed to be a surprise but she couldn't help herself. She probably felt like

cheering us both up and being able to look forward to it together.

I had to admit that her not making it a surprise really did reinvigorate our conversations. We'd been able to talk about what we'd do in New York, and that lit a fire in both our bellies.

It wasn't so much that I'd felt lonely. Not at all. The band and the entire crew got along like we'd been touring for years. I was having the time of my life, but still, at the end of every evening, when I lay down in bed, I'd turn over and wish Maeve's face was the last one I spoke to. She loved me in a way that nobody had before. All of this was because of her, and I never for one second forgot that. Maeve's love felt unconditional.

My flight was early the next morning, and I knew I'd have fierce jet lag, so I didn't want to look rough, too. We'd had a day off today again. I went to a souvenir shop to get what I needed, had one last hurrah shot with the gang, and came back to the hotel early to eat in my room and call Maeve.

After three tones, her face appeared. "Where are you?" she asked.

"My hotel room." I showed her my tray with a steak. "Steak and chips, as they say here in England."

"Wow, you're bilingual."

I laughed. "Yeah, you know. I try. Anyway, I wanted to get some beauty sleep since I have a hot date tomorrow."

She was at work again and wandered back outside to the bench she usually took. I had to go sit with her on that bench when I got back. The sunlight always hit her face perfectly in the mid-morning. I wanted to see that in person and kiss her eyes when the sun made them sparkle the way it did.

"What a coincidence," she said. "I have a hot date, too. Sadly, a red-eye flight means very little beauty sleep. I hope he's all about the personality."

"I'm sure he is. I bet all he cares about is having someone kind, honest, witty, and fun. If I may speak for myself..."

"Well, I'm a lot more shallow than that, I'm afraid. I need nice eyes and a big dick."

I burst out laughing. "You horny little devil..."

"It's been a long time." She smiled.

"It has. I've really missed you, my Fairy..." A surge of fuzzy warmth overcame my limbs, my core, and my head. Thinking about being with her again was like switching on the ignition.

She took something from her purse and held it in the air. It was her deck of cards. "This has kept us going, though. Don't you think?"

"Indeed."

"We never had a chance to bring up your dad again."

"Let's not. Not right now."

"It's just, I've been racking my brain about it. Not even over what you should do, if anything, just why your grandma would do that..."

"Mmm." I didn't want to bring that card up again. I wanted to ride this wave of gushing love that coursed through my body. Analysis would kill that vibe. "How about we pull a new card?"

"Yes, please."

Maeve was so enthusiastic about it, and in a way that was almost childish. For the first time since starting to exchange answers, I realized that these had been really good for Maeve on so many levels. She wasn't the best at sharing her feelings and didn't like being the center of attention in our conversations.

She'd spent so many years being strong and pretending to be strong that she might not even know the difference. The cards invited her to be the focus of our conversation and forced her to be vulnerable and tell the truth. The distance actually helped, too. Hard as it was, it was a blessing on our relationship.

I got up to grab my stack out of my satchel. I kept them on me at all times. Every single time Maeve and I'd had a call she'd asked to do a card, and I never wanted to be caught off guard. I pulled my top one. "Right... it says: what would you change about yourself if you could?" I thought for a moment. "That's a strange question..."

"Is it?" she asked immediately. "I know what I'd change."

"What? And for the record, I wouldn't change a thing about you..."

"Give it a few years." She smiled. "I'd worry less if I could."

I nodded. I saw this in her, too. "What kind of things do you worry about most?"

She took in a deep breath then let it out loudly. "Like... everything. Almost everything. Or maybe, if I really think about it, I'd change the fact that I think I can control everything. They kind of go hand in hand. I feel like I have the power to make people feel better, or conquer the world or whatever, and then I get anxiety when I worry that I actually don't have control. I guess this isn't a really good answer. Haven't figured it out completely yet, but it's definitely something to do with being a worrywart control freak."

"Now... I'm going to sound like an asshole."

"Why?"

"Because I'm not sure I'd really change anything about myself."

She rolled her eyes, but her smile never faded. "You're annoyingly perfect."

I popped a fry in my mouth and thought about it for a second. "No. I'm not at all perfect. But I guess, unlike perfectionists, I embrace the messiness in life. Not that I'm always happy, totally not the case just... every day is a gift, and every day is a chance to be whatever you want to be."

She turned her face to the sky. "I had to answer first." She laughed.

"Okay, I lie. I would change one thing."

"Great. Make me feel better."

"I have a double crown."

"Oh, shut the fuck up!"

"What?! Do you know how hard it is to get a haircut from anyone but Larry in Seattle?"

She tutted and drew one of her cards. "Good. Here's one that won't make me feel like a twat." She narrowed her eyes at me, then read, "What is your favorite family vacation? I'll go first again. Mine was going on safari in South Africa. My favorite animal is an elephant, and we saw so many there. Baby ones, too. I was like fifteen when we went, and even when I reflect on that vacation, my thoughts switch off when I imagine myself back in the safari truck, my chin on the side of it, in total awe of the size and majesty of those creatures."

She thought some more, and I loved when her eyes seemed to look up into her brain for more.

"And," she continued, "that was also the only vacation we had while living with my parents that Tyran and I hadn't argued, too. My dad also rented a car, and we drove ourselves through the safari park, and he let me and Tyran drive, like totally solo. It was amazing."

Reflecting on Maeve's self-professed control freak slash

worried nature, there were quite a few moments when we'd talk that she dug into her memories and a shower of calm drenched her. Her face relaxed, her shoulders lowered, and she seemed to almost float. This was one of those memories. I didn't want her to stop talking, but she did.

"What about you, my love?" she asked.

"My turn to be a twat. I don't think I really enjoyed my vacations very much as a child. So it would probably be Nakiki with the Uyu gang."

"Did you go on vacations with your mom?"

"I did. Yeah, she took me and Grams camping, and we stayed in a national park once but, I don't want to sound ungrateful for anything, but the truth was, in my mind's eye it was just a bit lonely. You know how kids are. They want to play with other kids. Sounds selfish, and looking back, I know how hard she worked to put that money aside and all, but I can't recreate my memories... I think my best vacation is yet to come." I licked my lips. "My best vacation will definitely be with you."

She smiled wistfully. "Where?"

"Hmmm... I'd imagined us in Japan before, but now... I'd say Thailand. An elephant sanctuary. We can help out with your favorite mighty beasts by day and get foot massages on the beach by night."

"You're speaking my language."

"But first stop, New York."

"Will you take me ice skating?"

"Is that your number one? I only have time for your number one, so we need to make it count."

"Definitely ice skating. Then, we have to have dinner with our friends and then, we need a *lot* of time in the hotel room. We'll be jetlagged and tired after all."

"Oh yes, we will…" I reached down and grabbed my dick. "In fact, I'm tired right now…"

"Wish I could help you with that." She smirked.

"Tomorrow, baby. You're in trouble."

"Promise? Because you know I love trouble."

"Promise. A Jackson promise is a Lewis promise. So get ready for it."

WE WERE on the side of a beautiful, Christmasy rink in the middle of New York City. Everything glistened around us, and a light dusting of snow still clung like virginal romance to streetlamps and awnings. Maeve wore a sexy black beret still bearing a few specks of the fluffy dust, and it was a wonder we'd made it out of the hotel at all, she was so damn perfect to me. We'd walked through the streets of this iconic city, hand in hand through the snow, making a monochrome holiday romance film.

Though I suspected ours might be a bit dirty for Hallmark.

Maeve had never told me she was good at it until we got ringside. But I should have guessed because she'd been so insistent upon ice skating.

While lacing up our skates, I said, "Do you remember that question about what I'd change about myself?"

She glanced over from her bent position, hair framing either side of her face. "Yeah?"

"This might be it. I'm pretty sure I might look like a double-jointed giraffe out there."

She giggled. "Aw… don't waste a wish on something you can learn to do. I'll teach you."

"Just how many times have you been?"

She stood onto the slices of metal like they were a pair of sneakers. "A few."

She arched a devilish brow and offered her hand, which I took, but was careful not to actually use. I pushed my way to standing and I was surprisingly stable... on the rubber matting.

I'd already seen several people fall immediately upon stepping onto the ice.

"Just a tip..." Maeve gestured her hands forward and backward. "Don't move your feet vertically back and forth. You'll go nowhere. It's a sort of pushing back diagonally movement that you need. Like this..." She motioned with her feet this time, perfectly balanced, even while on only one of them.

"Got it."

She made it seem easy.

I took her hand and tried my best to be cool, leading my dark ice fairy to the rink.

When we got to the opening of the rink, Maeve let go of my hand. "Let me go first. I want to watch you get on."

She floated onto the ice, pushed off twice, like a ballerina, and lifted a leg in the air as she did some sort of Olympic ice spin move, turning toward me, proud of herself.

"Oh. I see how it is. Is that how good I'll be after a 'few' times?" I asked.

"Something to work toward."

I managed to stay up on the ice when I stepped on, but I think if I hadn't watched others fall I would have myself, because I would have taken for granted just how slippery it was. The world below me was impossible to grip.

Maeve took my hand; she was an amazing teacher. Within a few laps, I wasn't doing a triple lutz or anything,

but we glided naturally, in tandem, hand in hand, like two lovers floating around some gravity-free planet.

It was heaven when Maeve broke away and flirted with a little twirl or skated backward in front of me for a moment, her pert nose and curly eyelashes smiling at me, a Christmas sprite coming to spread cheer on a perfect winter's day.

One moment, I couldn't take it anymore, she was absolutely gorgeous. Long leather-clad legs with the extra four inches on skates and her fucking delicious black shearling coat, sweet and spicy at the same time. The beret nearly sent me over the edge.

I stopped her at the next corner and urged her back into the side of the rink, grabbing either side of the edge. "You're really fucking turning me on right now." I bent down and kissed her. "I just want to rip your clothes off and watch you twirl around my dick in your bra and panties."

She kissed me back, hard, almost desperate, like underneath the surface of her perfect performance, she'd been gasping for my touch. Our lips kneaded, her warm mouth so delicious and comforting against the bitter air. I pulled my coat up as if shielding our faces and leaned my dick into her. My cock tightened in my pants.

I let my coat down and pulled back. "Let's go."

GETTING to the hotel was hard. I had an erection the size of the Empire State Building, and Maeve didn't give a fuck who saw her touching me. We made out the entire cab ride back to the hotel, her leg draped over my lap, but I imagined it was nothing a New York cabbie hadn't seen before.

I rushed Maeve through the lobby, her hand in mine, and drew her into an elevator where we pushed between two men in suits, to the back where we figured they wouldn't dare turn around.

Side by side, we suppressed feral smiles while I slid my hand underneath her coat and found the bare small of her back. She flinched a little, my fingers were cold, and it made the touch of her delicate warm skin all the more satisfying. Her skin was as soft as I'd remembered it, and I couldn't help but tease my finger along the waist of her pants, willing it inside just an inch, sliding it along her back and wrapping it around her and toward the front until I met her hip bone.

My arm wrapped around behind her, I eased my hand deeper into the front of her pants, and she prised her leg open more, wishing I'd make my way deeper, but the elevator dinged, and the two men, stiff-backed, walked out without looking behind.

We only had one more floor, and I wasn't a fucking one-minute man, but as soon as the doors shut, I inhaled her. I reached my hand deeper down into her tight pants, finally reaching that sexy bit of tidy pubic hair close to her slit, and just the thought of being so close to her pussy for the first time in weeks sent my dick into overdrive. I undid the button of her pants.

Suddenly, the elevator dinged, and I took my hand out. She straightened her hair and not a moment too soon.

The doors opened, and Quinn was there with Vanessa, waiting to enter the elevator. Maeve only just did back up her button as the ladies' eyes darted straight to her sneaky fingers.

Vanessa acted natural, but Quinn said, "Ah, rock stars and their women. Carry on. Nothing we haven't seen before."

I took Maeve's hand to leave as we'd gotten to my floor and nodded at them. "Ladies."

I rushed Maeve onward toward my room and couldn't get her in the door fast enough. I didn't give a fuck about the men in suits or Vanessa or Quinn. At this point I would have fucked her in the hallway if Maeve hadn't moved her little feet as fast as she had. I was absolutely wild for her.

She headed straight for the bed as I closed the door behind me, both of us throwing our winter coats to the floor. She had on a turtleneck made of some super thin fabric, and it clung to every curve... her bra must have been just as thin as I could see her nipples ready to be pinched and sucked, poking through like they could have cut glass. I stalked to the bed and went right for them, taking a nice pinch right through her top, and she sucked air through her teeth.

"My little girls... Daddy's home..."

I pushed her top up along the sides of her body, and she lifted her arms for me, revealing a see-through bra of sheer, black fabric and her nipples cutting devilishly against it.

I laid Maeve back down on the bed and, right through the fabric, took one of her perky breasts almost completely into my mouth.

"Mmm," she groaned, arching her back, spreading her legs, ready for me to ravish her.

I fingered the fabric aside and took her nipple into my teeth like I knew she loved. I circled my tongue around her nipple then took a gentle bite.

"Fuck. I missed you so much," she whispered with her eyes closed.

The tenderness in her voice softened the animal in me, and I released her breast.

Lowering myself over her body, I kissed her straight

from my heart. I urged every ounce of love it carried into her. Her fingernails clawed at my back, but not like a sexual beast, more one hanging on to a cliff's edge. I didn't want her to be like this. I could feel it had hurt her to be apart. I could feel every minute of her yearning dig into me painfully, hungrily.

But we were together now. I was with her and only her. And it was only for two days, so I'd force every ounce of my love inside her. I'd kiss her full. I'd make love to her so long, so hard until she felt me inside her, a phantom limb. We were never really apart. Not really. Love didn't work like that.

I eased down her pants, though it wasn't easy, they were painted on, and her matching sheer panties revealed her little pussy, making me think right back to the elevator and how close I'd gotten.

"You look delicious," I growled.

I took off my shirt and dropped my pants and boxer briefs to the floor. My dick stood tall and proud like a lion about to claim the alpha lioness for its own. And all at once I was a beast again.

I lowered myself on top of her, and my cock welcomed the warm fabric of her panties. She spread her legs wide for me, and I rubbed myself slowly against her, my dick alternating between the friction of her panties and the softness of her thigh. I raised her arms above her into the bed.

I told myself to slow down. I had this woman for twenty-four hours more and I needed to savor every moment, not wolf her down, even though my heart pounded like a predator. But I only found myself driving down harder, pushing into her desperately.

She lifted her pussy into me, grinding and writhing just as hard as I was, but she couldn't move much with me

securing her arms against the bed. I slid my hand up her thigh, over her hip bones, caressing the side of her stomach. I flicked her nipple and then grabbed her chin in my hand, forcing her to look at me.

"I fucking love you, Maeve. Don't let anyone tell you otherwise. Nobody. You hear me?"

She nodded, but it was there in her eyes; I'd exposed her uncertainty.

She whispered, "I fucking love you, too." Her voice cracked; her eyes were soft. "I don't even have the words to say how much."

I rubbed my nose against hers and trailed kisses along her cheek, her neck, and made my way down to the place every nerve ending in me wanted most right now. I tugged her panties down and dove in.

She smelled like home. Neither good nor bad, just that smell that was everywhere you wanted to be because it felt natural. My tongue slithered from her opening to her clit; she spread her legs wider for me, wanting, thirsty for it. The taste was familiar, the feeling of the smoothest skin in the world right there between the lips of her sex... I could have devoured her all day long.

I took her clit into my mouth gently, warming it, keeping it wet and circling my tongue around it, just how she liked. It grew harder, and I eased off the intensity to keep her going. Her hips gyrated, and I gave her clit kisses as I plunged two fingers deep inside her.

"Ahhh..." she gasped.

I eased my fingers in and out, while my cock grew more and more desperate to be inside. Even with it rubbing against the bed I thought I could come.

I licked her, tasted every inch of that slit, sucked in every ounce of the juices flowing out of her. Her clit was on the

verge, and I circled faster but still feather-soft. I wanted to make her come, make her scream my name...

"Oh God..." She moaned.

That would do. She tensed and drove her core into me, about to explode. I sucked her in to my mouth, and she pulsed around my fingers, cum gushing into the palm of my hand. I cupped her entire sex, kneading her clit gently in my palm.

Her eyes were closed when she reached down to tug at my shoulder. "I want you."

She opened them, sat up as I crawled closer to her, still smoothing my slick fingers around her opening, keeping it nice and wet for me.

She caressed my balls in her palm, playing with them gently, my dick gorged with hot blood. She urged me to sit up, maneuvering my ass until I was up on my knees in front of her.

She kissed my dick at first with sweet kisses, my thick dick so tight and full I had to grab a handful of her hair to brace myself. She took me into her mouth, sucked on my dick, taking it all the way to the back of her throat. I palmed her head, steadying it, enjoying her tongue on my cock. When I hit the back of her throat, each time I thought I was done.

Securing her head, I fucked her mouth slowly. The relief of her touch was too much, I need to be inside her. As much as I wanted to explode in her mouth and watch her swallow every inch of me, I wanted that pussy more.

I snatched my pants from the floor, found a condom, and rolled it on. I nearly came at the feel of my own hands. I was dying to be inside her. I'd craved her for so long. Seen her only in my dreams and jacked off pretending my cum was her juices all over my hand. It was about fucking time.

With her legs spread open, that glistening pussy brought out the animal in me, wet and pink. Admiring her, taking in a mental picture I could use for the next four weeks, I prised her legs further apart and licked my lips. Climbing on top, I eased my dick in, inch by inch, slowly.

She let out a sigh.

My dick dipped into the hot wetness of her core. I plunged as deep as I could. She clenched around me. I slid in and out while she grabbed my ass, pressing it into her, like I couldn't even get deep enough. The look on her face was a mix of pleasure and pain. She liked that, though.

I rode her faster and bent over to bite her nipple. Her insides firmly gripped my dick, every fold and ripple of her core giving me pure ecstasy.

I pushed harder, almost afraid I'd make her raw I shoved myself in so hard... I could never feel deep enough inside.

I dragged her to the edge of the bed, raised her legs into the air, holding them wide open as I watched her body writhe with every thrust. Harder and faster, I needed that relief. I had to have it all now. I had to release weeks of wanting and the pain of it all.

Her wetness made it easy, and I groaned, thrust, and finally, all at once, I pulsed and exploded inside her, a pleasure and relief all-consuming, my entire body sighed into her. I let go of her legs and steadied her hips, pressing my thumbs into her hip bones, securing her on the spot until my very last pulse.

We both breathed erratically, calming ourselves, and it all ended with us finally making eye contact.

Sliding out of her, I tossed the condom on the floor and scooped her up off the bed and into my arms. She wrapped her legs around my core. We were both wet and moist with sweat, but I felt like dancing with her coiled around me like

this. I swayed with her, her arms draped around my neck, her legs hanging on, her little butt in my hands, and I just held her close like we did a slow dance at prom.

She whispered in my ear, "I wish we could stay here forever."

I did, too.

When you loved someone this much, the rest of the world blurred into backdrop and felt insignificant. For a moment, even me, Drake Jackson, king of being present, wished for something other than what it was.

WE STAYED in bed for a few hours, savored a round two, and then realized that time was ticking before we'd said we'd meet Koa, Jasmine, and Drake's crew for dinner at a nearby restaurant. I didn't want to leave. I wrapped myself over Drake's beautiful brown abs and traced circles with my finger around the nipple of his perfect pec.

"It's hard to stay in shape for you while on tour," he said.

"You're perfect...

He cupped my ass cheek in his hand. "You, on the other hand, have been doing something with this ass. Did Tyran

finally drag you to some spin classes? This little peach is firm."

I nestled into the crook of his arm. I wasn't sure I wanted to talk about my mom and I knew the minute I mentioned her, he'd ask more. But I'd avoided talking about how serious things were with her on the phone, not wanting him to be distracted by me and my problems. We had too little time on the phone, and the last thing I wanted to do was be negative.

My considered pause was too long. I'd messed up because now he asked again.

"Are you keeping the best kept secret to a fine ass all to yourself now?" He lifted his head and to meet my eye.

"No... I've been hiking hills with my mom." I turned around, trying to get a view of my butt. "I didn't actually realize it'd had any effect until I tried to squeeze into those leather pants today." I did notice a difference. "Not quite Kim K, but it has taken on a peachy quality."

"Understatement... so you've been walking with Dix? That doesn't sound like either of you... I step away for four weeks, and everyone's reinventing themselves."

"It was Tyran's idea. I'm doing a charity walk with him."

"Why didn't you tell me?"

"I just did."

"Well, I need to make a donation to the cause." He pushed himself up further in the bed so we could chat. "What's it for?"

I teetered my head back and forth and shrugged. "Pancreatic cancer."

"Course." His face lit up. "Hey, why don't I mention it at the show tomorrow night?"

"No."

"Yeah... might get some serious donations..."

"Maybe..."

He laid his head back against the headboard. Man, he was beautiful. "So Dixie is doing the charity walk, too?"

"No." I thought back to my mom and her resistance. I wasn't sure what stage of grief she was in. Pain and guilt? Anger? Depression? These were supposed to be distinct stages of the seven, but she felt all of these things at once. "She didn't want to, but Tyran and I'd decided she needed to get out of the house more. And maybe exercise would help with her... you know..."

"Depression?"

"That and her alcohol... use."

"That's a great idea, babe." He stared at the ceiling and pulled me tighter into him with his arm. "Endorphins. Has it helped?"

We'd been having so much fun until now. Even though my heart sank, I didn't want to bring up such a downer, a serious and tender subject so close to us needing to shower and meet up with friends. I didn't want to weigh either of us down.

Drake wasn't the type to move on from any feeling until it was completely digested. But I'd also promised myself to tell him more, allow this time to bring us closer, so I gave him a snippet. "It hasn't helped. Not yet."

Should I tell him that she still filled her water bottle with vodka for every hike? Should I tell her that even after four weeks she had a two-mile maximum and hadn't gained any fitness because I was basically taking her on booze cruises?

"You're worried about her," he said. It was a statement. Not a question.

"Didn't I tell you? I worry about everything..." I put on a smile.

"Tell me more. I don't want to find out eight weeks' worth of life when I get back, Maeve."

I sighed, and out it came a bit more truth. "Babe, she has a problem. I'm not a professional but... she... she does drink all the time. I mean, all. The. Time. She brings alcohol on our walks even. It's bad... but... I have Tyran, and we're working on it."

"Fuck. I didn't know it was like that, but I'd be lying if I said I didn't think it would go in that direction. Using alcohol to cope is a downward spiral."

Drake drew his fingers through his hair and scratched his head. I knew this kind of talk dredged up memories of Jay. Since we'd known each other, he'd told me more about just how bad it had gotten with Jay before they'd spilt.

He'd stolen money from people. Had brought random crack addicts from the street to their band practices... Drake had helped him through two overdoses. It'd left a scar on him. Besides me not wanting to be a downer in general, this was the other reason I didn't want to bring up my mom much. I brought back painful memories for Drake.

"It's a downward spiral," I said clinically, "but Tyran's been through something like this with a friend, and we talked to our family doctor about it. I know we can't make her get better, but anyway... that's what this charity walk is about."

"Mmm..."

"Is that an 'mmm' good idea or 'mmm' good luck with that?"

"I'm not cynical, Maeve. You know that. I'm just thinking."

He did that. And I'd learned to appreciate it because he wasn't the kind of guy who had to take back shit that he'd said. But sometimes I'd sit there, my head reeling,

wondering what he was thinking. Like now. That time was now.

I filled the silence because I couldn't bear it. "Well, I guess it doesn't matter what you think because that's what we're doing. It's the only idea we had. And I have to do something, don't I? I'm pretty much the most responsible person in the family at this point. It'll be fine. My mom isn't the type to let herself slide completely. One day she'll see. We probably just need to get her through this... you know, her grief."

"Blind leading the blind."

"Oh, that's helpful." My defense mechanisms were up now. My skin stiffened like dried plaster of Paris. "I know I'm not a hundred percent either but I think I can help my mom, Drake."

"I didn't mean it to be rude, just there needs to be some third party intervention here. You need to deal with your own shit. She needs professional help for her issue. If you're saying it's grief and not alcohol, I'm not sure you're the one to help her if she's in that deep. But I'm not sure that's what you're saying. Sounds like she's alcohol-dependent, and I have to say, I know Jay isn't Dixie, but I wish I would have sorted out an intervention earlier. We all regretted it. If you get in too deep with drugs..."

"It's not drugs."

"Stop, Maeve. Semantics. If it makes you feel better, I'll call it a substance. My point is, and I'm trying to be helpful here, my point is it's scary to confront the situation. It's hard. I know. But when that pang goes in your chest and it hurts like a motherfucker because it's telling you they need help now, you got to listen. Don't ignore it. That's when you have to do it, even if it's scary."

He climbed on top of me and kissed me. "And trust me, I

hope it doesn't come to that, but if it does, you really can talk to me. I get it. I mean, not all of it, but I get a lot of it. Enough to be better than talking to a wall."

He stroked my bangs off my face and kissed my forehead. "And I'll be back in LA soon. Real soon."

I wrapped my arms and legs around his manly torso and hugged him. "Come on. This is depressing. I just nailed a rock star, he told me he loves me, and I'm in New York City. Let's get out of here."

JASMINE AND KOA waited in the cold outside the restaurant Drake's manager, Vanessa, had booked for us. They were like two babies poking their eyes and noses out of swaddling; they were bundled up so tightly.

I joked. "Shit, you two look like babies in a papoose."

Drake wrapped his arm around Koa. "This is true love. When your friend decreases the minimum temperature of their vacation for you? That's commitment."

"Can we go inside now?" Jasmine shivered.

Drake shoved open the door and gestured us all inside gallantly. I stepped through the doorframe, and the wash of ecstasy I'd bathed in in Drake's hotel room was instantly sullied, like being splashed by a car on the curb in my favorite dress.

As would be the case for every set of eyes entering the room, mine were drawn to Quinn at the bar. She was tall, beautiful, and her long, white-blonde hair was a beacon in a storm of people. I turned to my friends and, sure enough, we were all facing that direction.

She looked in ours, too, and waved us over. When we got

there, she embraced Drake as if she was some Swedish princess, with two kisses on the cheek and everything, and then proceeded to do the same with Koa and Jas as Drake introduced us all.

She ended with me. "Last but not least... of course I already know you..." Kiss. Kiss.

The sound of her lips smacking in my ear was as uncouth as someone chewing with their mouth open. But I was sure I was the only one whose senses were heightened and thought so. Jas offered her usual friendly smile, and Koa, who typically seemed serious, lifted a corner of his lips, too.

"Where are the others?" Drake asked.

"Everyone's here. We have a chef's table downstairs, but it's in a room with no windows... I said I'd wait up here for you guys because I just needed some light, you know? We've been living our lives in the dark for four weeks, it seems." She touched Drake's arm. "Especially in England. And Scotland was soooo dark. We didn't get any daylight there."

"It was," Drake agreed, clearly thinking nothing of her touch. "I said that to Maeve."

Yeah, he did. On the day you saw his dick.

"Anyway, so nice to meet you guys and to see you again, Maeve... let's go down. They already have wine poured. Or can I interest you guys in a shot? My treat?"

Of course, none of us turned this down, and she ordered some impressive flaming thing off the menu that probably cost twenty bucks a piece because she was showy like that. It did taste damn nice, though, and I welcomed the cinnamon warmth into my chest and the instant calm eighty-proof alcohol offered. Then, we followed her and her hair (because it was practically a separate entity, as if shadows were made of sunlight) to the table downstairs.

It was a long table for twelve. Drake's crew already drank wine at one end and stood to wave and welcome us onto the other end. I'd really hoped that Quinn would be as far away from me as possible at this dinner. I'd contemplated this dinner and whether or not to wiggle our way out of it for the past couple of weeks. It wouldn't have been strange to suggest just the four of us old mates had some time to ourselves.

But Drake really wanted us to meet everyone, and it made sense to. Graphic Temple was here to stay as far as he was concerned. This wasn't just an eight-week gig, this was potentially his retirement plan.

I'd dreaded it for ages but a few days ago told myself it was for the best. Getting to know Quinn could potentially help with my jealousy. It might just calm the edge and the nonstop thoughts I had about Drake. It had become all-consuming that just about every time I thought about him, I thought about her, too.

The five of us took the far end of the table, Jas and Koa opposite me, Drake in the middle, then Quinn. Of course she had to sit next to him. She should have sat next to me if she'd had any intention of easing the pressure here. She wasn't an idiot.

Quinn had always been socially adept. Even way back in high school, she had plenty of fools in her court. She'd know I would be uncomfortable, and this was her move? To sit on Drake's arm instead of mine?

As it was a chef's table, he came out to tell us about dishes, and food and wine simply flowed. Before long, we were all several drinks in.

Quinn spoke to Koa a lot, as she should have. He was as good-looking as Drake and had that stand-off grumpy vibe that most women took as a challenge. Jas had told me his

unrequited heart belonged to her sister, but that's why I'd expected Quinn to try. She was the kind of woman who wanted every man to adore her just so she'd have the pick of the litter.

"Drake told me you run a surf school in Nakiki?" she asked him. "I've never been. Embarrassed to say I've never even heard of the island…"

"It's small. It's a US territory that operates under the jurisdiction of Hawaii."

"So you're Hawaiian?"

Jas piped up. "That's what we all say. Same bloodlines and all. Koa has Kamehameha blood in him."

Quinn shook her head.

Jas explained, "He was the king of Hawaii."

"Not true," Koa said humbly. "Jas just likes the idea of it."

"Oh, wow…" She thought that was impressive, immediately picturing herself as queen, most likely.

"And you work with Koa at his surf school?" Quinn asked Jas.

"I'm living in Southern Cali at the moment. Long story. Not worth talking about now. But yeah, I'll head back. It's just temporary, and I'm not interested in living outside Nakiki."

"I probably wouldn't either if I lived in paradise." Quinn smiled a charming, let-me-win-you-over smile. "In fact, you make me want to move there now. Especially with this subzero weather."

Koa finally spoke. "You can come anytime, lessons on the house."

"Oooh. Sounds like a quid pro quo. Maybe all of Graphic Temple can go and we do a shoot or something? Publicity for your services?"

For the first time, Quinn spoke my language. We Los Angelians could be mercenary business people.

"That's actually a good idea," I said to Koa.

Quinn seemed almost surprised that I'd said anything at all. I'd been quiet and observing thus far.

Koa piped up. "The lesson comes no strings attached."

He didn't flirt. Or maybe he did, and I just couldn't tell because Koa's face always had the same serious expression on it.

I still hadn't been able to get the story, how such an eligible bachelor on a small island could still be single when he was the kindest and deepest soul (after Drake, of course) on top of fucking gorgeous. He must have had ladies crawling all over him.

Drake put his fist to Koa for a bump, and they did. "Man, I can't wait to be back there." He turned to me. "That should be our first stop after all this. Maybe take a long weekend? Bring that fifties bikini you had at Uyu?" He kissed my lips and nuzzled me.

The attention felt amazing, especially in front of Quinn. But it was exactly this attention that turned her toward me. She leaned in on Drake; it looked like her monstrous melon breast touched his arm as she pressed herself toward me. He didn't flinch.

Was it in my imagination? Or were they this close now? Like how he'd hug Jas or Flick or Helena, and they could put their head on his shoulder in pure, unadulterated friendship? Was this just how it was after spending four weeks, day and night, with someone?

"Maeve, Drake tells me you're a lawyer at RI now. I was sorry to hear about your dad."

"Yeah. Thanks."

"So is it your plan to stay there, in the legal department

at R.I?"

She made it sound unambitious. Something in her tone condescended, judged this as stagnant when in reality a shit ton of entertainment lawyers would love to end up at a place like RI But I wasn't about to tell her my dream of running the place one day. I didn't want to sound like I justified her judgment. I wasn't ready to share my goals, but Drake did it for me.

"Maeve's got her eyes on the prize. She'll be the boss of all of us one day."

Quinn's eyes grew, and she lifted her eyebrows as far as they could go, but it was as if like she'd already started getting Botox or something because her face hardly moved.

"Wow," she said slowly with a hint of cynicism. Her gaze turned to her glass of wine. As she picked it up and swirled, her words wafted over to me in a patronizing tone: "Those are big shoes to fill."

Bitch. Goddamn motherfucking or fatherfucking whatever fucking fucking... bitch. How dare she? How dare she patronize me and at the same time pretend she actually knew my father? What game is she playing?

Drake rubbed his hand up and down my thigh. He was looking at Quinn and thankfully hadn't noticed my heart had stopped and I was near a full-blown cardiac arrest.

"You can't begin to imagine how fierce my girl is," he said to her. "She's like Cinderella. She can magically slip her foot into any size shoe, so you better believe it. She'll be signing our checks one day."

He supported me, and it was sweet, but it did nothing to quench the forest fire under my skin. I was flaming... fuming. And I hated myself for it. How could I let one six-word sentence slay this entire evening?

I couldn't. I had to calm down. I took a sip of wine and

inhaled slowly, but as invisibly as I could, exhaling, being sure not to let the dragon fire out of my nostrils. Drake wouldn't like me being catty. I considered one of my mom's Southern insults that nobody got but Georgians, but instead, somehow found a speck of integrity. "Guess we'll see. Actions speak louder than words."

Quinn placed her arm along the back of Drake's chair and leaned in again to speak to me, her mouth only inches from Drake's face. Okay, maybe five inches, even six, but it was too close for me. "One of my favorite adages. Speaking of action, you guys are coming to the show tomorrow night, yeah?

"Of course. I wouldn't miss it for the world." I took Drake's thigh into my palm and squeezed. I smiled at him, and he smiled back.

He had no clue he was the rope in a game of tug of war. Or was I imagining all of this? Was Quinn actually just flirty and confident? Flick, Drake's festival friend, was a lot like that. She winked at everyone and hugged them and touched them, but it was meaningless because she did it to everyone. Maybe that's what Quinn was like?

I had to convince myself she was harmless. I had to, or there was no way in my fragile state I'd get through the next four weeks. I was working the typical ten-hour days and coming home most weeknights to walk with my mom afterward. The exhaustion and worry mixed into a toxic fume, spreading as invisibly and as deadly as carbon monoxide right through my system. It was all slowly eating me alive, and Drake took center stage when my thoughts were at their worst.

He was the only good thing in my life that gave me joy right now. And when you didn't want to lose something, that's all you ever thought about... losing it.

OUR NIGHT TOGETHER WAS INCREDIBLE. It was a warm, nurturing love like the kind that must happen when a soldier came back from war. There were moments of desperation, moments of tenderness so pure it brought tears to our eyes, and moments that were purely carnal.

New York. The city that never sleeps kept its electric energy on us all night long.

He'd fallen asleep before me, which was rare; in fact, perhaps it had never happened before. I'd been exhausted but the last thing I remembered, tipsy and tired, was gently

wrapping his Uyu do-rag around his head for him as I'd learned to do in a YouTube video.

His eyelashes had been curly and thick, his lips beautifully relaxed, before I'd fallen asleep. A surge of love overwhelmed the moment, and I'd known I would never ever feel so deeply about anyone ever again. He was perfect. Maybe he wasn't everyone's perfect, but goddamn it, he was my perfect.

Morning came, and we'd probably only been asleep for an hour. Poor Drake. The digital clock stared at me with its red, evil eyes, telling me we didn't have long before Drake needed to get to practice. He was going to feel this today. I hoped I didn't ruin his show.

Spooning him, I whispered in his ear, "Babe. Time to get up."

He didn't move, but our phones gave him an extra nudge, mine sounding out chimes and his the Jimi Hendrix intro to "All Along the Watchtower." Jimi's guitar blasted Drake upward. He looked around as if he didn't know where he was and immediately felt his hair.

I laughed. "Don't worry, Princess. I tied your hair up. Don't you remember?"

His body flopped over mine, heavy. He buried his head in the covers over my chest. "I don't wanna go to school..."

"But you have music class today..."

His eyes peeked up. "Oh. Favorite day of the week."

His soft lips kissed mine, and he moaned. "I wish we had time this morning... sorry I have to rush out."

"It's fine. I'll see you backstage tonight."

A moment of silence replaced a thousand sad words, because after his show, he'd hop on a bus to head off to Boston. And I'd come back to this hotel room without him.

"Now this I could get used to! Brah!" Jasmine shouted and grabbed Koa's shoulders and shook them as music blared from the stage. Graphic Temple was full force into their first song.

Koa wasn't immune to Drake's electric guitar and smiled bigger than I'd ever seen before. Both of them affected, as if adrenaline was being pumped through that smoke machine instead of fog.

"Backstage mo bettah!" Koa jumped up and down to the beat, letting himself feel the rhythms within his limbs.

"Yeah, brah!" Jasmine danced, too; she was incredible, her hips seemed to have a life of their own.

They were drunk on the experience but also nearly half bottle of Jägermeister.

I didn't tell them I'd only mostly been backstage at big concerts. I didn't know what it was like to be in the crowd, unless I wanted to be. But anyway, this *was* different. This time it was *my* man. This time it was *their* family.

I threw my hands in the air and two-stepped, and even though the intense drums and Drake's guitar initially had me in hypnotized, soon my brain kicked into overdrive, and I looked out at the crowd.

Graphic Temple was a new band; Drake, a new kid on the block. This crowd hadn't come to see them. They were openers, and it could be seriously hard to capture attention in an arena this size.

I knew Vanessa and Jules were here, too, but anything I could feed back to Drake would help. Did the crowd

respond when he spoke to them? Did they like song two? Should they carry out solos longer?

I would do anything to help Drake succeed, so as much as I wanted to relax and party with our friends, this was my contribution. My dad used to take me to shows and tell me to watch the crowd. I'd learned from the best and I'd pass all that on to Drake.

Saying that, he was a hell of a front man, and the people who were in the venue, which admittedly wasn't SoFi or MetLife but was about five thousand strong, had largely been coaxed back out of their seats and into the pit by their sound. Toward the end of the set, people had hands in the air and were already spilling their drinks on each other. Caring more about the music than their booze was a hell of a good sign.

I bopped my shoulders and turned my attention back to my man, leading this incredible new venture to stardom. I felt it in my Lewis bones. Drake had this.

It was their second to last song, one of Drake's from one of my few visits to Seattle. One he'd said he'd written for me... "Darkness."

"In your eyes
Over there
They hid something
I knew you couldn't bear
I wandered over
Gave you my hand
Yours felt cold
Didn't understand..."

It all had been going too well, Drake's vocal blowing into my heart like a full-flown Victorian swoon. When the chorus came on, Tae and Quinn stopping playing. Drake

went a cappella with his warm, honey tone. Quinn came off the drums and went to his mic to harmonize with him...

"But in your darkness
I'll give you light...
She was so close.
"No matter what it is
I can make it right...
She closed her eyes. Her lips were too near. And this was my song. She'd made it hers. Worse. She'd made it theirs. Did he even notice how close she was? Was this how they'd sung *my* song for the past four weeks? Practically kissing?

The crowd sensed this was the last or penultimate number, and some people put their phones in the air. Jas and Koa got their phones out behind me.

I, on the other hand, had been completely paralyzed by this shock of losing... whatever it was that I was losing. Watching Quinn sing with Drake like that, like it had been about her, or like it was about him for her, I couldn't even tell, but it was worse than her seeing his dick. This was intimate. Like having an emotional affair over a physical one. A million times worse.

Tears stung behind my eyes, but I attempted to keep swaying so the guys wouldn't notice. But as they continued to sing, Quinn took her hand and ran some fingers through Drake's hair. My chest became tight and heaved faster, trying to suck in air, but my lungs were made of iron.

Just then, someone took my hand. I turned and blinked back the tears.

It was Jas. "It's just a show." Her words were sympathetic, kind, and had responded exactly to every thought in my mind and the ones that were surely splattered across my face. "She's just playing to the crowd."

"I know..."

Neither of us were convinced by my words. Jas wrapped her arm around me and snuggled me in tight. Her strong surfer arms held me the way I needed to be held. She boarded me up and prevented the tornado inside me from letting it all fly.

"Don't let it get to you, sis. Drake loves you and only you. This song wouldn't exist without you. All of this wouldn't exist for him without you. He knows that."

I nodded and thanked God the song came to an end. Drake glanced over to where we stood backstage and smiled. It was still *my song*. That's what his smile meant. I just wished Quinn knew it was mine, too.

She ran back to the drums, and it went from gentle, soft vocals to total fury on stage in an instant as they all seemed to strum and drum some sort of intro. Suddenly, the singer, of the main band, Filly, came on with her microphone in hand.

The crowd, surprised, roared wildly. Two more lead guitarists came on as well and played into the loop Graphic Temple had created. Their drummer came out and rocked his shoulders, pulsing to the beat Quinn tapped with her sticks.

"How ya'll doin' tonight?" Filly shouted into her microphone.

The crowd roared.

"I need you to wake up and tell me... how ya'll doing tonight? Who loved Graphic Temple?"

A bigger wave of sound rippled throughout the space.

"We're gonna take this last song with these guys who fucking rock by the way... "

Rooooar.

"Getting serious for a minute. This last song is dedicated to someone we know who passed away too early. Someone

who gave me a start in this industry. He was taken too soon, and we want you to all grab a flyer before leaving, scan the QR code, and consider giving a little something to a pancreatic cancer research charity we're supporting to help fight this cruel disease."

Drake continued strumming the loop but stole a look over at me and winked. Our gaze didn't linger. I didn't want it to because most likely my mouth hung open.

Holy shit.

Koa came to the other side of me and bumped me with his hip. He pointed at Drake. "That guy loves you." Was he saying this because he'd supported my donation drive? Or because he'd just carried on a very public near affair with his bandmate, and Koa, like Jas, wanted to reassure me?

It was all too much. And the worst thing about all of this was that as soon as this song was over, Drake would run off into the tour bus parked and idling behind the venue, ready to drive to Boston. I had to find a smile somewhere in my body for him to take with him. It was all just showbiz. I knew that. It had to be...

The song blurred, the crowd blurred, and time passed without me knowing it.

Our goodbye was even more hurried than I thought it would be. Jules rushed them off. There'd been a tipped-over gas truck somewhere on their route, making for several hours' delay, so they had to leave immediately. Drake kissed me, breathed me in with the best goodbye kiss a woman could ask for, given the circumstances.

I excused myself early, telling Koa and Jas I didn't feel well. I knew they didn't believe me, but they didn't press either. They'd leave that till morning.

That night, pushing myself down inside the cold sheets

of the bed, where only hours ago I'd made love to the man I wanted to spend forever with, I was crushed.

The cool sheets reminded me that he wasn't there. They'd been changed by housekeeping, so his smell was gone. His satin pillow wasn't on the bed anymore. His underpants weren't on the floor. The notebook he always kept on the nightstand for sparky ideas was gone.

I pulled the covers up as far as I could. Maybe if I couldn't see he was gone it wouldn't hurt so much. But when I closed my eyes, I realized his song was all wrong.

It was in the darkness that I saw all my greatest nightmares and all my fears, and he wasn't taking them away, he was putting them there. I peeked my eyes out, and the room blurred as they filled with tears. I didn't even try to hold them back. They weren't the kind of tears that were going to blink away or suck back with a snuffle.

I cried hard. Sobbed. With every pump of my heart another gush came out. I wiped my face, but as soon as old tears were dry, new ones arrived. How could this be happening?

Why did I have to share the best of Drake with everyone else? Why did Quinn have to be such a flirty, disrespectful, showy bitch? Why did my mom have to be a fucking alcoholic so I couldn't just be a silly twenty-six-year-old and run off to be a groupie with my rock star boyfriend?

When the questions started to repeat themselves with the monotony of counting sheep, my eyelids grew heavy. Totally exhausted, I shifted my face on my pillow looking for a dry patch, then finally slid down off it, under the covers, and let the night gobble me up.

18

Drake

I HADN'T BEEN able to see Maeve for a week, and our conversations had been briefer than ever. But now that I was in the States again, I had a plan. A surprise to be exact.

She hated surprises, I knew this, but she needed this in her life. Some spontaneous fun. Especially in light of all she'd told me about her mom. It was pretty dark where she was.

I thought it would be hard to contain my excitement and to pull off a shocker, but in actual fact, since our New York visit, we'd hardly spoken. It seemed as though she'd had a

meeting whenever I called or it was after work and I knew that her time with her mom was important so I didn't dare interrupt that.

The two times we'd spoken on the phone in the past week, Maeve seemed distant. I didn't think it was me at first but then I couldn't help but ask. I knew that my move to get donations in New York was bold and maybe a bit intrusive, but I'd asked her (sort of) beforehand, and she'd said maybe.

Anyway, since then, she'd insisted it was only a good thing and thanked me as thousands had been donated as a result of that. So I only guessed that she'd been having a hell of a time with her mom.

Even though her mom was important, Maeve was, too. And we couldn't care for others unless we cared for ourselves first. Maeve had put her mom's oxygen on first and forgot to breathe herself. I planned to resuscitate my beautiful woman, one breath at a time. One kiss at a time. One touch at a time. One thrust at a time... damn, I missed her.

I'd worked out the plan with Tyran, who although I loved like a brother, wasn't sure I trusted to keep a secret. I hoped could. I'd even gotten everyone else in on it.

Vanessa put a fake publicity meeting into our schedule, and according to that, we were still supposed to be in Northern California. Jules, Tayo, everyone was to say that we were meeting with *Next* magazine today. I'd even dared to ask Gina to help me get a full day fake conference into Maeve's schedule so she'd have to meet me at Loews Hotel in the lobby at nine-thirty a.m.

My plan, with less than twenty-four hours between our true next gig, was to fly down to LA, take my woman out for walk on Santa Monica pier and back to my hotel room on the beach, and even drive her to work the following day just

to pinch every lemon drop of zesty life out of myself and give her back some zing.

Life had become heavy for my little Fairy. I'd be the wind beneath her wings. If she didn't like that surprise then... well, I'd never do one again.

It was a mild winter day, and the sky was a lot clearer when I landed at LAX than it had been in San Francisco. It was a perfect sixty-degree morning as I put the plan into action.

Two taps, and Tyran's mobile was buzzing.

"Yo," he answered.

"ETA?"

"Yeah, I'll sign it today." He didn't let a thing slide, with Maeve in the car next to him. "Just having a quick breakfast with my sister in Santa Monica before heading in. I'll be at Loews in twenty-five minutes, so an hour there... should be in by ten-thirty, eleven latest."

Perfect. Tyran had spent the night with Maeve and Dixie in order to get Maeve out the door on time. She had to walk in at nine-thirty because I wasn't the only one who was going to be in the lobby.

I checked in at eight forty-five and rushed my things to my room. The mirror told me I wasn't quite the fairest, but it was nothing a little curl spritz and cologne couldn't fix. I headed downstairs and got the rest of the surprise items assembled.

Bing. My phone alerted.

TYRAN: The eagle has landed. At the valet.

One more minute, and she'd be walking through the door. I looked on either side of me, and my fellow surprisers of eighteen strong nodded with anticipation.

With a light December breeze, the door opened, and in walked Tyran with Maeve. They spoke about some-

thing, her eyes on the floor as she walked. When they got closer, her nerve endings must have sensed the crowd in which I stood. It wasn't any ordinary crowd. It was an a cappella group I'd hired to help me serenade the hell out of my girl.

When her eyes lifted, they widened and shifted back and forth quickly, until they landed on me. The shock was pure. When something was so unbelievable, our brains told us to blink, rub our eyes, and open them to something more expected. Her mouth parted slightly, and she brought a hand to it.

"One, two, one, two, three," I whispered like a conductor, getting the a cappella group on cue.

I picked one of the best all-time love songs. One every person on the planet knew and probably sang at karaoke. Aerosmith's "Don't Wanna Miss A Thing." The group sang with me.

Aerosmith's words, and the easy, uncomplicated harmonies of my slapstick group had Maeve blushing. I'd known she would. I loved seeing her squirm, though, and she needed to feel something different for a while. She needed a break from stress, worry... from missing me.

If she needed a hero, I wasn't going to let her down.

Somehow, miraculously, my few times listening to this group's a cappella version, and I'd been able to fit in. It tugged at even my heartstrings as passersby stopped to watch and took out their cells to record. Maeve had her face buried in her hands, peeking out between two little fingers.

Our final note filled the foyer, closing off with a harmonious hum that would fill this space with love and positive energy for months to come. Maeve shuffled toward me, her face still buried in her hands. I took her into my arms. She was rigid, and I tried to prize her hands away.

"Baby, I came all this way to kiss you," I said softly into her ear.

"I can't..."

She finally let me take one finger off. There were tears in her eyes.

"Oh, babe..." I kissed her salty cheek. "Do you still hate surprises?" I pulled her in and kissed the top of her head.

"I love it... how did you...?"

"I found these guys online, set a date, and we practiced a few times on Zoom."

"I'm speechless." She turned to Tyran. "Were you in on this?"

Tyran put his arm around Maeve. "You needed this. Now, I actually need to leave you two lovebirds alone because I don't have an imaginary meeting at eleven, I have a real one in forty-five minutes." He walked off. "Amazing job," he said, putting his arm on one of the singers, then he shuffled off to make money.

Most of the singers had other places to be, I doubted this was any of their full-time income, and they trickled out quite quickly, leaving me and Maeve in the sun-drenched lobby alone, holding each other like we were the only ones who existed.

Even if people didn't have anywhere else to be, they wouldn't want to be with us. This was a party for two.

"Come, Fairy." I took her hand. "Let's pop your things in the room and have a big walk... I'm your training buddy today." I quickly added, "Tyran's hanging with Dixie tonight, so no need to think about anything but right here, right now. Relax yourself and be with your lover boy."

She reached up on her tiptoes for a kiss. "I love you. Thank you... but I need to call work? I'm supposed to be there in..."

"All sorted. You have the day off. Gina helped me."

"She did?"

"The perfect surprise leaves no loose ends."

Her eyes searched mine for something, though I couldn't tell what.

We headed to my room, and I opened the door for her to reveal several gift-wrapped boxes on the bed.

She looked at me with curious eyes. "Whose birthday is it?"

"Every day is a day for gifts. Open them."

I took her work bag off her shoulder and ushered her to the bed.

"Any particular order?"

"Small to big."

She unwrapped the small box, in which there were toiletries for the evening. A toothbrush, some girlie face washes and creams, the makeup I was pretty sure she wore, and everything she'd need for an overnight after which I knew she'd have to head straight to work.

"Wow, you *have* thought of the details," she said, lifting up a bottle of porcelain foundation. Thankfully, her skin was predictably vampire shade because when I'd gone to the Chanel website to look at foundations, turned out there were a billion hues.

She opened the next package. Inside was an outfit for today. Sneakers, some sexy Lycra (I hadn't known workout clothes could be quite so hot until I went hunting for some and I couldn't wait to watch Maeve's ass climb a hill in this).

I'd been watching her standing, taking mental pictures of each surprise as it entered her, lighting up her eyes with a brightness I hadn't seen for weeks. I sat on the bed next to her and handed her another box.

She shook her head. "I can't believe this, Drake. I honestly feel like I'm dreaming. This is very *Pretty Woman*."

"Except I prefer the bob to curls."

"And I prefer Drake to Edward..." She kissed me. "I... I don't know what to say."

I tapped the biggest box. "Open it." It was the gift I'd taken the most time to choose.

A woman like Maeve had a million little black dresses. She had very little color in her wardrobe, and coming from a family where before her dad died they'd gone to a lot of industry parties, it was pretty intimidating picking out an LBD for the queen of LBDs.

As she slid the lid off the box and unfolded the crepe paper, for a moment, I felt something like nerves. I wasn't really sure because I wasn't one to get nervous, but my belly flopped like I'd dropped into a sudden dip in the road.

Maeve held up a Valentino leather minidress. It had a skater-style skirt, cute with heels or maybe even a pair of black Converse to be sassy, not that I'd ever seen Maeve in sneakers, but I could envision her on a skateboard cruising down the boardwalk.

A 3D leather flower sat right between the cute cups, perfect for hugging her breasts when they weren't in my hands. I was a fashion guy, and since meeting Maeve at Uyu, completely imagined her in a variety of black dresses I'd seen in ads. Every time I saw an outfit I liked, I'd always wondered what it would look like on Maeve instead of the model.

Now, I could afford to spoil her.

A surge of pride lifted my chin. "You like?"

"You shouldn't have... this is... it's too much."

"Nothing is too much for you, babe. Nothing. I swear I couldn't buy you the Taj Mahal and feel I was done."

Her hand caressed my jaw. "I love it. It's..." She looked down at the dress again, and I had to admit, I'd outdone myself.

She climbed on top of my lap. ""I guess this means we're going out tonight? Or I'd be happy to slip into it for room service?"

I slid my hand up her pencil skirt. "Naked will do."

Rolling her onto the bed, I threw myself on top of her, locking her hands down above her head. I pressed into her, just enough for her to feel me, to know I was in charge now. Her silky top crumpled under my fingers as I slithered it up and inhaled her perfume from her neck.

She arched her back and rolled her head backward, craning her neck with the deceptive innocence of a swan. I inched her top all the way up and over her arms, her hands, and traced my fingers down along her arms, watching her shudder, and by the time I reached her ribs, there were tiny goosebumps. Her eyes were closed as they usually were when I was on top. I didn't know if it was because she was self-conscious or if she wanted to soak in the experience through her other senses. I'd never know with Maeve. She was a mystery still, in so many ways, luring me in with wonder.

Taking my time, I perched above her, unclasping her bra. It whispered to down her sides, her perky breasts, some Lolita making me feral with wanting but at the same time had this forbidden, youthful quality. I'd never had myself down as a pervert until Maeve. I think she loved her breasts as much as I did.

I brought my lips to her delicious skin, taking nibbles around her nipples, the tip of my nose gracing her nipple until it was so hard it cut against me with urgency.

She moaned, "I can't fucking stand when you tease me..."

"You love it..." I searched under a pillow, and I pulled out a nipple clamp.

Her eyes were still closed, and she sucked air when I pinched her little tit. "Fuck." She finally opened her eyes. "What else do you have hidden around here?" She smiled at me, a total vixen.

I worked my hand around the back of her skirt and tugged down her zipper. The waist of her skirt loosened, and before I could even do the job myself, she wiggled herself out of it, panties and all. I loved every inch of that skin, so soft and unblemished she seemed to be made of perfect porcelain. All I wanted was to press mine against her.

Throwing my own clothes off with abandon, my dick was already thick and hard for her. I knelt at the edge of the bed, yanking her legs off the edge, easing them wide open so I could taste her already glistening pussy.

I dove in, kneading her clit with my lips, reaching up with my fingers to take her other nipple in them. I squeezed hard, pinching relentlessly just like she liked, and she writhed, lifting her hips, urging her core toward my mouth, and I sucked her pebbled clit in gently, taking it between my lips with tension, rubbing the tip of my tongue over it at the same time.

I plunged two fingers inside her and she clenched around them. The smoothness of her insides made me mad, feeling my fingers grew wet with her desire. She shoved harder toward me, wanting it more. I couldn't take it anymore. My cock was fucking rock-hard, it had waited fucking forever to have her.

Pushing her down into the bed, I turned myself upside

down and climbed on top of her. She opened her mouth for me, and I eased my dick inside. The warmth of her mouth was enough to make me let out a groan, and I pressed in deeper, bending down to find her pussy again. When I spread her lips apart, her clit came out to play. I licked it madly as she ran her mouth up and down along the length of my cock, taking it deep, right to the back of her throat. It was all fucking too much. To be able to taste her pussy and fuck her at the same time was a dream come true.

Her hand played with my balls, and I had to hold back from fucking her face hard. My lips were soaked with her juices now, and after such a long time, I couldn't help but give her clit a light bite. She moaned, and I wanted more of that. I wanted to make her fucking scream.

I eased my index finger into her pussy and let the middle one play with her ass. She spread her legs wider, and I eased her juices over her asshole, massaging it. She gyrated and sucked my dick even harder. I knew she liked it, I knew she wanted it. I wanted to fill every inch of her up with me. I pressed my finger inside her, filling her up slowly, igniting all her senses, and she took me in deeper into her mouth, sucked hard. I had to clench back my urge to explode into her mouth, to make her swallow me whole.

I'd waited so long to have her. I needed to have her. I took my fingers and my dick out. Maeve sat up and pushed herself deeper into the bed, looking at me with her crazy sexy brown eyes like fucking Bambi. I grabbed a condom from under my pillow of tricks and ripped it open with my teeth, rolling it on to my tight, desperate cock as quickly as I could. My God, I could have come in my hand if I wasn't careful. Especially went she went on all fours.

I climbed into her and, on one knee with the other bent, I plunged deep inside her. So deep, every inch of her swal-

lowed my cock. Every velvety stroke of her pussy along the length of my thick cock felt like it would be the last, I was so hard for her. I wanted to be consumed by her. I urged her back lower, her face now against the bed, and she took me in an inch more. My balls tapped her clit, and I thrust into her. In and out, I had to brace her hips. I couldn't help but pound harder and harder, the urge inside me to explode and release making me feel more and more helpless.

I pulled her up onto her knees, still balls deep. I wanted her body flush with mine, I wanted her warm back against my torso. I reached my hand around to tighten the nipple clamp.

"Fucking God..." she groaned.

I reached down to play with her swollen clit, circling it while I thrust in and out. She grabbed the hair at the nape of my neck, sending a fucking shiver right down through my cock, and I couldn't take it anymore. I filled her harder, circled her clit with just the right amount of restraint, which was a miracle because I felt fucking crazy for her.

"Ahhhhh..." She let out a groan, and with it, her clit pulsed underneath my fingers, her cum wet around me.

Pushing deeper, faster, harder than I was sure she could take, she felt like ecstasy. My whole body shook. I felt ferocious with wanting. With taking... I exploded deep inside her.

THAT AFTERNOON and evening reignited something in Maeve. I wouldn't have said that the spark had gone out, at least not for me, but Maeve's had been fading. Or losing momentum. I couldn't tell exactly what it was, but I'd been

determined to bring it all back again, and this morning, after a perfectly executed surprise date, sitting in the lobby curled up with each other like two entwined cats trying to stay warm, it felt like we were back on track.

We waited for my rental car, the one I'd gotten so I could drive Maeve to work, then myself to the airport, when I noticed Quinn at the reception desk.

"Ey! Yo!" I shouted and waved.

Maeve's eyes glanced over in the direction I yelled then stiffened. Fuck. I was right. It was Quinn that was setting her off.

She muttered, "What's she doing here?"

Though admittedly she succeeded in her words coming out neutral and curious, I knew better. "We flew down together. She wanted to hang out with friends."

I pulled Maeve in deeper for a snuggle, but it might as well have been hugging a plank of wood. By this point, I'd very much regretted waving at Quinn and making our presence known.

Quinn sauntered over in her high heels and tight bodycon dress. "Hey, you two... how did the surprise work out?"

Yes. Thank you, Quinn, for that. Now Maeve knows I talked about her. That she's my number one. That Quinn Hartley knows I pull out all the stops for my girl.

I didn't move from my spot with Maeve, and although she tried to shift away from me slightly, I locked my arm around her. We were united. A couple. We came as a unit when we were together as far as I was concerned, and PDA was the only thing that could come between us.

"Yeah, perfect," I said. "The group was on point. But doesn't matter what I think. Did you like it, babe?"

"The a cappella group was nice... the rest was better."

She looked up into my eyes slyly but also with something else in hers.

I couldn't be sure, but if I had to name it, I'd use the word vexed.

"Gah. TMI." Quinn pretended to be disgusted but smiled. Merely alluding to sex was not enough to pain this one. She put a hand on her hip. "Well, I got to dash this morning. Squeezing in one last coffee with my mom. Don't be late for our flight, big boy."

She started to walk off then turned. "Oh, and check your messages. They booked us another tour on the back of this US one." She lifted her shoulders with excitement. "Japan!" She left us with a wave that said goodbye with only her fingers.

19

BIG BOY?

Was this something she called him all the time? Why the hell did she have a term of endearment for my boyfriend? And why big boy? Where the hell did she get that from?

I held in my screams, and the heat of them could have melted metal. I'd just started to feel slightly better about all of this. More secure in Drake's love. In our ability to wait it out, and here she was, inserting herself into my future memories.

Until fifteen minutes ago, I'd planned to hang on to this twenty-four hours like a lifeline. But now...

Drake picked up his phone off the couch we sat on and opened some messages. "Shit. Wow..."

"Japan?" I asked. "When does that tour start?"

He stared at his phone, but I knew he'd already read the message. My underarms prickled. My Aesop Herbal Deodorant was no match for the combination of being pissed off about Quinn and him being gone again.

"Fuck. Wow." He scrolled a bit through the message. "Looks like we go straight from our last US date in Chicago."

"Well, that's good. More tours is a good thing." I didn't mean it. I didn't mean it one little bit, but I tried to. And I should have. I should have been happy that Drake was in demand. I should have been happy that his dream was coming true, but as many times as my mind warred with my heart, I just couldn't negotiate a truce. There was no peace, and there probably wouldn't be until all this was over.

Wrong as it was, disgusted as I was with myself for thinking that way, much as I could *never* say that out loud to anyone, I thought it. And even though this thought kept me company day and night, never leaving my side, a faithful and very annoying companion, it made me feel like the loneliest woman in the world.

"It is a good thing," he said, still reading his phone. His eyebrows knitted together, and he finally looked up. "Three weeks. How am I going to go three more weeks on top of the few we've still got left?"

"*You'll* be fine."

Passive-aggressive was a term that was highly overused. People always said it even when, in actual fact, the person saying the supposedly passive words was being overtly

aggressive and the recipient just wanted to ignore a fight. This time, it was apt.

He would be fine. Drake had Quinn. *He* had the thrill of achieving his lifelong dream and chicks throwing their souls and virginity at him at after parties. *He* had the experiences and joy of creating and living in the moment and the finest life a twentysomething man could ever dream of.

Drake wasn't stupid. He picked up on the nature of my comment and was smart enough to let it go. There was absolutely nothing he could say right now. I didn't even want to know when he'd get back. As far as I was concerned, a minute past the time I'd been working toward for the past five weeks was more than I could bear.

A man in an Enterprise polo shirt came in to the lobby, looked around, and spotted Drake. "Hey! Did you order a rental car?"

I untangled myself from Drake and stood so he could, too.

Enterprise Man handed Drake some keys and asked Drake to sign a few papers. My thoughts continued to reel in the beat of silence. How did I go from feeling solid to as combustible and chaotic as propane? My brain was flying off in all different directions, my logic floating away like a sad birthday balloon from a crying child. And I felt just as spoiled and rotten and ungrateful as that little kid who hadn't enjoyed what they had when it was actually within their grasp.

How could I be thinking of myself right now? When Drake needed me to be cool? When my mom needed me here anyway? Why couldn't I just let fate and life take its course and be patient? Let time reveal all things? Why did I hate Quinn and why did I think about her nearly as much as I did Drake when they were away?

Drake finished up with his documents, and we walked out to where a sleek, black Mercedes sat with its top dropped. It was a luxurious choice to get around town, and I knew Drake wouldn't have gotten something like that just for himself. It was yet another thing he'd done for me. So why, with all of this... with all this wonderfulness that he'd put together just for me could I not feel settled?

Because in all of this there were too many uncontrollable factors, and I was a woman who thrived on predictability. Touring was unpredictable. Fans were unpredictable. Quinn was definitely unpredictable.

My mom had told me a long time ago, the only other time a guy in a band went for me, that I'd never be able to deal with being in a relationship with a musician. My mom had had a lot of bits of advice throughout the years, and she'd always been right, apart from Uyu. That she'd gotten completely wrong.

But wearing lipstick did make me feel prettier. That magic mushroom tea was a drug that my brother had found fun and I could not handle. My brother and I did eventually become friends "when we grew up," and I was better suited to law than finance. Just like she'd said. Wolford stockings were worth the money, my hair was nicer when I didn't wash it every day, and I got over being attracted to bad guys by the time I was out of college. Just like she'd told me.

Maybe she was right this time, too. Maybe steady, boring, formulaic Maeve couldn't thrive with all this variety. All these questions. She'd told me a performer would drive me insane. It certainly felt truer than I wanted it to. I hadn't been able to properly concentrate since the day Drake had left LA.

We popped my parcels and Drake's carry-on in the trunk, and Drake came around to my side to open the door

like the gentleman he was. I lowered myself in and stole a glance at his stunning chiseled cheeks, beautiful lips, and hell, I even loved his nostrils, for fuck's sake. Everything about him was perfect... except the timing.

I wanted to be the woman for him. I wanted to be confident with chaos. And I really believed that before my dad died, I was getting pretty damn close to being one hundred percent comfortable in my own skin. But when I met Drake, I'd hit a wrinkle in time, and I was still trying to iron things out at home. I tried hard to hide it, but my eyes were probably green by now.

I hardly even noticed that we were already off the 10 headed up the 101. Neither of us said much. Maybe his balloon had floated away, too. Or maybe he felt like he'd just been given a thousand of them and was flying away toward his fairy-tale ending.

Either way, we both pretended to listen to the radio, and I'd never been more thankful for oversized sunglasses being in fashion.

Drake drove through the security gates at Reckless Integrity and to my parking spot. They'd given me my dad's, and for the first time since parking in it, I thought less about how I planned to make him proud here at RI and more about how much I missed him. I knew that it was unlikely I'd ever have met Drake if he hadn't died, and at the same time, I knew he'd make all of this better if he was still here.

Drake turned off the engine. He breathed in through his nose then let out a heavy sigh. "This hasn't all ended the way I planned."

What hadn't ended? Us?

"I thought this would have given us a boost to get to the end of the eight-week tour."

Oh. Phew.

He continued. "I'm trying really hard not to sound ungrateful for all this but..." He looked me in the eyes. "I know you need me here. And I can't help but feeling I'm abandoning you. But I don't know any other way to take care of you but this. I hope you don't think it's easy for me."

"At least *you're* having fun." Shit. It had come out wrong. I'd tried to say it like: hey, look at the bright side, at least it's entertaining. But it came out as I'd really felt it: oh, give me a fucking break.

"What's that supposed to mean?" he let out, clipped and curt.

Oh shit. This sentence is the entry point to every argument.

But I wasn't one to shy away from that. I was a lawyer after all. "I guess it means I really don't want to hear you complain about living your best life and have you tell me you're sorry you can't be with me. It's absurd."

"Absurd? Wow, Maeve. There's a word choice." For the first time ever in my time meeting Drake, he sounded exasperated.

"My turn to ask... what's that supposed to mean? It is absurd, Drake. The word choice is perfect if you ask me."

Oh no. The brakes were off, and I could feel us rolling toward to edge of the cliff.

"So you really think it's absurd that I'm torn between the girl I love and the career I love? Maybe you don't get how love works."

His blood simmered beneath his skin. The temperature rose in the cockpit. I'd never seen Drake like this before. Ever. I should have taken a deep breath and picked apart what was happening. I should have been more sympathetic. Empathetic. But my ego had kicked in.

"You're saying I don't know how love works? Or do I know better than you do how it works, Drake? I'm

wondering how you can't see how I could question your sincerity. I mean, you've had this dream for like, a decade. You only met me five months ago..."

"A hundred and sixty-five days ago..." he said. The fact that he'd crossed off calendar days should have been romantic, but he'd said it to defend himself. "But you wouldn't know that, would you, Maeve? Because I'm always the one chasing the next day. Not you."

My jaw dropped. For the third time in a span of five minutes, the same question arose. "What's that supposed to mean?"

Drake threw his head back, ran his fingers through his hair, and sighed. "I shouldn't have said that. I'm just frustrated. I didn't think I'd be gone even more. And I'm feeling all sorts of shit right now and I only have a few minutes to talk about this... fuck."

He lifted his head, considered me, and put his hand on my leg. "It's not easy to have zero control over your destiny. That's what this feels like. Like... fuck... this Japan thing... coming in like some casual email owning my life, my time. Is this how it's going to be? How fucking long could they just keep tacking on two weeks? Four weeks?"

"Two years I think is the longest..."

"I know! I fucking know... the fucking Grateful Dead lived on tour..."

The problem for Drake wasn't that he didn't want to tour. It was the push-pull factor. It was that something waited for him at home. A needy, dependent, feeble woman waited for him.

He'd be better off without me. He could cope with all this without me. Drake liked control as much as I did, but without me in the background, he would focus on what was within his control. And there was plenty. The songs they

performed. How they performed them. The clothes they wore and the look they'd curated. How they interacted with the crowd... he had a lot of power and only felt he didn't because of me. A wave of guilt drowned me.

I looked at my nameplate signpost for the parking spot. They'd only had to replace the Mitch with Maeve. You could see they'd kept the Lewis. Maybe they'd even kept the M.

Suddenly, a quote of my dad's seemed like the one to describe everything that happened here between me and Drake. "If you chase two rabbits, you won't catch either one."

Drake laughed lightly, but not because he thought it was funny, just out of place. "I'm not going to ask what that's supposed to mean."

"Good. Because you know what it means. If you really think about it. And so do I."

His nostrils flared as a flash of understanding sparked in his eyes. Then a fierce, almost scary look took over, and his brown eyes went black. "Don't go there. I'm not that guy. I don't play that game."

"What game?"

"You know. The daisy game. He loves me, he loves me not? I have a one-track mind. We're together or we're not. I'm not about this..."

"It's not an ultimatum by the way."

"Good." He sounded mad again.

"What I meant was..."

"I know what you fucking meant, Maeve. I'm not better off without you. Some problems don't have a solution, you just have to live with them. Life gets uncomfortable sometimes. That's all I was saying."

He gazed out the driver's-side window so I couldn't really see his face, but his jaw clenched, and he rubbed the

back of his neck. He threw his hands onto his lap with a loud clap. "Jesus, I want to be able to talk to you without you going off the deep end. Can we do that, or are you always going to be looking for the exit when things get hard?"

"I'm not looking for the exit..."

He turned to face me, his features rigid and eyebrows tense. "Could have fooled me with your clever little quote."

An apology was perched at the edge of my tongue, but I didn't know why. I wasn't sorry for thinking that Drake might have a better time without me. I wasn't sorry for thinking that this would be easier for him if he was single. I wasn't sorry for being focused on my only remaining parent.

This was going nowhere. And worst of all, when I checked the clock, it was time for Drake to leave. He must have noticed the time, too. He let out a big sigh and ran his thumb along the length of his lips. The ones I used to kiss instead of fight with. This felt so shitty. We'd never argued before.

He shook his head quickly, and his shoulders along with it, then turned to me with a smile. Not a big smile from the heart but one from the head. One that hoped to gain some kind of resolution before he said goodbye. "I don't want to leave you like this. I love you."

"I love you, too. So much." I grabbed his hand. "It's just, not everything is about love. Is it?"

He left shortly thereafter with mine being the last significant words uttered between us.

I'd regret saying them till the day I died. Which felt very soon, judging by the strain of my heartbeats when I stood on the curb watching him drive away.

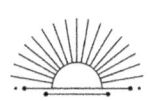

Drake

I DIDN'T CHALLENGE HER. I just wanted to wrap up our conversation and time together as nicely as possible before I took off for another huge stint, not knowing when I'd see her next.

But after I settled into my airplane seat, said hey to Quinn, popped on my noise-cancelling headphones and eye mask to block out the fury of the world, I couldn't help but replay her words in the blank space.

"Not everything is about love."

What did she mean by that? Love certainly guided

everything for me. And up to this point, I'd sworn it was everyone's lighthouse. Love, or hate (which could arguably be the same thing if you looked it at hard enough) motivated everything I did.

I wished we'd had more time. I'd wished we hadn't argued and I hadn't let my frustration get the best of me. I should have managed that situation like the man I wanted to be for Maeve.

From the minute I'd heard that story about her dad on the pirate ship at Uyu, I'd wanted to take care of her. I wanted to put her first. Even the Jay situation and my best friend stealing my songs didn't compare with my urge to comfort her.

But she was making it harder and harder. Maybe I was refusing to take a hint. "Not everything is about love" and her two rabbits quote? Was she trying to tell me something, force my hand, or did she need reassurance?

Either way, I'd pretty much failed in doing both. And the coal of anger I held on to over her acting that way kept telling me she needed to be a big girl, too. This was hard for both of us.

Which felt a slightly ridiculous comment as I reclined in my first-class airplane seat. But I wasn't going to pretend that this wasn't complicated. Or that it was comfortable for me. She didn't realize how my heart ached not being able to make a single promise anymore. RI owned me. Today, when that Japan tour came through over email, was the first time it had really sunk in.

If I wanted this dream to come true, I'd sacrifice my freedom for it.

And now, maybe the love of my life, too.

LATER THAT NIGHT, while I sat in my dressing room with my feet up on a sofa, knuckles rapped my door. I looked at it and sighed. "Come in."

It was Tae and Quinn with a bottle of champagne.

Tae held it up. "Dude. I know you don't like to really drink before shows, but we thought it was time to celebrate Japan."

Quinn gave a smile that was one I'd never seen before. Was it meek? Maybe. I'd completely ignored her on the flight to Colorado, hadn't said a word through fetching suitcases, and I was pretty sure I'd said something to our driver before I really talked to her. I was in my head about Maeve, and that wasn't a great place for me. I got tunnel vision when I started trying to figure out unsolvable problems.

Tae continued. "Might loosen you up?"

He didn't know what was wrong either, but it was impossible to miss I'd basically been an automaton at warm-ups tonight. Tae lifted the bottle toward me with concern in his eyes. I looked back to Quinn and realized that's what her smile was about, too. Concern.

Being present was the best gift you could give yourself. If I took this moment out of context, it was perfect. I had two bandmates who only a couple of months ago had been total strangers, and now we were all achieving our biggest dreams together. It could have been so much worse. These two were such a serious improvement on Jay and the dynamic I'd been dealing with for the better part of my twenties. How could I let them see me sulk? I was supposed to be the leader of this pack.

It meant a lot that they'd sought me out to cheer me up. I'd spent so many years being the one to do that for Jay that to have these people with me on an even footing, proper peers who could jam and contribute like equal partners... this felt amazing.

"Too right," I said. "Tonight we need to bring the house down."

Tae poured into some plastic glasses.

I toasted. "To new friends, new adventures, and taking the world by storm. To Graphic Temple..."

The guys clinked my cup with an uneventful sound, but their voices had plenty of hope. "To Graphic Temple."

We drank, and that was the first bottle of many. When the alcohol hit my system, it seemed a hell of a lot easier to be present and do the job I was meant to do.

We sipped from our glasses, and I perked up, not only because of the drink but because these two didn't deserve to be dragged down. For them, getting the news about Japan was everything going to plan. It was more than we'd all dreamed of the first time we'd tried to play together back in LA. We'd come a long way in a short amount of time, and my bandmates deserved to feel happy, and for me to share the part of me that was, too.

A stage manager poked their head through the door Tae had left ajar. "Five minutes."

"Better get cracking..." Tae poured the remaining bottle into our Silo cups, some of it spilling over as we downed it.

Before we left the dressing room, I grabbed the guys into a huddle. "Thanks. Seriously... I just want you to know I'm grateful. You two work hard. You're smart. You're fucking amazing at what you do. Nobody I'd rather do this with than you two."

They squeezed me back.

Moments later, the three of us ran out on stage. Quinn went straight to the mic and shouted, "What's up, Deeeeenveeeer!"

Even if I hadn't been buzzing, her energy would have been infectious. Tae had some groovy lip pout thing going on as he plucked his strings. Quinn ran to the drums and pounded, and I wailed on my guitar with abandon. The songs flowed like never before that night.

Everything was different. It couldn't have been simply sharing a drink beforehand in the dressing room. We'd done that at least a couple of times before. Especially in the early days.

That's when I realized it was me. It was me who had been holding back. Sure, it was only a fraction, a minuscule thing, but that's often the difference between a megaband and one that didn't make it. One percent. It wasn't that one group's songs were bad and one's good. It was a difference so imperceptible that people just called it the X factor. Or even "je ne sais quoi" which literally meant "I don't know what." Nobody seemed to know exactly what made an international success over a band that never cruised out of Seattle, but I could tell you now. It was this one percent.

I held back one percent for Jay. And Maeve was right, I'd held back that one percent for her. Hell, probably even more.

I hadn't wanted to admit it. I hadn't even known it, but she'd been speaking the truth. It wasn't that I was better off without her but that I had been holding back because of her.

Still, as I sang a song inspired by her sleek black bob and tortured, Goth-like soul, I knew we could do it. We could both have it all. We just had to believe. I needed to go full

throttle, and so did she. We needed to stop simply being infatuated teenagers and start being partners. An upgrade.

In fact, I thought about upgrading the whole damn thing in more than just my mind. In more than just hers.

Maybe a ring would make this all different.

LATER THAT NIGHT, we came offstage on a total high. We'd played better than ever before. Tae and Quinn felt like family all of a sudden. Like my crazy assortment at Uyu. They felt it, too.

Tae cracked open a beer and handed me one, then lifted the cap off another for Quinn. He gave it to her. "So, Queen Quinn... I know Big Daddy convinced us after parties would make us tired and ruin our sound, but I need a wingman tonight."

She lifted a brow with feigned curiosity because we both knew what the hell he meant. "Oh? Whatever would you need a wingwoman for?"

"I have a feeling the girl with the afro in the front row will be waiting by the tour bus."

"Oh, you dirty boy. I was starting to think you were celibate. But even I noticed her... that hair..."

Tae took a swig and nodded, thinking about the hair. "There was a lot of eye contact going on." He turned to me. "What do you say, Big Papa? I know we've been on strict curfew, and I'm not complaining, because up till now we've all sounded tight, but we need to celebrate Japan, bro. This shit's kicking off, and we need to ring it in."

They didn't know I wasn't just some totally focused, type A lead singer. I had so many reasons for keeping fans off the

tour bus. Sleep, performance. Maeve. Fears around Jay point 2 developing. But they were right. This was their dream, too. And just because I had my issues didn't mean they should own them.

"I was going to take a walk anyway. Need some fresh air. Do what you want."

I was going to say they didn't have to ask me for permission but held that back. It was probably better that they'd felt they should. I wasn't their dad but I didn't mind them thinking I was the boss.

Tae and Quinn hugged each other with a silliness that made me realize just how much they'd wanted to party with fans.

I finished off my beer in one long pull then went over to Tae and Quinn and put my hands on their shoulders, joking. "Make sure Vanessa cards everyone."

They shoved off to the bus giddy, skipping like newborns foals. It made me smile. I hoped the one with good hair waited for Tae. Not sure what Quinn was looking for, just attention most likely, but I didn't hate her for it. We were supposed to be having fun in our twenties.

But it didn't work out like that for everyone. It wasn't working out like that for Maeve.

I managed to leave the building unnoticed, since people probably expected me to be with the Graphic Temple entourage. The air was dry and arctic in Denver that night, and the hot air from lungs, still full of spilled drinks and human humidity, breathed smoke into the black air. I walked quickly, to where I didn't know, but far enough away to escape any people who actually thought Graphic Temple was worth missing the main show.

It'd seemed like a totally industrial kind of area, but within a few blocks, I hit a river. I couldn't see it that well but

I could hear it rushing, and the strange combination of a sound I usually associated with leaves and nature, against the backdrop of buildings and manmade structures made me yearn for Snoqualmie. It brought back the days when I'd had my quiet alone-time walks on the outskirts of Seattle when things, despite being complicated, were simpler than they were now.

I leaned my forearms against a railing, so cold with Colorado winter I could feel it through my leather jacket. With my cell in my hands, perched and ready to see her face more than maybe ever before, I pressed the button next to her Pulp Fiction pose.

Booooop.

Booooop.

Two rings was a lot. Girl was making me sweat.

Booooop.

Don't tell me she was going to leave me hanging? Give me the silent treatment?

Booooop.

Shit.

Booooop.

I'd never known this, and very few people did, but Face-Time rang eleven times before telling you they were unavailable. I looked it up. Guessed if it rings less it meant they declined your call. At least she hadn't done that.

Where could she be at just after ten on a school night? I knew Maeve. We'd been up nearly the whole night before, and she couldn't handle full-on benders even if she was irresponsible enough to partake. She was a workaholic.

A text was all I had. It had to be good. It had to say what my entire conversation meant to say. I took in a breath of air so cold it burned my insides. Looking at my cell, I typed: *My*

Beautiful Dark Fairy—the only rabbit I need to catch is you. Stop running away from me. I love you.

I took one last look at the river and walked back to the bus, my ears and nose feeling they were on the top of Everest. Seattle winters were wet and got into your bones. Denver winters froze your blood and made your balls want to drop off.

I was actually okay with getting back on the bus by the time I reached it. The windows were partially steamed up already, and music blared from the inside. Our bodyguard Diego gave me a fist bump.

"What am I getting into in there?" I asked.

"About twenty extra bodies. Tae told me to card them, but there might be one fake ID."

"Ha. He took me seriously?" I shook my head. "Not sure they'll be happy Dad is home then."

He let out a gravelly laugh, and the bus door opened for me. The heat from inside instantly soothed my chapped face, and Quinn noticed me immediately. "Dray!"

She was half cut, or maybe whole cut, because my couple of drinks felt sober at this point. What were they doing? Beer bongs?

She pushed her way through a sea of mostly women and a couple of men who were either gay or wore a lot more glitter than the typical men coming to our shows.

Quinn wrapped her arm around me. "Hey, everybody, Daddy is back!" She gave me a silly kiss on the cheek.

She unraveled her arm, and my eyes were drawn to the back corner table where Tae lifted his hand to greet me, then turned back to the glorious mane of hair he'd been waiting for. I smiled inside for him and searched around for a seat, but there weren't any.

Quinn grabbed my arm. "Come on. Sit with us."

She led me to one of the long sofa benches. There were two that faced each other, and both were full of bodies. She led me to a half spot and shooed a girl over a bit to make room for my ass.

Then, to my surprise, she sat on my lap. "Ladies," she said to two women next to us, "and ladies..." to the two glittery men opposite, "I'm sure you already know Drake."

Quinn's bony ass shifted on my thigh when she reached over to a table at the end of the couch and grabbed her cell. She lifted it high, women circled me for the frame, and snap! She captured her selfie.

The gal to my right poked Quinn in the arm. "Oh. Can you tag me or send that to me? Please?"

"Yeah..." Quinn focused on her phone. She seemed to examine the photo like all social-obsessed people did as soon as they took one. She seemed satisfied, then turned around to speak to me.

Her face was close. Her arm draped around my neck, and she was one position away from being a lap dance. I'd had lots of my girlfriends sit on my lap before. But this one had to wait until I talked to Maeve.

"Yo. Your tailbone is like fucking Excalibur," I said.

"Is that your clever way of saying I'm no Kim Kardashian? I'm bringing back the waif look, Drake." She laughed.

The fans laughed with her.

"Well, go waif on someone else's leg while I get a drink. Want one?"

She wiggled her face into mine, not in the least bit offended by my joke because the woman had a wicked sense of humor. "Yes, please. Passionfruit vodka and tonic. But make it full-fat tonic. Apparently, I need it."

She got up.

I replied, "You need something more like a milkshake. And a burger and fries. But I'll get you going on that tonic to start."

I walked to our mini-kitchen, opposite the table where Tae sat, his girl's leg wrapped around one of his; she played with his hair while they spoke like the third wheel next to them didn't exist.

And now it had begun. This is what real rock stars lived like. Never in a million years would I have thought I'd be the geek of the group.

I started to make myself a drink then decided not to, pouring some plain soda. I went to give Quinn her drink and stayed standing, listening and considering which conversation I'd like to be a part of and picking none. The only conversation I wanted right now was with the woman I loved.

I missed her the way I imagined old people ached.

I REPLAYED the Mercedes drop-top conversation a million times and I replayed it yet again as I waited in the parking lot by my undeserved premium spot, waiting for my brother.

Although I regretted being such a petty child for moments of the fight, mostly, I knew what I'd said was true. I thought after a bit of time, scrubbing my brain with clauses and signatures, I'd be able to see that Drake loved me, and that I should apologize and tell him I was being foolish and stressed. I'd hoped that somewhere between

then and now I'd think that love *was* enough to get us through. But something in my tin can heart wouldn't let me.

Self-preservation. I knew that's what was going on from a logical point of view. I'd resigned myself to this not working out as if that way it would hurt less if it didn't.

Still, this wasn't the way I'd want to go out if we did. With Drake accepting some parable-like quote and maybe just dropping me a text? Or worse—ghosting me? Not that he'd ever do that, but leaving angry was not good. I felt caught in no-man's-land. Purgatory. I had no idea what was happening now. What was going on in his head?

And fucking hell. Would this be the crack that Quinn was waiting for? A weakness for her to take advantage of?

Before, Drake had called me, completely oblivious and totally on a happy high at the end of each day. He'd tell me about his day like some kid coming home after being picked first for the baseball team. Now, we'd have to hash out our first argument from hundreds of miles away. Maybe thousands. I yearned for the oblivion right now.

But no matter how hard I tried, I couldn't take back a feeling I justified over and over again. I stood in the chill of an LA night in a sea of concrete and cars, and he was basking in the stage lights, being cheered by a crowd of strangers. It might have been petty, but any woman in my position would be feeling just like me. It was impossible not to feel jealous and that he had the long stick in this situation. I wasn't Mother Teresa, for fuck's sake. Martyrdom was not a Gen Z trait.

I waited by my parking spot for Tyran to fetch me since I didn't have my car. I looked at my watch, and he was only five minutes late, so that meant he'd be another fifteen. I imagined Drake would have told him, when planning the

surprise, to make sure to be on time. Tyran would have lied and said he'd be here.

Suddenly, my heart felt less like a tin can and more like an over-filled water balloon. What had I done? Why couldn't I have controlled my tongue today? I'd tried to scare off the only man in the world to make me love surprises.

Tyran rolled up only ten minutes late and pulled into my parking spot so quickly I'd thought he'd knock down the sign.

I threw my things in the trunk and then myself into the passenger seat. "Only ten minutes late. Impressive. If I was some pathetic date of yours thinking you were God's gift to women, I'd be charmed by your near punctuality."

Tyran widened his eyes. "Eeeeeh... what the hell? I thought you'd be in a good mood tonight. I could've sent an Uber."

"I would have preferred it."

He turned off the car completely, put two hands on the steering wheel, and braced himself. "Talk. Spill it, because we both know this isn't about me."

I crossed my arms, trying to hold in some of the pain and the start of a sob that bubbled in my belly. "Drake and I had a fight..."

He took off his seat belt and turned himself toward me. "That was bound to happen eventually."

"What do you mean?"

"I know you don't want to hear it. Ladies go mental at the J word, but you're jealous."

"Misogynistic much? Men don't like being called jealous either."

"Not the same. Women have all sorts of devices to make men jealous. Women are attracted to jealousy. Men usually

aren't. Call it misogyny if you want, but it's fucking true. You know I'm right."

"Makes me sick."

"Is it more Quinn or the thought of fans or what?"

I examined my nails and picked the side of one because it was hard to look Tyran in the face. But I wanted to be honest. Having a male perspective right now would be helpful. But if I wanted it to help, I'd have to tell the truth.

"Mostly Quinn. I know Drake can resist attractive women, but if he develops a connection? That's what makes me worried. I don't trust her and I guess it's more I think that maybe he'd be drunk and he'd regret it, but the damage would be done from my perspective... then also, this is all so much easier for him. He probably doesn't even notice I'm not there most of the time. Meanwhile, I notice his absence every second of the day. It just feels unfair. That's me just feeling sorry for myself, I know, but that's how I feel, so there's no point in sugar-coating it."

It wasn't easy to say these things, but it did make me feel better. I registered this feeling in hope of creating some muscle memory. Being open wasn't all bad. In fact, not being totally open was what got me into this trouble in the first place.

"So I'm guessing the fight was because you told him something along the lines of 'you got it good?' And you probably left the Quinn thing out completely so that's still a mystery to him."

I cracked a meek smile. "You're pretty damn good, bro. Pretty much. That's it."

Tyran pointed at me with two fingers. "Only you know he knows, right? How you feel about Quinn? He probably didn't say anything because he still thinks you two are 'friends.'"

"What?" Mortification snatched my smile. "Did he say something?"

"No, he's just not dumb. You might as well talk about it because I'm sure he suspects it."

"I tried and failed."

"You tried to save face is what you tried. I know how these things go. I've been through how many breakups now? Like as many as I am years old. I'd have to be pretty dense to not see the pattern. Woman will pretend the fight is about anything but jealousy."

He was right. For weeks now, I'd avoided talking about Quinn. In my defense, it was partly because I'd thought it would go away. But now, the thought of saying it aloud, somehow admitting that I felt inferior in some way was humiliating. Tyran was right. I'd rather fight about anything than my low self-esteem.

I punched Tyran in the arm. "You should have been a therapist. You're wasting a super power."

"You kidding? I use psychobabble all the time in real estate. Plus, it pays better."

"Mmm."

He started the car back up. "Come on. I'm getting you home. You're going to stay up till whenever Drake's set is over and then call him. Tell him the damn truth and get over this. You two are good together. I'm usually a sceptic about these things and... you know." He sighed. "I see a lot of Mom and Dad in you two. It's magnetic. Beyond it all you're a good team. Be a team. Trust is only built when you take the fall. Now you gotta fall and let him catch you."

Tyran's words pumped me up. His faith in me and Drake as a couple shored up my foundation. I was ready. I was ready to call Drake and have a big-girl conversation. Be honest and vulnerable and trust that he'd totally get how hard this was for me.

But I never got the chance.

Tyran dropped me off, and by the time we'd gotten to our gate at nine p.m., he'd coaxed a few smiles out of me with stories of his silly office politics.

I opened the door, shoved my shoes in the hall closet, and immediately, something didn't feel right. It was very, very quiet. Quiet the way that pitch-dark is dark.

My mom always had a TV on these days or some music playing over Sonos when I came home. But there was nothing. She was definitely in. She'd texted me at eight, only an hour ago, asking if I wanted her to pop some salmon in for me for dinner.

"Mom?" I wandered deeper into the darkness, not a light showing the way, and with the sun deeply set, the eerie feeling I already had brewing inside me swelled. "Moooom?"

That's when I heard her. Her voice sounding feeble and old like a ninety-year-old woman calling from a hospital bed. "Maeve?"

I ran. I didn't know why I ran, but a sudden urgency took over. That wasn't her voice. It was her voice in trouble. "Mom?"

"Maeve…"

I followed the quiet trail of her murmured voice. I turned on lights in every room like I was scared of the dark. I searched around with a weird feeling, like when I'd find her she'd be tied to a chair by some kidnapper asking for ransom. Something was wrong. Very wrong.

I turned a corner, tapped another light on at the control pad, and I saw the something wrong. My mom was at the bottom of a staircase, facedown on her stomach, not moving a muscle.

"Mom!" I ran to her and knelt next to her. A lump formed instantly in my throat. "What happened? Are you okay?"

"Maeve?" she asked as if she didn't even know it was me beside her.

"You're at the bottom of the stairs, Mom. I'm calling an ambulance. Don't move."

I dialed 911 as apart from my name, my mom didn't say anything else, and she kept closing her eyes and disappearing. She didn't remember anything when I asked, or really, she didn't even respond. But she was alive. They were sending help right away.

I texted Tyran: *Mom had a horrible fall.*

Tyran called immediately. "What's happening? What...?"

I kept my voice as calm as possible in case my mom was more conscious than it seemed. "Mom is at the bottom of the stairs, and she can hardly talk or anything. There's no blood, but I... I just don't want to move her without professional help in case her back is broken or something."

My mom uttered my name again. "Maeve..."

"She keeps saying my name... I need you..."

I stroked my mom's head, gently, as to not move a single vertebrae. "I know you're okay, Mom. Just telling Tyran what's up. We're not worried, and you shouldn't either. Help is on the way."

I turned my attention back to Tyran. "Just pull over when you can, and I'll let you know what hospital we're going to when the medics arrive. Can you meet us?"

Of course, he said he'd drop everything.

That night, Tyran and I didn't talk much as we waited to be told that our mom had a fractured neck and a blood alcohol level of .22. The doctor said this was blackout level. Near loss of consciousness. Stairs weren't a good idea.

But before we had to contemplate how to put a baby gate over a grand staircase, the doctor told us they'd be keeping her in for at least occupational therapy with her halo and for an ASQ.

"What's that?" Tyran asked.

"Suicide Screening Questions," the doctor replied, still focused on his chart. When he did look up, he added, "Have you seen her drink to this level before? You both reported she was alone at home... we do see blood alcohol like this a lot in the ER, but she didn't come here from a frat party."

We nodded because that was all either of us could bring ourselves to do.

This wasn't how I'd wanted it to happen. But at least in the short-term Dixie would have no choice but to sober up. But had she done this on purpose? Had she tried to drink herself into darkness?

One thing was for sure. She was officially an alcoholic, and even when I looked at her with the huge halo contraption around her head, I was happy she'd been lucky enough to be given a chance to fight it. Maybe a broken neck would be easier than rehab. Or maybe this would be the most painful rehab anyone could experience.

That's when you knew you were really fucking low. When breaking your neck was the best thing that could happen to you, it didn't get much worse. Sitting next to the bed in the hospital, my mom sleeping and attached to a beeping machine, I saw what love did to a person.

Love wasn't always this wonderful thing that lifted us up and made us feel powerful. Love did hurt. I remembered at

Uyu when Drake had said love was the only thing that didn't hurt. But love had done this to my mom.

I stayed in the hospital next to my mom that night. I knew Drake would wonder where I was, but I didn't have signal, and I wasn't about to go outside to get some. I wasn't ready to talk about this. I would be. I would be tomorrow. But tonight, all that mattered was my mom.

And sleep. Sleep mattered. My body was limp with exhaustion and emotion. It was done.

22

I woke up with a start in the chair next to my mom's bed, the crick in my neck not giving up when I pushed my head to the opposite shoulder. It was bright in the room, and a slice of sunshine from the window was hot on my knee.

I looked at my mom who was still sleeping. I wasn't sure I was ready to talk to her first or if I wanted to speak with Drake first. This had all been such a crazy whirlwind, but the smell distinct to hospitals that was probably some sort of cheap antiseptic worked a bit like smelling salts.

Shit. I really needed to talk to him. Drake first.

I checked my watch, and it was eight in the morning. Probably too early to call. I didn't want to wake him before nine. But some fresh air wouldn't go amiss. My skin felt that cakey, greasy sort of feeling when you slept without taking off your makeup and had only junk food to eat.

Instead of a hospital coffee, I ventured out into the streets in hopes of finding a coffee cart or chain or anything that didn't taste like instant coffee granules like that thin, brown water of the hospital cafeteria.

I lucked out with a cart literally across the street and I found a bench just to breathe in any air that didn't taste like chemicals. Though I imagined I sucked in just as many outside as in. My phone had pinged a number of times as soon as I hit signal on my way out, so I opened it up.

Eight messages from Tyran this morning. But it was really one because he always texted like this:

Make sure you text
When you wake in the morning
And the doctor comes
To tell you more
About what we should do
Love
Y
You
PS It's going to be okay

And then there was one from Drake. And also a missed FaceTime call. I dreaded opening the text. I knew it wasn't great that I hadn't answered last night. He'd totally have the wrong impression. Maybe think I was giving him the cold shoulder. Nobody would be able to guess this. And until now, I'd had no regrets in not leaving the hospital to call him. It hadn't felt right to leave my mom's side.

But when I opened the text from him, I had the kind of dread that made me bite my bottom lip.

It read: *My Beautiful Dark Fairy—the only rabbit I need to catch is you. Stop running away from me. I love you.*

My breath stuttered letting out the breath I'd been holding on to. It meant everything to me, that message. I needed it more than anything right now. I needed to think that one thing in my life was going to be okay.

I thought about what to message back, but by now it was eight-thirty, and I only had a half hour to wait to call. It was silly to text and possibly wake him. My body was still stiff from sleeping on the vinyl upholstered chair in my mom's room, and it would do me good to take a little walk.

I checked some work messages. Fortunately, there were very few as I assumed Gina had intervened on that front. I'd told Tyran to buzz her. She was like an auntie to us and our only local "family." I was sure she would have told my department I wouldn't be in and to take care of anything on my desk.

I flipped over to social media because I always checked on Graphic Temple's antics now. Drake never really posted about himself, but I usually got a vibe check for the city and how it had gone. I was his biggest fan after all.

But upon opening the page, I saw quickly he had a lot of "biggest fans." There were tons of photos posted from last night. Maybe more than ever because it wasn't only just of the show, but of some sort of after-party on the tour bus.

I flicked through, looking for Drake, and when I found him, I could have spontaneously combusted. It was a selfie of him with what appeared to be Quinn on his lap and girls on either side.

The caption read: "Daddy extended our curfew."

What the hell? This was what Drake was doing when at

the same time he'd sent me that message as if I was the only thing that mattered? It didn't look like he was chasing two rabbits, it looked like he was chasing twenty. Or however many he could shove into that damn tour bus.

We had a fight, and he went off to party? I was dealing with my mom in the ER, seeing her with some cyborg Saturn rings around her head, being asked if I thought she'd tried to kill herself, and he was hanging out with women calling him "Daddy?"

I was not down with this. No, no, no. He had the wrong girl. This girl was not about to be the fool. This girl wasn't going to let the sweet talk woo her. This girl would not...

Thoughts reeled through my mind when a passerby peered at me with sympathetic eyes, making me wonder what my face did. Was I angry? Sad? Frustrated? Or did I look like a serial killer, because there was a bit of that kind of psychotic rage mixed in there, too.

Drake was not the guy I thought he was. I didn't expect him to stop enjoying himself. I didn't want him to not live his best life. It wasn't that. It was that all this time, for so many weeks on tour, they'd *never* had fans in the bus or in their hotel rooms, and now, the night of our first huge ding-dong argument was the first time he'd extended invitations? And what the fuck was this "Daddy" business?

My heart pounded so hard I nearly clenched it. It was heavy with pain and five sizes too big for my ribcage.

My cell rang. It was Tyran. I shook my head and took in a deep breath.

"Hey."

"Hey, sis. Any news?"

"I'm..." I did a U-turn and headed back toward the hospital. "I'm just going back in now. Maybe you should just

come down here, too. I don't want to be here alone anymore."

That was a big statement coming from me. Loner for a lifetime and obvious introvert, I'd never ever said I didn't want to be alone. It even sounded like I'd just spoken a foreign language to my own ears.

"What's wrong?" Tyran asked. "Are you okay? Is Mom okay?"

"Mom was fine and stable when I left. It's just... fuck, I know this sounds petty at a time like this, but I'm just... spinning over Drake."

"What happened?"

I walked with quick steps and could hardly breathe at this point. "He had groupies on his bus last night."

"Maeve, this is going to happen. He can't control Tae and Quinn..."

"I know! Don't you know I know that?"

"You don't sound like you know that."

I hit the automatic hospital doors. "I'm going to lose reception. Can you come here? I won't crumble without you but... I can handle this. You know I can, but I just don't want to miss any of the important stuff the doctor has to say. You know? And I'm not in the best frame of mind right now, plus I only slept an hour or two and am having sympathy pains for Mom's halo."

Tyran's office was only twenty minutes away since he went against traffic. He agreed to come, and I dragged my feet. I didn't want to face Mom without him. Nor the professionals. I was sick of having to be such a grown-up and so responsible and be strong for everyone but me.

Drake certainly wasn't. He was off being a twentysomething rock star. And I should be some rich girl living it up in

Hollywood ordering flaming drinks like Quinn had in New York.

It wasn't fair. Life had been hitting me with the hard stuff for well over a year now. And it only made it harder seeing how green the grass was over there. I knew my hysteria was just jealousy. But now wasn't the time for personal growth and additional emotional challenges.

By the time I reached my mom's bed, yet another few hours from talking to Drake, I'd formulated what I needed to say to him. I just had to get through this doctor appointment and I could get through with the rest, too.

THAT AFTERNOON, I got home and threw my shoes off down the hall. I didn't bother to pick them up. Nobody was home to tell me I was being a slob. Nobody was there to care, and I almost wished I'd scuffed the wall.

Tyran had told me not to call Drake today. He'd said silence was better than whatever words I'd had for Drake. He'd told me I'd feel better in the morning after a good night of sleep. He'd even joked and said if I could handle my week sleeping near the Kink Dome I could surely handle a few groupies.

I grabbed a sparkling water from the fridge, twisted the cap, and the noise practically echoed because there was nobody there to catch the sound and ask if I was home.

It was around two in the afternoon, more than twenty-four hours since I'd spoken to or texted Drake. I dreaded it. The sweat under my arms wasn't particularly sticky, but it smelled pungent. I always wondered what exactly made the body smell the way you were feeling when terror struck

through. Maybe it was sent to shock your nose and tell you to snap out of it.

Should I snap out of it? Yes, of course. But telling myself to stop feeling awful and thinking the worst about what happened when Drake was away was about as effective as telling someone with ADHD to stop fidgeting. You couldn't just tell yourself to think or feel a certain way and expect it to be so. Maybe I needed therapy. Probably I *did* need therapy. But one thing was certain, I loved Drake enough to step away.

I didn't want to drag Drake's trophy through the mud. I didn't want to rain on his parade. Burst his bubble. I didn't want to sully this beautiful moment in time. I knew he thought he wanted to help, but he really couldn't. Certainly not while on tour, but maybe not at all.

Sometimes, we met the right person at the wrong time. Distance. Career logistics. Grand life changes. Despite our undeniable spark, there were so many external factors weighing us down. I couldn't help but feel a sense of impossibility.

"Soulmates are made, not found." That's what my dad had always said. It was something he'd said once in a while and had always felt incongruous with his romantic soul. It'd conflicted with his attitude of living from a place of abundance and all that.

I'd considered whether or not now was the time to really listen to this advice. We all wanted to believe it would be easy when we found "The One." Maybe that was all he'd meant by it: Don't think you won't have to work just because you're with the right person.

Walking deeper into the house, I went to my room to throw off my wrinkled, smelly work clothes from yesterday. I hopped in the shower to wash off the stench of the hospital,

the reek of the doctor's words, and the heavy shroud of guilt that had somehow layered over me when I'd told my mom I was heading home.

I dried myself off and threw on a bathrobe, which felt like a very unfitting last image to give Drake, but the fact that I didn't care what I looked like anymore proved how low I'd gotten.

My dad was probably right. Long-term relationships and what outsiders called "soulmates" probably took crafting. But I was too tired for that. My arms were weary. My legs were weary. Literally, that's how bad it was. I was using the word weary.

A person only had so much to give before their tank needed filling up. Unfortunately, every eight to ten weeks wasn't enough for me.

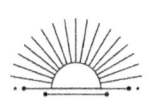

THANKFULLY, I didn't have to be the one shouting last call because after about forty-five minutes of being in my bunk listening to the music blare, checking I hadn't put my phone on silent, Vanessa told people to go. Not long after, the engine revved, and the constant purr of the tour bus engine sent me into an hours' long Wordscapes session because I just couldn't sleep.

When I woke up in Albuquerque, I slapped around on my bed for the phone, feeling sure I'd missed a call from Maeve.

I hadn't.

What the hell was going on with her? I'd thought we'd left with love still between us. It was just a frustrated, stupid argument which ultimately was only had because we loved each other and wanted to spend more time together. That was a good thing. At least I'd deduced that was a good thing. Hadn't she?

This was the longest I'd ever gone without hearing from Maeve since the moment I'd laid eyes on her at Uyu. Even at Uyu, when fate, without her cell phones and mystical Wi-Fi, somehow pressed us together. Since then, we'd talked or texted multiple times a day. And even though I knew Maeve was likely to be the one who was pigheaded in this relationship, my gut told me something was wrong.

But if something had happened to her, I was pretty sure Tyran would have texted me by now? I probed.

ME: Hey, did you get Maeve back in one piece last night? I haven't heard from her.

It could be hours before I heard from him. He often had meetings... I should've called. He could have answered then if he was in the car.

But this time, I didn't have to wait long.

TYRAN: She got back all right but there's been something we've been dealing with. I'll let her tell you, but as far as I know, she's at home.

She was at home? In the afternoon of a weekday? And what could they have been collectively dealing with? Why wouldn't she just drop me a goddamn text? My stomach knotted, and I rubbed my forehead.

Some knuckles rapped against the wood outside my bunk. "Wake up, sunshine."

I pulled the curtain aside to see Tae standing there with

a coffee. "You're the last one up. You okay? Not like you to need an alarm clock."

I took the coffee and looked around the bunk bay. Empty. Crazy that everyone had gotten up without me noticing. "Guess I really didn't fall asleep until maybe three or four. Still in the deep sleep. Thanks for the caffeine."

Tae sat the best he could across from me with his coffee; he perched on the edge of one of the bunk beds. "So what's up with you? Not that I figured whatever it was could have been cured with that champagne we served up yesterday, but the fact that you're still in bed now has me asking. It's like some girl just called your penis cute."

I laughed. "Is that your material?"

"Nah. Quinn's. She just said it to a security guard who was being moody. Thought it was worth recycling."

"It is, actually." I tapped my head as if storing it in my brain, then took a sip of coffee. "Anyway, to answer your questions—my dick is still called Moby, and Maeve and I had a fight while I was in LA. I just want to talk to her and make up, you know? Sorry if I've been in a mood. Trying not to be, but it's our first one. Hopefully the last."

"Don't waste hope on that. If you love each other, you'll fight again."

"Wiser words were never spoken. Though I hate to have it happen often because I'm dating a lawyer. You gotta be smart to outwit one of those."

He nodded. "So let me guess. Japan set it off?"

"Yeah. Set me off, too. Can I be honest with you?"

"Shoot."

"This might be as hard for me as it is for her. Don't get me wrong, man. I wanted this. But I'd be lying if I said I'm taking it in my stride. It's..."

"Unsettling?"

I saw in his hooded eyes. Tae understood. It was probably the same understanding he'd had last night when he'd brought us together with that bottle before we hit the stage.

I nodded but didn't really want to say much more.

He said it for me. "Dude, I seriously get it. I miss my girl, too."

I thought back to him cuddling with Good Hair Girl from last night.

He donned a wistful look, like a princess pining in a tower. "There's nothing like the smell of my mom's kimchi."

I chuckled.

"All kidding aside, though, it isn't easy. That's probably why Quinn and I were desperate for some numbing. We all miss home a little bit. But this thing with Maeve is pretty fresh, eh? That's harder."

"Yeah. Only met her five months ago."

"Oooh. Yeah, and this isn't your everyday long distance."

"That it is not. But I have a plan."

"A plan? What do you mean?"

"Just need to let her know I might be gone but I'm going nowhere."

He lifted an eyebrow and smile crookedly. "All right... I think I see where you're going with this..."

Tae stood, stretched, and cracked his neck. We had to get to rehearsal in an hour and we usually all took in some fresh air first. I definitely wanted some of that.

"You can talk to me, dude," Tae said, walking toward the front lounge. "I'm pretty good with jewelry, too."

"I'll keep that in mind."

I GOT my clothes on and was relieved I didn't have to tell anyone I wanted to be alone. I went for a walk, and New Mexico wasn't as warm as its namesake. But it was sunny as hell, and it felt good to get some Vitamin D before heading back into the night.

I slept away most of my free time, and whenever we arrived at a city, I never knew where to go. We'd always be parked by the venue, and I'd only wander within a one-mile radius. This one-mile radius showed promise on my Google Maps.

This venue was almost exactly that distance to the Rio Grande which sounded better than grabbing another view of concrete.

When I sat at the bench, though, I was unimpressed with the dried-up patch of river. I'd thought the Rio Grande was a mighty beast river known for its rafting, but the sad, mucky stretch before me wasn't better than the pond in Jay's grandma's backyard. What had happened? Global warming? Was it tidal? Either way, it wasn't my lucky day.

Bummer.

Boooop.

Boooop.

Maeve. Calling on WhatsApp. Finally.

"Hey, love. Why are you calling and not showing me your gorgeous face? I want to see you."

A pause. And not a good pause. A pause like the one that had stopped filling up this dried-up riverbed.

"Drake... We need to talk. Do you have time?"

Shit. Shit. Shit. I leaned forward, perching my elbows on my knees, ready for something heavy to be loaded on my back.

"Yeah. I have time. And we do need to talk. I'm really sorry with the way things were left the other day..."

"Stop."

"And, Tyran told me something happened. I'm worried about you..."

"You spoke to Tyran?"

"Just a text. I was worried about you when you didn't contact me for so long."

She drew in a breath. "Yeah. My mom fell down the stairs and broke her neck last night."

The news shot my body upright. "What? Maeve, why didn't you text me or something? Is she okay?"

"It was all such a whirlwind. We went off in an ambulance, and I didn't have reception in her hospital room..."

"You could have called me. You know you could have. Is she still in the hospital? What's the situation?"

Like a train slamming on the brakes, she said, "That's not what I called about. We need to talk about us."

"Yes, we do, but I just want to know if your mom is okay..."

"Drake. We can't be together anymore."

How did it feel when someone dropped a bombshell like that? Totally unexpected? It was called a bombshell for a reason. I felt blasted. Like a ton of bricks had just landed on me. Heavy as it was, though, I broke the hell out of the pile like the Hulk. "If you're going to break up with me, Maeve. Put on your video."

Silence.

"Put on your video, Maeve, and say it to my face. I want to look in your eyes when you take this away from us."

"Don't put this on me like that," she defended herself. "It's a two-way—"

"I said put on your video, Maeve!" I hadn't meant to raise my voice. I was usually so good at controlling it. But my

heart pounded so madly, my face hot with an intense burning. I had to release the steam.

My phone made the telltale blooping with her request to change to video call. When I accepted, her face was more beautiful than ever.

It was raw beauty. She was totally disheveled. Her hair was wet and unbrushed. She had dark circles under her eyes, the rims light-pink, and her lids were slightly swollen, making her wide eyes appear even bigger. She didn't wear a speck of makeup, so the beauty mark on her cheek was even more visible. Her eyes, unadorned by eyeliner, seemed younger. Innocent and hopeless,

I wanted to reach through the phone and have this Maeve more than I'd ever had any other. "You're so beautiful," I said, taken aback and almost forgetting about the shrapnel in my chest.

"Don't say that now," she whispered back, pushing hair behind her ear.

We gazed at each other, through this device which was the only thing that bound us. I didn't say a word. Maybe she was having a moment of madness and just needed to blurt out everything that was going on with her. Maybe I'd reacted too quickly to something she didn't mean...

But no. She bit her top lip and when she opened her mouth, she repeated, "We can't be together."

"We can, though. And we will. Maeve, you know we belong together. I can't let you do this. I know I kind of offered an ultimatum in LA, like not letting you say what you were really feeling."

"The daisy game."

"Yeah. I didn't mean it like we can't talk about our doubts and fears. But just to be clear. I have fears. I have fears like anyone else but I don't have one fucking doubt in my mind

that you're the one for me. I've never been able to talk to anyone the way I talk to you. We look outward and stare at the same things, in the same direction. When I think of my love for you, it leads me back to the best of me. You bring out the best in me, Maeve."

I hadn't intended my little speech to be a persuasive one but if I had, it wasn't.

"You're right. And that's exactly why we can't be together. I need to stop staring out with you at this invisible, intangible, imaginary future in the distance. I need to start focusing on what's before me. Life is screaming for me to pay attention to my family, and I keep ignoring it."

"We can pay attention together. I'm here for you. I don't need to be next to you to support you."

She rolled her eyes. "You don't get it. You'd never get it because you're Mr. Hopeful."

"What's that supposed to mean? Of course I'm hopeful. When life gets uncomfortable, it's what keeps us going. Hope has a life of its own."

Her second eye roll. "Pzzt. It sure does. It sure does, Drake. And I don't want to be its friend anymore. I'm sick of hoping."

"Don't say that..."

"Why the hell not? The best thing that could happen to me is if I stop hoping and start accepting."

"Accepting what? That somehow me not being in your life will make it better?"

"No. That being without hope would make it better. I have to get rid of some of this goddamn hope. It's killing me. Hope is fucking cruel, Drake." She shook her head, and her eyes glassed over with sadness.

She looked to the ceiling and composed herself. "You want to know about all my hopes? I hope that one day I'll

get used to my dad being gone. I hope my mom will get better. I hope that my brother and I keep getting along because he's all I've got. I hope that after all these months of living your best life you come home and still want *me*. You know what hope leaves me with? Absolutely nothing. The reality is that I have nothing, Drake."

"You do have me. What are you saying? You don't need to hope for me to come home to you..."

"I do, though!" She shouted so loudly through my phone a passerby glanced in my direction. "You have no idea what it's like to watch you performing with Quinn. Sharing you with her and every other woman in the world with eyes for you."

"So is that what this is really about? You don't trust me?"

"It would be a lot easier to trust you if you weren't hanging out with women who call you Daddy."

My whole body came to an emergency stop. Yes, both Quinn and Tae referred to me as the "dad" of the group. But it wasn't sexual, emotional, or anything.

"It's a joke, Maeve. Tae and Quinn both joke about that. I can't control the world around me. And I don't want to. You can see for yourself how crazy it makes you to try."

She furrowed her brow. Did she actually think I'd cheat on her?

"How can you not trust me? After all we've been through? All you know about me? You can trust me to the end of the earth and back, Maeve. I'll never do you wrong."

She softened a little. "It's not about trust. It's about my own insecurity. I get it. I've listened to enough podcasts to know it's my ego. But now isn't the time for me to add another challenge to my life. I need to just let it go. Can't you see..."

"Give me a chance to..."

"Just because you can't accept it? Accept it, Drake. Please. I'm not strong enough for all of this. I'm not! I'm tired. I'm tired of being strong for everyone and feeling like shit. I have no choice but to be strong for my mom but I don't have to be strong for you."

That stung. It stung like a million wasps, and I could feel the venom of her words spreading slowing through my every cell.

"I've been trying to swallow this all down for weeks now," she continued. "All of it. My jealousy, my own... my own *everything!* And it's taken me away from focusing on the one thing that matters most. My mom. She's it. I have one parent left and I can't let her fall deeper because I'm distracted over some guy."

Now that was fucking it. I knew she had to say her piece, but she'd crossed the line. How dare she belittle us that way? "Some guy? Who the fuck are you kidding, calling me *some guy?* I've been here, too. Every dance, every kiss, every touch... I'm not just some guy to you, Maeve, and I'll never be just some guy no matter how many more you go through. And you'll never be some girl. You're *the* girl. *My* girl."

I met the eyes of a walker, and they narrowed theirs, thinking I was the bad guy. I'd been talking loudly. I quietened down. Jesus. I couldn't believe I was being broken up with in public. Over the phone. When we were still in love. "Don't do this. You don't have to do this to help your mom. You don't need to feel guilty for living your life..."

She put the phone facedown on something, and the screen went black. Fuck. I hated being so far away. Why couldn't I just fuck off this show tonight?

Her face reappeared, calm and determined. Clinically resigned. "Haven't you ever heard of duty? It binds us together, Drake. It's what makes family, family. If you love

me like you say you do..." She paused, and it seemed like it was in order to remember her speech. "I love you enough to let you live your life and want the best for you even if it's without me. I need you to walk away. I need you to make the most of this opportunity. I need you to run off and be a global megastar and never look back, because I couldn't deal with the guilt of ruining you, too."

Too? What did she mean, "too?" Was she blaming her mom's depression on herself? Her dad's death? What was going on here? She sounded both lucid and insane at the same time.

Finally, self-control came over me again, and I was able to stop. To think. This was as overwhelming as it seemed impossible. How could everything have seemed so perfect from my point of view and be at the point of breakup from hers? I knew she'd had trouble with her mom. I knew she found it hard being apart and I'd even noticed her narrowed eyes and singular raised eyebrow around Quinn. I hadn't called it out because no woman liked being called out for jealousy. And also, there was no reason for it. Quinn was like a little sister to me. Or maybe even a little brother. There was nothing there.

Everything inside me was geared up to fight for this. My skin prickled like I'd been out for a run, and my heart beat just as hard. There had to be something I could say to change her mind. "Maybe we should just come back to this conversation later. Just... we're both emotional, and I don't want to say anything I regret."

Fuck. Now her narrowed eyes were on me. "What do you mean? Something you'd regret?"

"Nothing in particular just... you're being a fucking idiot, Maeve. Why the fuck you think you're better off without me supporting you is... it's fucking stupid."

And there it was. Something I'd regret.

Her eyes widened. Even though I'd thought I'd calmed my emotions, I hadn't. And anyway, it was the truth. She was being stupid.

"What about you being part of the problem don't you understand?"

She used some sort of courtroom tone on me, and I didn't like it. "This isn't some logical debate, so don't start. None of this makes sense, and you know it. I honestly just think we need a breather."

Her nostrils flared with anger. Insulting Maeve was a mistake, but I'd meant every word.

"That's exactly what I was proposing," she said. "A breather. A permanent breather. So we're agreed then."

"I didn't mean it like that."

Her anger pixelated and drifted away. "I know you didn't. And I don't mean to be angry either, but please don't. Please don't keep fighting for this. Please don't make it harder than it already is. I can't handle this right now. That's all I'm saying. It isn't you."

The time on my cell blared at me. I had fifteen minutes to get into rehearsal. "Look, let me call you later. Tonight. We'll talk some more..."

"Don't. Don't call me later." Her face contorted, her trying to hold back tears, which she did unsuccessfully. They trickled down her baby-doll cheeks. "Drake, you deserve this. Let me just feel happy about this. Let me just walk away feeling like I had a part in making someone's dream come true. In loving you unconditionally. In giving you a life worth living. Let me walk away with that feeling. Please..." Her face was wet with emotion, and she wiped one of her eyes. "Please."

"Okay."

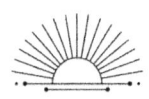

"OKAY."

Me saying a word so vague, so liquid and formless, made me want to gag on my own sick. "Okay" was the favorite word of average people. Months later, I'd still regret leaving her with that as my last two syllables.

Christmas had passed. New Year had passed with only sloppy kisses on both cheeks. One from Tae and one from Quinn, both at the same time. Our friendship had grown

and was now a solid bond through sharing this once-in-a-lifetime experience.

We finally stopped touring in late January, just for a month, but I couldn't face going back to LA. I'd spent a couple of weeks crashing in what was meant to be paradise. I slept on Koa's couch, waking up to him telling me to man up and never let anything stop me from getting what I want and who I wanted.

But he didn't understand. Pursuing Maeve would have been like constantly ripping off the scab of an open wound. For both of us.

I did text Tyran, though, respectfully checking in on Dixie who was about to have her halo off and apparently booked tickets to spend a month in an ashram in India for when it did. He'd alluded to her healing but not to her cure.

That family was tight. He probably danced on a wire, not wanting to piss off Maeve with anything too much more than a polite response to me. I'd never be able to piece together what Maeve was thinking now by merely texting her brother. Lewises didn't commit treason.

I gave her the space she needed. Nearly two months of it, and she'd made me a social-media junkie. Checking for a thumbs-up on goddamn every post. My life was moving on, but my heart sure as hell wasn't.

I'd promised my mom a Valentine's Day date, and on February fourteenth, flew from Koa's Nakiki bachelor pad to the cold humidity of Seattle. I booked out the best restaurant in town for us and bought my mom a new dress for the occasion.

Showing up at her house, the one inherited from my grams, the one she refused to move out of even though I'd offered her something new, I was actually so relieved she'd held on to her roots. They were my roots, too, and a sense of

warm comfort enveloped me when I walked into the small, unassuming, two-bedroom bungalow.

With Chanel bags in tow, I let out a huge breath I hadn't known I'd been holding since before this all happened. Maybe that I'd been hanging on to even since the day I'd taken Mitch's card from Maeve back at Uyu.

Seeing my mom in a dress I'd bought her with money brought to me by that card made me think of Maeve even more. I knew I didn't owe all of this to her, but she'd given me my break. She'd believed in me. I wondered what Maeve would have thought seeing my mom prance like some lady coming home from a day on Rodeo Drive.

I smiled when my mom twirled in her outfit, but she stopped and sat next to me on the couch. "What's up with that weird smile? Because I know I'm damn fine in this dress, so it isn't that. This kind of dress could make anyone look good."

"You know you're gorgeous. Standing-ovation gorgeous."

"So what's the deal?"

"I'm smiling."

"Yeah, like a statue smiles. Not like my Drake smiles. Still brokenhearted?" She took my hand.

I nodded. "I've actually been okay. I'm fine... but who wants to be fine. Right?"

"Nobody ever is just 'fine.' They just don't bother to find the words to describe the mood."

She put her arm around me.

"Go on, Mom. I came here to be your date not your downer. I'm all right. And we have so much to talk about. Plus, you've always wanted to try Opal."

"True, but not as much as I want to make sure you're able to talk. I'll make macaroni and cheese and stay here all night if need be. Though I will keep the dress on."

I chuckled. "You better."

She smoothed it. "Think I might even wear it to bed." She put her hand on my knee. "Now talk to me."

"I just still worry about her but I'm trying to give her space to heal. Going from her dad dying to her mom being ill to in a relationship was a bit much. Sometimes, if you love someone, you gotta let them go and swim on their own."

"Yeah, and sometimes you have to lead them to shore. Anyway, you haven't let her go so you might as well stop pretending you have. You haven't. You can't. Don't."

"It's not my choice."

"Well, I liked her a lot the two times I met her. She seemed sincere, considered, and totally in love with you. But might I add she's an idiot?"

I laughed. "My words exactly, but they didn't go down well. Go on, Mom. Finish getting ready. We can talk more over caviar or whatever else rich people like to pretend tastes nice."

She popped up with my hand still in hers and stood before me with that loving, unique expression that only moms seemed to know how to give you. "Baby boy, go and get her. She didn't leave because she doesn't love you. If anyone can find the words to make her see that, it's you." She let go of my hand. "I'm going to go curl my hair so might be a minute."

She walked off, and I let myself fall back into the corduroy couch that she'd had since I was seventeen. Life had been so much simpler then. Get up, go to school. Come home. Buy a couch every ten to fifteen years.

I ran my fingers along the cords and came to a small, almost imperceptible stain that I might not have noticed if I hadn't already known it was there.

I wanted this with Maeve. I wanted to make messes and clean them up and live daringly, not caring if we left a few scuffs behind because they were our scuffs. Damn, I was lucky nobody could hear the way I was thinking. I was like a goddamn sulking teenager. Good thing I'd never loved anyone until now.

My cell rang. It was my manager. "Hey, Jules. All good?"

"So... tell me... does the name Jason Fry mean anything to you?"

I sat up slowly, almost as if my body descended carefully into a haunted house. I said nothing, expecting Jules to say more, but all he did was repeat himself. "Does the name Jason Fry mean anything to you?"

I trod carefully. "It probably matters more what the name means to you."

"Interesting answer. You'll do well in court."

"What?"

"Man, I'm sorry to say, but we've been served. He filed a lawsuit against you and RI for copyright infringement."

I stood like a rocket. "What the hell? You're joking, right?"

"Is there a basis for any of this? I'm not accusing you, Drake, I just need to know so we can handle this appropriately. No... don't tell me. Actually, really do *not* tell me. In fact, don't say anything to anyone but the lawyers. Someone will buzz you tomorrow."

In the midst of being served, of potentially losing it all, the only thing I wondered was whether or not that lawyer would be Maeve.

"Who is it?" I asked, my heart racing. "Who's calling me?"

Jules never had much time to spare, so he said what he had to say in as few words as possible. "I got the name in my

phone. Hang on... says Hunter Rodrigues. He's junior but good. A senior lawyer will represent you in court..."

I interrupted. "In court? Are you serious right now? We have to go to court over this? Jay is just some..." I stopped myself from saying druggie, junkie, or any of the other things I wanted to say about him. Worse things than having a drug problem were wrong with Jay. Plus, his drug use wasn't a defense.

"I'm dead serious," he continued. "Anyway, Hunter will contact you first. We'll go from there. But safe to say, no more touring for the time being unless you guys whip up an album real fast. Even then..." He grumbled something but stopped himself. "Gotta run. Just try not to worry about it. RI is a helluva lot bigger than the production company behind Mr. Fry. That means a lot with these things. Money is muscle. Talk soon."

And he hung up. Shit, I knew Jules was my manager, not my therapist, but sometimes he was downright brutal in his delivery.

Ping. Fuck, something from Quinn.

My mom hummed in her room.

Ping. Man. One from Tae.

What was I going to say to these guys? I'd brought all this drama into our new little family. They shouldn't have to be dealing with this right now. And how was I going to act normal on Valentine's Day, let alone like the Prince Charming my mom actually deserved to be on a date with?

Ping.

Holy shit...

Maeve.

HEY READER! I swear I didn't mean to hurt you. And I'll put you back together again in Surge. Total promise. books2read.com/surgebook

And if you'd like to receive offers such as free or discounted books and my general news and author antics, why not join my newsletter? https://www.subscribepage.com/sjsnewsletter

Also if you could be so kind as to let me know what you thought of this book, reviews really help readers decide what books to buy. Maybe yours would be just what they need to hear to push them to buy! And that means I can keep writing... https://www.amazon.com/review/create-review/error?ie=UTF8&channel=glance-detail&asin=B09SPNPZ3T

ALSO BY SJ CAVALETTI

The Way We Were

Path Less Taken Series

ABOUT THE AUTHOR

SJ Cavaletti is an American contemporary romance author. She lives on a small farm in England with her husband, three kids, ponies, cat, dogs, chickens and likely many more animals by the time you read this.

When she's not writing, she can be found hiking and swimming in the sea. Like every respectable woman she also loves drinking champagne and eating half of every chocolate in a truffles box.

ACKNOWLEDGMENTS

Emmy Ellis thank you so much for your amazing editing support. I love how I learn through your editing process and each book gets better and better. This one feels like the best one yet but as there are many more to come so I know it won't be. Merci beaucoup!

Cover Designs
Torso Cover- Paideia Art
Discreet Cover- by Emily Wittig

14287812R00161